JUDICIAL ENIGMA

JUDICIAL ENIGMA

The First Justice Harlan

TINSLEY E. YARBROUGH

New York Oxford   OXFORD UNIVERSITY PRESS   1995

Oxford University Press

Oxford   New   York
Athens   Auckland   Bangkok   Bombay
Calcutta   Cape Town   Dar es Salaam   Delhi
Florence   Hong Kong   Istanbul   Karachi
Kuala Lumpur   Madras   Madrid   Melbourne
Mexico City   Nairobi   Paris   Singapore
Taipei   Tokyo   Toronto

and associated companies in
Berlin   Ibadan

Library of Congress Cataloging-in-Publication Data
Yarbrough, Tinsley E., 1941-
Judicial enigma: the first Justice Harlan / Tinsley E. Yarbrough.
p.   cm.
Includes bibliographical references and index.
ISBN 0-19-507464-5
1. Harlan, John Marshall, 1833-1911.
2. Judges—United States-Biography.
[1. United States. Supreme Court—Biography.]
I. Title. II. Title: Harlan 1.
KF8746.H3Y36 1995
347.73'2634—dc20
[B]   [347.3073534]
[B]   94-11443

2 4 6 8 9 7 5 3 1

Printed in the United States of America
on acid-free paper

To the memory of

my mother and mother-in-law

Preface

*

F or the first Justice John Marshall Harlan the Supreme Court was truly a bully pulpit. Throughout his 34 years on the high bench (1877–1911), and often in solitary dissent, the devout Presbyterian lay leader regularly offered up noble lessons of justice, fairness, and common decency for his brethren and the nation— whether they were willing to listen or not. When a majority in the *Civil Rights Cases* of 1883 suggested that it was time for the former slave to cease being "the special favorite of the laws" and assume "the rank of a mere citizen,"[1] Harlan's pen fairly dripped with righteous indignation:

> It is, I submit, scarcely just to say that the colored race has been the special favorite of the laws. What the nation, through congress, has sought to accomplish in reference to that race is, what had already been done in every state in the Union for the white race, to secure and protect rights belonging to them as freemen and citizens; nothing more. . . . To-day it is the colored race which is denied . . . rights fundamental in their free- dom and citizenship. At some future time it may be some other race that will fall under the ban. . . . [T]here cannot be, in this republic, any class of human beings in practical subjection to another class, with power in the latter to dole out to the former just such privileges as they may choose to grant.[2]

When the *Plessy* majority, 13 years later, embraced the sophistry that segrega- tion laws treated blacks and whites alike, abridging no constitutional guarantees, the justice's reaction was equally vehement:

> [I]n view of the constitution, in the eye of the law, there is in this country no superior, dominant, ruling class of citizens. There is no caste here. Our constitution is color- blind, and neither knows nor tolerates classes among citizens. In respect of civil rights, all citizens are equal before the law. The humblest is the peer of the most pow- erful. The law regards man as man, and takes no account of his surroundings or of his color when his civil rights as guaranteed by the supreme law of the land are involved. It is therefore to be regretted that this high tribunal, the final expositor of the funda-

mental law of the land, has reached the conclusion that it is competent for a state to regulate the enjoyment by citizens of their civil rights solely upon the basis of race.

In my opinion, the judgment this day rendered will, in time, prove to be quite as pernicious as the decision made by this tribunal in the Dred Scott Case.[3]

Nor were such appeals confined to the racial arena. In numerous dissents, Harlan argued that state officials, no less than their federal counterparts, should be required to obey the guarantees of the Bill of Rights,[4] urged extension of those precious safeguards to the people of the U.S. territories,[5] supported broad national authority over corporate excess,[6] and championed the cause of the weak against the powerful in a variety of other issue areas as well.

In general, Harlan's colleagues and era embraced neither his rhetoric nor his legal positions. Several justices questioned his ability and the almost mystical underpinnings of his opinions. The acerbic Oliver Wendell Holmes, Jr., dismissed him, derisively if accurately, as "the last of the tobacco-spittin' judges" and likened Harlan's mind to "a great vise, the two jaws of which could never be closed."[7] During remarks delivered at a dinner given by the Supreme Court bar in honor of Harlan's completion of 25 years on the high bench, Justice David J. Brewer observed affectionately, but probably only half-jokingly, that his colleague "goes to bed every night with one hand on the Constitution and the other on the Bible, and so sleeps the sweet sleep of justice and righteousness."[8]

Given such contemporary impressions and Harlan's status as one of the Court's most frequent dissenters, it was hardly surprising that his image for many years following his death in 1911 was at best that of an intriguing "eccentric"—as Justice Felix Frankfurter dubbed him in a 1947 opinion rejecting his predecessors's controversial contention that the Fourteenth Amendment was intended to extend the Bill of Rights to the states.[9] Within two decades of Frankfurter's observation, however, a Supreme Court majority had extended most Bill of Rights safeguards to the states;[10] largely adopted Harlan's *Plessy* dissent;[11] accepted the Thirteenth Amendment as an adequate basis for congressional assaults on all forms of racial discrimination,[12] a position Harlan had argued for in the *Civil Rights Cases*; and also come close to accepting Harlan's argument that congressional authority under the Fourteenth Amendment extended to private as well as state interferences with the rights its provisions guaranteed.[13] Years before, moreover, the Court had embraced the broad concept of congressional regulatory authority over the economy that Harlan had urged,[14] and it had largely rejected—as Harlan generally, though not invariably, had[15]—the notion that the Constitution's due process guarantees clothed the Court with "super-legislature" review power over economic regulations.[16]

With belated endorsement of his jurisprudence came greater recognition for Harlan the justice. In 1970, 65 judicial specialists were asked to evaluate the performance of the 96 justices who had served on the Supreme Court from 1789 to 1967. Twelve were ranked "great" justices. The first Justice Harlan was among them.[17]

Irrespective of his current judicial reputation, Harlan as justice, politician, and human being remains an enigma. The author of the compelling *Plessy* dissent also spoke for the Court in dismissing, albeit on narrow grounds, a Georgia county's denial of a high school education to black children;[18] the staunch proponent of national power over corporate excess rejected a congressional ban on yellow-dog contracts.[19]

Harlan's political record is even more complex. He was not named John Marshall Harlan for nothing. His father was a staunch Whig, the close friend of fellow Kentuckian Henry Clay, that state's preeminent nationalist. Harlan would embrace a broad Whig conception of national power throughout his political and judicial career. But in other respects, his political posture was hardly stable and consistent. In the 1850s, when the sectional tension pushing the nation toward war was also bringing on the collapse of the Whig Party, Harlan not only joined the Know-Nothing movement but became an enthusiastic defender of its anti-foreign, anti-Catholic platform. During the Civil War, he opposed secession and raised a Union infantry regiment. But he was also a harsh critic of emancipation, extension of the suffrage to former slaves, and federal programs designed to relieve their plight. As Kentucky's attorney general during and after the war, he persuaded its court of appeals that a federal provost marshal's removal of slaves from the state was an indictable offense under Kentucky law[20] and that the Union commanding general for Kentucky could be indicted for aiding in their escape.[21] When a lower court, considering itself bound by the federal Civil Rights Act of 1866, allowed the introduction of a black's testimony against a white defendant, contrary to state law, Harlan refused to defend that position in an appeal of the court's holding.[22] While he later represented the United States in civil rights prosecutions, he also defended whites accused of violence against blacks. Nor was he entirely above race-baiting. In at least one stump speech, for example, he delighted his audience with the story of "ze little black nigger."[23]

In the aftermath of the war, Harlan renounced many of his earlier positions, enthusiastically embraced the Republican Party, ran for governor of Kentucky on the party's ticket in 1871 and 1875, and became a staunch defender of the Reconstruction statutes and the newly adopted constitutional amendments on which they were based. But his detractors vehemently questioned the sincerity of his conversion, charging that he was motivated principally by a desire for control over local distribution of federal patronage and national influence, now that Washington was dominated by the party to which he had recently pledged allegiance. When President Rutherford B. Hayes chose him to fill a Supreme Court vacancy in 1877, a former close friend charged that in an 1866 conversation the nominee had bitterly denounced emancipation, asserting that "he had no more . . . scruples in buying and selling a negro than he had in buying and selling a horse . . . and that the liberation of slaves by our general government was a direct violation of the Constitution of the United States."[24] His critic conceded that Harlan's remarks were "directly opposite" unionist sentiments the nominee had expressed when they served together during the war and that he blamed Harlan for his failure to secure a federal post. But he was by no means the only opponent of Harlan's confirmation to challenge the integrity of the future justice's professed commitment to Republicanism and the goals of Reconstruction.

Darker elements of Harlan's personal life further complicate the noble image of the justice his judicial opinions project. Like his sons, whose financial difficulties are recounted in my study of his grandson, the second Justice Harlan,[25] Harlan was bedeviled with money problems throughout his adult life. He was well aware that his judicial station insulated him from such pressures and was not above taking advantage of his position. In a letter regarding a mutual debt, for example, he assured a relative "that the Bank would never bother me—had charged off the debt as lost— and . . . would be content with whatever it got from your father's estate."[26] Harlan preferred, in fact, to avoid even acknowledging his debt. "I do not wish by any paper or release," he wrote, "to give [the bank] any additional capacity to annoy me." On another occasion, a frustrated Kentucky banker wrote to a Washington lawyer who had failed to collect a debt from Harlan, "If you have done or are doing anything with the matter please inform us. If timid about it return us the note and we will send it to an atty who is not afraid of the Justice and who will sue for us."[27]

Unappealing elements of the justice's life extended to at least one member of his family. His brother, James, two years Harlan's senior, was an accomplished lawyer and chancery judge. But he also became a hopeless alcoholic and, later, a morphine and opium addict, largely dependent on the charity of others. In letters to his brother, James repeatedly vowed to reform, bemoaned the shambles he had made of his life, pleaded for funds, hinted at suicide, complained of the justice's indifference toward him, and made veiled threats to expose his situation—the pauper-like existence of a Supreme Court justice's brother—to the public at large.

The justice's reaction to his brother's plight was a complex mixture of pity, contempt, impatience, and embarrassment. Pleading difficulties of his own, Harlan made only limited financial contributions to James's support. Before leaving on a trip to Europe, he informed a friend that, should his brother die before his return, he should be "decently buried" in the family plot in Kentucky, "with as little expense as possible."[28] When James's son, Henry, faced discharge from a patronage position for intoxication on the job, the justice's response was harsh and uncompromising: "My creed from now forward is to let such a drinker go his own way and destroy himself if he will do it."[29] When a mutual friend suggested placing James in a Washington, D.C. hospital or the justice's home, Harlan declined, citing the embarrassment his brother's presence might cause Mrs. Harlan and their daughters, who were "in society."[30]

Harlan's relationship with his putative mulatto half-brother, Robert Harlan, apparently the product of a liaison between the justice's father and a slave, is equally intriguing. John and Robert Harlan—whose descendants, interestingly, include the daughter-in-law of James Nabrit, Jr., one of the Howard University law professors who played a pivotal role in *Brown* v. *Board of Education*—maintained at least limited contact throughout their lives. When one of John Harlan's white clients was charged in 1871 with shooting a prominent black, the future Justice turned to Robert Harlan for assistance.[31] The two also regularly corresponded about Republican politics, in which Robert was very active, about patronage, financial matters, and related subjects. Yet John obviously never treated Robert as a member of his family.

In fact, for all the rhetoric of his judicial opinions, Harlan may well have embraced racial stereotypes common to whites of his era. The unpublished memoirs of his wife, Malvina Shanklin Harlan, are filled with anecdotes reflecting the traditional Southern image of blacks as happy, simple folk devoted to the whites they served.[32] There is evidence that Harlan was of a similar mind and remained so throughout his life. Nor, it appears, was he free of the prejudices of caste and class: for example, a secretary who made arrangements for the family's return from a trip to Europe in 1892 assured the justice that the steamer on which he had booked passage "will not carry immigrants on this trip."[33]

Particularly in view of the modern acceptance of the moral premises underlying his opinions, Justice Harlan's judicial reputation is not likely to diminish. In many ways, his judicial handiwork embodies the best aspirations of Reconstruction and the monumental revolution in constitutional liberties that era ultimately, if belatedly, spawned. A full understanding of the justice, however, requires investigation of the complexities of his personality as well as his judicial record. What follows, it is hoped, will cast further light on those complexities.

Greenville, N.C.   T. E. Y.

Acknowledgments

Many individuals and institutions helped to make completion of this book an immensely enjoyable as well as rewarding experience. For this study as with my earlier biography of the second Justice Harlan, the encouragement and assistance of Harlan I's granddaughter Edith Harlan Powell and great-grandson Roger A. Derby were invaluable. Mrs. Powell offered family photographs and memories, while Mr. Derby gave me access to important family papers, read the entire manuscript, and shared with me his immense knowledge of Harlan family history and provocative insights into the personalities of its members. Roberta Harlan Nabrit, great-great-granddaughter of Robert Harlan, Justice Harlan's slave half-brother, was equally crucial to my project, providing me with important materials regarding her ancestor's roots, life, and descendants. I am forever grateful to these and other Harlan family members.

Grants from Earhart Foundation and the East Carolina University Research/Creative Activity Committee provided critical financial support. The staffs of the Library of Congress and the University of Louisville, repositories of the John Marshall Harlan Papers as well as the manuscript collections of Harlan contemporaries, were indispensable, as were those of The Filson Club Historical Society, the University of Kentucky, the Kentucky Historical Society, the Kentucky Department of Archives, Western Kentucky University, the Cincinnati Historical Society, the Cincinnati Public Library, the Rutherford B. Hayes presidential library, and East Carolina University.

Sincere thanks is extended, as always, to Cynthia M. Smith, for invariably flawless secretarial assistance; to my superb editor Helen McInnis and other members of Oxford's fine staff; to Henry Abraham, Kermit Hall, Woodford Howard, and A. E. Dick Howard for friendship and encouragement as well as wise counsel and support; to Loren Beth, Alan Westin, David Farrelly, and other Harlan scholars for penetrating insights into our mutual research interests; and to Mary Alice, Sarah, and Cole, for their constant love and support.

Finally, I appreciate the encouragement and affection of my dear mother-in-law Letha Irene Thompson, whose recent death caused me as much sorrow as the 1991 passing of my own beloved mother. This book is dedicated to the memory of those great Alabama ladies.

Contents

JUDICIAL ENIGMA

Beginnings

In physical appearance, the Harlan men and women generally fell into one of two groups, the "Big Reds" or the "Little Blacks." The latter were of medium size with rather dark skin, whereas the former were large and tall with sandy, reddish hair and bright complexions. When John Marshall Harlan was born on June 1, 1833, it was immediately evident to which group he belonged. Aunt Betty, one of the family slaves at the Harlan home in Boyle County, Kentucky, near the headwaters of the Salt River, emerged from the birthing room to announce the appearance of "another big red-headed boy."[1]

Harlan's mother, Eliza Shannon Davenport Harlan, was born in Boyle County in 1805. Her father, a native of Spottsylvania County, Virginia, had migrated to Kentucky in the late 1700s and was a Boyle County farmer; but little else is known of Harlan's maternal ancestry. The future justice's father, James Harlan, was a member of one of Kentucky's original pioneering families. The earliest Harlan (first spelled Harland) known to the family in America was born in England around 1625 and lived and died on English soil. A member of the Church of England, he had three Quaker sons who migrated to Ireland. In 1687, two of the sons, Michael and George, left Ireland and settled in what is now Chester County, Pennsylvania. George Harlan was active in politics, serving as a provisional governor of colonial Delaware in 1695 and as a member of the colonial assembly in 1712.[2]

John Marshall Harlan's grandfather, also named James Harlan, was a descendant of George Harlan. Born in Berkeley County, Virginia (now West Virginia) in 1755, James was 19 when he and his older brother, Silas, joined a company of adventurers from Virginia and Pennsylvania raised by Captain James Harrod, an ally of Daniel Boone, for a trek into the Kentucky wilderness. The band left Virginia by canoe in May of 1774. Roughly four years later, Silas and James built a stockade fort on a hill overlooking the Salt River, about seven miles from what is now Harrodsburg, Kentucky. Called Harlan Station, the "Old Stone House," as it became known in family and local lore, would be the birthplace of both John Harlan and his father.[3]

Of the two brothers, Silas acquired a more distinguished place in the history of the Kentucky frontier. As a major in a company commanded by General George Rogers Clark, Silas fought in the Illinois Indian campaigns of 1779 and other battles and skirmishes. According to his biographer, Silas did not play an important role in such engagements; instead, he was "a second-in-command who capably backed up his leader, but who rarely had an important mission in his own right." Even so, Silas apparently fulfilled that function with distinction. General Clark termed him one of "the best subalterns" he ever commanded; and another associate said of the popular, good-natured soldier, "No man stood higher in the estimation of the people." Silas's death at 29, in the battle of Blue Licks Springs, confirmed his high standing in Kentucky lore. In 1819 the state legislature laid off the boundaries to Kentucky's sixtieth county, placing it along the Virginia line, north of the Cumberland Gap. It was named Harlan in honor of Silas, the "hero" of Blue Licks.[4]

In longevity, if not reputation, James Harlan was more fortunate than his brother. James married Silas's sweetheart, Sarah Caldwell, raised a large family, achieved some success in farming, and lived a comparatively long life for that period, dying August 8, 1816, at the age of 60.

The couple's son, James, John Harlan's father, was born June 22, 1800, in the "Old Stone House." His education, he later wrote, was a "very imperfect" but "good English education embracing mathematics." Initially planning to pursue a mercantile career, James clerked in a dry goods store from 1817 to 1821, but soon decided that his future was in law. After reading law for approximately two years with John Greene, a prominent state jurist, he was admitted in 1823 to the Kentucky bar.[5]

The year before his admission to the bar, James Harlan married Eliza Davenport. Theirs was to be a happy and prolific union. In their first year of marriage, Eliza presented James with a son, Richard Davenport. Richard's birth was followed in rapid succession by the arrival of William Lowndes in 1825, Elizabeth (or Lizzie, as she early came to be known) in 1828, Henry Clay in 1830, James in 1831, John in 1833, Laura in 1835, George (who died in infancy) in 1837, and Sallie in 1841.

The progress of James Harlan's career was equally swift. He established thriving practices, first at Harrodsburg and then at Frankfort, Kentucky's capital. For many years he enjoyed the largest practice of any lawyer before the Kentucky court of appeals, the state's highest court. In 1850 he was appointed by the governor to a committee charged with simplifying the rules of practice in the state courts. Drawing on his work with the committee, he published in 1854 *The Code of Practice in Civil and Criminal Cases*. The previous year, he and an associate published a two-volume digest of all common law and equity cases decided by the Kentucky court of appeals since its creation in 1792.

Late in life James Harlan would scorn politics as a "ruinous business" and advise a younger friend to enter that arena "under no circumstances."[6] By that point in his career, he clearly had a basis for such judgments. In 1829, 43 citizens submitted a petition to Governor Thomas Metcalfe, urging James Harlan's appointment as commonwealth attorney. Many of the signatories had known their candidate "from his infancy." He was, they assured Metcalfe, "a gentleman of unquestioned integrity" who "possesse[d] such requirements and such a habitual industry and attention to business as will secure the interests of the Commonwealth."[7]

Following four years as prosecuting attorney for the circuit in which he was born, James Harlan resigned from that position. In 1835, however, his fellow citizens elected him to the U.S. House of Representatives; in 1837 he was reelected without opposition. Although his brief congressional career was generally uneventful, during his second and last terms he chaired a committee investigating highly publicized charges that the collector of customs and a federal attorney in New York had misappropriated funds in their custody.

On leaving Congress, James Harlan returned to his Harrodsburg law practice. In 1840, Governor Robert Letcher named him Kentucky's secretary of state, a position he held until September of 1844. The next year he won election to the lower house of the state legislature, where he served as chairman of the judiciary committee. He declined nomination for another term in Congress, but in 1850, Governor John J. Crittenden named him state attorney general, an office to which he was later twice elected by the voters, as required by Kentucky's new constitution of 1850. During the Civil War, President Lincoln named the staunch unionist and opponent of secession federal attorney for Kentucky, a post he held until his death in 1863.

For a time it appeared that James Harlan might occupy another federal position. In 1851, President Millard Fillmore—"without any solicitation on my part," Harlan later wrote[8]—sent the Kentuckian a commission to serve on a board recently created by Congress to investigate the complex matter of California land claims. If Harlan wished to accept the post, interior secretary Alex H. H. Stuart informed him in an accompanying letter, he should take the oath of office before a federal judge.[9] Henry Clay, Kentucky's most prominent national politician and James Harlan's close friend and political ally, had apparently suggested Harlan to President Fillmore and now urged his friend to accept the offer. Joshua F. Speed, another close associate with important Washington connections, sought to persuade Harlan that he could give up the office after a few years—it carried a three-year term—and return to law practice with sufficient knowledge of land law to make a large fortune. So confident was Speed of his friend's potential that he guaranteed Harlan $15,000 annually for the first five years of his practice, stipulating only that Harlan turn over to him all his earnings in excess of that figure.[10]

But James Harlan was skeptical. He asked Stuart to supply a copy of the law creating the land commission and details regarding salary, expenses, and staff.[11] Stuart readily obliged but to no avail.[12] The $6,000 annual salary was a handsome sum in those days, but unfortunately, other information about the position was sketchy or dependent on further congressional action. Thus, Harlan remained unconvinced. In late May, Stuart pressed him for a decision, citing the president's desire that the commission begin its work.[13] At that point, apparently, Harlan declined the post. As Justice Harlan once noted, had he accepted it and moved his family to California, his son "would not, perhaps, have become a Justice."[14]

Although James Harlan and Henry Clay parted company on the land commission venture, their Whig nationalist political leanings were virtual mirror images of each other. Like Clay and the great chief justice for whom his fifth son was named, James Harlan was "uniform in [his] opposition to the so-called Democratic Party."[15] Years after the elder Harlan's death, Justice Harlan aptly captured his father's political philosophy in a letter to his family:

My father was an ardent admirer of John Marshall, and held to the views of constitutional construction which that great jurist embodied in the opinions delivered by him
as Chief Justice of the Supreme Court of the United States. He was equally ardent in
his opposition to the views of constitutional law . . . entertained by Thomas Jefferson.
Marshall, my father always contended, held to views which, all concede, would give
to the country a government that would be supreme and paramount in respect to all
matters entrusted to the General Government. . . .

My father adhered firmly to these views and opposed to those maintained by Jefferson, because he believed that Jefferson's views were based upon a narrow, literal
construction of the words of the Federal Constitution which, in time, would so minimize the functions of the Government intended to be established by that instrument as
to place the National Government so completely at the mercy of the States that it
could not accomplish the objects of its creation. He regarded "Jeffersonianism" as an
evil that needed to be watched and overcome. He so thought during his entire life. . . .
He gloried in being a Whig.[16]

James Harlan's Whig nationalist sentiments pervaded every aspect of his political life. During his tenure as attorney general, for example, Governor Crittenden
sought his advice regarding the possible impact of the newly adopted Kentucky
constitution on the state's contractual obligations with a bank. Harlan's response
drew heavily on the broad construction John Marshall's Supreme Court had given
the constitutional ban on state laws that impair the obligations of a contract:

[I]ndividuals, companies, and corporations who subscribe stock in said Bank and advance their money, [have] done so in the faith of the law that the state would comply
with her *contract* by subscribing an equal amount. If the constitution should be construed as repealing or changing [such] acts of incorporation . . . , "[s]uch a proceed-
ing" (to use the language of Chancellor Kent) "would be repugnant to the letter of the
Constitution (U.S.) and to the principles of natural justice." And the fact that the state
is one of the contracting parties cannot alter the principle. The Supreme Court said in
Fletcher vs. Peck [Chief Justice Marshall speaking for the Court] that a sovereign
state was as much bound by its contracts as are individuals.[17]

Given the parallels in their political views, it is not surprising that James Harlan
became an ardent follower of Henry Clay, even naming one of his sons after him. In
the 1844 presidential election, the "Great Commoner" had lost to the Democrat
James K. Polk. In 1848, Clay again sought his party's nomination. But many
Whigs, including his fellow Kentuckians, were doubtful Clay could be elected. At
the Whig convention in Philadelphia that year, all the Kentucky delegates but one
abandoned Clay and voted for General Zachary Taylor. That sole exception was
James Harlan, who continued to vote for his friend until the end, becoming the convention's lone holdout against making Taylor's nomination unanimous.

Clay's desertion by the convention and loss to Taylor, a war hero who had never
voted and whose sole appeal appeared to be the votes his military record was expected to garner, incensed the great Kentuckian. In a letter to Harlan, his frustrations bubbled to the surface. He was sickened at the spectacle of politicians willing
to "ridicule and degrade themselves in the presence of Gen'l Taylor" and "to denounce [the] party in the same breath in which the Whig party is called on to support the General as a Whig, that is, a party man!" In Clay's eyes, Taylor's nomina-

tion was a disaster for his beloved party. "It is mortifying to behold that once great party," he exclaimed, "descending from its lofty position of principle—known, avowed and proclaimed principle—and lending itself to the creation of a mere personal party, with a virtual abandonment of its old principles."[18]

But Clay was as admiring and grateful to Harlan as he was contemptuous of Taylor. Shortly before the Philadelphia convention, Clay had written his friend a letter of introduction, describing James Harlan as "a gentleman worthy of all confidence and respect." In the convention's aftermath, Clay's friends raised funds for a silver pitcher, which they presented to Harlan as a token of admiration and affection. Following Clay's death in 1852, his son, James B. Clay, presented Harlan with a fine cane New Orleans Whigs had given the "Great Commoner" years before. Clay had instructed his son to extend the gift to Harlan as evidence of his "love and confidence."[19]

Such feelings, of course, were fully mutual. In 1855, James B. Clay, who had become a Democrat, had written to Harlan, apologizing for failing to vote for him in his successful bid for reelection as attorney general. "I assure you," Harlan soon replied, "that your failure to vote for me . . . has not, in the least, diminished the respect I entertain for you and for every member of the family of your distinguished and venerated father. My veneration for his character is such that I could never entertain any other but the most kind feelings and highest respect for his children, and nothing, I am sure, will ever occur to change my mind."[20]

The 1848 experience to the contrary, James Harlan was usually on the winning side of the political battles in which he became embroiled—but not always without controversy or challenge. Robert R. Letcher, a leading Whig politician for many years in Kentucky, had first been elected to Congress in 1822 and was repeatedly reelected until 1835. James Harlan managed one of Letcher's congressional campaigns against a Democratic opponent, Thomas Moore. Harlan was then living at a hotel in Danville, and Moore resided nearby in Harrodsburg. At one point in the campaign and for reasons now obscure, Moore became enraged at Harlan and challenged him to a duel. At two o'clock one night, Moore's second aroused Harlan from a sound sleep to deliver the challenge. Clad in his nightgown and reading by candlelight, Harlan immediately accepted the challenge. The choice of weapons was his. He selected rifles—the barrel of each to be placed at the opponent's chest![21] The embarrassed, and apparently prudent, Moore withdrew the challenge and dropped out of politics.

Although the Moore incident was James Harlan's closest brush with death in the political arena, his political activities were not without frustrations, albeit, of a more mundane variety. In June of 1855, his son William Lowndes, who intermittently practiced law with his father, wrote a letter to several friendly newspaper editors. James Harlan was then seeking reelection as Kentucky's attorney general. When his father accepted his party's nomination for another term, William wrote the editors, he had assumed that a stump campaign would not be necessary. The elder Harlan was then heavily involved in cases pending before the state court of appeals and would be unable to even begin a canvass for several more weeks. Meanwhile, his novice opponent was "going about making a schoolboy declamation of his prepared speech." William did not want his letter published but hoped the editors' readers could be "informed or reminded of a fact or two," especially about the candidates' comparative credentials:

> The present incumbent you know. He has had more than thirty years legal experience in the laborious practice of his profession. . . . He is well acquainted with the organization of all the state offices, for which he is the legal adviser; not a day passes that [he] does not have to give some of them a legal opinion; some of which require hours of investigation. His opinions often affect every county in the state, clerk, sheriff, surveyor or Judge, etc.
>
> Now who has the Dem. convention set up to fill this office? Who is asking the people to turn out this officer, and to put himself in [the] place . . . ? Why, a young man not 28 years of age, who has been practicing law about 4½ years, most of which time was taken up in attending to local politics in his county. This game about to be played off in the *people*, is too serious for a farce, it is a *fraud*, involving a man [unequal] to the people's interest.[22]

On at least one occasion, Harlan's effort to balance his private practice and official positions was also a source of concern. In 1857, a Cincinnati client wrote to him about a claim he had asked James to collect two years earlier. The client had written Harlan several follow-up letters but received no reply. He had recently asked mutual friends, he now wrote Harlan, what their experience had been with the prominent lawyer. They assured him Harlan had been a "prompt correspondent" in the past but stressed that he now occupied a "high position." "Perhaps that's the difficulty!" the frustrated client exclaimed. "He can't see objects so near the surface!"[23]

The Cincinnati client's consternation was understandable but minor. A rumor about Harlan's law practice that began circulating around the state in the summer of 1851 could have been devastating to both his practice and political career. In August a friend wrote to him about gossip of "a most slanderous character." It was charged, the friend related, "that you have an agent travelling over the State hunting up negroes claiming their freedom for the purpose of instituting suits in their behalf. . . . It has also been stated that you are an *Abolitionist* and that you have now deposited in the jail at Lexington a negro woman and child for whom you have brought suit for [their] freedom . . . on the ground that in coming from the State of Virginia they were brought through the State of Ohio [a free state] by their owner." Harlan's friend had registered "a flat and unqualified denial" to each of these "ridiculous" charges, as well as the claim that Harlan had confined other blacks in jails for the same purpose. But he wished to substantiate his assertions in his friend's behalf and urged Harlan to provide "a full statement of the facts."[24]

James Harlan's reply was swift and blunt. The charges, he declared, were "as palpable falsehoods as ever were concocted or uttered by mortal man." Whoever called him an abolitionist "lied in his throat." In a scratched-through passage of his response, he added that he had "the same opinion of an abolitionist that I have of a disunionist—Each deserves the gallows." He also asserted, however, that "nothing which may emanate from Negro traders or others will ever prevent me from instituting a suit for *freedom* if I believe the laws authorize it."[25]

The rumor apparently had little discernible effect on Harlan's practice or political future. His responses to the charges, however, reflect the complexities of his views on slavery—views his son, John, largely embraced, at least through the Civil War years. The Harlan household maintained roughly a dozen slaves, all of whom James and his wife had acquired from their parents. By all accounts, Harlan was a kindly master. In her unpublished memoirs, Justice Harlan's wife Malvina, an Indiana native of New England Puritan stock, recalled being surprised to find, on moving to Kentucky following her marriage, that her father-in-law's slaves "were all carefully looked after, not only physically but morally. . . . The close sympathy existing between the slaves and their Master or Mistress," she wrote, "was a source of great wonder to me as a descendant of the Puritans, and I was often obliged to admit to myself that my former views of the 'awful institution of slavery' would have to be somewhat modified."[26]

James Harlan remained an opponent of immediate abolition throughout his life. Moreover, while he did seek freedom for slaves legally entitled to such relief under existing law, his practice also included slavery transactions. In 1834, for example, he drew up an elaborate deed for the transfer of slaves from one estate to another.[27] Harlan made it possible, however, for at least two of his slaves to purchase their freedom. Moreover, he abhorred the cruel treatment to which the slaves of others were often subjected. An incident reflecting his concerns was repeated often in family lore. In her memoirs, Malvina Harlan gave the following account:

> One Sunday morning, on his way to church, he passed in the main street a company of slaves that were being driven to the "Slave Market" in a neighboring town. The able-bodied men and women were chained together, four abreast, preceded by the old ones and the little "pickaninnies" who walked un-bound.
> This pitiful procession was in [the] charge of a brutish white man belonging to a class which in those days were called "Slave-drivers." . . . Their badge of office was a long, snake-like whip made of black leather, every blow from which drew blood.
> The sight stirred my Father-in-law to the depths of his gentle nature. He saw before him the awful possibilities of an institution which, in the division of family estates, and the sale of slaves, involved inevitably the separation of husband and wife, of parent and children; and the dreadful type of men which the institution of slavery developed as "slave-drivers," seemed to my Father-in-law to embody the worst aspects of the system.
> My Father-in-law could do nothing to liberate the poor creatures then before him; but he was so filled with indignation that any one calling himself a man should be engaged in such a cruel business that, walking out to the middle of the street and angrily shaking his long fore-finger in the face of the "Slave-driver," he said to him, "you are a damned scoundrel. Good morning, sir." After having thus relieved his feelings, he quietly pursued his way to the House of Prayer.[28]

There is also at least indirect evidence that James Harlan favored a gradual elimination of slavery. Toward the end of his life, his friend and political ally Henry Clay advanced a plan for gradual emancipation and shared with Harlan his frustrations about the disruptive effect the "peculiar institution" might have on his beloved union. In early 1850, for example, Clay wrote Harlan that slavery was "the all engrossing theme" in Washington and expressed his growing despair "whether any comprehensive plan of adjustment could be devised and proposed" to resolve the "vexed question."[29] Harlan's son and Clay's namesake, Henry Clay Harlan, once wrote to a family friend describing his frustrations at slavery "perpetualists" who would tolerate no compromises on the issue. Delegates were then being selected to draft what was to become the 1850 Kentucky constitution, and Henry Clay Harlan feared that intransigents would dominate the process:

> It is to be hoped that the Lord is not afflicting our people with the most terrible visita-
> tion of his wrath, namely; "giving them over to strong delusion that they believe a
> lie." Perhaps out of the foolishness of the counsels of slavery perpetualists, he intends
> to spring forth the success of Emancipation doctrine. I did at one time think that some
> ground of compromise could have been taken, and the pro-slavery party would con-
> cede. . . . But the new Constitution will contain the most ultra provisions for the per-
> petuation of slavery and if I mistake not it will be most terribly mangled when it
> comes before the people for ratification.[30]

Presumably, James Harlan's views substantially tracked his son's feelings.

The Other Harlan

Growing realization of the threat slavery posed for the Union and the Whig Party, and his association with such moderates on the issue as Henry Clay, undoubtedly contributed to the complexities of James Harlan's racial views. An element of his private life, however, may also have influenced his thinking, as well as that of his son, the future justice. In her memoirs, Malvina Harlan reported that one of the slaves her father-in-law had permitted to purchase his freedom had found work as a railroad porter, becoming a "most valued employee of the company." The other had gone to California in 1849, "and was fortunate enough to 'strike gold' almost im-mediately." Her husband's sister, Elizabeth, Mrs. Harlan added, had received "a fine new piano as a . . . gift from this grateful quasi-member of the household!"[31]

What Mrs. Harlan neglected to mention was that "this grateful quasi-member of the household" was probably her husband's half-brother, progeny of a liaison be-tween her father-in-law and a mulatto slave named Mary. Accounts of Robert Har-lan's life are replete with inconsistencies. At least one source has suggested that James Harlan's father might have fathered Robert.[32] But the elder Harlan died in 1816, the year of Robert's birth, or two years before his birth, depending on the ac-count examined. It thus seems more likely that Robert was John's half-brother rather than his uncle, and most versions of Robert's roots make this conclusion re-garding his paternity. Robert Harlan spent much of his adult life in Cincinnati, and a study of that city's black population, first published in 1926, referred to Robert as the "reputed half brother of . . . Justice Harlan."[33] More important, a thoroughgoing recent study, drawing on voluminous tax and census records, as well as physical re-semblances (six feet tall, "high yellow," blue-gray eyes) and much additional evi-dence, has concluded that Robert was John's half-brother.[34] And while the author of that fine effort was unable to locate Robert Harlan's descendants, a relation whom I contacted confirmed her family's long-held belief that her ancestor and Justice Har-lan were half-brothers.[35]

One profile of Robert Harlan indicates that he was born in Harrodsburg, on De-cember 12, 1816.[36] The most thorough obituary published at his death in 1897 confirms that account of the date of his birth but lists his birthplace as Mecklenburg County, Virginia.[37] Other sources concur with that site for his birth; but the court record of his emancipation on September 23, 1850, indicates that he was born on December 12, 1818.[38] Mecklenburg, situated in southern Virginia along the North Carolina border, was a considerable distance from the Berkeley County ancestral home of the Harlans in what was then northern Virginia. But it was relatively close to Prince Edward County, from which John Harlan's maternal grandparents had migrated to Kentucky. It is probable, therefore, that Robert Harlan's mother was a slave on that side of the family. Robert may have been conceived during a visit by James Harlan to his mother's family in Virginia. James would have been only 15 or 17 at the time, but the liaison may have been intended to provide the young man with sexual experience.

A Harlan family scrapbook of unknown origin contains an undated clipping from the *Cincinnati Enquirer* that provides a different version of Robert Harlan's initial association with the family. According to this account, a Crab Orchard, Kentucky, man prominent in horseracing circles brought Robert and his mother from Virginia and convinced Justice Harlan's mother to accept them in exchange for a Harlan slave who was a fine horseman. "Mrs. Harlan, Judge John M.'s mother was so much pleased with the fine looking and smart boy," who was only "very slightly colored," the story claimed, "that she purchased him. Hence Bob took the name of Harlan."[39] Such a story avoids the sensitive matter of Robert's paternity, and indeed may have been concocted for that purpose. The evidence suggests, however, that Justice Harlan's father sired Robert and that he and his mother were taken to the Harlan home near Harrodsburg when he was a child, perhaps as young as three.[40]

On occasion, of course, masters acknowledged their slave children, but not always without risk. In 1836, such candor almost cost Kentucky's Colonel Richard M. Johnson the vice-presidency of the United States. A popular politician and war hero, and the reputed slayer of Chief Tecumseh, Johnson had lived with a mulatto woman. She later died, but Johnson educated their two daughters and presented them socially. For his temerity, Andrew Jackson's running mate failed to win the electoral vote majority necessary for victory, surviving the race only by election in the U.S. Senate.[41]

James Harlan never formally acknowledged Robert as his son. Their relationship may have been widely known, or suspected, in the family and among close associates; but there is little direct evidence bearing on the extent to which their relationship was public knowledge. In 1868, following Robert's return from an extended stay in England, a Harlan family friend, O. S. Poston, wrote John Harlan from Chicago with the following news: "I saw Robert Harlan, late of England, here this week. He seems to have improved by eating English beef and breathing British air."[42] But Poston was hardly a casual acquaintance. He had lived in the Harlan household while reading law with James Harlan and was virtually a family member much of his life.[43]

Whatever the degree of general public awareness of their relationship, James Harlan was apparently an unusually generous and solicitous master to Robert. According to one account, Harlan even attempted to enroll the youth in the village school at Harrodsburg with his other sons, but was promptly rebuffed by local authorities. Given the deepseated taboo against schooling for slaves, that story is probably apocryphal. But Robert Harlan delighted in telling it, remarking that he had only "a half day's schooling" in his entire life.[44] Although he was denied formal schooling, James Harlan's oldest sons—presumably Richard and William—reportedly shared their lessons with Robert, giving him at least the rudiments of an education.

By the age of 18, Robert had managed to save enough to open a barber shop and later a grocery store. With proceeds from these enterprises, he purchased the first of many race horses he was to own. A skilled horseman, he began to enter races in Kentucky and other states, winning large purses at the principal tracks of the day. At times, too, he posed as a "free man of color."[45] James Harlan undoubtedly knew of such activities and permitted them at considerable risk, given the mounting legal obligations of masters to curb the activities of their slaves. Perhaps for that reason, the elder Harlan filed a deed of emancipation in the local county court on September 18, 1848, granting Robert his freedom in exchange for 500 dollars.[46]

In 1849, the discovery of gold in California enticed Robert to join a party of white men who sailed around the Isthmus of Panama, bent on striking it rich on the Pacific coast. Malvina Harlan's memoirs, along with several other sources, state that Robert quickly amassed a fortune in the gold fields. Another account indicates, however, that Robert opened a store in California and acquired his wealth from gold-seekers rather than by prospecting for the valuable mineral himself. The most probing study of Robert's life to date suggests that he won his fortune at the gaming table.[47] He amassed a fortune estimated at $50–90 thousand, and then returned east, settling in Cincinnati.

Building on the capital he had accumulated in California, Robert speculated in Cincinnati real estate, ran a hotel, occupied one of the city's larger homes, and purchased its finest photographic gallery as well as the services of a number of the nation's premier photographers. He also became the owner of an impressive stable of thoroughbreds and was for years, according to several accounts, the only black owner permitted to enter races at Louisville, New Orleans, and other southern cities.

In 1852, Robert Harlan married Josephine Floyd, said to be the daughter of John B. Floyd, Virginia governor and secretary of war in the cabinet of President James Buchanan. Floyd and his wife had only two adopted children, a son and daughter. It is thus likely that Miss Floyd, like Harlan, was the offspring of a relationship between her father and a slave. The couple had a son, Robert James Harlan, Jr., in 1853, but Josephine Harlan died when the boy was six months old. Harlan also had three daughters by a previous marriage.

During the early days of the Civil War, Robert Harlan played an important role in defending Cincinnati from Confederate forces. In August of 1862, fifteen thousand rebels under Kirby Smith occupied several cities in northern Kentucky. General Lew Wallace, who had been placed in command of Union forces at Cincinnati, issued a call for volunteers to assist his troops in protecting the city from a rebel siege. Black citizens were among the first to volunteer, and Robert Harlan was one of their leaders. "The negroes," according to one account, "were organized into a working brigade and did most effective service in the trenches . . . under the control and leadership of Judge William M. Dickson. The landlord of the famous Dumas House, the retreat for so many colored people, Colonel Harlan, led the corps down to Broadway on its daily march to labor and, rough-clad and vari-colored as they were, they were never surpassed in the contribution they made to the preservation of the town."[48] Their march, another source relates, was headed by "the stalwart, manly form of the landlord of the Dumas House, Colonel Harlan."[49]

To escape the racial prejudice of the period, Robert Harlan ultimately moved his family to England, returning to the United States several years after the hostilities had ended. He had first traveled abroad in 1851, as a visitor to the first World's Fair in Sydenham, England. One account indicates that he next left the United States for England in 1859, but the siege of Cincinnati, in which he is reported to have played a part, did not occur until 1862. It is probable, therefore, that he sailed for England in 1862–63. Accompanying him were his children, eight thoroughbreds, a trainer, and a jockey. By selling his Cincinnati real estate and gallery and investing all his money in securities, he was able to establish a handsome annuity for life in England; and he apparently maintained a gracious lifestyle there, complete with a fine home, retinue of servants, and a stable that he augmented with a number of English thoroughbreds. Harlan's entries in British races proved profitable, but the impact of the war on his securities holdings was devastating, forcing him to return to the United States in 1868.

Both before and after his sojourn in England, Harlan was extensively involved in civic and political affairs. Through negotiations he initiated with the philanthropist Nicholas Longworth, he was responsible for building the first school for blacks in Cincinnati. He also served for years as a trustee of the city's schools and its orphans' asylum. In 1870, he delivered an oration urging the adoption of the Fifteenth Amendment, banning racial discrimination in the suffrage. He would become the first black selected to a seat on the Republican state committee in Ohio. In 1872, he was a delegate-at-large to the Republican national convention that nominated Ulysses S. Grant for a second term in the presidency. In 1875, he raised a battalion of 400 black soldiers, for which effort Governor Rutherford B. Hayes commissioned him a colonel in the state militia. His detachment was a forerunner of the Ninth Ohio Battalion, which became part of the 372d infantry regiment in World War I. Narrowly defeated in 1880 for a seat in the Ohio legislature, he was an alternate delegate-at-large to the 1884 GOP national convention, and then won a state assembly seat in 1885. As a member of the Ohio legislature, he joined other black leaders of his era in obtaining repeal of state laws that imposed special disabilities on black citizens. Invariably active in conventions called to consider the plight of blacks, he was temporary chairman of a national conference convened for that purpose in Nashville in 1876.

Robert Harlan's political activities led to federal patronage positions in a variety of Republican administrations. Shortly after his return from England, President Grant appointed him special agent-at-large with the postal department. In 1881, Chester A. Arthur named him a special agent with the U.S. treasury department in Cincinnati. He was removed from that post during Grover Cleveland's terms as president, but occupied the office again following the return of the GOP to power.

By the time of his death on September 21, 1897, he was retired and residing with his son in Cincinnati.[50]

Like his father, Robert Harlan, Jr., benefited from involvement in efforts in behalf of the Republican Party. In the 1880s the younger Harlan graduated from the Cincinnati law college and obtained a law license. During most of his adult life, however, he held a variety of government jobs. Before his father's death, he served as a surveyor with the Cincinnati water works, as a license deputy with the auditor's office, and as a deputy in the county treasurer's office. Through his father's sponsorship, he developed an image in national Republican circles as someone who could help deliver the black vote in the Midwest. During the 1888 presidential campaign, he was president of his ward's Republican organization. On one occasion he wrote to Benjamin Harrison, the party's nominee, that his group "propose[d] by earnest work to carry the ward in the coming election for the nominees of the republican party," adding: "As colored men we thank you for your expressions of friendship toward the race, and renew our assurances of fealty to the cause you so ably represent."[51]

Robert Harlan, Jr., and William Howard Taft were reared on the same Cincinnati street and were classmates at the city's Woodward school.[52] Before and during Taft's successful 1908 presidential campaign, Harlan frequently wrote to the candidate, professing his "unqualified loyalty" and detailing his efforts to marshal black voters in Taft's behalf. In May of 1908, he assured Taft "that the opposing element among the colored people [was] becoming rational" and expressed confidence that "if intelligently influenced after your nomination even those who have strayed far from the fold will return without being tempted by the husks of democracy."[53]

In 1906, Brownsville, Texas, erupted in gunshots, presumably fired by black soldiers of an infantry regiment stationed there. One man had been killed, another wounded; and while the evidence of guilt was unclear at best, President Theodore Roosevelt had dismissed three entire companies of black soldiers when they refused to expose the culprits in the incident. Deciding against seeking a third term, Roosevelt threw his support to Taft in 1908. Partly for that reason, opponents of Taft's nomination at the 1908 Republican convention in Chicago charged that Taft's selection would cost the party many black votes.

In a letter to Taft dated August 1, 1908, Robert Harlan, Jr., blamed the opposition on the "emotional nature" of blacks and on the venal "negro preachers" who had "grown . . . large in self-importance." He agreed that much work would be necessary to "correct false impressions and the erroneous belief that [the nominee had] no interest in and kindly feeling for the negro." Ultimately, however, he doubted that many members of his race would abandon the GOP for the Democrats, "a party that has given them no consideration except a guarantee of their 'treaty rights'. . . . [W]hile there may be some deserters, the large body of negro voters will remain in the ranks of the Republican party and do their whole duty on the 3d of November next."[54]

At the beginning of the fall campaign, Robert Harlan, Jr., shared with Taft letters he had received from Indiana and Illinois in response to his inquiries regarding Taft's chances among black voters in those states. One such missive, from a prominent black Chicago surgeon, offered a pessimistic assessment of Taft's standing in Illinois: "There is absolutely lack of enthusiasm for Taft among the supposed Taft leaders . . . ," he wrote. "On the other hand the opposition is getting in its deadly work. . . . The negroes feel that Taft is a Roosevelt tool."[55] Taft soon responded, thanking his classmate for the intelligence he had provided. "I have to take the bitter with the sweet," he wrote, "and I am glad to get all views."[56]

By that point, Robert Harlan, Jr., was living in Washingon, D.C., and working for the treasury department. Promptly after Taft's victory and inauguration, he sought a promotion and salary increase. Taft's secretary, Frank W. Carpenter, made appropriate inquiries in Harlan's behalf, but to no immediate avail. When Taft was defeated by Woodrow Wilson in 1912, Harlan became fearful that his "long and faithful service and good record will not be sufficient protection to insure my safety from the storm now raging."[57] Taft did some checking and then wrote Harlan that his fears were unjustified; at worst he could expect a transfer, not a discharge. "You ought not to make any effort to prevent this," advised Taft, "but take your medicine in this regard as it is dosed out to you."[58]

Ultimately, Harlan's position was saved. By 1916, however, he was again writing Taft for assistance, this time urging the former president to intervene with the Wilson administration for a transfer to a more stable position, less vulnerable to elimination or reduction in salary than his current post. On this occasion, Taft demurred: "I have uniformly declined to write to members of this administration on subjects of patronage." When Harlan was later transferred and his salary cut, he attributed the action to his lineage, writing Taft: "[B]ecause of a moral lapse made by my Grandfather, why should I pay a vicarious atonement? I believe if the Secretary knew the facts in the case he would reinstate me in my former salary."[59] There is no evidence, though, that Taft sought to help his former classmate on this occasion either. Even so, Harlan continued over the years to write Taft lengthy, cordial letters, which Taft acknowledged with polite, if brief and unelaborated, replies.[60]

Certain descendants of Robert Harlan, Jr., remained in Washington and were connected by marriage to a number of significant figures in the first and second Reconstructions. The maternal great-grandfather of Robert Jackson Harlan, a grandson of Robert Harlan, Jr., was John Mercer Langston, a black congressman from Virginia, U.S. minister to Haiti, and the first dean of Howard University's law school. In 1955, moreover, Robert Jackson Harlan's daughter, Roberta, married James M. Nabrit III, son of the Howard law professor who, along with Thurgood Marshall and others, played a key role in the school desegregation cases of the 1950s.[61] Those rulings, ironically enough, began the dismantling of the *Plessy* precedent, against which the first Justice Harlan had vigorously dissented.[62]

In 1956, the year following the second Supreme Court decision in the school desegregation cases, Robert Jackson Harlan wrote to the second Justice Harlan, requesting an interview. "By way of introduction," he began his letter, "let me say that the similarity of our surnames is due to no mere coincidence. My great grandfather, Robert Harlan, was a slave in the home of your great grandfather. He was a boy when your grandfather, John Marshall Harlan, was a boy."[63] Justice Harlan readily complied with Robert Jackson Harlan's request for an interview, read his visitor's family scrapbook, and attempted to assist Harlan in securing a position as an assistant U.S. attorney in Washington. Those efforts were not immediately fruitful. Beginning in 1963, however, Robert Jackson Harlan held various civil-rights related positions with the General Services Administration. From 1970 until his retirement in 1976, moreover, he was deputy director of the office of civil rights in the Federal Highway Administration.[64]

Whether Robert Jackson Harlan broached the subject of their probable familial relationship during their conversations is unknown. The journalist Drew Pearson carried a brief item on a later visit of the two Harlans in his column, but noted only that Robert Jackson Harlan's "great-grandfather had taken the name Harlan from the slave owner, as frequently happened in those days."[65] Barrett Prettyman, Jr., Justice Harlan's clerk at the time, could not recall any discussion of the matter with the justice.[66] The justice's daughter, Eve Dillingham, was surprised to first learn of the connection only years after her father's death.[67] Justice Harlan's sister, Edith Harlan Powell, "vaguely" recalled learning of the relationship from older members of the family, but also remembered that little was said about it since "it was, of course, illegal."[68]

Justice Harlan must have been aware of his familial ties to Robert Harlan. If accounts of Robert's birth are accurate, he was born in 1816 or 1818, while John Harlan's birthdate was 1833. Robert's childhood associations with James Harlan's sons were thus primarily with John's older siblings. As adults, though, the two half-brothers corresponded regularly and probably had personal contacts as well.

The racial views of Robert Harlan and his son are not entirely clear. Passages from the correspondence of Robert Harlan, Jr., with William Howard Taft suggest a stereotypical attitude toward poorer blacks common among most whites of his era. As noted previously, he referred to the "emotional nature" of blacks. On more than one occasion, moreover, he shared crude racial humor with Taft, written in the dialect of uneducated blacks. In a 1928 letter written to Taft following a speech by Democratic New York Governor Al Smith about corruption in the Republican Party, Harlan told of "an old colored man in Cincinnati who thought election day was for 'revenue only' and would not vote until paid." On election day he received more bribes from Republicans than Democrats, yet voted Democratic. When asked to explain his choice, he replied, "'Boss, dem publicans is so much more currupt dan de demmycrats, I had to vote 'cordin to mah conscience.'" In the same letter, Robert, Jr., described the visit of a black couple and their 11 children to a county fair. When they asked the price of photographs being taken at one booth, they were told that pictures were a dollar a dozen. "Looking over the brood of 11 with a sigh the wife said, 'Come on chillun, we's got to wait til next yeah.'"[69]

Whatever his racial or class biases, however, Robert Harlan, Jr., obviously supported the Reconstruction amendments and efforts to secure equality before the law. In a 1929 letter to Taft, for example, he complained of the way a "prejudiced South" ignored the amendments, adding: "Civil rights are the basis of good government and disenfranchisement of a part of the electorate because of race or previous condition, weakens the foundation of the Temple of Liberty."[70]

Robert Harlan, Sr., Justice Harlan's half-brother, had also resented the nation's racial record and its refusal to recognize blacks of whatever complexion as full members of the national community. His correspondence with Frederick Douglass, the most prominent black leader of his era and a personal friend, provides evidence of his racial attitudes. When Douglass was appointed minister to Haiti in 1889, Harlan penned his friend a letter of congratulations but expressed "regret you did not receive a place commensurate with your ability and position," adding: "The office does not honor you and I trust as soon as the diplomatic difficulties between Hayti and this country are arranged that you will resign and return home."[71] Even more revealing was a letter Harlan wrote Douglass the next year, in response to a letter from his friend and a speech Douglass had given criticizing the use of the term "Afro American" to label American blacks.

> It was coined [wrote Harlan] . . . to classify us under a head to which we do not belong. We are Americans simply, with guaranteed rights which if enforced would place us upon an equality with all citizens of our common country, so far as our civil and political rights are concerned. We might just as well speak of Afro Germans and Afro Irish as Afro Americans. While our ancestors came from Africa, we did not, and we are just as thoroughly natives of this country as the descendants of the pilgrims who landed on Plymouth rock. There is no sense in the name Afro American, unless it refers to blood and mixture, and that would make us part Indian and part African, for the Indian is the only aborigine of this country. Therefore the absurdity of the term is apparent.[72]

There is no direct evidence that Robert Harlan shared his views and frustrations with the future justice. Following the Civil War, however, as John Marshall Harlan gradually moved into the Republican Party, the two had frequent contact on matters of mutual political concern. Certain of their correspondence involved mundane patronage opportunities. During the period Robert was a special postal agent, for example, he reported to John that another agent had recently been removed from the service. "If you have a friend that wants the position," he wrote, "now is his time to apply for it. Nothing must be said in regard to Dobbins having been reported as drunk. Please let me hear from you when convenient."[73] But Robert's letters at times concerned John's political fortunes and those of his friends as well as Robert's value to the Republican Party. When John's former law partner, Benjamin Bristow, was seeking the GOP presidential nomination in 1876, for example, Robert wrote his half-brother that Bristow had many black Ohio friends who "pretend to be for [Rutherford B.] Hayes." He also assured the future justice that he was "working quietly" for Bristow. Robert was then preparing to attend a Nashville convention on the political interests of blacks. He invited John to contact him before his departure for Tennessee: "I can do much good among the colored delegates as I know the prominent men of the South."[74]

When Hayes won the presidency with the support of both Harlans, moreover, Robert Harlan was among the first to conclude, based on a conversation with a Hayes intimate, that the president was planning a Supreme Court appointment for John Marshall Harlan. Several days after Hayes's inauguration, Robert wrote his half-brother, expressing "great" disappointment that he had not been named attorney general. He also reported, though, the impression of a mutual friend that John was on the president's "slate for anything you wanted." His source had "further said that he could not understand [the president's inaction] in any other way [than] that Hayes intended to offer you Judge [David] Davis's place on the bench."[75] This was the seat to which John was ultimately appointed.

But their contacts were not limited entirely to electoral politics and patronage matters. On one occasion, John Marshall Harlan apparently sought his half-brother's assistance in a case with racial overtones. In 1871, Captain James M. Davenport, a relation of John's mother, was charged with assaulting a black justice of the peace in Washington, D.C. The victim was Captain Orindatus Simon Bolivar, or O.S.B., Wall, brother-in-law of John Mercer Langston, who was then dean of Howard University's law department. Like Robert Harlan, Langston and Wall were the offspring of white masters and slave women. Following the death of Langston's parents, a friend of his father had raised and educated the youth, who became the first black graduate of Ohio's Oberlin College. While at Oberlin, Langston married O.S.B. Wall's sister, Caroline, who, along with Langston and Wall, would also graduate from Oberlin. During the Civil War Wall had been one of the few blacks to receive a commission and had devoted most of his wartime attention to the recruitment of southern blacks into the Union army. Like the Langstons, Wall was an outspoken critic of slavery and racial prejudice. Davenport's assault on Wall, unprovoked and committed in a drunken rage, could thus have had serious political implications.[76]

In late August of 1871, John Marshall Harlan received a letter from Thomas F. Miller, a Washington attorney representing Davenport. The prosecution, Miller reported, would be able to make a strong case against his client, whose only possible successful defense might be "mental incapacity . . . to commit wrong" at the time of the incident. Davenport hoped that his kin might come to Washington and take over the defense. Given Harlan's growing political influence, Miller felt the Kentuckian might be able to persuade the authorities "to relax what we have reason to believe will be a very vigorous prosecution." Otherwise, Miller could "not see . . . how a conviction can be avoided."[77]

On receiving Miller's letter, if not before, Harlan contacted his former law partner, Benjamin Bristow, who was then serving as treasury secretary in President Grant's cabinet. Bristow's response was hardly optimistic. One of the Washington newspapers had already reported that Harlan was expected to defend Davenport! Bristow had been told, moreover, that the defendant "expects and very much desires it." But Harlan's former partner was hardly pleased at that prospect. "I do not think he has any right," wrote Bristow, "to require such a sacrifice of business and time at your hands." Bristow promised to do "cheerfully" what he could to secure bail for Davenport, but doubted "very seriously the propriety of his being released before trial," adding, "My great fear is that he could not resist the inclination to drink." The treasury secretary predicted that the case would be "a *very bad* one," resulting in a conviction. "The attack was wanton and reckless," he wrote, "[induced] no doubt by craziness from drink which is regarded here as no excuse for crime and the courts always so charge." Bristow also warned that "[t]he wounded negro is a brother-in-law of John M. Langston, who takes an interest in the prosecution." The treasury secretary, however, was not entirely pessimistic. "Perhaps," he suggested, "after trial we can get the Prest to pardon."[78]

Several days later, Bristow penned Harlan a further report. He had seen Davenport, who looked "quite well" and talked "rather cheerfully," and had "tried to impress upon him the great inconvenience that it would be for you to quit your business and come here to defend him—to say nothing of the pecuniary costs." Bristow had also told the defendant that Harlan was anxious to help him and that if Davenport would select a lawyer for his trial, Bristow would secure the fee. Harlan had written and telegraphed Davenport that he would visit Washington in his kin's behalf; and Bristow assured Harlan that he was not attempting to discourage him from making the trip, but only "to justify your not coming, if you see proper not to come."[79]

Bristow seems to have been hopeful that Harlan would not become directly involved in the politically sensitive case; and Harlan ultimately concurred. In a letter dated mid-September, Bristow noted that Davenport was "greatly disappointed at your not coming" but understood the considerations underlying the decision. Bristow reported that he was seeking trial counsel for the defendant, since Miller, while "unselfish in his devotion . . . [did] not amount to much." The treasury secretary had little success finding new counsel. One, presumably black, attorney declined to accept the case because he and Langston were colleagues at Howard, and his relations with Wall were "very intimate." A Kentuckian attempted to enter the case, but Bristow considered him to be "a great liar & drunkard & a dead beat." As he had stated on previous occasions, Bristow continued to think it wise to leave Davenport in jail, where he was reasonably comfortable and "certainly improved in health." Warning that Davenport's "thirst for whiskey amount[ed] to a *disease*," Bristow feared he "would soon fall into his old habit," if released. If Harlan wished to have him released, however, Bristow offered to assist in raising bail. "Of course," he added, "I wish not [to] be known as taking any part in the case."[80]

The morning of the day Bristow wrote to Harlan, Charles P. Pennebaker, another lawyer connected with Davenport's defense, secured a continuance of the case until December. The following day Pennebaker wrote to Bristow, informing the treasury secretary that he had spoken with the "negro squire" the previous day. Pennebaker was hardly sympathetic with Wall's situation: "He professes to have no enmity whatever against Davenport. Talks that sickly sentimental talk—the Lord does all things—the law must have its course and that he could not in conscience do anything or fail to do anything in the way of the law—protests that if Davenport was turned out on bail that he would be in constant fear of his life so much so that he would be greatly [distracted] in the discharge of his important official functions." Pennebaker stated that he sought to convince Captain Wall that he need have no fear of the defendant, but to no avail. He reported that Wall claimed that "the *nigs* all love him as they love their own hearts," and that Wall took credit for saving Davenport from mob violence at the time of the incident—an assertion Pennebaker branded "wholly untrue." In Pennebaker's view, Davenport could be released on bail without danger to himself or Wall.[81]

While the case was pending, John Harlan apparently discussed the matter with his half-brother. In late October, while the case awaited trial, Robert Harlan visited New York on business and stopped off in Washington, he later wrote John, to "see what I could do for Mr. Davenport." Robert Harlan and Professor Langston had been friends in Ohio. From a conversation with Langston during his Washington visit, Robert concluded that Davenport had "taken altogether a wrong course" in the case. "[H]e had reported that you had written to the President and other governmental officials in behalf of Mr. Davenport and that you had also authorized other parties to draw on you for large amounts of money for the purpose of clearing Mr. Davenport."[82]

John Harlan had contacted not only Benjamin Bristow but also Secretary of War William W. Belknap, and perhaps others in President Grant's cabinet as well. Belknap's inquiries led him to conclude that Davenport's assault on Wall was indeed an "outrageous one" but that the growing prominence of the future justice—whose 1871 Kentucky gubernatorial campaign had made him "famous" in national Republican circles—might be helpful to Davenport.[83] Robert Harlan however, denied to Langston that his half-brother was attempting to influence the case.[84]

After visiting Davenport in jail, Robert Harlan went to Captain Wall's residence. Wall was absent, but Harlan did speak with his wife, Amanda, whom he described as "an old acquaintance" and a "most intelligent" woman. Amanda Wall's feelings toward Captain Davenport were bitter at best. She "seemed to think," wrote Robert, that "Mr. Davenport shot her husband because he was a colored man and held an office." When Harlan spoke with Captain Wall the following day, he was "pleased" to learn that "his feelings [were] not so hostile toward Mr. Davenport as his wife's." Like Langston, Wall informed Robert that the future justice's "influence and money had been thrown up to him," adding that "no amount of the latter could influence him." The police lieutenant who arrested Davenport had told Wall that the defendant would harm him again if given the chance, that he had threatened to shoot other blacks, that his neighbors feared him, and that the defendant had so viciously abused his own wife that she had returned to Kentucky. Davenport, Wall added, had shot him without warning or "a cross word."

Attempting to calm Wall, Robert Harlan assured him that he had known Davenport "almost from childhood." The defendant came from a "very respectable family" made poor by the war. Their kin's imprisonment would disgrace the family and be "of no earthly benefit" to Wall. Wall agreed, but explained that he had political ambitions and wanted to avoid any appearance that he had been "bribed in any way." The law, he insisted, must "take its course."

The following day, Robert Harlan again visited Captain Wall. On this occasion, he drew heavily on John Harlan's contributions to "the Republican party and the colored people in Kentucky." He also offered to raise money for Wall's medical expenses and lost income. If freed, he assured the victim, Davenport would leave the District of Columbia.

Education and Marriage

With Robert Harlan's assistance, the Wall–Davenport case was apparently resolved to John Harlan's satisfaction. As much as any other facet of their relationship, the affair illustrates the extent of Robert's ties to his half-brother and suggests his influence on the future justice's growing attachment to the Republican Party and the principles of Reconstruction during the years following the Civil War. Numerous events and personalities from his youth also played an important role in determining the direction of John Harlan's career.[85]

John spent his earliest years in the old Harlan home near Harrodsburg and Danville. During the period his father served in Congress, the family moved to Harrodsburg. Then in 1840, when James Harlan was appointed Kentucky's secretary of state, they moved to Frankfort in Franklin County, capital of the commonwealth. At that time Franklin's 2,493 slaves comprised about one-fourth of the county's total wealth. Slaves were the primary products for sale and barter, and newspapers of the day were filled with advertisements of the following kind: "For sale—a very likely negro woman; a first rate cook, washer, &c., and three children"; or "a likely negro girl who is a good cook, washer and spinner; she is also honest"; or "a very likely and intelligent mulatto boy, twelve years old. . . . I will sell a bargain, for cash in hand."[86]

James Harlan's thriving law practice and official positions provided his family with a comfortable, if not lavish, lifestyle; house servants performed the more arduous tasks. The childhood of John Harlan and his siblings was largely uneventful and pleasurable. Future prominent Missouri politicians George G. Vest and B. Gratz Brown, both red-heads like John, were among his childhood playmates. A contemporary newspaper account described the childhood of the "three remarkable red-headed boys": "After school was out, and the darkness of night had thrown a veil of comparative protection over the apple orchards of the neighborhood, the boys would gather on the front porch of the Vest mansion and 'talk.' They used to make wishes and resolves, and no resolution stopped short of the presidency of the United States."[87]

Like most privileged young Frankfort men of their era, the three boys attended the academy of Professor B. B. Sayre, where a strict regimen was the order of the day. Sayre had a terrible temper and "when in a bad humor" was a "terror" to his students. According to a local newspaper account,

> One day when the class was called, he was so plainly out of temper that the lesson was frightened out of the head of every pupil, as David Copperfield "felt whole pages slipping away."
>
> "Spell mouse!" he called out to the head of the class. "M-o-u-s-e," was nimbly passed over. "Very well—what is the plural?" was the next question fired at the boy with the precision of a bullet. "Mouses!" answered the frightened lad. "Next," cried the teacher, and every boy in the line lost his head, and one after another answered "mouses," including Vest, Harlan, and Brown, all very close to the bottom.
>
> Mr. Sayre's rage was complete. Beginning at the head of the class, he took every boy, one after another, by the ears and bumped his head against the wall.[88]

John attended Professor Sayre's school until 1848, when he enrolled at Centre College in Danville. Founded in 1819 as a state institution, by 1830 Centre had become the first college in the nation to be directly supported by the Presbyterian Church. The key figure in Centre's operations during Harlan's tenure there was John C. Young, who was appointed president the year the college affiliated with the Presbyterians. Like James Harlan and Henry Clay, Young, a Pennsylvania native and Princeton seminary graduate, was a slavery moderate. On two occasions, he had freed groups of his own slaves. He publicly supported the inclusion of a clause in the Kentucky constitution of 1849–50 providing for gradual emancipation. At the same time, he opposed what he considered to be the radical demands of the abolitionists. And although his students were mainly Southerners, many from the Deep South, whereas Young and most of his faculty were northern men, he "got by with his moderate antislavery views," as one history of the college put it, "without giving offense to either side on the slavery issue."[89]

Harlan entered Centre as a junior. The curriculum for juniors at that time included the Greek and Roman classics, rhetoric, chemistry, political economy, calculus, and "moral" and "natural" philosophy. Seniors undertook more of the same, as well as courses in zoology, architecture, and constitutional and international law. Harlan's interests seemed primarily directed to American and world history, for in 1849 he compiled an impressive list of biographies and other historical studies he had read.[90] Presumably, he also observed the strict discipline Centre demanded of its students, including one regulation under which each student was expected to be employed in study at least 7 out of every 24 hours, "exclusive of the time occupied in recitation."[91] Naturally, Centre gave its students' moral development considerable emphasis as well. Each student was exposed to Bible instruction, including daily chapel, church attendance, and a Sunday Bible lesson. Beginning in 1848, the year of Harlan's admission, students "also [had] an opportunity of attending a religious lecture from the [college] President, once during each week."[92]

Nor was deportment neglected. The school was proud of the "moral and religious habits of its students" but was eternally vigilant against the rare unwholesome influence of "boys of bad habits (formed elsewhere) and ungovernable dispositions." Certain taverns and related establishments were "off limits" to students; attendance at theaters, balls, or horse races was strictly forbidden, as was the possession of weapons. "Profane swearing, intemperance, obscenity, licentiousness, impiety, playing at cards or at any game of wager . . . boisterous noises, [and] all wearing of disguises" were also banned. College discipline, however, was mild. "[N]o severe or disgraceful penalty [would] be awarded, except when the paramount interests of the Institution demand it."[93]

Harlan thrived at Centre, graduating with honors in 1850. He was now obliged to choose a career. Professor Sayre had urged James Harlan to train John for mercantile pursuits. His four older brothers were lawyers, an ample number for any family, Sayre reasoned.[94] John's mother shared the professor's preferences. While James Harlan was serving in Congress, Eliza Harlan had met a distant relation of her husband from Philadelphia. At the time of John's graduation from Centre College, Mrs. Harlan wrote this kinsman, who arranged an apprenticeship for him as a clerk in a Philadelphia mercantile house. Travel plans were made, and Mrs. Harlan even packed her son's trunk for the trip east. Only then, apparently, did she broach the subject with her busy husband. "Without hesitation," Justice Harlan's wife later related in her memoirs, "[James Harlan] said that 'it would never do, but that John too was to be a lawyer'; he had not named him 'John Marshall' . . . only to have him spend his life in the counting room of a mercantile house."[95]

Presumably with the young man's approval, if not his mother's, John thus began reading law with his father following his graduation from Centre. But his legal studies were not limited to the apprenticeship approach to legal training common in that period. He soon entered the law department of Lexington's Transylvania College for more formal instruction. During a 1908 visit to Transylvania, Justice Harlan would recall his law professors in laudatory terms, declaring, "If George Robertson and Thomas Marshall had been placed upon the bench of the Supreme Court of the

United States in their early years, they would have left a reputation as great as that of Chief Justice Marshall."[96]

The justice's assertion may have been an exaggeration, but Robertson, Marshall, and the other faculty Harlan praised that day were distinguished students of the law and prominent politicians and jurists of their time. Robertson, who joined Transylvania's law faculty in 1834, was born in Harrodsburg in 1790, the son of parents who had recently migrated from Virginia. Orphaned as a small boy, he had triumphed over his humble origins, serving in Congress and as speaker in the Kentucky house of representatives. But Robertson achieved his greatest distinction as a justice of Kentucky's court of appeals, the state's highest tribunal, on which he served from 1828 to 1843 and 1864 to 1871; from 1829 to 1843 he was chief justice. So prominent was Robertson in his state's history, in fact, that a Kentucky county was named after him.[97] The career of Thomas A. Marshall, who joined the faculty in 1837 and also served on the state court of appeals, was similarly illustrious.

As a young boy, John Harlan had sat at the feet of the "Great Commoner," Henry Clay, during one of his stirring stump speeches, "charmed with his magnificent, bugle voice."[98] But Harlan was moved by more than Clay's voice. By the time he entered Transylvania, he had thoroughly embraced the Whig nationalist teachings of Clay, his father, and others prominent in Kentucky and national politics. His Transylvania professors would reinforce and refine those leanings.

Of the school's law faculty, George Robertson was a particularly staunch nationalist. In a widely publicized 1836 lecture to students, he elaborately explained and defended his views, declaring at one point in his address,

> The Federal Constitution, to the extent of its provisions, is thus fundamental and supreme. It was made by the people, not by the States; is subject to modification or abolition by the people alone; . . . and belongs to the people of all the States, as one common and entire mass, and not to the several States as separate and corporate bodies. It cannot, then, be subject to State power or State will, or even to the power or will of a majority of the people of all the States, except for amendment, or by revolution.[99]

Robertson had hardly modified his thinking by the time of John Harlan's arrival at Transylvania. Indeed, his address to Harlan's graduating class resounded with nationalist themes; and in a request that the address be published, Harlan and three other students praised Robertson's contempt for "the monstrous doctrine of nullification and secession, which threatens . . . to undermine the fabric of our government."[100]

Like Harlan's father and Henry Clay, Robertson also possessed complex feelings regarding the increasingly controversial slavery issue. While seeking election as a delegate to Kentucky's 1849 constitutional convention, Robertson underscored his revulsion at the institution of slavery in seemingly uncompromising language:

> I am not one of those who believe that domestic slavery is a blessing, moral or physical, to the white race. I cannot believe that it makes us richer, more moral, more religious, more peaceful, more secure, or more happy—nor can I admit that, under its

various influences, our children become more industrious, more practical, or more useful; and I am sure that free labor is degraded and laboring freemen greatly injured by slavery. If, in the dispensation of an all-wise Providence, it could be obliterated from the face of the earth, I should consider the achievement as most glorious and beneficent to mankind; and trusting in the benevolent purposes of that overruling guardianship, I cannot doubt that the day will come, when all mankind will be prepared to enjoy, and will therefore enjoy, civil, religious, and personal liberty and light.[101]

Nevertheless, Robertson doubted that he would live to see "even Kentucky" a free state, much less, he might have added, the Deep South. Nor did he favor emancipation. Instead, Robertson supported a ban on the importation of slaves from abroad and believed that "if let alone—if neither increased by importations, nor tampered with by fanaticism—it will run its race in Kentucky and find its appropriate grave."[102]

By the year Harlan completed his studies at Transylvania, Robertson had grown defensive at the charges of "selfish and unscrupulous demagogues" that he was soft on the slavery issue. In an address to the Kentucky house of representatives, he rejected again the notion that "the enslavement of the black can be a blessing to the white race" or "an individual or social good." At the same time, though, he expressed the belief that slavery in the United States would "eventuate in the ultimate civilization of doomed Africa—and in the aggregate welfare of mankind." Nor, he insisted, had he ever doubted that "when the white and black races live together, as they now co-exist in Kentucky, the welfare of the inferior and the security of the superior race would both be promoted by the subordination of the former to the tutelage and dominion of the latter." Only when "all mankind shall become civilized" could "all be free." Slavery's elimination must be gradual and "the spontaneous result of a moral, peaceful, and progressive causation." Mandated emancipation was thus "altogether hopeless in Kentucky for years to come. . . . If . . . slavery in Kentucky be a curse, premature and compulsive emancipation would . . . be, to both races, a greater curse."[103]

As a member of Congress in 1819, Robertson reminded his listeners, he had opposed an antislavery provision in the bill to organize the territorial government of Arkansas. The next year he fought attempts to forbid slavery in Missouri; and in 1848 he had been an opponent of the Wilmot Proviso, the proposal to prohibit slavery in territory acquired from Mexico. He had thus, he declared, consistently "opposed any agitation of the question of emancipation, instant or prospective—and [had] probably suffered as much, by that course, as any other citizen."[104]

With what learning and politics he had absorbed from Robertson and other Transylvania faculty, Harlan graduated in 1852 and entered his father's Frankfort law office. His older brothers were all associated with the practice at various times. By 1852, however, their number had begun to dwindle. In September of 1849, Henry Clay Harlan died. The previous month he had written a friend of the devastation visited on Frankfort by a cholera epidemic,[105] and he had apparently fallen victim to the same disease. At the time of his death, Clay was considered one of James Harlan's most promising progeny. In 1847, at the age of 17, he had raised a company for the Mexican War; and although his men were not accepted for the campaign, since Kentucky had already filled its quota, the youth was widely applauded for his valor. On learning of his namesake's death, Henry Clay wrote the elder Harlan of his "great distress" at the "lamentable event," adding stoically, "Time and a patient resignation and submission to the Will of Him who, having given us our children, has the right to take them from us when he pleases, can only heal the wounds inflicted, and mitigate the sorrows which the bereavement necessarily excited."[106]

Richard Davenport Harlan, the oldest Harlan child, had been a lieutenant in the Mexican War, fighting valiantly with a cavalry detachment in the battle of Buena Vista. Richard seemed destined for an outstanding career, but in 1854, he, too, died. James Harlan, Jr., practiced law with his father during the earliest years of John's career, but following the marriage of their sister, Elizabeth, to Dr. James G. Hatchitt, James moved to Evansville, Indiana, where the couple resided. He practiced law in Evansville from 1854 to 1859–60. James, Sr., of course, was Kentucky's attorney general during the 1850s. Owing to these events, John and his brother William Lowndes were primarily responsible for the family practice during the years preceding the Civil War.[107]

Harlan's practice in those early years was devoted heavily to probate matters, contracts, property transactions, and claims against the war department and other government agencies. Firm ledger entries for 1857, for example, include a $11.25 fee for the sale of mining privileges and $37 for a property transfer. As Kentucky's capital, Frankfort had more than its share of seasoned attorneys, many of them prominent figures in state legal circles. To build up his practice, therefore, Harlan was obliged to "ride circuit" extensively, traveling by stagecoach or on horseback, his clothes and papers stuffed in saddle bags, to courthouses throughout the state. But the tall, powerfully built counselor with the sonorous voice made a striking appearance in or out of court, and the prestige of his father's name and client list was no hindrance either. Soon, he was considered one of the state's most promising young attorneys.[108]

Although Harlan's caseload included criminal as well as civil cases, his practice was generally free of the violence that often arose in the arenas of frontier justice. On one occasion shortly before or after he began his legal career, however, he became involved in a case fraught with personal risk. One of his cousins, John R. Harlan, was given, as the justice later put it, to "irregular habits." Once, while visiting an "improper place" in the hills of Boyle County, John R. killed a man named Pitman during a quarrel. The kinsmen and friends of the deceased vowed to kill John R. at their earliest opportunity; and when his murder trial began, they were scattered throughout the courtroom, whispering and muttering angrily to each other as though planning mischief. But John Marshall Harlan, his father, the defendant's brother James (or "Big Jim," as he was commonly known), and Wellington Harlan, another cousin, were also present for the trial. When John R. entered or exited the courtroom, Justice Harlan later reported, his cousins and brother "were immediately around [him] every step . . . and at his side in the courtroom during the trial. Our purpose was to make it impossible for the Pitmans to get at him, without encountering his brother and two cousins in deadly conflict." Following John R.'s acquittal, his kinsmen again surrounded him, escorted him out of the courtroom, and kept him in Frankfort several months, until local animosity had subsided. "I should, in candor, say," Justice Harlan later conceded, "that during the whole of John's trial, Big Jim, Wellington and myself were heavily armed. The man the other side most feared was Big Jim, who was believed to have on his person (as he did) an enormous bowie knife, which he had the strength, skill and willingness to use, if necessary."[109]

As his law practice began to grow, the future justice also embarked upon a long and, by all accounts, happy marriage. Harlan's sister, Elizabeth Hatchitt, as noted previously, had moved with her husband to Evansville, Indiana, following her marriage; and their brother, James, was also an Evansville resident at the time. On one of his frequent visits there, in the late summer of 1853, John took a fateful walk by the home of Malvina French Shanklin. A young girl of 15, Malvina had been confined to her darkened bedroom with an eye infection. As John walked by, she happened to be peeping out a window through a narrow crack in its shutters. "That was sixty-one years ago," she later wrote, "but, as clearly as if it were yesterday, she can still see him as he looked that day—his magnificent figure, his head erect, his broad shoulders well thrown back—walking as if the whole world belong[ed] to him." To her young eyes, he was "A Prince of the Blood."[110]

The following February, Malvina attended a supper at the Hatchitts's home. While talking with her hostess, her "Prince" pranced into the room—a rope to each arm, as he "played horse" for a delighted nephew. Although embarrassed at being caught "playing the boy," the young lawyer was as attracted to his sister's guest as Malvina was to him. He called on her daily the following week and at week's end asked for her hand in marriage.

At her parents' urging, the couple agreed to delay their wedding two years, while Malvina attended a boarding school near Cincinnati. Had the Shanklins been aware that their future son-in-law was obliged to borrow $500 from his father to finance the wedding and the couple's "start in life," Malvina later wrote, they might have looked on the approaching marriage as "a trifle unwise and hasty." But John Shanklin had been impressed with John's letter asking her parents' approval of the marriage, and a prominent Kentucky friend of the Shanklins had been enthusiastic in his estimation of the prospective groom. In December of 1856, the Shanklins mailed invitations to their friends announcing simply that they were to be "at home" the evening of December 23. Enclosed with the invitations were two cards, tied together with a bow of white ribbon and bearing the names of the bride and groom. At nine o'clock that evening, friends and family gathered at the Shanklins' home to hear the couple repeat their vows for a marriage that was to endure for more than half a century.[111]

Consistent with the custom of the day, the newlyweds spent the first week of their marriage with the bride's parents, while a number of parties were given in their honor in the homes of friends. Malvina, or Mallie as she would more commonly be known, then moved with her husband into the Frankfort home of his parents, where the couple would reside for the first several years of their marriage. The elder Harlans' household was quite large, including not only the newlyweds but also, at various times, James, Jr., and his family, the Harlans' unmarried son, William Lowndes, their two unmarried daughters, Laura and Sallie, and a dozen or so house servants.

Elizabeth Hatchitt and her children spent the greater part of every summer with her parents, too.[112]

The elder Harlans' Frankfort home was a large frame mansion with spacious rooms, situated at one corner of an unusually wide and deep lot. The family spent their summers, however, at a country house located about a mile from Frankfort, on Harlan's Hill, one of the many steep promontories surrounding the Kentucky capital. Originally quite small, the summer house was steadily enlarged as the family grew.[113]

James Harlan, Sr., and his wife were noted for their hospitality. Friends, family, and political associates were frequent overnight guests at both their homes. The Harlans and their friends also hosted occasional evening parties and formal suppers. Attending sessions of the state legislature was another amusement among their circle of friends. In such an atmosphere, Mallie soon established a warm relationship with her husband's family.[114]

Mallie Harlan readily embraced the Harlans' avid interest in Frankfort's religious life. Her father-in-law was not a church member, but John's mother and sisters (and presumably his brothers as well) were members of the city's Presbyterian church, and his father regularly attended its services. Mallie had been a faithful communicant at Sunday services and weekly prayer meetings of her Presbyterian congregation in Evansville. Shortly after her arrival in Frankfort, she agreed to teach a Sunday school class and began a long tenure as church organist. Her husband, "wishing (as it seemed) to be always near me," attended all services with his bride; and a number of the congregation's leaders soon prevailed upon him to become superintendent of its Sunday school as well as teacher of an adult Bible class.[115] From that day forward, Harlan was a devoted Presbyterian lay leader and Bible teacher, acquiring national prominence in those roles during his years on the Supreme Court.

The Know-Nothing Movement

Mallie Harlan's close relations with the Harlan family were fortuitous, given her new husband's increasingly hectic professional schedule. The circuit-riding portion of his law practice required him to be away from home days and weeks at a time, and his growing involvement in Kentucky politics meant that he was away from Frankfort nearly as much as he was in town.

Harlan's active participation in government and politics had begun, however, even before his marriage to Mallie. In 1851, Governor John L. Helm had invited Harlan, who was then a clerk in the state auditor's office, to become Kentucky's adjutant general. Harlan was then only 18 and certain the governor was joking. But on November 14, 1851, he received his commission.[116]

The position was hardly one of consequence. Kentucky had no military, and as adjutant Harlan was responsible only for maintaining custody of some military papers dating from the War of 1812 and for certain duties relating to two privately operated military academies—the Kentucky Military Institute, located near Frankfort, and the Western Military Institute at Drennon Springs in Henry County. Under their charters, the governor appointed a board of visitors to visit each institute annually, review the cadets, and report to the governor its conditions and prospects. As ex officio chairman of the board, the youthful, and thus slightly embarrassed, adjutant supervised these yearly tours and presided over board meetings "with all the dignity I could command." The position did carry a $250 annual salary, though. Thereafter, until his elevation to the Supreme Court, Harlan would normally be addressed as "General" in correspondence and conversation.

The adjutancy, of course, was not to be Harlan's only public service position prior to his appointment to the Court. In 1854, the year following his admission to the bar, he was elected city attorney of Frankfort, a post to which he was reelected in 1856. In that capacity he prosecuted minor criminal offenses such as breach of the peace, public drunkenness, and liquor sales to slaves, winning convictions and the imposition of fines in most instances. In a hard-fought 1858 campaign, moreover, he won election as a Franklin County judge, winning the post against Robert A. Thompson, his Democratic opponent, by a 119-vote majority. One of 11 judges in the county's court system, he would hold the position until his resignation on May 4, 1861.

As the Whig Party began to collapse under the weight of the slavery issue and related conflicts that would soon embroil the nation in its bloodiest war, Harlan and his father also made a fundamental shift in party loyalty—a particularly ironic one for the son, given the reputation he was to forge on the Supreme Court as a staunch defender of equal rights. In 1854, a friend asked John Harlan to join the Know-Nothing Society, a secret organization dedicated to the destruction of Roman Catholic and foreign (non-native) influence in American politics and thus committed to the motto, "Put None but Americans on Guard." On the night of his initiation in the grand jury room of the Frankfort courthouse, he took an oath to vote only for native Protestant candidates for public office. "I was very uncomfortable when the oath was administered to me," he explained late in life. "My conscience, for a time, rebelled against it. For a moment I had the thought of retiring; for while I was intense, as I am still, in my Protestantism, I did not relish the idea of proscribing anyone on account of his religion." When he saw that his father and other Frankfort Whigs were present for the ceremony, however, he "had not the boldness to repudiate the organization." He decided, moreover, "that, *all things considered*, it was best for *any* organization to control public affairs rather than to have the Democratic party in power."[117]

However "uncomfortable" Harlan may have found the experience, he and his father played a vigorous role in the Know-Nothing movement and the American Party, which it spawned. James Harlan was the party's successful candidate for attorney general and promoted the movement in other ways as well. Since adoption of the first Kentucky constitution in 1792, naturalized citizens had enjoyed the right to vote in the state immediately following issuance of their final citizenship papers. When antiforeign sentiment swept the state in the 1850s, Know-Nothing leaders argued that new citizens should be obliged to meet the state's two-year residency requirement for voting before being granted the franchise, however long they might have resided in the state prior to their naturalization. Foremost among those assuming that stance were James Harlan and Justice George Robertson, John Harlan's law professor. In 1857, James Harlan issued an attorney general's opinion declaring that a former alien's "political existence" dated only from his naturalization and that "his residence here, while an alien, ought not to be taken into consideration in ascertaining whether he is entitled to vote." Two years earlier, he had issued an opinion denying the authority of county courts to conduct citizenship proceedings. Justice Robertson was more demagogic. Naturalized aliens, he asserted in a published letter of 1857, should be made to fulfill the residency requirement, just as would "a secret agent of abolitionism, a citizen of Ohio . . . here two years in the execution of his diabolical mission," who later decided to obtain Kentucky citizenship.[118]

Following a major Know-Nothing victory in the Louisville election of August 6, 1855, a Democratic newspaper charged James Harlan with fraud favoring American Party candidates. Called "Bloody Monday" in Louisville's history, that election day was marred by riots in which the homes and businesses of foreigners were vandalized and burned, and several persons, including children, lost their lives. Attorney General Harlan was never formally charged with any responsibility for the riots. The *Louisville Times* claimed, however, that he and members of the city council had effectively disenfranchised between 1200 and 1500 Democratic voters by refusing to establish additional polling places in a number of precincts. Apparently, no legal action was taken on the charge.[119]

John Harlan became a Know-Nothing speaker and candidate. In 1855, the movement ran Charles S. Morehead, a veteran state legislator and congressman, for governor. James Harlan was on the ticket as the incumbent candidate for attorney general. During the campaign, Thomas L. Crittenden, another prominent political figure, agreed to speak across the state in behalf of the American Party ticket. One day when he had a speaking engagement at a country schoolhouse in Bridgeport, near Frankfort, Crittenden asked John Harlan to accompany him. After speaking to a crowd of around 100 people for about three-quarters of an hour, Crittenden, as Harlan later put it, "seemed to have run dry." A hard rain was falling, and the audience could not leave. "Immediately," Harlan would recall, "some one cried out, 'Let's hear from John Harlan.' This surprised me, but I said nothing. The demand for me to speak became general and persistent. I said that I was only twenty-two years of age and had never made a political speech of any kind. They replied, all over the house, 'That don't matter; tell us what you think.'" Harlan obliged, speaking without notes for nearly an hour, to enthusiastic applause.

Bolstered by the experience, John Harlan first conferred with his father and then had a printer run off copies of a handbill announcing that he would give a speech at the Frankfort courthouse. The evening of the event, every seat was filled, and his hour-and-a-half speech was well received. Deciding that he had "a capacity to say what I desired to say, and to make myself understood by those who heard me," he next scheduled speaking engagements in 20 mountain counties of the state. As he was accustomed to doing when riding circuit for court appearances, he traveled by horseback, his clothes stuffed into a pair of saddle bags thrown across his saddle.

The speaking tour honed Harlan's skills as a speaker and whetted his appetite for politics. He drew large crowds at every stop—as well as requests from local Democrats—who were often seasoned debaters and politicians—for a division of time. "Those debates," wrote Harlan, "were of great value to me as a speaker. They destroyed whatever bashfulness I had, and gave me readiness of speech and a steadiness of manner that served a good purpose when addressing juries."

The American Party's 1855 national platform thoroughly embraced Know-Nothing principles. The party favored "cultivation and development of a sentiment of profoundly intense American feeling; of passionate attachment to our country, its history, and its institutions; of admiration for the purer days of our national existence." It supported "radical revision and modification" of the immigration laws, offering a "friendly reception and protection" to the "honest immigrant," but "unqualifiedly condemning the transmission to our shores of felons and paupers." It favored "earnest modification" of the naturalization laws, including repeal of state laws permitting aliens to vote, denial of federal land grants to unnaturalized foreigners, and a ban on voting rights for aliens in the territories. Nor, of course, was the Roman Catholic or foreign influence on politics overlooked. The party urged opposition to the church's "aggressive policy and corrupting tendencies" through support for measures confining all political offices to "those only who do not hold civil allegiance, directly or indirectly, to any foreign power whether civil or ecclesiastical, and who are American by birth, education, and training." Since Christianity, on the other hand, was an important element of the nation's political system, "every attempt to exclude it from the schools" was also to be opposed.

On the increasingly important question of slavery, the party embraced a position approximating that of James Harlan and other Whig moderates: support for maintenance of the Union but opposition to federal interference with state slave policies. The platform declared,

> Congress possesses no power, under the Constitution, to legislate upon the subject of slavery in the States where it does or may exist, or to exclude any State from admission into the Union because its constitution does or does not recognize the institution of slavery as a part of its social system . . . [or] to legislate upon the subject of slavery within the territory of the United States; and . . . any interference by Congress with slavery as it exists in the District of Columbia would be a violation of the spirit and intention of the compact by which the State of Maryland ceded the District to the United States, and a breach of the National faith.[120]

Whatever misgivings John Harlan may have entertained regarding the Know-Nothing movement were carefully concealed from his enthusiastic audiences. A correspondent for the Frankfort *Commonwealth* filed the following account of Harlan's appearance in Columbia, Kentucky: "He traversed the whole range of discussion between the American and anti-American parties, and left the poor antis prostrate at the feet of his 'Holiness' and the Foreigner begging for office." His rejoinder to his opponent, the correspondent added, "amounted to the 'abolition' of Mr. Caldwell, as a debater."[121] In the same issue of the paper, a former classmate, identifying himself only as a "Native," predicted that "if he lives, [Harlan] will leave a name enrolled with the brightest in Kentucky's history." Georgetown Know-Nothings termed an early Harlan speech "the clearest and ablest exposition of American principles which has been given in this place,"[122] while an admiring journalist declared that he "came amongst us unknown to fame, and utterly unheralded, but he left an impression behind him that will not be effaced for a long time."[123]

John Harlan's debut year in electoral politics was a banner season for the Know-Nothings. American Party candidates carried every statewide office against their Democratic opponents in 1855. Harlan's contributions to that victory were not ignored. The following year, the "young giant of the American party," as an enthusiastic reporter dubbed him,[124] was selected as an assistant elector at-large for the American Party, which obliged him to canvass the state for its Millard Fillmore–Andrew Jackson Donelson national ticket.

The party and its press organs continued to be vehemently anti-foreign. The *Louisville Daily Journal* decried as "absolutely unbearable," "[t]he disrespect and impudence displayed by foreigners, who choose to come and live amongst us. . . . We give them the right to enjoy liberty and property and perfect self-protection when they come to our land, and the moment they have come under our banner they have sought to tear it in shreds." The specific target of the correspondent's ire was an article in a German newspaper, published in New York, that condemned the maxim, "No Union without slavery." The correspondent complained: "Just to think of the audacity of this European who comes here under the protection of our generous laws, and in his foreign, and so far concealed language, aims at the destruction of that of which it is with our native people profane to speak but in reverence and awe."[125]

John Harlan again pursued his responsibility vigorously, vehemently denying the charges of Democrats that his party's leaders were abolitionists or religious bigots, but just as fiercely proclaiming that "Americans should rule America" and that he would always vote for native Americans over foreigners. The American Party press was again enthralled. "It was orthodox . . . Know-Nothing Scripture," declared the Frankfort *Commonwealth*, adding: "We are ready to stand by and swear to every word he uttered."[126]

On this occasion, however, the efforts of Harlan and other Know-Nothings were to little avail. By that point, Kentuckians were becoming increasingly fearful that American Party inroads on the pro-slave Democratic vote might lead to the election of an abolitionist Republican president. Moreover, while favoring officeholding for natives only and a 21-year residency requirement for naturalization, the American Party's 1856 platform endorsed popular sovereignty in the territories on the slavery issue. Nationally, the Fillmore ticket garnered only eight electoral votes; the victorious Democratic candidate, James Buchanan, whose running mate was Kentuckian John C. Breckinridge, won 174 votes; and John C. Fremont, the Republican candidate, 114. In Kentucky, Fillmore lost by over 6,000 votes. Nativism had failed completely as a national issue, and apparently in Kentucky as well.

In the face of such defeat, John Harlan, his father, and other Kentucky Whigs quickly abandoned the Know-Nothing movement and certain planks of its platform, and established the Opposition Party as a state counterpoint to the Democrats. One of the "new" party's goals was to regain control of Kentucky's eighth congressional district, the famous Ashland district, which Henry Clay had served for many years and which was named, in fact, for Clay's Lexington estate. Until the 1850s, Ashland had been safe Whig territory. In 1851, John C. Breckinridge's election pushed Ashland into the Democratic column; and Breckinridge won reelection in 1853. But in 1855, the year Harlan campaigned so vigorously for the Know-Nothings, the Amer-

ican Party candidate won the Ashland congressional seat. Two years later, the
Democrats regained control with James B. Clay, son of the Great Commoner, as its
candidate. After a single term, however, Clay decided against seeking reelection,
leaving the Opposition with considerable cause for optimism—and Harlan with a
potentially promising opportunity.

The party held a district convention in Lexington on May 18, 1859, for the purpose, among other things, of choosing a congressional candidate. Harlan attended as
a member of the Franklin County delegation. Of several candidates for the Ashland
seat, Roger W. Hanson of Fayette County, who had run a strong race for the position
in 1857, and George S. Shanklin, a promising state legislator, were the clear front-
runners. But neither was to win the nomination.

Toward the end of his life, Harlan gave the following account of the convention's decision on a congressional nominee:

> In the progress of the balloting, Thomas T. Vimont, of Bourbon, to my great surprise,
> rose and said, with great vehemence of voice and manner, that the party needed a
> young man as its candidate, and he placed me in nomination. I was sitting at the time
> in the rear of the hall; greatly agitated by the fact that I was to be voted for by some of
> the delegates, I started to jump up and say that I was not a candidate and could not
> think of being one. But a member of the Franklin County delegation, who was de-
> lighted at the suggestion of my name to the Convention, pulled the skirt of my alpaca
> frock coat so strong as to tear it nearly off. The balloting proceeded before I could say
> anything, and to my amazement I was nominated. Immediately a cry arose that I
> should take the stand. I did so, and when I turned to address the delegates, the condi-
> tion of the skirt of my coat was so manifest that I referred to it as proof of my efforts
> to prevent my being nominated. I commenced my talk, intending to decline. But the
> crowd said, "No, no," and I concluded by accepting.[127]

A correspondent for an unfriendly newspaper offered a decidedly less sanguine
version of the proceedings. Initial balloting, he reported, had produced no victor;
and other candidates gradually withdrew until only Harlan and Hanson remained in
the race. At that point Harlan won the nomination, but only by a vote of 36 ⅔ to 35
½. The convention was "largely attended," the correspondent conceded, and as "in-
expressibly funny" as it might appear, "the no-party party [even had] strong hopes
of electing their candidate." But he had never before seen, the correspondent declared, "a more inharmonious, incongruous, unsettled body of men . . . gathered together."[128]

The correspondent's derision not withstanding, Harlan had considerable cause
for optimism early in the campaign. The Democrats had selected as his opponent
Captain William E. Simms of Bourbon County. Simms was a seasoned politician
and Mexican War veteran. But Democrats had genuine reason to doubt his commitment to their party, for Simms had been raised as a Whig and had served two terms
as a Whig representative in the state legislature, defecting to the Democrats only
when the Whigs denied him nomination to seats in the Kentucky senate and U.S.
Congress. A third candidate, Stephen Fitz J. Trabue, who ran as a Know-Nothing,
was considered something of an eccentric and certain loser. Indeed, at least one
Democratic newspaper, while praising Trabue's "considerable energy, much zeal,

and fair ability," decided "that it would be a waste of time to discuss the issues he attempts to intrude into the discussions."[129] An Opposition paper agreed, declaring that Trabue was "of no consequence in the race except to be in the way and consume time that might be more profitably as well as more agreeably occupied."[130]

In mounting his campaign, Harlan abandoned, or revised, Know-Nothing positions that had lost voter appeal. He did favor preventing poor immigrants and those with criminal records from entering the country and also supported a citizenship requirement for public land grants. In the face of growing numbers of Roman Catholic, immigrant voters, however, he dropped the anti-Catholic fervor of earlier campaigns and championed the cause of naturalized Americans forced into foreign armies during return visits to their native land.[131]

Harlan also embraced a number of issues likely to attract voter interest without generating political controversy. In 1858, the federal government had prepared to dispatch a military force against the Mormons of Utah, whose endorsement of polygamy and related practices was a continuing national concern. The expedition was disbanded when Mormon leaders agreed to Washington's demands. But Kentucky, with Harlan as its adjutant general, had been unusually successful in attracting volunteers for the effort, raising 21 companies of troops—more than twice the number needed. The enthusiasm with which the call for troops had been greeted by Kentuckians apparently convinced Harlan that the Mormon question was ripe for political exploitation and carried no risks in a state with few, if any, members of the unorthodox faith. "He is for destroying the Mormons without law or form," one Democratic paper reported in late July; "thinks that Brigham Young ought to be hung by the Federal Government for having 64 wives when Capt. Simms has not even one."[132]

The alleged waste and extravagance of President Buchanan's Democratic administration presented another easy target. One supportive newspaper summarized a Harlan stump speech in which he "showed from documentary evidence the vast and alarming increase in the public expenditures since the close of Mr. Fillmore's term, and especially during the existence of the present administration," and demanded that his opponent "show what had become of the money." Harlan also favored annexation of Cuba but opposed putting the $30 million needed for the project "in the hands of the President in advance, for purposes of bribery and corruption."[133]

Slavery, of course, was the overriding issue for all the candidates, with each attempting to outdo the others in defending that institution. In an important exchange with his opponents at Paris, Kentucky, in June, Harlan addressed the slave question first. He asserted that the *Dred Scott* case—a decision he was to condemn as an embarrassment to the Supreme Court and the nation in his *Plessy* dissent—had judicially settled that vexing issue by holding "that the owners of slaves had the right, under the constitution, to take that kind of property into the Territories and that there was no power in Congress . . . to exclude it—indeed, no power on the subject matter except the power to protect." He scorned Simms, moreover, as a Stephen Douglas Democrat who would permit the people of each state and territory to determine their own slave policy, and challenged his opponent repeatedly to deny that he would support Douglas and his "squatter sovereignty" philosophy were Douglas the Democrats' 1860 presidential nominee. Harlan favored a national law "to punish negro stealing, if the legislature of any Territory in which such a law might be necessary, should fail to enact one."[134]

It was difficult, however, to best the Democrats, many of whom were clamoring for secession, in their devotion to slavery. Harlan preferred a law punishing "negro stealing." Simms declared that he would "vote to hang the nigger-stealer as high as Haman"—a recommendation an Opposition newspaper considered "rather beyond what is thought necessary or humane in most civilized States."[135] Pro-slave voters seemed increasingly concerned, moreover, that abandonment of the Democratic Party ultimately would mean simply an abolitionist Republican in the White House.

For the first time in his career—but not the last—Harlan became the target of charges that he was woefully inconsistent in his political positions. One Democratic newspaper reminded its readers that he had supported the American Party platforms of 1855 and 1856 that approved local option on the slavery issue in the territories and denied congressional authority to protect the rights of slaveholders there.[136] Another sarcastically marveled at his "facility to drift in the current popular sentiment, and change his opinion as the hour demanded," adding: "Once a Whig, then a fanatical and violent American, and now a hybrid opportunist, he has accomplished as many somersaults in his brief career as any man in the country."[137]

A number of incidents plagued Harlan's efforts as well. Early in the contest, the Simms campaign charged that in 1856 Harlan had written a letter to the *New Albany Tribune*, a Fillmore paper in Indiana, urging members of the American Party in that state to vote for "[Oliver P.] Morton, Black Republican," in Indiana's gubernatorial election. Harlan immediately wrote a reply to the offending paper, with copies to others, declaring that he was not the letter's author, was "never consulted in reference to, nor did I ever endorse or approve the writing of any such letter," had not been informed that the letter would be, or had been, written until several weeks after its publication, and, in fact, had addressed a large crowd urging the election of the American Party ticket on the very date (September 12, 1856) the letter bore.[138] Other statements indicated that Harlan's brother William Lowndes had written the letter, and the candidate vowed never to support the Republicans on any issue vital to the South.[139] But the charge may have damaged his campaign.

An equally damning rumor charged that Harlan had attempted to win the freedom of a slave in 1853. In that year, Nathan Williams, a slave owned by R. B. Logan of Fayette County, had brought suit for his freedom in the Louisville chancery court. Logan believed that the Opposition Party's congressional candidate had represented WIlliams in the case, and the Simms campaign circulated that rumor. Bland Ballard, a Harlan family friend who would later win a federal court seat, promptly acknowledged that he had been Williams's counsel, that the petition for Williams's freedom had carried only his name and that of Harlan's brother, William Lowndes, and that he was "quite certain" he "never wrote or spoke to" the candidate about the case. Logan, an Opposition paper reported, was "entirely satisfied" with Ballard's explanation and "immediately set about repairing the injury which he had done Gen. Harlan."[140] But that incident may have cost Harlan votes.

S.F.J. Trabue's published letter withdrawing from the campaign in mid-July was no help either. Trabue had found that many voters who "so recently professed to be native-Americans politically" were ready to abandon the cause and unite with the

Opposition Party. He naturally opposed such a move. The Opposition "faction," he declared, would "be powerless for good, and only powerful for evil." In Trabue's judgment, the Democratic Party was the only "truly national" party, "and the only one capable of fighting successfully the many factions of the day, and the black republican party particularly." He urged all "true constitutional national men, and the people of the south especially," to support the Democrats, rather than those "now the most willing to wholly and shamefully abandon" American principles.[141]

Perhaps most damaging to Harlan's chances, however, was an incident involving his other opponent and one of Harlan's staunchest supporters. Immediately after his nomination, Harlan had arranged a series of speaking engagements with Captain Simms, to extend over a 40-day period. When they opened their joint canvass in Georgetown, Harlan observed John C. Breckinridge, a prominent citizen of the Ashland district and the leader of Kentucky Democrats, in the audience. Breckinridge hoped to win his party's presidential nomination in 1860, and his presence at Georgetown indicated to Harlan that he attached great importance to the Ashland congressional race, and perhaps even believed that a Democratic defeat there would harm his presidential prospects. Harlan did well in the Georgetown exchange; in fact, an exasperated Breckinridge reportedly told Simms afterwards, "If you don't do better that young fellow will beat you."[142] Within ten days, Harlan had concluded that he had Simms "on the run."

Then, a particularly venomous anonymous letter scorning Simms's inconsistencies and betrayal of Whig principles appeared in an Opposition paper.[143] The following day, the candidates made one of their joint appearances at Ruddel's Mills. At the close of his remarks, Simms denounced the letter's author as a scoundrel and liar. Whereupon, Garrett Davis, a member of the Kentucky legislature and one of Harlan's most ardent and fearless partisans, arose from his seat in the audience, revealed that he had written the letter, and excoriated Simms, as Harlan later put it, "in merciless terms."

Two days later, Harlan traveled to Cynthiana for another debate with Simms. On arriving at his hotel, he learned, to his surprise and annoyance, that Davis was already registered there. When Harlan went to the local courthouse for the scheduled engagement later that day, moreover, he was distressed to see Davis sitting on the front bench of the courtroom in which the debate was to be held. Realizing that Davis's attacks were likely to arouse sympathy for Simms among Democrats, he feared that any further confrontation might be disastrous to his campaign. To Harlan's relief, Simms made no reference during the debate to his difficulties with Davis, who sat quietly in his seat. Afterwards, however, Davis sent Simms a personal note which the Democratic candidate construed as a challenge to a duel.

Word soon came to the agonized Harlan that the two antagonists had left the state to pursue their plans for the duel. When Simms failed to appear at their next scheduled debate, Harlan explained the situation to the large crowd assembled for the event and declared that, under the circumstances, he would not speak. After Harlan was obliged to follow this routine at the next nine engagements, two prominent friends of Davis and Simms located the antagonists in Cincinnati and arranged an agreement by which both simultaneously withdrew their intemperate charges.[144] Simms then returned to the stump with Harlan.[145]

For the remainder of the campaign, Harlan pursued his opponent relentlessly, speaking every day, and at least twice a day the last month of the contest; he stumped three times daily during the final two weeks before the election. He was convinced, however, that the Davis-Simms dispute had done him serious harm. "I recall with distinctness the occasion when [Simms] joined me [again]," Harlan later wrote. "He had a warm welcome from his political friends. The Democratic leaders who, up to that time, were lukewarm and indifferent [toward the former Whig], were aroused at what they regarded as the attempt of one of my supporters to 'bully' their candidate."

As he perhaps expected, Harlan did lose the election, but by a very narrow margin. The Democrats elected a governor, six of the state's ten congressional representatives, and an overwhelming majority of the Kentucky legislature. But Simms's margin of victory was only 67 votes of the 13,797 cast.[146]

Not surprisingly, Harlan's supporters cried fraud. Indeed, a newspaper friendly to him had warned even before the election that the Democrats were importing ringers into the district to assure Simms's victory.[147] Following the election, the Frankfort *Commonwealth* reported that 683 more votes had been cast in the congressional race than in the 1856 presidential election; 353 of those votes had come from Harrison and Nicholas counties, and the remaining 330 were gained from the other six counties in the district. Had the Democratic majorities in Harrison and Nicholas "not greatly exceeded the most sanguine calculations of the best informed Democrats in those counties," the paper declared, "John M. Harlan would have been elected by about three hundred majority."[148]

In his own investigation of Harrison County voting records, Harlan found nearly 300 names on the county rolls "of persons whom no one knew and of whom no one in the county had ever heard." He also obtained statements indicating that many men, believed to be Irishmen from Cincinnati and Covington, had arrived by train at various polling places on election day, voted, then left the district, "never [to be] seen again." Similar findings were made in Nicholas County.

Harlan's supporters quickly raised $10,000 to finance a formal contest of the election results. Democratic newspapers raised allegations of their own, however. One reported, for example, that "nearly the whole naturalized vote of Frankfort," except those willing to vote for Harlan, was excluded from the election, "wantonly knocked down, bruised and maimed for no other reason than that they were Democrats."[149] Harlan may thus have been concerned about challenges to his vote were a contest undertaken.

There were other considerations as well. His party was part of no national political alliance. "If I had been given the seat in Congress," he later reasoned, "it would have been by the votes of the Republican or Free Soil party, and that fact alone would have sufficed to destroy our party in Kentucky and would have ruined me politically—so bitter was the feeling in Kentucky, at that time, against the Republican or Abolition Party." Another concern was the burden a contest would have imposed on his law practice—"the taking of several hundred depositions, the loss of more than a year's time, and a practical abandonment of my profession while preparing." Ultimately, such considerations were controlling. Harlan decided not to initiate a formal protest, and the money raised in his behalf was returned to his supporters.

In later years, Harlan speculated on the effect his election to Congress might have had on his life. "Most probably one session of Congress in Washington at my then age, would have given me such a taste for political life as would not have been consistent with professional success. On the whole, the men who conceived and carried out the frauds which gave my opponent a certificate of election did me a great service." On another occasion, he stated, "[If] I had gone to Washington at twenty-six I might have lost all the character I had."[150]

War

The presidential contest of 1860 suggested that the Union had already been split into two independent nations. The Republicans chose Abraham Lincoln as their candidate. Following internecine conventions at Charleston and Baltimore, the Democratic Party's southern and northern wings seceded from each other, with the latter selecting Stephen Douglas as their nominee and the secessionists opting for John C. Breckinridge of Kentucky. Whig–Americans organized a Constitutional Union convention, at which they picked John Bell of Tennessee and Edward Everett of Massachusetts as their candidates. In most states, however, the campaign was a two-party battle—Lincoln against Douglas in the North, Bell against Breckinridge in the South.

In Kentucky, John Harlan and most other Whig–American–Oppositionists joined the Constitutional Union movement. With a commitment to "the Union, Constitution and Enforcement of the Laws," including existing safeguards for slave property, the Kentucky contingent of the Constitutional Unionists pursued a platform emphasizing preservation of the nation over all other considerations. Harlan was a leader in that effort. As a member of the party's state committee, he signed an address pledging the group's support of the Union and "unalterable hostility to [both] Northern Republicanism and Southern Secession." In a resolution he helped to draft for the party's state convention, moreover, he and other Unionists agreed that the South had been treated unfairly, but urged resolution of sectional grievances "inside the Union and not out of it."[1]

As an elector pledged to the Bell–Everett ticket in the fall campaign, Harlan canvassed his entire congressional district, appearing in numerous debates with electors committed to Breckinridge and Douglas.[2] Such efforts bore fruit. Bell carried Kentucky by a substantial majority, while Abraham Lincoln, the national victor, won less than one percent of the vote in his native state.

The Bell–Everett Kentucky triumph in no way meant, of course, that the state's commitment to the nation was final and irreversible. Lincoln considered Kentucky's loyalty a key to the Union's survival, remarking on at least one occasion, "I hope to have God on my side, but I must have Kentucky." Although the state ranked ninth in numbers of slaves, only 70 of its 38,645 slaveholders owned more than 50 slaves.[3] Its citizens could thus have been expected to be somewhat less committed to the perpetuation of slavery than their more southern neighbors. Contrary to the myth that would develop during and after the war, moreover, unionist forces in Kentucky included many of the state's most influential citizens. As Justice Harlan himself later declared,

> The Union leaders in Kentucky . . . constituted a body of men of whom it may justly be stated that, in respect of social standing, family history, character, education, and intellectual power, they could be favorably compared with any like number of men living at any time in any State of the Union. Many of them were born or were reared in counties popularly known as Blue Grass counties, while the others were, as Lincoln was, born or reared on "thinner soils." But whatever the nature of the soil on which they were born or reared, they were of noble nature, gentlemen in the best sense of that word, and of the highest social position.[4]

But Kentuckians had become more defensive of slavery in the 1850s. Mobs ran more than one abolitionist leader out of the state. The state's legislature repealed its ban on the importation of slaves and prohibited the distribution of abolitionist literature. Free blacks were forbidden to enter Kentucky, and slaves permitted to purchase their freedom were required to leave the state.[5]

Ultimately, Kentucky would remain in the Union; in fact, more than twice as many of its white citizens served in the federal army as with the Confederacy.[6] On the eve of the war, however, Kentucky's status was by no means certain. South Carolina, Alabama, Mississippi, Georgia, Louisiana, Florida, and Texas had seceded even before Lincoln's inauguration on March 4, 1861. Following the fall of Fort Sumter and the new president's call for troops to suppress the rebellion, four additional states—Virginia, Arkansas, Tennessee, and North Carolina—joined the Confederate cause. Whether Kentucky would go with her sister states was a matter of intense concern in the state and nation.

Although he was always to be strong in his devotion to the Union and never a supporter of secession, the intensity of John Harlan's sentiments varied over time. Prior to the attack on Fort Sumter, he seemed primarily dedicated to preserving the peace and the productive commercial relations that had long existed between his native state and the rest of the South. On January 8, 1861, the Constitutional Unionists and Democrats opposed to secession held separate conventions in Louisville. The Constitutional Unionist gathering, with Harlan as its secretary, approved an anti-secession resolution drafted by a committee selected from the two conventions. But Harlan also led a move to defeat a resolution calling for federal coercion of the slave states.[7]

The following month Harlan moved his law practice and family from Frankfort to Louisville, with plans apparently to devote his entire attention to his career, despite the impending crisis confronting the nation. His friends were pressing him for a rematch with Captain Simms for the Ashland District's congressional seat. As he would later explain, the move to Louisville was prompted largely by a desire to avoid the distraction from his profession and the severe drain on finances, time, and energy such a contest would entail.[8] The move to a growing city with a smaller population of lawyers than Kentucky's capital city had attracted also offered Harlan an opportunity to enlarge the size of his practice and reduce, if not eliminate, the onerous circuit-riding portion of his work.[9] But he may have desired simply to escape for a time difficult decisions regarding the extent of his involvement in the developing struggle to preserve the Union.

Nor was his choice of Louisville law partners likely to sharpen his unionist sentiments. A Fayette County native more than a quarter century Harlan's senior, William F. Bullock was a distinguished circuit judge and professor in the law department of the University of Louisville who had played a key role in the establishment of Kentucky's common school system.[10] Once, several years before Harlan's move to Louisville, a mob had lynched three blacks on the courthouse lawn in protest against Judge Bullock's dismissal of a deadlocked jury and his decision to reschedule the blacks' case for another trial. According to one account of the incident, Bullock calmly "walked through the midst of the mob to fill his seat in the courthouse as if that angry assembly had been a smiling crowd of picnickers."[11] But Bullock was no radical unionist. Although he remained loyal during the war, his son joined the Confederate army and Bullock eventually became a southern Democrat.[12]

The ambivalence Harlan may have felt in the first months following Lincoln's election is suggested by a letter he wrote to Joseph Holt on March 11, 1861. Holt was completing his tenure as secretary of war and postmaster general in President Buchanan's cabinet. From his vantage point in Washington, however, he was also the leader of Kentucky's staunchest unionists and would be a bitter critic of the neutral posture his native state initially assumed in the war.[13] In his letter to Holt, Harlan urged the immediate withdrawal of all federal troops from the secessionist states, "especially the troops at Forts Sumter and Pickens." Were the troops withdrawn, he predicted, the rebellion would die in Kentucky and all the other slave states that had not yet formally seceded. Harlan was certain that the chief cause of southern anxiety was "the constant fear that Lincoln's Administration will attempt coercion, or war between 'him' and the Seceding states." Any outbreak of hostilities would thus be a terrible blow to the Union, one "from which it may never recover." Withdrawal of the troops, on the other hand, would strengthen the Union cause in the border states and trigger a "formidable" movement in the seceding states "in favor of a return to the National Union."[14]

Harlan did not question the federal authority to maintain troops in all the states, but he urged their withdrawal as a pragmatic "display [of] magnanimity to a misguided people which [could] but be followed by the happiest results." If such efforts failed, however, secession should not be resisted: "[W]henever it becomes a settled fact that the people of the seceding states are unalterably opposed to the Federal Government", he declared, "they should be allowed to go in peace."[15]

Whatever the depth of Harlan's unionist leanings at the time he wrote Holt, the Confederate firing on Fort Sumter a month later strengthened his opposition to secession and destroyed his commitment to peace at any price. With that incident, he later wrote, union loyalists became convinced that the "purpose of the extreme men of the South was to provoke a war that would ultimately disrupt the Union. Hence the firing upon our Flag. *Then* the people in the non-slaveholding states and the Union men in the Border States felt that any more efforts to keep the peace and prevent bloodshed was useless. They felt that the time had come when further forbearance was out of the question. They rose, as one man, and resolutely determined that the rightful authority of the Union should be maintained over every foot of American soil, cost what it would in men and money."[16]

The Battle for Kentucky's Soul

The degree to which Harlan actually embraced such sentiments in April of 1861 is obviously open to question, particularly in view of his letter to Joseph Holt the previous month. Nor were such sentiments unanimously held even in his own family. While traveling by boat to Evansville to visit her family following her husband's enlistment in the Union army, Malvina Harlan encountered one of Harlan's cousins. "[Her] welcome to me," Mrs. Harlan later wrote, "was that she felt 'disgraced' that any one of the Harlan name should be 'enrolled in the Yankee Army.'" [17] In the months following Fort Sumter, however, Harlan took part in a series of efforts designed to preserve Kentucky's ties with the Union.

A particular object of unionist concern was Beriah Magoffin, the state's Democratic and intensely pro-southern governor. Before South Carolina's secession, Magoffin had circulated a letter to other slave state governors urging adoption of a constitutional amendment dividing the territories into slave and nonslave enclaves as well as assuring recovery of runaway slaves. As the secessionist movement gained momentum, however, Magoffin became a leader in the movement to secure Kentucky's commitment to the Confederacy. In his January 17 message to the legislature, the governor declared, "We, the people, of the United States are no longer one people, united and friendly." He proclaimed his state's "sympathies" with the seceded states, and promised that "Kentucky [would] not be an indifferent observer of the [federal] force policy."[18] Later, when Lincoln called forth state militia units to assist in suppressing the rebellion, Magoffin defiantly responded that "*emphatically*, Kentucky will furnish no troops for the wicked purpose of subduing her sister states."[19]

Harlan and other unionists were determined to block the secessionist efforts of Magoffin and his allies, although, "as a general rule," the future justice would later concede, they "did not approve of all the methods suggested by the Union men of the Northern States for the prosecution of the war, particularly those relating to the institution of slavery."[20] At his father's request, Harlan returned to Frankfort where he and others lobbied the legislature for weeks in a successful effort to defeat plans for a "sovereignty" convention and related attempts to push Kentucky into the secessionist camp. During the summer, moreover, he joined James Speed, who later would serve as Lincoln's attorney general, Speed's brother, Joshua, the president's longtime and especially close friend, and other unionists in educating the citizens of Louisville, which was then a hotbed of secessionist sentiment, on the "horrors and dangers" of disunion and war. "Meetings were arranged for the street corners in Louisville," Harlan later remembered. "A band of music[ians] was employed to bring the people together. The speaker usually stood on a box obtained from some storehouse near by. It is safe to say that during the summer of 1861 I made at least fifty 'store-box' speeches for the Union cause."[21]

At one point, Harlan also bolstered the unionist commitment of one of Kentucky's most distinguished newspaper editors. A Connecticut native and Brown graduate, George Dennison Prentice had first visited Kentucky in 1830 while compiling a biography of Henry Clay. Whig politicians were so impressed with the young journalist that they persuaded Prentice to take charge of a paper established to counter the spread of Jacksonian democracy in the state. Prentice's Louisville *Daily Journal* became the most influential Whig newspaper in the South and West, and he is known as one of the greatest editors of the era.[22]

In the early months of 1861, Prentice, like Harlan and other moderate unionists, urged a Kentucky policy of strict neutrality toward the mounting conflict. In an April issue of the *Journal,* Prentice declared that anyone who moved from that stance "into the line of apology for the Republicans becomes the ally of anti-slaveryism, and he who deviates from it into the line of apology for the seceders becomes consciously or unconsciously the ally of disunion."[23]

During the summer, however, Prentice's young assistant, Paul Shipman, an easterner and staunch unionist, became concerned that his mentor might yield to pressure to join those opposed to the use of federal force against the seceding states. Prentice's wife, although an Ohio native, was apparently a thoroughgoing rebel, and his two sons would later serve in the Confederate army. His home, therefore, was hardly a hotbed of unionism. Recent financial reversals, moreover, made him vulnerable to offers to purchase his support for the rebel cause. Among other difficulties, he had lost a large part of his interest in the *Journal* to its current principal owner, Isham Henderson, a wealthy businessman essentially unconcerned with politics.[24]

After a conversation with Prentice convinced Shipman that his fears had substance, he went to John Harlan and told him of the campaign to secure the *Journal*'s support for the Confederate cause. According to Shipman, former Kentucky governor Charles Morehead, who had a substantial investment in a Mississippi cotton plantation and believed war would bring him financial ruin, had recently sought to enlist Prentice in the secessionist cause. In a meeting with the *Journal* editor, Morehead had declared that the Union could not be preserved by force and that civil war would be destructive of Kentucky's interests. In return for writing an editorial opposing war against the secessionists, Morehead promised to pay Prentice $100,000 which would allow him to leave the country with his family for the duration of the hostilities.

Advancing age and what Harlan would later vaguely term Prentice's "bad habits" had led the editor largely to give up editorial writing for the paper; and Paul Shipman, although only 27, was then generally regarded as the *Journal*'s real editor. Perhaps for that reason, Prentice shared the details of Morehead's proposal with his assistant. Shipman promptly warned his mentor that he would not only oppose such a scheme but expose it as well. The young journalist also mentioned the matter to Isham Henderson, the *Journal*'s owner, who hotly responded that he would see his paper "sink into hell" before allowing it to be put to the use Morehead had proposed. But Shipman remained concerned, he now told Harlan, that financial woes and the pressures of family members might push Prentice into the secessionist camp. And in recent days, in fact, Prentice had begun to weaken in his support for the Union cause, suggesting editorially that the federal government should permit the southern states to leave the fold and arguing that the use of force against the secessionists was an unwise policy.

Harlan immediately telegraphed his father as well as Orlando Brown and Joshua F. Bell, leading Whigs and lifelong Prentice associates, urging them to take an early train to Louisville. When Harlan informed the three of the situation, each visited the *Journal* editor separately, alluding to rumors about Morehead's scheme, condemning such a course as "treasonous," and, in general, as Harlan later put it, attempting "to stiffen Prentice's backbone."

As Prentice's assistant, Shipman would read each of his mentor's editorials before they went to press and thus could attempt to kill any smacking of secessionist thinking. Fortuitously, Prentice was then confined to his home because of illness. To Harlan's alarm, however, Shipman was soon obliged to journey east. At that point, Shipman arranged for Harlan to write editorials supporting the Union cause as well as screen Prentice's pieces; and Isham Henderson instructed the printer to print whatever Harlan wrote without consulting the *Journal*'s editor. For two to three weeks, Harlan visited the newspaper every evening, at times until past midnight, screening editorials, contributing brief unsigned commentaries of his own, committing the paper ever more firmly to the Union cause, and making it increasingly difficult for Prentice to modify the *Journal*'s editorial posture. Soon, according to Harlan, Prentice regained his courage and was again writing editorials critical of the rebellion and encouraging to the unionist cause. At least one column, moreover, attacked the "oily-tongued Ex-Governor" Morehead for preaching neutrality in Kentucky but a decidedly different message during a tour of the secessionist states.[25]

The foregoing account of Harlan's role in assuring the *Journal*'s support for the Union is based on the justice's own reminiscences. Correspondence between Harlan's eldest son, Richard, and a descendant of Paul Shipman tends to confirm the accuracy of Harlan's version. Those letters indicate that the following notation relating to the incident, in the handwriting of Shipman's wife, was found among Shipman's papers: "The inside history of those days remains to be written, and but two men so far as I know possess the knowledge. One is Justice Harlan of the Supreme Court. It is but just and proper the World should have it."[26] On reading the proceedings of a dinner honoring Justice Harlan's twenty-fifth year on the bench, moreover, Shipman wrote the justice a warm congratulatory letter, commending his "unsurpassable" legacy and the "glory" of his life.[27]

Harlan also played a significant role in an early effort to secure arms for Kentucky unionists. As tensions between the state's unionist and "disunionist" forces— as rebel sympathizers were often called—continued to mount, Union supporters became increasingly fearful that members of the state militia might ally with the Confederacy, taking all of Kentucky's weapons and munitions with them. The political leanings of General Simon Bolivar Buckner, the militia's commander, provided ample cause for concern. A West Point graduate who fought with distinction in the Mexican War and other campaigns, Buckner was appointed to his post by Governor

Magoffin in 1860. His sympathy for the rebellion, like Magoffin's, was common knowledge.[28]

Upon his appointment, Buckner immediately moved to organize the militia into a large and well-armed state guard, recruiting new companies to his command almost daily.[29] In an effort to counteract Buckner's efforts, unionist leaders promoted the establishment of local military units known as home guards. In Louisville, a home guard of two regiments, with Mayor John M. Delph, a strong Union man, as its commander-in-chief, was organized on May 25, 1861. Harlan became a captain in the Crittenden Zouaves, one of the Louisville units.[30]

The day before the Louisville guard was formed, unionists had pushed through the Kentucky legislature provisions removing military power from Governor Magoffin's hands and placing it in a five-man board. Under the arrangement, the board was to have complete control over the state's armaments; and the state and home guard units were to participate equally in a fund established for military supplies.[31]

Before their legislative victory, however, the Union sympathizers, fearful of their vulnerability to General Buckner's state guard units, had secretly appealed to the federal government for arms and ammunition. In early May, William Nelson, a navy lieutenant, Kentucky native, and ardent unionist, called on President Lincoln in Washington and convinced him that the Union's Kentucky supporters should be provided arms immediately. The president ordered an initial consignment of 5,000 muskets—the "Lincoln Guns," as they were to be known forever in state lore—sent to Cincinnati, from whence they were to be dispatched to various parts of Kentucky. In the course of making arrangements for the transfer, Lieutenant Nelson traveled to Louisville for a meeting with Lincoln's close friend, Joshua Speed. The two then took a train to Frankfort, where they met with Harlan's father, James Speed, and other prominent unionists in the elder Harlan's law office. At that meeting and through correspondence, Nelson and his allies determined the details for distribution of the arms. At James Speed's urging, moreover, Indiana governor Oliver Morton agreed to furnish ammunition for the "Lincoln Guns."[32]

General accounts of the "Lincoln Guns" incident mention only James Harlan's role in the episode, not his son's involvement; and the most thorough study indicates that Mayor John Delph received the 1,200 weapons dispatched to Louisville. By his own account, however, Harlan played a significant role in the muskets' distribution in the Lexington area. According to Harlan, Lieutenant Nelson shipped several boxes of the arms by rail from Cincinnati to Lexington, from whence they were to be transported by wagon to loyalists at nearby Camp Dick Robinson. When the train reached Cynthania, midway between Cincinnati and Lexington, the conductor spotted a mob of rebel sympathizers, led by a captain of the state guard, and ordered the engineer to return to Cincinnati. After conferring with Kentucky court of appeals judge Joshua F. Bullitt, a prominent opponent of the rebel cause who would later part company with the Lincoln administration on the slavery issue, Harlan asked Lieutenant Nelson to ship the guns by boat to Louisville, addressed to Harlan. When the shipment arrived at the city wharf at one or two o'clock one morning, Harlan and Judge Bullitt, heavily armed, met the boat, transported their precious cargo on drays across town to the railroad depot, and loaded it on the next freight for Lexington. There, after a tense, if brief, standoff between state guard and home guard forces, the arms were delivered into the hands of troops from Camp Robinson.

With the help of state funding, the "Lincoln Guns" maneuver, and other devices, neutral Kentucky was soon armed to the teeth. Indeed, one citizen was moved to remark, "If it requires all these men and all this money, to keep up an armed neutrality, God save the Commonwealth from active war."[33]

As a captain in the Crittenden Zouaves, Harlan did his part to protect his state from early rebel encroachments. President Lincoln initially declined to send Union troops into Kentucky. In late summer of 1861, however, rebel forces under General Leonard Polk and Simon Buckner entered southwestern Kentucky and occupied Bowling Green. At that point, Union troops under the command of General Robert Anderson were dispatched to the state in large numbers.

Anderson's department included William Tecumseh Sherman, who was to become one of the Union's outstanding generals during the war. Sherman established a camp at Lebanon Junction, southeast of Louisville, and immediately made an excellent impression on Kentuckians, Harlan among them. "He was full of life and aggressiveness, and seemed anxious to meet the enemy," Harlan later recalled, adding that the general possessed "more genius for war than any soldier of his day."[34] Several companies of home guards, including Harlan's Crittenden Zouaves, were ordered to Lebanon, where Sherman assigned Harlan's unit to guard his headquarters at the local hotel. Harlan slept on the floor in Sherman's room for the week to ten days the general remained at Lebanon. "He was not at all informed as to the physical geography, or roads, or the sentiments of the people in particular localities of the State," Harlan later wrote. "He found that I was, the result being that he had me up at all hours of the night in order that he might obtain information. . . . He was a diligent student of all the county maps that he could lay his hands on. His energy was extraordinary, and he seemed to sleep but little."

Sherman's immediate objective was to resist any advance of rebel troops from Bowling Green northward toward Louisville. Toward that end, he advanced his troops 15 miles south toward Bowling Green and established a position at Muldraugh's Hill. Of home guard units, only the Crittenden Zouaves remained at Lebanon Junction. Soon after Sherman had established his new position, however, he ordered 5,000 rounds of ammunition dispatched to his new camp. Harlan was directed to execute the order.

At first, Harlan decided that compliance with the general's order would be impossible. Rebel troops had destroyed the railroad bridge over the Rolling Fork of the Salt River near Muldraugh's Hill, and the river was unusually broad and deep there. Ultimately, however, he and his men placed a farmer's wagon bed on a railroad handcar, loaded the bed with the ammunition, and forded the river with a team of four horses, Harlan riding one of the lead horses. Once they gained the other side of the stream, they mounted the railroad car on the track, and pushed it through a mile-long tunnel to Sherman's forces at the top of Muldraugh's Hill.

After delivering their cargo, Harlan and his men mounted the handcar for the return trip to Lebanon Junction. Just as the car was about to enter the mile-long tunnel near Sherman's camp, the group encountered several men walking along the track.

Harlan and the others immediately recognized one as Basil W. Duke, a Confederate officer and brother-in-law of John H. Morgan, the noted rebel cavalry officer. Harlan had first met Duke while attending Transylvania University and knew him well. Duke described the encounter in his memoirs: "I was immediately recognized, and . . . ordered . . . to surrender. I tried to seem astonished and look as if it was a case of mistaken identity, but was very much puzzled about what I should do. Greatly to my wonder and relief, however, the car, instead of being stopped, rolled on into the tunnel. . . . By the time that the hand-car with its occupants had returned to the spot . . . , I was beyond immediate pursuit."[35]

Only years later did Duke learn the reason for his good fortune. "When Judge Harlan recognized me," Duke was later told, "it at once occurred to him that I was trying to make my way to Lexington to see my wife; but he also realized that if captured I would be in great peril of being tried and punished as a spy. . . . So he quietly placed his foot under the brake, and the efforts of his companions failed to stop the car. Judge Harlan's foot, like everything in his make-up, mental, moral, and physical, is constructed on a liberal, indeed, a grand scale, and might affect the motion of a passenger coach, not to mention a hand-car. It was an exceedingly generous and kindly act, and I, of course, can never know exactly how deeply I am indebted to him."[36]

Kentucky Colonel

Harlan's activities at Lebanon Junction and Muldraugh's Hill were not his only missions with the Crittenden Zouaves. When the Harlans moved to Louisville with their two children, Edith Shanklin and Richard Davenport, born in 1857 and 1859, respectively, they established a residence in the National Hotel on Jefferson Street. One evening Harlan arrived at the hotel with news that rebel forces were threatening the city and that the home guard units were to guard Louisville's businesses and residences through the night. Unwilling to leave his family at the hotel alone, Harlan took Mallie and the children through troop-lined streets to the home of his law partner, Judge Bullock. "That night, which was dreadful enough in itself," Mallie later recalled, "was a most horrible one for me. My dear host and hostess were alone in the house. Their son . . . had enlisted in the Confederate Army (though his parents were Union people) and he was then in the far South. Added to my own anxiety was the agony I heard expressed in dear Mrs. Bullock's tears and prayers throughout the whole night."[37]

The following day the crisis abated, and Harlan returned to his family. By that point, he had come to realize that his involvement in the war could not be limited to occasional service with his home guard unit. In congressional elections that summer, unionist candidates had been victorious in every contest. At the end of the summer, following further elections bolstering the Union cause, the state legislature formally abandoned neutrality and brought Kentucky actively into the struggle against the Confederacy. Harlan now knew that he, too, must assume a greater role in the conflict.

"That night," according to Mallie's memoirs, "he paced the floor until dawn, his duty to his wife and little ones and his duty to his country wrestling within him in bitter conflict." Finally, he placed the matter entirely in Mallie's hands, telling her that she and the children were his first duty, but also conceding, in response to her inquiries, that had he neither wife nor children, he would enlist. "I knew what his spirit was," Mallie continued, "and to feel himself a shirker in the hour of his country's need would make him most unhappy. Therefore, summoning all the courage I could muster, I said, 'You must do as you would do if you had neither wife nor children. I could not stand between you and your duty to the country and be happy.'"[38]

The following evening, or shortly thereafter, Harlan visited George Prentice at the *Journal* office and asked the editor to draft an address announcing his plans to raise an infantry regiment. Prentice, whose own commitment to the Union had been substantially restored, readily obliged, praising his friend for his patriotism. The next morning, September 27, 1861, Harlan's announcement appeared in the paper. Each company in his regiment was to be composed of not less than 84 nor more than 101 men, who would select their own officers. Any individuals who wished to do so were invited, without further written authority, to raise a company and then report to Harlan the names of unit officers.

Harlan's—or Prentice's—call to the colors was rousing and moving:

And now I appeal to my fellow Kentuckians to come forward and enroll themselves for service. Their invaded State appeals to them. Their foully-wronged and deeply-imperilled country appeals to them. The cause of human liberty and of Republican institutions everywhere appeals to them. All that is most glorious in human government is now at stake, and every true man should come to the rescue.

The time, fellow-citizens, has come, when even the unpatriotic and selfish should hasten to take up arms for the common defence of their State and country. Every consideration of enlightened self-interest calls us to the field. If our enemies triumph, all our trades, all our professions, all our avocations of whatever character, all our possessions of every description, become valueless. To save ourselves and our families from ruin, not less than to save our State and our country from degradation and shame, we must rally now where the National flag invites us. Come, then, let us gird up the whole strength of our bodies and souls for the conflict, and may the God of Battles guide home every blow we strike. For one, I am unwilling to see the people of my native State overrun and conquered by men claiming to be citizens of a foreign government. I cannot be indifferent to the issue which an unnatural enemy has forced upon Kentuckians.[39]

Harlan established his headquarters at Lebanon, and then traveled to adjoining counties, making unionist speeches and recruiting soldiers. By November, he had attracted nearly 1,000 men to the cause. On November 21, three days before the Harlans' third child, James Shanklin, was born, Harlan's regiment—the Tenth Kentucky Volunteer Infantry—was mustered into the service of the United States. As head of his unit, Harlan, then only 28, received a commission as colonel.[40]

The Tenth Kentucky Volunteers were part of a division under the command of General George H. Thomas, whom Harlan would come to consider one of the four great Union generals of the war and whose "boys" referred to him affectionately, albeit behind his back, as "Old Pap Thomas." Shortly after Harlan's regiment was mustered into service, Thomas's division began a march toward Mill Springs, south of Lebanon on the Cumberland River, where Confederate troops and fortifications, which had entered Kentucky from east Tennessee, were situated. The brigade to which the Tenth Kentucky Volunteers were attached lay at the rear of Thomas's line of march. When the head of the division reached Logan's Field, three or four miles from the Cumberland River, Harlan's troops were ordered to pitch camp for the night, then move out early the following morning to capture a Confederate supply train.

Harlan and his soldiers lay concealed in the woods an entire day, but no train appeared. The following morning, however, a cavalryman from Thomas's advance unit dashed into Harlan's camp with an order for his unit and an Ohio regiment to hurry to the front to meet rebel forces then advancing on Thomas's troops from their Mill Springs fortifications. By the time Harlan and his soldiers reached the battlefield, the rebels had been defeated and were in full retreat. At daybreak the next morning, Thomas's division, with Harlan's troops and the Ohio regiment at the front, as Harlan had requested, marched toward the Confederate forces' river fortification. To their disappointment, they discovered that the rebels had crossed the river during the night and were now beyond their reach. Even so, the previous day's battle was the first decisive Union victory of the war and made General Thomas the man of the hour.[41]

For a short time after the Mill Springs engagements, General Thomas's troops camped in the abandoned rebel fortifications. The division was then ordered to join the army of General Don Carlos Buell at Nashville, Tennessee, where they remained encamped for several weeks. Soon, however, Thomas was directed to join the army of General U.S. Grant, then embroiled in a campaign against rebel forces in west Tennessee and Mississippi. Constant rain so delayed Thomas's progress that the major battle of the campaign, bloody Shiloh, was substantially over before his troops joined Grant's. But shortly after their arrival Harlan was able to strike a blow in behalf of his soldiers' comfort.

Harlan's men had made the last miles of the trip to Grant's headquarters at Shiloh Landing by boat. When they docked late one evening, the soldiers were ordered to disembark immediately. Thomas's troops had no wagons or tents with them, nothing but army blankets to protect them from the persistent rain and cold wind, and Harlan considered the command that they leave the shelter of the boat a "cruel order." His men spread hay over the ground, but were soon soaked and chilled. Meanwhile, a brilliantly lit steamboat, occupied only by a few officers and their aides, was docked nearby. Harlan called his men into line, marched them to the steamboat, and prepared to board. When a guard attempted to interfere, Harlan brushed him aside and ordered his men to "pitch into the river" any guard who resisted them. His men quickly boarded the vessel and were soon sleeping soundly. Only later did Harlan learn that the steamboat was serving as General Grant's headquarters and that he could have been shot for his temerity.

During his stay at Shiloh, Harlan toured the battleground and renewed his acquaintance with General Sherman. Through Sherman, he also had the opportunity to meet General Grant. Eventually, Thomas's troops advanced on Corinth, Mississippi, excited at the prospect of a major confrontation with the rebels. But again they were to be disappointed. "Not even a barrel of crackers," Harlan later recalled, "was found for the use of our soldiers." Harlan soon would confront a more formidable foe—a fiery Alabama cleric and a bevy of southern belles.

Following the advance to Corinth, Harlan's regiment was stationed briefly at Eastport, Mississippi. Then, however, General Buell was ordered to concentrate his forces, including Thomas's division, in east Tennessee to prevent an anticipated rebel march into Kentucky. During their march east, Harlan's regiment found itself encamped one Sunday morning at Florence, Alabama. The devout colonel suggested to an aide that they attend services at the local Presbyterian church. When they arrived, they were pleased to see that at least three-quarters of the congregation that morning were officers and enlisted men from Thomas's division. But the pastor, Dr. Mitchell, was not one to play to his audience. During a lengthy pastoral prayer, he pleaded for a Confederate victory and beseeched God to smite to the earth the remorseless invaders of his beloved South.

The soldiers sat quietly until Dr. Mitchell ended his prayer, then stalked out of the church and gathered outside, grumbling bitterly about the pastor's outrageous behavior and recommending his immediate arrest, or worse. As the senior officer present, Harlan cautioned the men against any disturbance of the congregation, then rushed to General Thomas's tent for instructions.

Thomas's sentiments apparently paralleled those of his men. "Go back and arrest the old scoundrel," he ordered Harlan; "no rebel preacher shall behave in that way in my lines." Harlan reminded Thomas that Dr. Mitchell would be delivering his sermon when he returned to the church. "No matter," the general rejoined. "Arrest him at once and deliver him to the 1st Ohio Cavalry with my order to send him at once to the north, not to return until the war is over."

Harlan executed Thomas's order promptly, but not without resistance from women of the church who, the future justice later recalled, "gathered around me and pleaded feelingly for the Doctor's release from arrest, saying that the old gentleman meant no harm." One beautiful Alabama belle was particularly incensed at Harlan, who had not shaved in months and sported a thick, sandy-red beard. "She got mad and called me a red-whiskered Yankee. I disclaimed being a Yankee, saying that I was a Kentuckian. I said to her that I could not quarrel with so handsome a woman as she was. This did not satisfy her. She stamped her feet on the floor in rage and went off." Dr. Mitchell then took Harlan's arm and walked with him to the camp of the First Ohio Cavalry. In less than an hour, the outspoken pastor was en route to St. Louis, where he remained in custody until after the close of the war.

Not surprisingly, the march to join Buell's forces occasioned frequent engagements with the enemy. In a July 31, 1862, report from Pulaski, Tennessee, future birthplace of the Ku Klux Klan, Harlan indicated, for example, that he had engaged a rebel force near Courtland, Alabama, where his men had "fought until completely surrounded and overwhelmed." His losses had included one killed and four wounded, while the Confederate losses were believed to be seven killed and more than 20 wounded.[42]

As the trek continued and a growing number of Harlan's men, feverish and exhausted, fell behind the main body of march, the young colonel also made an effort to prevent their capture by Confederate troops and civilian guerrillas. Thomas's division was to meet General Buell's forces at Decherd, Tennessee. When Harlan's regiment reached Shelbyville, the number of active soldiers in his unit had been reduced by several hundred. At least 75 were so sick or weak they could not carry a rifle.

On the outskirts of Shelbyville, Harlan spotted to his horror two blacks, dressed in Union uniforms and hanging from a roadside tree. This grim spectacle, in particular, made Harlan fearful for the fate of the sick and exhausted men trudging along behind the main body of his troops.

Entering Shelbyville later that morning, Harlan discovered 30 to 40 well-dressed citizens sitting quietly under spreading shade trees. Their presence immediately gave him an idea. At his order, his troops arrested a half dozen young men who appeared to be influential and well-to-do. He then warned the others that he would execute two of the arrested men for every one of his soldiers murdered or captured by rebel guerrillas. Harlan adopted this arrangement at every town through which his troops passed on the march to Decherd. He later wrote that he had no intention of carrying out his threat. But the ploy was entirely successful. No more of his sick soldiers disappeared or were killed. Later, however, he learned that the hostages taken in Shelbyville had been among the few Union sympathizers in the town.

Once all the troops under General Buell's command had gathered at Decherd, they advanced along the track of the Louisville and Nashville Railroad through Nashville and on to Louisville. While Buell's army of 75,000 to 80,000 men was encamped at Louisville, Mallie Harlan traveled from her parents' home in Evansville, Indiana, to her husband's side, bringing their son, James, with her.

The visit of his wife and baby no doubt bolstered the young colonel's spirits. Harlan and his comrades were becoming increasingly disenchanted, however, with General Buell and certain of his principal officers. Buell's troops had reached Louisville in advance of Confederate forces under General Braxton Bragg. But during his march into central Kentucky and after his arrival in Louisville, Buell had passed up several opportunities to engage Bragg's troops and remained at the rear of his army during the bloody battle of Perryville, fought near Harlan's ancestral home, until the fighting had substantially subsided.

Harlan had been situated within 100 yards of Buell's headquarters during the battle at Perryville. He thus realized that the direction of the wind that day made it impossible for the general to hear musket and cannon fire from Perryville; the wind, not cowardice, had accounted for Buell's delay in reaching the scene of battle. But Harlan also doubted Buell's military prowess and that of his lieutenants. In a letter to his brother James, dated September 17, 1862, he complained that General Charles C. Gilbert, whom Buell had selected to head the corps to which Harlan's regiment was attached, and another of Buell's principal officers had "no common sense and are wholly worthless for the emergency," adding, "Without a General nothing can be done against the invasion of the rebels."[43] When the field officers in Gilbert's corps held a meeting at a small schoolhouse near his camp the day after the Perryville engagement, Harlan was invited to attend.

Those attending the meeting first focused their ire on General Gilbert. Calling him incompetent and a disgrace to his uniform, several of those present recommended that a telegram be sent to President Lincoln, urging his immediate removal. Finally, an officer with an Illinois regiment rose from his seat and impassionately branded the group "a pack of cowards." He declared, "[W]e have spent all this evening talking about Gen. Gilbert, when our real objection is to Buell as our commander. In my opinion, Buell is a traitor, is untrue to the army, and untrue to the country."

Harlan immediately registered a partial protest. Buell, he insisted, "no doubt has made mistakes, and may have views that I do not share. But I do not believe that he is untrue to the army or that he purposely or treacherously allowed Bragg's army to escape." Nor, he added, would he sign any telegram questioning Buell's loyalty.

"What sort of telegram will you sign?" the Illinois officer retorted. "Put down on paper what you are willing to say." Harlan then drafted a message to the president indicating that Buell had lost the confidence of his army and urging a change of commanders in what he termed the "public interest." All those present signed the document and then suggested that Harlan transmit it to Washington.

Harlan rode the next day to the Lebanon telegraph office, prepared to send the message but increasingly apprehensive that he and his comrades were risking serious difficulty by their temerity. Fortunately, however, he happened to read a morning newspaper first and learned that Buell had been superseded by General William B. Rosecrans and temporarily deprived of his authority. Harlan quickly pocketed the telegram and returned to his troops.

Shortly after Buell's replacement, Harlan was put in charge of Union troops camped at Castalian Springs, Tennessee, northeast of Nashville and about ten miles from Hartsville, another Tennessee community. At that time, about 2100 Union soldiers were stationed at Hartsville. The officer commanding them was exceedingly lax. His men were permitted to roam the countryside, preying on the property of civilians, and no pickets were maintained around the encampment.

While the Hartsville troops were quietly eating breakfast one morning, cavalry detachments under the command of General John H. Morgan, the daring Confederate raider, burst from the woods and quickly killed or captured the entire unit. On hearing the sound of musket fire from the Hartsville vicinity, Harlan rushed to the scene with his men. By the time they arrived, however, the ground was covered with the dead and wounded, and Morgan's cavalrymen, with Union prisoners on the backs of their mounts for protection, were already across the Cumberland River and racing up the hill from the river bank. Harlan's foot soldiers were no match for Morgan's cavalry.

One of the rebel soldiers left dead on the battlefield had passed through Harlan's camp the previous day, disguised as a farmer with chickens for sale. Just before the Hartsville raid began, General Morgan issued a warning to his men based no doubt on intelligence the friendly "farmer" had supplied him. The battle, he cautioned, must end in an hour. By that time, "John Harlan will be here from Castalian Springs . . . with more men than we have."

Hartsville was not to be Harlan's last encounter with General Morgan. In December, the Confederate raider moved his men along the L & N railroad line, destroying bridges over which supplies for General Rosecrans' army, then encamped at Chattanooga, were being transported. General Thomas, whose headquarters were at Gallatin, Tennessee, north of Nashville, ordered Harlan to leave Castalian Springs in pursuit of Morgan's forces. That same day, Harlan and a brigade of men reported to Gallatin and boarded a train for Louisville. The distance from Gallatin north toward Bowling Green was not great, but the locomotive's progress was repeatedly delayed, prompting Harlan to become suspicious that its engineer was a rebel sympathizer. When Harlan and his troops finally did reach Bowling Green, Harlan shared his suspicions with the depot agent and warned that any further unnecessary delays would be summarily punished.

With a new engine and no further delays, the train continued on to Munfordville, where Harlan's men scattered a portion of Morgan's troops, and then proceeded to Elizabethtown, where inquiries were made as to the location of the balance of the rebel officer's forces. From intelligence pieced together at Elizabethtown, Harlan elected to march his men at a fast pace down a road leading to Johnson's Ferry, where they joined a cavalry detachment, a company of artillery, and part of another infantry regiment.

When the colonel leading the cavalry unit reached the top of a hill overlooking the ferry landing, he discovered some of Morgan's men resting along the Rolling Fork of the Salt River. At the colonel's order, the artillery squad began firing, while Harlan hurried his men forward, marched down the hill, and gave battle to the rebels, who, at the first sound of artillery fire, had hidden along the river bank and in the woods.

Morgan's mounted troops were again able to escape Harlan's infantry. When the firing began, however, the rebels had abandoned their plans to destroy the Rolling Fork bridge. At one point in the skirmish, moreover, bullets whistled past Harlan's face as he dashed on horseback in search of rebel troops. For his success in helping to rout Morgan's forces, he received a military commendation and became something of a war hero in the eyes of Kentuckians.[44]

Apparently, Harlan also enjoyed the affection of his soldiers. Champ Clark, the colorful speaker of the U.S. House of Representatives, was a boy during the war. A company of Harlan's regiment had been raised in Clark's community, and he recounted the stories they told:

> When the soldiers came from the war they had divers tales to tell of their beloved colonel. Among other things they said he could outrun, outjump, and outwrestle any man in the regiment. They told with much glee how, before they were ever in battle, the colonel would make them speeches about how bravely they should perform under fire, and how, after their first engagement—the battle of Mill Springs—the colonel told them frankly that if any of them felt like running he did not blame them, for all that prevented him from fleeing was his shoulder-straps.[45]

The soldiers especially delighted in telling, to the staid Harlan's chagrin, the story of a bellicose Baptist preacher who served as chaplain with the regiment. In the midst of battle, the chaplain rushed up and down the lines. "[B]elieving that some swearing was necessary, and not being willing to swear himself, he would yell, 'Boys, give them hell, as Colonel Harlan says!'"[46]

The feeling was mutual. Whatever elitist, anti-immigrant, anti-Catholic biases Harlan's Know-Nothing experience may have reflected gave way during the war to growing egalitarian leanings and admiration for the German immigrants and Kentucky mountaineers in his regiment. His war reports underscored "their willingness, even eagerness, to endure any fatigue or make any sacrifice." In a dispatch on the battle of Mill Springs, he declared, "Although the men of my regiment were entirely destitute of provisions, and on that morning had not received half enough for breakfast, my summons to them to fall into line and march to the aid of our brethren was obeyed with commendable alacrity." Once his men had taken possession of the woods near the rebel fortifications, he described how they "lay on the ground during the whole of Sunday night without fire, tents, overcoats, or blankets, and with nothing to eat except about one-fourth of a cracker to each man."[47]

Years later, Harlan would recall his men's exhausting struggle with the elements on the road to the same engagement: "[T]he earth was so thoroughly soaked with rain that Thomas's troops could only make a few miles each day. The regimental wagons sank into the earth up to the hubs of the wheels, and had to be lifted out by the soldiers. There was not a day when I did not myself join in that work in order to encourage my men. All along the route we had to cut down trees and saplings and make what were called 'corduroy' roads, over which the wagons, when lifted out of the mud, would be placed by the soldiers." Of the "many Catholics" in his regiment, he wrote: "It was a magnificent sight to see how the boys struggled through mud and rain to reach the field of battle. The ground was so wet and muddy under them that their feet slipped at every step. I see now with great distinctness old Father Nash pushing along on foot with the boys. Equally earnest with him was a Catholic priest from Washington County, who had come with Catholic soldiers from that county."[48]

Harlan's regard for his men did not extend, however, to the citizens of Louisville, or perhaps to Kentucky's civilians and home guards generally. In September of 1862, when General Bragg's Confederate forces were threatening to seize Louisville, Harlan wrote his brother James, complaining that the "people [there] will do nothing for themselves—not more than a lamb when seized by the butcher. . . . I do not intend," he vehemently added, "to fight for these people when they manifest no disposition to help themselves. You may not be surprised if I come to Evansville in a few days—I am out of all patience with the military and people of Louisville."[49]

Whatever his frustrations with those he was endeavoring to defend, Harlan remained in uniform for the balance of the year and into 1863. In early March, however, he resigned his commission. During the previous summer, Frankfort and the surrounding countryside had been under rebel control, and Harlan's father, who was then serving as U.S. attorney for Kentucky, was compelled to remain in Louisville. In the early fall, the Confederate forces left the area, and James Harlan decided to join his wife, whom he had not seen for several months, in Frankfort. Seeking to evade rebel capture, the elder Harlan first traveled to Cincinnati and then by rail to Lexington. The remaining 20 miles from Lexington to Frankfort he traveled in an open buggy, a Henry rifle across his lap for protection but without an overcoat against the weather. When he reached home about midnight, he was thoroughly chilled.

At first, his condition did not appear serious. When John Harlan visited his parents, he found his father ill with a congestive chill but, apparently, in no immediate danger. By mid-February, however, his condition had worsened; and on February 23, he died.

In Harlan's eyes, his father's death left him with no choice but to leave the army. "His death," the future justice later wrote, "was a great calamity to his family and left my mother practically without anything upon which to live. He had only a small estate, and he had not fully paid for his residence. His uncollected fees as a lawyer were all that my mother could look to for support, and as I had no estate, the prompt collection of those fees was therefore absolutely necessary. I alone of my father's family was in condition to meet the emergency."[50]

On March 6, 1863, after conferring with General Rosecrans and the general's chief-of-staff, James Garfield, Harlan resigned his commission. Fearful perhaps that his action might be construed as evidence of declining faith in the Union, he stated the reasons for his decision in his letter of resignation and had the letter published in the Louisville *Journal* and other papers.[51] The letter read in part:

> I deeply regret that I am compelled at this time to return to civil life. It was my fixed purpose to remain in the Federal army until it had effectually suppressed the existing armed rebellion and restored the authority of the National Government over every part of the Nation. No ordinary considerations would have induced me to depart from this purpose. Even the private interests [relative to his father's death] to which I have alluded would be regarded as nothing in my estimation, if I felt that my continuance in or retirement from the service would to any material extent affect the great struggle through which the country is now passing.
>
> If therefore I am permitted to retire from the army, I beg the commanding General to feel assured that it is from no want of confidence either in the justice or ultimate triumph of the Union cause. That cause will always have the warmest sympathies of my heart, for there are no conditions upon which I will consent to a dissolution of the Union. Nor are there any conditions, consistent with a republican form of Government, which I am not prepared to make in order to maintain and perpetuate that Union.[52]

Harlan had recently learned that President Lincoln was sending to the Senate his nomination for advancement to the rank of brigadier-general. By a letter to Kentucky Senator John J. Crittenden, Harlan asked that the nomination be withdrawn.

If the enlisted men of his regiment were proud of their colonel, the officers of the brigade Harlan was commanding at the time of his resignation were, too. In an enthusiastic resolution, they expressed deep regret for the "private affliction" that had led to his separation from the army, extended a "fond farewell" to their "friend and companion in arms," and applauded "his amiable manners, unflinching integrity, and indefatigable" sense of duty, "courage, skill ... genius, and ... unswerving devotion to the Union." But the praise heaped on him by *Journal* editor George Prentice was even more effusive. In January, following John Harlan's visit to Louisville, Prentice published a brief "Tribute to Colonel Harlan," in which he declared that his young friend deserved "the lasting gratitude of the whole country for his invaluable services in arresting the depredations of John Morgan and his fellow-brigands."[53] When Harlan announced his resignation, Prentice focused on the "gallant" colonel's selfless devotion to familial as well as national duty:

> Nominated for promotion to the office of Brigadier-General, and assured of the preferment if he but continued in the service, he has retired at the very moment when a brilliant military career was opening before him. Colonel Harlan has manfully sacrificed inclination to duty. The sacrifice must have cost him many sharp pangs, but he was equal to it. Now, as ever, he is true to himself. In the golden opinions and loving

wishes that accompany him from the Army we most cordially unite. May health and prosperity ever attend him![54]

"Ze Little Black Nigger"

Following his father's death, Harlan returned with his family to Frankfort and established a law practice with his brother, James. Their duties as co-administrators of their father's estate also consumed a considerable portion of their time.[55] In April 1863, moreover, they announced plans to produce *Harlan's Selected Cases*, a volume of important unpublished opinions of the Kentucky court of appeals, which the justices of that tribunal, in a letter published with the Harlans' announcement of the project, predicted would be of "as great value as any volume of the Kentucky Reports."[56]

But John Harlan would not long elude politics. At a March 16 meeting of Union State Party members in Frankfort, he was selected as a delegate from the Ashland congressional district to the party's state convention in Louisville.[57] Three days later, the state body chose him as its nominee for attorney general, the position his father had long held in Kentucky politics.[58]

Harlan's commitment to the Union and opposition to secession was undoubtedly firm and sincere. His war reports were replete with unflattering references to the enemy and their "evil" goals. In one dispatch, he wrote proudly of driving "back in dismay . . . the vandal horde of secession and treason" and "those wicked and unnatural men who are seeking without cause to destroy the Union of our fathers."[59] In his convention speech accepting nomination as attorney general, according to a newspaper report, he vigorously "recommend[ed] an earnest prosecution of the war with all the energies of the nation" and rejected the "idea of peace on any terms less than the submission of the rebels to the laws they had outraged."[60] By this point, he no doubt sensed that there was no chance of ultimate success for the secessionist cause. In a March 28 letter, a friend Harlan had asked to dispose of some Confederate currency urged him to send the funds immediately, "as the money is getting worse every day."[61]

On January 1, however, President Lincoln's Emancipation Proclamation, declaring freedom for slaves in the secessionist states, became fully effective. Politically, commitment to the Union—and any hint of support for Lincoln—had thus become extremely risky in Kentucky. Indeed, the tiny contingent of pro-Lincoln unionists in the state did not even attempt to field a slate of candidates for the 1863 elections.

Harlan may also have had a personal motivation for opposing emancipation. According to his wife's memoirs, he personally purchased only one slave before the institution's demise. Under Kentucky's inheritance laws, however, his mother stood to receive only one-third of his father's estate, and thus only four of the family's dozen or so slaves. To assure that she retained all the family servants, Harlan had assumed a heavy debt.[62] One close student of Harlan's pre-judicial career has suggested that his immediate financial stake in the perpetuation of slavery may help to account for his opposition to the Emancipation Proclamation.[63]

During the 1863 campaign, Harlan and other moderate unionists pursued a stump strategy that scorned both the "Secessionist" Democrats and the anti-slavery program of the Lincoln White House. As one moderately unionist Democratic paper put it, the goal was to "*choke to death*, those twin sisters of infamy and deviltry Secession and Abolition."[64] On several occasions during his bid for attorney general, Harlan delivered stridently pro-Union speeches. But he also condemned the president's suspension of habeas corpus and charged that the Emancipation Proclamation was unconstitutional.[65]

For the time being at least, the ploy worked. Every Union Democratic candidate for state office won. Harlan beat his opponent by over 50,000 votes.[66]

The campaign had also given Harlan the opportunity to bolster his reputation as a formidable platform opponent. Champ Clark recalled playing hooky from school in order to hear Harlan and gubernatorial candidate Thomas Bramlett speak in a sugar grove on the outskirts of Mackville:

> [Harlan] was as magnificent a specimen of a physical man as one would have found in a month's journey—standing six feet three in his stockings, weighing two hundred avoirdupois without an ounce of surplus flesh, red-headed, blond as any lily, graceful as a panther. . . . Governor Bramlett was a large, handsome man and made a good speech, but Harlan easily overtopped him mentally, physically, and oratorically. Mere chunk of a boy as I was, I could see that Harlan was the greater man, and I thought that therefore he ought to have been running for the greater office.[67]

Nor had Harlan's increasingly vocal opposition to Lincoln's policies dampened his devotion to the Union. In early June of 1864, Governor Bramlette, who had headed the ticket on which Harlan was elected attorney general, informed the future justice that a detachment of General Morgan's Confederate raiders was then advancing on Frankfort. Determined to set a good example for his townsmen, Harlan seized his father's old Henry rifle and, along with John S. Hays, the pastor of his Presbyterian congregation, rushed to the "Fort"—a few rows of earthen breastworks situated on a hill behind the capitol building, overlooking the city. Soon, a small squad of rebel soldiers made an advance; but Harlan and local militia, armed only with two small cannons, rifles, and sidearms, forced them to retreat. Later, Harlan and the others spotted a large number of Confederate horsemen in the yard of the Harlan summer home on a hill across the Kentucky River from the capitol. After making certain that the cannon would not hit the Harlan house, which his mother occupied, Harlan ordered the militia to fire on the cavalrymen, who soon retreated.[68] In the incident's aftermath, he led efforts to bolster the city's fortifications, organized an all-night vigil to protect key bridges against sabotage, and moderated a meeting to create a more permanent city militia.[69]

In the following year, Harlan became even more vehement in his attacks on Lincoln's emancipation policies. In January 1864, longtime family friend O. S. Poston cautioned him not to "attach yourself to[o] fast to what is called the Conservative Party."[70] But Poston's warning fell on deaf ears. The previous month, the national committee of the Conservative Union Party had met in Cincinnati, with Governor Bramlette and other Harlan associates in attendance. The committee endorsed General George B. McClellan for the presidency and declared that restoration of the Union was the war's sole legitimate objective. Harlan became a member of the party's state central committee, and when General McClellan became the presidential nominee of northern Democrats, he endorsed his candidacy and actively campaigned for his election.[71]

Under normal circumstances, the notion that Harlan, a man of unblemished Whig credentials and heritage, might embrace Democratic candidacies would have been unthinkable. But these were not normal times. Relations between Kentuckians and their national government were growing increasingly hostile. In fact, beginning July 5, 1864, the state officially was under martial law—for 15 frustrating, resentment-breeding months.[72] It was thus not surprising that in his speeches for McClellan and other Democratic candidates, Harlan lashed out repeatedly at Lincoln and his policies, particularly his efforts to abolish slavery.

Harlan did not limit his canvass to Kentucky. He also toured neighboring Indiana, speaking in support of McClellan and General Mahlon Manson, a wartime comrade and Democratic candidate for lieutenant governor of the state, while excoriating Lincoln and Oliver Morton, the radical Republican Indiana governor who had supplied Harlan and other Kentucky unionists with ammunition during the early days of the crisis.

A speech Harlan delivered in New Albany, Indiana, on October 4, 1864, was perhaps his most vitriolic effort. For the record, he reaffirmed that he was "an unconditional Union man, unconditional for the Union and the Constitution," but in the main, he attacked his opponents. The Republican Party, he declared, "should never have triumphed [in 1860], because it was based upon the single idea of hate and hostility to the social institution of one section of our country." But once that party won the election, Lincoln and the nation were entitled to respect; and when the secessionists fired on the nation's flag, the president was justified in using force to restore the Union and maintain the supremacy of national law. But the war was intended only for that "high and noble goal" of preserving the Union, and "not for the purpose of giving freedom to the negro." Lincoln had "perverted" the war's character and was now "warring chiefly for the freedom of the African race." The president, in Harlan's judgment, would "not be content with simply re-establishing the authority of the Constitution and restoring the Union" and was opposed to "peace upon any terms which [did] not embrace the abandonment by the South of its local institutions." Such a goal, declared Harlan, was "impossible of achievement." Union forces might quash the Confederacy, "but under the policy of Mr. Lincoln the Union [could] never be restored in the hearts and affections of the people of the South." Lincoln should have pursued policies that would divide Southerners and their "wicked leaders." Instead, his punitive policies and disregard for fundamental rights of liberty and property had created "a divided North and a united South."[73]

Harlan's campaign activities frustrated the most intensely unionist of his old allies. The Frankfort *Commonwealth,* now a staunch pro-Lincoln paper, reminded its readers that Governor Morton, against whom Harlan was campaigning, had sent thousands of troops into the state to protect Kentuckians, including "the property and interests of Colonel John M. Harlan," from "rebel hordes." "Is it not inconsistent and ungrateful," the *Commonwealth*'s editor asked, "for any citizen of Kentucky professing Unionism—much more so for an incumbent of State office—to take an active part in the attempt to defeat Governor Morton?" The paper wanted the unionists of Indiana to know that Kentucky's Union men were in no way responsible for such behavior. "Col. Harlan, once an unconditional union man, has cast in his lot with those who were from the first with the rebellion."[74]

Perhaps in anticipation of such reactions, George Prentice's Louisville *Journal* had earlier recounted Harlan's Whig heritage and loyal military service. The paper assured its readers that Harlan "acts with the Democratic party in this struggle from simple devotion to his country."[75] On another occasion, Prentice was less delicate. In supporting McClellan, he declared, Harlan was simply choosing the lesser of two evils: "[N]ecessity requires that he do it in order to defeat . . . the machinations of the *Nigger* Republican party."[76] For his part, Harlan asserted that he had simply "buried the hatchet" with the Democrats because he considered McClellan the only hope for preserving the Union and the Constitution "in all parts of the nation."[77]

Lincoln's supporters were hardly persuaded. In its account of an October 10 debate in Frankfort between Harlan and a Lincoln elector, the *Commonwealth* opined that McClellan's spokesman "labored and worried along like a man who had no heart or spirit in what he was doing, [whose] entire effort bespoke a man who was sorely striving to uphold a cause he felt and knew to be wrong, and in opposition to which every impulse of his convictions and his principles arose [as] an impossible barrier." He seemed "like himself," the paper concluded, only "in a single instance when he gave the rebels a lick or two that reminded his hearers of the ancient ring of his Union voice."[78]

Whether for reasons of personal conviction or political expediency, Harlan continued his attacks on the Republicans throughout the campaign. On at least one occasion, he even indulged in a bit of crude race-baiting. In late October, Colonel Philip D. White, a Kentucky native then residing in Philadelphia, visited the state for speechmaking in behalf of the Lincoln presidency. During debate with White in Anderson County, Harlan told an anecdote about a Frenchman and his "little black cow." The Frenchman's anxiety about his cow, he told his delighted audience, reminded him of the Republican Party's concern for "*ze little black nigger.*"[79]

In the end, McClellan carried only three states. But Kentucky was one of them, giving the Democratic candidate 11 of his 21 electoral votes. The state's Conservative Unionists continued to consider Harlan one of their more promising political weapons. In 1865, his friends urged him to make a run for Congress. One assured him, in fact, that he "would suit the people of [his] district better by far than" other likely candidates and noted that the "besetting sin" of another prospect was "that he gets a little *tight* sometimes," although the same could also be said, he conceded, of "most of our great men."[80]

In declining another congressional bid, Harlan cited "[c]onsiderations . . . of a private nature, relating to my professional and other duties." In a published letter explaining his decision, however, he also scorned the abolitionist movement and the proposed Thirteenth Amendment ending slavery—which was to win ratification by the year's end. "[I]f there were not a dozen slaves in Kentucky," he declared in a letter to Colonel John W. Combs, a Versailles supporter, he would oppose the slavery amendment on principle. That provision, he asserted, was based on the theory "that there is no local or domestic policy of any State, however dear to the people or however unimportant in a national point of view, which may not be abolished, interfered with, or regulated by other States, under the cover of an amendment of the Constitution." For him, the practical consequences of abolition were equally daunting:

Our State has suffered much during the civil war through which the nation has just passed, but she will suffer much more, and, unnecessarily, if, by the action of other States, her large slave population is suddenly freed in our midst, and the power taken from the State . . . to effect the removal of the blacks to other localities, or protect her white citizens from the ruinous effects of such a violent change in our social system. With the hands of the State tied, and the control of the black population transferred to the appointees of a Freedman's Bureau, the white men of Kentucky will regret that any of them ever assented to the surrender to other States, through Congress, of our undoubted right to regulate our own local concerns.

Kentucky was then under martial law, and General John M. Palmer, the abolitionist commander of federal troops in the state, had recently embarked on a policy of enlisting blacks in the Union army in order to free them from their masters. Palmer's action and other elements of the abolitionist agenda, Harlan charged, meant "the subsistence of large bodies of negro men, women, and children in this State, at the expense of the nation, and with a watchful care which has never been exhibited for the wives and families of the white soldiers of Kentucky." Left alone and "unterrified by armed bands of negro soldiers," Kentuckians would eventually resolve the slavery question "consistently with the interests of the whites and blacks, and soon enough for the comfort, security and happiness of both races." But they would "not bow in humble submission . . . to a *forced*" compliance, nor, in Harlan's judgment, should they. Instead, those who were interested in a lasting, peaceful Union, but opposed "admission of the negro to the ballot-box, or to the enjoyment of other political privileges," should unite to "secure the *cheerful* and *willing* obedience of the people to the Constitution and laws."

Harlan stated his belief that the triumph of such a goal could be achieved only through policies of conciliation and mutual respect:

The Union must be restored in the hearts and affections of the people of the States lately in rebellion, before we can expect the nation to recover from the effects of the war through which it has passed, and enjoy uninterrupted and substantial peace. To effect results so desirable, we should remember that the people with whom we have been at war possess the same feelings and pride which we do, and are descended from the same ancestry; and, while our vast military power may force them to submit to all which may be done, we can, by a liberal and magnanimous policy, and with due regard to the authority of the National Government, win their confidence and secure their hearty co-operation in restoring law and order, and in perpetuating our matchless system of Government.[81]

Although Harlan made no election bid in 1865, his brother, James, sought a seat in the state house of representatives as an anti-abolition candidate. Harlan stumped the district in his brother's behalf, reiterating the themes of his letter to Colonel Combs—and again infuriating the staunchly unionist Frankfort *Commonwealth*. In a series of editorial snippets comparing the Harlans to James's opponent, William H. Gray, the *Commonwealth*'s editors attempted to paint the brothers as opponents of Kentucky whites. "The Harlans want to keep the negro here by keeping him enslaved, and compel the laboring white man to seek some other place where labor is free," read one, while another charged that "The Harlans think, and so do the Rebels, that the slave is better than the laboring white man, and therefore they want

to keep him on the best lands." But the *Commonwealth* was most effective in excoriating the brothers' defection from the Union cause:

> Both of these gentlemen were out and out Union men as long as they believed that
> was the winning side. No persons in this county were more denunciatory of rebels
> and rebel sympathizers than they were until they believed they could turn rebel votes
> to their own advancement for office; and now, there are no rebel sympathizers in Ken-
> tucky who are more blatant contemners of the Government, and those who are admin-
> istering it, than John and James Harlan.[82]

As clerk of the U.S. district court, the paper reported, James was receiving 20 to
25 cents for administering rebels the amnesty oath, while his brother was assisting
rebels for a $10 fee. Indeed, so pro-rebel was one recent speech by James Harlan,
it claimed, that one sympathetic member of the audience was moved to shout,
"Huzza for Jeff Davis," before being knocked from his horse by "a sturdy, honest
Union man."[83]

In the August 7 elections, conservative, anti-amendment candidates, including
James Harlan, generally won, if by narrow majorities. They elected five of the
state's nine congressmen, narrow majorities in both houses of the legislature, and
the state treasurer—the only statewide office being contested.[84]

As attorney general, John Harlan also attempted to defend Kentucky's slavery
policies against the advancing movement of abolition. In July, 1864, the provost
marshal of Harrison County, acting on orders from the district provost, seized a
slave named Mariah and her three children from their owner and placed them in
federal custody. In *Jones* v. *Commonwealth* (1866),[85] the Kentucky court of appeals
upheld an indictment brought against the county provost and accepted Harlan's contention that federal officers could seize private property, including slaves, only on a
showing of imminent danger to the national government.

In another case, *Bowlin* v. *Commonwealth* (1867),[86] a state circuit judge, concluding that the recently enacted federal civil rights act of 1866 superseded state
law, allowed the introduction of testimony by a black witness against a white defendant in a larceny case, despite a state law forbidding such testimony. In a "Suggestion for the Commonwealth," written and signed in James Harlan's handwriting but
presumably reflecting Harlan's views, the attorney general refused to defend the
trial court's position when the defendant appealed his conviction before the state
court of appeals. "The only question on this appeal is as to the propriety of the
Court admitting the testimony of a negro against a white person," observed Harlan,
adding: "Not feeling at liberty, according to my views of that question as a legal
proposition, to uphold the judgment of the Court below, the case is respectfully submitted to the Court without argument on behalf of the Commonwealth."[87]

The state high court, speaking through Harlan's mentor, Justice Robertson,
shared the general's concerns. Reversing the white appellant's conviction, Justice
Robertson ruled that the U.S. Constitution forbade any congressional meddling with
Kentucky's law on black testimony. "Now," he pointedly added, "the danger has
shifted from an undue State supremacy and consequent disintegration of the national government, to an undue supremacy in the national head, usurping the reserved rights of the States and destroying their government by a concentration of
their power in it."[88]

Harlan's most celebrated case with political and racial overtones involved General John M. Palmer, the controversial military commandant of Kentucky. In the eyes of Kentucky blacks, Palmer was the key to freedom. As July 4, 1865, approached, rumors swept through the black population that Palmer would grant freedom to any black who came to Louisville by Independence Day. By that morning, at least 20,000 blacks were gathered in and around the city, singing, shouting, and praising Palmer's name. The experience made a tremendous impact on the head of Kentucky's Union forces. "I determined," he later wrote, "'to drive the last nail in the coffin' of [slavery] even if it cost me the command of the department." Standing in the midst of the black throng, Palmer declared, "My countrymen, *you are free*, and while I command in this department the military forces of the United States will defend your right to freedom."[89]

General Palmer undertook several measures to hasten freedom for Kentucky's blacks. When Louisville's mayor and council complained that the large number of blacks crowded into their city posed a serious threat of pestilence, he ordered train and ferry owners to permit blacks carrying military passes to leave congested areas. The order became a favorite device of slaves seeking their freedom and, like other Palmer edicts, infuriated white Kentuckians. It was hardly surprising, therefore, that when a slave named Ellen escaped to freedom in Indiana via one of Palmer's passes, a circuit grand jury indicted Kentucky's federal commandant for violating a provision of state law carrying a sentence of up to 20 years' imprisonment.

Taking judicial notice of the Thirteenth Amendment's adoption, a circuit judge quashed the indictment and Palmer soon left the state and the custody of its courts. In *Commonwealth* v. *Palmer* (1866),[90] however, the Kentucky court of appeals, speaking again through Justice Robertson, agreed with Attorney General Harlan that Palmer was indictable under state law. Aiding slaves to escape their masters served no legitimate military purpose, Robertson declared. Besides, so many blacks had obtained passports that "but few were left at home, and farmers generally, and many residents of cities and towns, were suddenly left without their accustomed and necessary help, the long-established system of labor terribly disturbed, and citizens excited almost to revolution." The disruptive impact of the order, he concluded, was "so universally notorious as to be stereotyped as local history, of which this court, if it know anything, must have judicial knowledge."[91]

Although Harlan continued to assume an anti-abolition posture as Kentucky's chief law enforcement officer, the honeymoon between his Conservative Unionists and rebel Democrats was shortlived. When the legislature convened in December, 1865, following the election of James Harlan and many other opponents of the Thirteenth Amendment's adoption, unionist delegates joined with Confederate sympathizers on several matters connected with the rebellion, including repeal of the state's expatriation act. The repeal restored to former rebels all the privileges of state citizenship, including the suffrage. The immediate enfranchisement of thousands of rebel voters swelled the ranks of the rebel Democrats, who began to consider themselves strong enough to stand alone, without the support of Conservative Unionists. As one Kentucky contributor to a Cincinnati paper put it, their battle cry became, "We will beat you and the radicals both."[92]

In 1866, the only state election contest was that for clerk of the Kentucky court of appeals. Now estranged from the rebel Democrats, Conservative Unionists joined with radical unionists to run General Edward H. Hobson for the post, while rebel Democrats chose Alvin Duvall as their candidate. Harlan became assistant state canvasser for the party and campaigned vigorously for Hobson. In a major speech at Glasgow, in Barren County, he depicted the campaign as essentially a contest between "Unionists" and "Disunionists" of the sort that had first raged in 1861. The disunionist Democrats, he charged, were *"par excellence* States Rights men" whose leaders, "with scarcely an exception, during the entire war sympathized with the rebellion, and desired the dissolution of the Union." He accused them of telling voters that they must be "for the South or Abolitionists"—that there could be no middle ground. "From such 'Democracy,'" exclaimed Harlan, "may a kind Providence deliver the people of this noble old Commonwealth." For Harlan, it was critical that Kentucky not become isolated from the Union and that the nation know that Kentuckians would not support those who favored the rebellion. "The political events of 1860," he asserted, "should teach us to beware of forming entangling alliances with Southern sentiment parties. Countenance no political organization which is not eminently national, and which will not do equal and exact justice to every part of the country."[93]

For Harlan and other Conservative Unionists, it was becoming increasingly difficult to convince Kentuckians of the wisdom of the "middle ground." Even before the Hobson–Duvall campaign began, Harlan and other prominent conservatives had sponsored a public rally at Frankfort to praise the moderate Reconstruction policies of President Andrew Johnson.[94] Both the radical and conservative factions of the party agreed, moreover, to denounce publicly proposals to extend the suffrage to the former slaves.[95] In his stump speeches, Harlan also emphasized Hobson's long support of the Democratic Party and regard for President Johnson's politics of moderation.

Hobson's connection with a coalition composed in part of radical unionists made his campaign a difficult venture. When Harlan, Hobson, and company, in an effort to make Hobson's candidacy more palatable to Kentuckians, began to attack elements of the congressional reconstruction program they had earlier promised to leave alone, their tactic threatened the fragile coalition they had forged with the radicals.[96]

Meanwhile, rebel Democrats once again bombarded Harlan with charges of political inconsistency for his alliance with the radicals. The Louisville *Daily Courier* scorned the "halting, doubting, dubious course of Harlan during the whole of his political career."[97] During an appearance at Elizabethtown on July 16, moreover, an unfriendly member of his audience asked, "Did you not promise in a speech in Lebanon, when making up your [Civil War] regiment, that if the war should be directed against slavery, that you would break your sword and make war upon the Abolitionists?"[98] One of the closest students of Harlan's pre-Court career found no evidence to support such a claim.[99] But, as another has noted, Harlan was certainly no friend of abolition at the time his regiment was mustered.[100] A Democratic newspaper carried an item by a Confederate sympathizer, who signed his dispatch "Old Line Whig," reporting that Harlan, on hearing the question, "was excessively confused and failed to give any direct answer." The correspondent expressed hope that Harlan's brand of unionism was not the "kind . . . which justified . . . atrocity and outrages ... the Freedmen's Bureau bill; the Civil Rights bill; the recent amendment of the Constitution, which, if adopted, will clothe negroes with all the rights belonging to the white man ... ; [and the right] to treat the Southern States as conquered provinces, denying them representation, and yet imposing upon them taxation."[101]

Kentucky voters were apparently as skeptical of the conservative–radical alliance as Harlan's critics were of his motives. Hobson went down to ignoble defeat in the August, 1866, elections, losing to Duvall by nearly 40,000 votes. Politically, Harlan fared no better in the debacle's immediate aftermath. The Republican *Cincinnati Gazette* accused him and other Conservative Unionists of breaking their agreement with the radicals and attacking most vehemently the very people with whom they supposedly were allied.[102] In protracted state legislative balloting for a U.S. Senate seat the following January, he garnered only eight votes, the fewest of any candidate.[103]

To break a deadlock in the legislative balloting for the Senate seat, the Conservative Unionists had again allied with the Democrats, enabling Harlan's old friend Garrett Davis, a staunch unionist who had become a particularly outspoken critic of emancipation and Reconstruction, to win over Benjamin H. Bristow, the radical who would later become Harlan's law partner and, for a time, his close friend and political ally.[104] But this alliance, too, would be brief. When the rebel Democrats met in February to nominate candidates for state offices, they filled all but one position on the slate with Confederate veterans or stay-at-home rebel sympathizers. For governor, they selected John L. Helm. A bitter critic of the national administration, Helm had not served in the Confederate army. But his son was killed in behalf of the Confederacy, and Helm had advocated secession, "the sooner ... the better."[105]

Conservatives of Harlan's persuasion now realized that they must either assume a secondary role in the activities and decisions of a Democratic Party dominated largely by rebel sympathizers or launch a separate party. Not surprisingly, they chose the latter course. On March 6, 1867, members of the Union Democratic Party of Kentucky, which generally became known as the Third Party, met in Frankfort and approved a series of resolutions condemning both the rebellion ("a crime and a blunder, and the fruitful source of the calamities that now afflict the country") and "any party that proposes to reduce any State or States to the condition of territories, or compel them to adopt negro suffrage, or place them as subjugated provinces under military government."[106]

Several days after the Frankfort meeting, an "Address of the Committee of the Union Democracy to the People of Kentucky" appeared in numerous newspapers. In their message to voters, the Union Democrats appealed to the "large majority" of Kentuckians who had no "genuine sympathy" for either radical Republicans or those with "an unwavering purpose to vindicate and consecrate the principles which led to the late rebellion." Condemning the civil rights bill then pending in Congress and the statute creating the Freedmen's Bureau as "unconstitutional, unwise and oppressive," they also rejected the notion "that bestowing the right of suffrage upon the black man, would benefit either the white or black man," adding: "It needs no argument to convince Kentuckians, who are well acquainted with the black race, that much evil would result from the establishment of such law."[107]

Harlan was not a member of the committee that drafted the party's address to the people, but he presumably had a strong hand in its preparation. He also drafted a widely circulated letter soliciting local organizers as well as funds to assure broad distribution of the address and the new party's effective functioning.[108] And when the Third Party held its nominating convention in Louisville on April 11, he was nominated to serve another term as Kentucky's attorney general.[109]

Harlan's efforts were of no immediate avail. In May, he campaigned in behalf of Union Democratic candidates for several congressional seats;[110] each was resoundingly defeated. He also waged a hard campaign to retain his post as attorney general—appealing to the unionist sentiments of fellow war veterans, scorning radicals and secessionists alike, and warning that the federal government offered Union men their only effective protection against vindictive rebels.[111] The August, 1867, elections were a devastating defeat for the politics of moderate unionism. Harlan and other Union Democratic candidates lost by wide margins, while rebel Democrats became even more solidly entrenched in Kentucky government.

In late November of that year, B. S. Sinclair, a family friend, sought Harlan's advice:

> Well, General [asked Sinclair], where are we drifting politically? And what can we do with ourselves as a party? If we continue to keep up our separate party, we . . . become a stumbling block to some good end. To go with the Radicals I can't and will not do. To go with the Reb. Democracy, would be very humiliating. . . . As there are nationally but the 2 parties, we will be compelled to go with one or the other, which virtually disfranchises me, for with my present convictions & prejudices against both, I can't feel satisfied to identify myself with either. . . . We know we have been right and . . . are still so, but our party has so drifted & weakened as to render us of little political significance. . . . I feel mortified and hope something may yet turn up for good.[112]

As 1867 came to a disappointing end, Harlan's mind no doubt was filled with the same uncertainties. Soon, however, he would make a decision that would have a momentous impact on the future direction of his life.

C H A P T E R   3

Redemption

He may have been attempting to escape the rebel Democratic atmosphere increasingly prevalent in Kentucky's capital. Or he simply may have desired to reestablish the law practice he began before entering military service. Or he may have believed that Louisville offered a wider range of professional opportunities than did Frankfort. Or a combination of such factors and others may have been instrumental in his decision. But whatever his motivation, in November, 1867, John Harlan opened a law office in Louisville with Judge John E. Newman, a staunch Conservative Unionist 14 years Harlan's senior who had held a circuit judgeship during the war.[1]

Soon thereafter, Harlan would make a fundamental change in party loyalty. On January 21, 1868, his cousin, Wellington Harlan, wrote to him from Harrodsburg with news that Wellington's wife, Jinkie, had given birth "to as handsome a baby [girl] as you ever saw," but also to speculate about John Harlan's political future. "There is much surmise and conjecture among your friends here," wrote Wellington, "as to whether you are included in the late sale made by [former unionists] to the rebel Democracy. I have uniformly expressed the opinion that you will not go into that concern and that if the Republicans nominate [General Ulysses S.] Grant you will support him."[2]

Wellington was right. In a late March issue, the Frankfort *Commonwealth* reported, "from *undoubted authority*," that Harlan intended to support Grant for the presidency and Republican R.T. Baker in the state's upcoming gubernatorial contest. "This patriotic determination on the part of this able and distinguished lawyer and former Union officer," exclaimed the paper's editor—apparently now convinced of the sincerity of Harlan's return to the unionist fold—"will be hailed everywhere throughout the State with satisfaction and pleasure by the friends of the Republic."[3]

By midsummer, Harlan was being touted as one of the prominent ex-Union officers and Conservative Unionists who had declared for the Republican ticket; and in the fall, he campaigned actively for Grant in Kentucky and southern Indiana.[4] In late November, W.N. Wadsworth, another Conservative Unionist recently converted to the Republican cause, wrote Harlan that he "was powerful glad when I heard you had opened on the Ku Klux Democracy," adding: "I see the future as you do, for dear Kentucky. Just now she is in the hands of a stupid . . . leadership; but not for long. In an age when great events are born every day, this leadership does nothing but say no, to the yes of 40 millions."[5]

In his speculations about Kentucky's immediate political future, Wadsworth was a poor prophet, yet his assessment of the developing transformation in Harlan's party leanings proved to be markedly perceptive. The future justice's high regard for the candidate's consummate skills as a military strategist could easily have accounted for his support of General Grant in his victorious 1868 campaign. Indeed, in 1869 Harlan would lead an effort to secure the new president's presence at a gathering of the Society of the Army of the Tennessee and the Cavalry Corps of the Military Division of the Mississippi; and although the president was unable to oblige, he noted in a reply to the former officer that he considered his service as commander of those units an "honor which I feel and shall always appreciate."[6]

But Harlan's canvass for Grant was a reflection of more than mere loyalty to a wartime commander. He was now becoming a full-fledged Republican; and by mid-1870, he was even chiding family members about any hint of sympathy for the hated Democrats. In a letter to a young relative of Mallie's, written on July 12 of that year, he quickly progressed from an account of a recent Sunday school picnic he had been unable to attend—an affair in which "a general license was given to all to make as much noise and have as much fun as they chose"—and advice about the relation's career plans, to politics. "What has become of him?" he asked of his in-law. "I fear from his silence that he is confederating with our Robert Shanklin to betray the Republican party. I have always had some doubt about Jim's being a true Republican. You may inform Robbie that he may talk about anything to Jim but politics, and, upon pain of being tried and convicted of treason, he must not get Jim into the Democratic party."[7]

The Making of a Radical

To a substantial degree, Harlan's relatively rapid move to the party whose policies he had recently and vehemently scorned was, most likely, motivated by considerations of sheer expediency. In the aftermath of their disastrous 1867 election defeats, Conservative Unionist leaders sought assurances that some of their numbers would be included as delegates to the February, 1868, state Democratic convention and that they would not be excluded from consideration as Democratic nominees for elective office. All they got was a vague promise that "all other good Democrats" were welcome to *attend* the convention.[8] Shortly thereafter, the Conservative Unionists disbanded.[9] Harlan's only remaining options were to assume a role—and probably a secondary role at that—in a party he and his father had long repudiated, or join the party which offered him the greatest opportunity for some degree of national influence. As a pragmatic political act, his choice thus appeared eminently logical—in fact, virtually the only decision he could have made.

Several events and associations also contributed to Harlan's growing commitment to the Republican Party and the goals of Reconstruction. The increasing influence of the Ku Klux Klan in the state and frequent incidents of Klan violence against blacks and sympathetic whites obviously played a role in Harlan's transformation. In May of 1870, a Richmond, Kentucky, lawyer asked Harlan to file a suit against a white man who allegedly beat an 11-year-old black girl so severely that she lost her eyesight and the use of her limbs. "She failed to dress to work as soon as [Wells] desired," the lawyer seeking Harlan's assistance explained; "and Wells became enraged on account of her delay and sprang upon her bed, kicked and bruised the child terribly."[10]

Another letter to Harlan's firm that same year sought federal protection for blacks brutalized when they sought to participate in the August, 1870, elections. On appearing at the Harrodsburg courthouse to exercise their right to vote, they had been attacked by a mob with guns, stones, and clubs, and then were chased back to the black quarters on the outskirts of town, where two were murdered and several other seriously wounded. "Reports are rife," the letter's author reported, "that there is to be a general massacre of [Harrodsburg's blacks] through the Ku Klux organization, and the most intense excitement prevails. The affair should be thoroughly investigated by the U.S. authorities and the guilty parties brought to justice. The colored people look with great interest to see whether they are to be protected in the exercise of their rights, and they say very frankly and freely that if the Government is passive and permits them to be butchered in cold blood then they can not be expected hereafter to stand by the Government."[11] Such incidents were hardly atypical and undoubtedly helped to sensitize Harlan to the need for federal intervention to protect even the most rudimentary individual rights in the postwar South.

Harlan's association with Judge Newman may have exerted an influence as well. Several months after their partnership was established, Newman declined an offer to become a candidate for reelection as circuit judge on the Republican ticket. In a published letter to the party, however, he excoriated the Democratic Party as "bitter and unrelenting in its opposition to the friends of the Federal Government" and condemned its "principal object [of] making . . . the 'Lost Cause' glorious, and Unionism or adherence to the Federal cause during the rebellion, odious forever." Henceforth, Newman proclaimed, he would devote his efforts to "the triumph of the candidates of the Union Republican Party."[12]

Of Harlan's associates during this critical period of his life, perhaps none was more influential than Benjamin Helm Bristow. An Elkton, Kentucky, native a year Harlan's junior, Bristow was educated at Pennsylvania's Jefferson College. His father was a leading Whig lawyer, politician, and Kentucky congressman, as well as an antislavery unionist during the war. Benjamin Bristow studied law with his father and was admitted to the state bar in 1853. After service as a Union officer during the war, he was elected in August of 1863, without his knowledge, to a seat in the Kentucky senate. As a legislator and politician, he supported all unionist measures, fought for ratification of the Thirteenth Amendment, and canvassed actively for President Lincoln's 1864 reelection. In 1865, Bristow resigned his state senate seat and moved to Louisville, where he was appointed assistant U.S. attorney. On May 4, 1866, he took the oath as U.S. attorney for Kentucky. As chief federal law enforcement officer for the state, he made war on Ku Klux Klan violence, securing 29 convictions under the first federal enforcement act, including one capital murder sentence.[13]

On January 1, 1870, Bristow resigned his federal post and joined the firm of Harlan and Newman. Shortly thereafter, however, Congress established the office of solicitor general to represent the United States in Supreme Court proceedings, and President Grant appointed Bristow to the position. In November of 1872, after arguing several important constitutional cases before the supreme bench and establishing a reputation for mastery of federal jurisprudence, he submitted his resignation as solicitor general to take a lucrative position as counsel to the Texas & Pacific Railroad. Quickly realizing that he had little taste for the largely administrative duties that assignment entailed, he soon left Texas & Pacific, returning to Louisville to resume private law practice. On July 3, 1874, however, he again joined the Grant administration, on this occasion as secretary of the treasury.

Bristow's tenure in that post was to be stormy. His reform of the department's internal organization and operations, and especially his exposure of the Whiskey Ring, a notorious conspiracy of western distillers and internal revenue agents to evade compliance with the whiskey tax, gave him a national reputation as a reformer but incensed ring members and their supporters. The target of repeated rumors designed to poison the president's mind against him, and repeatedly obstructed in his reform efforts by other members of Grant's cabinet, he resigned his post on June 17, 1876, and returned to the private practice of law for the remainder of his life.

It is uncertain when John Harlan and Bristow first met. They corresponded on several occasions, however, before establishing their brief partnership. In the fall of 1866, Bristow, in his capacity as U.S. attorney, notified the future justice that a suit was to be filed against James Harlan's estate for $90.55, the amount the elder Harlan, while U.S. attorney, had received from several defendants and allegedly had not deposited with the federal treasury. The tone of the letter was not unfriendly. "I trust," wrote Bristow, "you may be able to find among your father's papers some satisfactory explanation of the matter."[14] Were Bristow certain about the deficit, Harlan responded, "I would pay without a suit."[15] Later that year, Bristow wrote Harlan again, predicting on that occasion "that the Rebel Democracy of Ky. will not much longer continue their *professions* of friendship for the President," and adding, "Of course, they never were sincere in those professions." The "Union men of Ky.," he asserted, "should get together and form a [competing] party."[16]

In 1867, Bristow informed Harlan that he had suggested him as counsel for a friend seeking to create a new county from "loyalist" territory "made up of detached portions of the most Rebel counties in Ky." Bristow advised, "Perhaps it would be well not to mention this [motive] publicly to the present Legislature, which is strongly suspected of not being entirely in sympathy with loyalty."[17]

Once they became law partners, and particularly during Bristow's Washington tours, the two became regular correspondents on the state of Kentucky and national politics, the fortunes of the parties, Bristow's growing frustrations with the president and other members of his official family, and, of course, the ongoing struggle for racial equality.[18] Although Bristow's commitment to Republicanism and the goals of Reconstruction clearly antedated and was more intense than Harlan's, at least at that point in their respective careers, there were limits to Bristow's Reconstruction agenda. At times, moreover, his letters betrayed a certain cynicism regarding the nation's newest citizens. Ironically, given the stance Justice Harlan would assume on the Supreme Court, Bristow opposed legislation forbidding racial discrimination in public accommodations. "[I]f white people want to go to churches, theatres, schools and hotels with negroes or *even to marry them*," he wrote Harlan in March of 1872, "I would not prohibit them by law, but I will not commit to a law *forcing* anybody to do either. Nor do I believe that the . . . colored people desire such legislation. Certainly the effort to force social equality by law will result injuriously to them. Moreover, I do not believe that Congress possesses any such power." In fact, such concerns may have entered into Bristow's decision to resign as solicitor general later that year, for in his March letter to Harlan, he wrote, "Now what is one holding these opinions to do? I can't join the democracy. . . . It seems to me that the best course to pursue is to [leave] quietly and go to practicing law."[19]

When the Supreme Court, speaking through Justice Samuel Miller in its first construction of the Fourteenth Amendment, gave the amendment's provisions a narrow interpretation, limiting its scope largely to the protection of the newly freed slaves, Bristow again objected. In the famous *Slaughterhouse Cases* of 1873, a majority dismissed the claim of New Orleans butchers that the state's conferral of monopoly rights on one slaughterhouse company denied them equal protection of the law, violated privileges of national citizenship, and deprived them of liberty and property without due process. "If Miller's reasoning be correct," Bristow rejoined, "then indeed was the late war fought solely for the benefit of Sambo, and *all* the work of reconstruction has been in his interest. I think I am disposed to deal out favor and benefits liberally enough to the 'nigger,' but I am not prepared to admit that the white man is not equally entitled to the [amendment's coverage]."[20]

Nor was Bristow entirely satisfied with the radical Republican leadership in Congress, including Massachusetts Senator Charles Sumner, whom he once dismissed as a "learned fool" who had "scholastic, literary and scientific attainments almost beyond any man of this age," but not an ounce of common sense.[21] And Bristow's patience, limited under the best of circumstances, became exceedingly strained when black leaders questioned whether the Republican Party shared any responsibility for the shortcomings of Reconstruction. When three black Kentuckians wrote the treasury secretary in February of 1875, declaring that the "colored element" of their state had lost confidence in the party and its leaders in Kentucky as a result, among other things, of the suspension of the Freedmen's Bank, Bristow registered a hot reply. "[A]ny colored man," he asserted, "who believes the Democratic party, in view of its past history, is more friendly to his race than the Republican, has become so beclouded and befogged that it would be idle to attempt to reason with him." The antislave elements of the North, he pointedly added, were "becoming very restive under the belief that the party has already done enough for the colored people and that they should now be left to take care of themselves. While I do not myself sympathize with this idea, it is nevertheless undeniably gaining strength day by day throughout the North, and there is real danger that any further extraordinary exertion to give the colored people political control of the Southern States will so far disgust their earliest and best friends in the North that the Republican party will lose entirely its power to maintain even what has been done for the colored man." Bristow's advice to blacks: "accept with gratitude the great results that have been accomplished for them by the courage and heroic efforts of the Republican party, and . . . wait with patience future developments."[22]

In the main, however, Harlan's association with Bristow would serve to buttress the future justice's growing attachment to the Republican Party and its egalitarian goals. As justice, Harlan would dissent when the Supreme Court upheld Kentucky's authority to forbid racially integrated education at private Berea College.[23] In an 1876 letter accompanying a donation to Berea, Bristow, albeit not for public circulation, declared, "If I had the power I would not allow any local prejudice or race etiquette to stand in the way of the education of every child in the Commonwealth. Regarding as I do, the education of the youth of all races as the paramount duty of the State, I would not hesitate to place the facilities within the reach of every child of the State, of whatever color. . . . I regard all laws discriminating against colored people on account of color or previous condition as antagonistic to the spirit of the age, and at war with the true philosophy of government."[24] As his vigorous prosecution of the Ku Klux Klan while U.S. attorney attested, he was particularly vocal in his opposition to racial violence and official indifference to such outrages. When one version of the Klan, the White League, was running rampant in 1875, he reminded Harlan of his contempt for such groups:

> Of course you know my feelings and opinions, with reference to the White League. I have not abated one jot or tittle of my detestation of that organization. On the contrary, I regard it as the highest and most solemn duty of the Government to enforce their disbandment and the punishment of their leaders. In a government of laws there can be no such thing as an organized force outside of duly constituted authorities, without immediate danger to the very existence of the government itself. I do not believe there was ever organized in any part of this country a more wicked and inexcusable organization. . . . I am firmly persuaded that its purpose is to overthrow the late amendments to the Constitution, and reduce the colored people to actual, if not nominal slavery; that is to say, they mean to reduce them to the condition of subordination to the will of the white men wherein they shall be left no choice but to vote the Democratic ticket, and to perform the labor of the white man on such terms and for such compensation as he may dictate. Entertaining these views I cannot fail to favor the most vigorous measures for the suppression of the organization and the punishment of its leaders and participants. In doing this I would go to the very verge of Constitutional power, upon the most liberal construction of Constitutional provisions.[25]

Bristow's disdain extended to John Harlan's clients. In the summer and early fall of 1871, Klan nightriders embarked on a series of raids in the Frankfort area, lynching several blacks and beating and terrorizing many others. Following a visit to the area, Harlan wrote Bristow that the incidents had created an atmosphere of "universal dread amongst Republicans, white and black," who feared for their lives and property if they denounced the Klan and sought federal protection. A federal grand jury "in perpetual session" was, in Harlan's judgment, the "only road to root out the evil."[26]

Several days later, Harlan urged aggressive federal intervention against Klan violence during a conversation with President Grant at Covington, Kentucky, albeit to little avail. "I explained to him," Harlan later informed Bristow, "how difficult it was for the U.S. officers to accomplish anything with the inadequate means at their command. He said he would write to the Atty Genl and seemed to think that the fund under his control was the only one to be looked to. He said nothing about the secret service fund, and I of course did not feel at liberty to do so. But my opinion is that the Dist. Atty ought to have quite a large fund & with it I believe he can do something."[27]

Colonel Gabriel C. Wharton—the U.S. attorney for Kentucky, Harlan's close friend, and a staunch unionist of the Bristow stripe—had obtained indictments in the incidents and sought Bristow's help in securing Harlan's assistance with the prosecutions.[28] By that point, however, Harlan had already made other commitments. In part perhaps because of his growing attachment to the Republican Party, Harlan was now often approached by whites seeking relief from civil disabilities imposed on former Confederates[29] and counsel in criminal prosecutions growing out of incidents of racial violence. In November of 1870, for example, a friend asked him to defend a railway brakeman charged with assaulting a black who had attempted to gain entry—shades of *Plessy*—to a passenger car reserved for whites.[30] Such, apparently, was his association with such cases, that one lawyer asked to defend three men charged with beating blacks wrote him as to the appropriate fee for that sort of case.[31] (Harlan replied that he "would go in for $100 received in each case."[32]) And when Gabriel Wharton secured indictments in the Frankfort cases, Harlan agreed not to assist the prosecution but to represent a number of the defendants.

His decision shocked area blacks and Kentucky Republicans. One black woman exclaimed to Gabriel Wharton, "Before God, I thought the Custom House would not hold enough money to employ General Harlan for those men!"[33] Perturbed at such reactions, Harlan sought to explain his position to Benjamin Bristow:

There are some matters connected with this Ku Klux business which embarrass me. I must urge the govt. to "go for" the Ku Klux—and yet I am being applied to defend as counsel, some who are charged with being Ku Klux. I once thought that I would have nothing to do with cases of this kind, but, upon reflection, I find that I must play lawyer in those as in other cases [or] abandon good fees which I am not able to do.[34]

The first to approach Harlan was D. Howard Smith, an old friend he had recently assisted in removing disabilities imposed on rebels and whose son was one of the defendants. The younger Smith, declared Harlan in a letter to Bristow, had "clearly established an *alibi* and nobody believes him to have been guilty." Evidence against his other three clients was "very conflicting & not enough yet developed to convict before a petit jury. At least it so strikes me."[35]

In a second letter to Bristow, written two days later, Harlan resumed his defense of his position: My colored friends, some of them, cannot understand how *I* defend Ku Klux. Some of them think, in their ignorance, that I have deserted them. Altogether my position is embarrassing politically, but I cannot help it, for I cannot afford to decline practice in my profession. Whoever I defend, must pay."[36]

But the characteristically blunt Bristow was hardly sympathetic. "I read the Commercial's report of the testimony against your Frankfort clients last Saturday," he declared, "and have made up my mind that they are guilty. I hope they will not escape the punishment they so richly deserve." For Bristow, the "only remedy" for racial outrages of the sort perpetrated in Franklin County was "the prompt arrest & speedy punishment of such fellows by the Federal Courts. If these fail national law will become a necessity & I trust will not only be *proclaimed*, but vigorously enforced."[37]

His Frankfort clients not withstanding, Harlan would become increasingly outspoken in his alarm over Klan violence. In 1874, when the White Leagues were attracting considerable support, he expressed the hope in a letter to Bristow that their success "in the South will startle the North to form a compact organization against the return of the Democratic Party to national power." A Democratic triumph nationally, he predicted, "would make the condition of the Union men and the negroes of the South as intolerable as that of the children of Israel during their bondage in Egypt. We would then have taskmasters indeed who would seek to have us fall down and worship the devilish spirit of Southern rebellion."[38] Through violence and intimidation, he asserted in a later missive to his friend, the Democrats were bent on forcing blacks into their ranks or driving them from the polls, giving the South to the Democrats in 1876. "The North," he insisted, "must bristle up in the protection of the colored people—otherwise, we will drift into a state of utter helplessness and anarchy." The answer to the civil rights problem for Harlan was not racially "mixed schools" but vigorous federal protection of life, liberty, and free elections. "If the persecution of the colored people will unite the North in 1876, in opposition to the Democratic party, all will be well."[39]

Nor was Harlan's support for federal protection of civil rights merely rhetorical. In 1873, Attorney General George H. Williams named him "to assist in prosecutions for violations of the Enforcement Acts of Congress."[40] In that capacity, he participated with Gabriel Wharton in several cases, including a suit to oust Lexington officials for voting rights violations.[41] Involvement in such cases, like his association with Bristow, Wharton, and other staunch Republicans, no doubt strengthened Harlan's commitment to Reconstruction.

The events, personalities, and issues with which Harlan became connected during a protracted dispute between the northern and southern wings of the Presbyterian Church were probably equally influential. To a greater degree than other Protestant denominations, the national Presbyterian organization had supported the Union and emancipation, condemning slavery and the Confederacy during and after the Civil War. At its 1865 meeting in Pittsburgh, the church's General Assembly adopted resolutions requiring Southerners seeking positions as ministers or missionaries to demonstrate their loyalty to the Union and rejection of slavery. Naturally, many southern Presbyterians found such regulations highly offensive; and, like other Protestant denominations, the Presbyterian Church split into northern and southern groups. Within individual congregations in the South, the battle lines were soon drawn between those committed to maintaining ties with the national church and the "rebels," as their detractors generally termed sympathizers with the church's southern faction.[42]

In Kentucky, such strife was particularly bitter. In suit after suit, church members loyal to the national organization challenged the authority of local congregations to move their affiliation—and property—into the southern fold. Harlan and

Benjamin Bristow represented pro-Union church factions in a number of suits, most notably in a dispute involving Louisville's Third or Walnut Street Presbyterian Church, which was to culminate in a landmark Supreme Court decision regarding the reach of civil court jurisdiction over ecclesiastical questions.[43]

Like many other Protestant congregations, the Walnut Street church split into two factions, each bent on controlling its policies and operations. On February 2, 1866, elders recognized by the Presbyterian General Assembly filed suit to protect their interests in Louisville's chancery court. The following month, the chancellor issued a ruling in their favor, holding that a civil court had no jurisdiction to decide religious disputes and that he thus could not reverse the General Assembly's recognition of the plaintiffs as the congregation's true elders. The Kentucky court of appeals reversed the chancery decision and threw its support to the claims of the pro-southern faction.[44] In 1868, the appeals court reaffirmed its position in a related church case[45] and also issued a second ruling in the Walnut Street case, in which it emphasized that control of the church's property was to be returned to the congregation's pro-southern wing.[46]

But Harlan was not ready to concede defeat. Bland Ballard, the local federal district judge, had been appointed to his post in 1861 by President Lincoln. Ballard was a devout unionist, strong Republican, vehement opponent of slavery, and longtime Harlan family friend. Federal trial courts are authorized to hear so-called diversity of citizenship suits involving citizens of different states. Three members of the Walnut Street congregation—a married couple and the wife's mother—lived in New Albany, Indiana. With that trio as plaintiffs, Harlan was able to take the case into a federal forum—and a decidedly friendly one at that.

In the summer of 1868, Harlan filed a federal circuit court suit before Judge Ballard and Supreme Court Justice Noah Swayne. Counsel for the defendants complained that a federal court could not hear a dispute already pending in the state courts. In a number of preliminary rulings announced on October 12, however, Ballard concluded that the federal and state suits concerned different legal questions and could be heard concurrently.[47]

In May of 1869, Ballard ruled in favor of his friend's clients on the merits. Since the Walnut Street church was part of the national (now northern) Presbyterian organization before the split, he declared, it was subject to control only by those members who supported the northern church. The defendants were thus forbidden to interfere with Walnut Street's property in any manner inconsistent with the wishes of members loyal to the national organization.[48]

Walnut Street's southern faction then appealed the federal court's decision to the Supreme Court. Nearly three years were to pass before the high tribunal announced its own ruling in the case. In March of 1871, following what Harlan and Bristow considered unforgivable delay in the suit's progress,[49] Bristow wrote Harlan of a social call he and his wife had paid to the home of Justice Samuel Miller, during which the Justice noted that he had begun writing an opinion in the case.[50] The next month, Bristow learned that Justice Stephen Field had "expressed an opinion in our favor on the merits."[51] But a decision would not be announced for another year. On April 4, 1872, Harlan shared with Bristow what little he knew of the suit's progress, conceding, "I am nervous about the delay and hope for the best."[52]

By April 15, however, Harlan was aware that the ruling would be announced that day and anxiously awaited a telegram from Bristow in Washington with news of the decision. "My conclusion," he wrote his friend that day, "is that the court is reading the opinion and that you have not yet had time to telegraph." Nor was Harlan the only apprehensive person in Louisville that day. "Ballard is about to start to Covington, and is very anxious to hear the result." Harlan was optimistic about the outcome, though. Anticipating a favorable decision, he prepared an article for the *Commercial*, Louisville's Republican organ. "Success will be a grand thing for us," he exclaimed. "The city will hardly hold our friends, all of whom feel blue and doubtful about [the] result."[53]

The article Harlan drafted was not wasted. As he was writing Bristow, Justice Miller was indeed announcing a favorable ruling in the church case. Sensing no doubt the frustrations Harlan and others connected with the litigation experienced over the Court's exceedingly deliberate pace, Miller cited as justification for the justices' schedule "[t]he novelty of the questions presented . . . , their intrinsic importance and far reaching influence, and the knowledge that [the] schism in which the case originated [had] divided the Presbyterian churches throughout Kentucky and Missouri." The justices had also been influenced, he added, "by the hope that since the civil commotion, which evidently lay at the foundation of the trouble, has passed away, that charity, which is so large an element in the faith of both parties, and which, by one of the apostles of that religion, is said to be the greatest of all the Christian virtues, would have brought about a reconciliation. But we have been disappointed."[54]

Harlan, Bristow, and their clients were not disappointed with Miller's opinion. Civil courts, Miller held, could resolve property and related secular disputes involving religious organizations, but civil authority did not extend to ecclesiastical questions. When the highest organ in a system of church government decided such an issue, "the legal tribunals," declared Miller, "must accept such decisions as final, and as binding on them, in their application to the case before them."[55]

News that the Supreme Court had accepted the arguments he and Bristow had advanced elated Harlan. "I am the happiest man in Christendom tonight," he wrote his friend on learning of the ruling. "Our Presbyterian folks feel good all over."[56]

The Walnut Street suit, as noted earlier, was not Harlan's only involvement in the divisions the war and emancipation had created in southern churches. In early 1867, before his conversion to Republicanism, he was a leader of a successful campaign to kill a state legislative bill designed to place his beloved Centre College under the control of the Presbyterian Church's southern wing. Addressing the judiciary committee of the Kentucky house of representatives, he declared:

> With some persons it is a high moral crime for a church to declare it to be a Christian duty to stand by the country in its struggle with the rebellion, while the same persons regarded it to be a Christian duty to sustain the rebellion which had for its object the destruction of the Union. But this Legislature has nothing to do with churches. It is not your province, directly or indirectly, to regulate them. . . . [Kentuckians] insist that you shall not officiously meddle in their church matters, and shall not violate the chartered rights of a venerable institution of learning. . . . They say, hands off. . . .[57]

At times the church suits involved black communicants. Between 1871 and 1874, Harlan defended a black Methodist congregation from the title claims of the southern wing of the denomination.[58] And earlier, he had welcomed the opportunity to bring black members of a Shelbyville congregation into a church case, noting, "If our friends have or will conclude that we may put the darky into this fight, we will be glad to do so."[59]

The struggle between the Union and rebel wings of southern churches represented a microcosm of the national debate then raging over Reconstruction and the status of the newly freed slaves. Harlan's advocacy of the former's cause surely strengthened his Republican resolve, as did, no doubt, his association with leading figures in the pro-Union factions. Harlan had frequent contact, for example, with Robert Jefferson Breckinridge, leader of the northern wing of Kentucky Presbyterians until his death in 1871.[60] Breckinridge was a state leader of President Lincoln's 1864 reelection campaign and an uncompromising foe of the Confederacy, even refusing to save members of his own family from Union capture.[61] Nor, of course, was Breckinridge the only zealot attempting to save his church from ecclesiastical secession with whom Harlan became closely associated during his conversion to Republicanism.

The 1871 Gubernatorial Bid

While events, issues, and associations were solidifying Harlan's Republican resolve, he also assumed an active role as party booster, campaigner, and candidate. In 1869, Republicans had established the *Louisville Commercial* as a party organ dedicated, according to its inaugural issue, to "the fullest application of the doctrine of 'equal rights to all' as the highest good to each, . . . the adoption of the Fifteenth Amendment as the crowning victory of the right in the long struggle between Republicanism and caste . . . [and] universal amnesty as the fitting complement of universal suffrage."[62] By 1873, the paper was in deep financial difficulty, its owners faced with suspending operations.

Harlan became a leader in an effort to restore the *Commercial* to solvency, writing letters to potential benefactors[63] and at one point urging Henry Van Ness Boynton, influential Washington correspondent for an Ohio paper, to become the *Commercial's* editor.[64] In 1874, Harlan and W.A. Meriwether, the *Commercial's* president, assumed control of the paper.[65] "I feel that I am incurring great risk and responsibility in this matter," Harlan had indicated in his letter to Boynton the previous year. "But I am unwilling that the only daily Republican paper in the state shall fall without an effort on my part to make it a success." Although constantly strapped financially, the *Commercial* continued operations.

Harlan also corresponded regularly with fellow unionists, seeking to secure their commitment to the Republican cause. "You said in your last letter to me," one responded, "that you hoped I was still steadfast for the Union; I am and grow in that sort of grace every day." There was a certain cynicism to this adherent's Republican fervor. "What do you think," he wrote, "of the darkies now? . . . What do you think of the Mississippi darky as United States Senator? And the South Carolina darky

Judge of the Supreme State Court. And the New Jersey darky Judge of the Supreme Court of the United States? Would not such success and elevation of the darkies in this State give the *Rebs* Typhoid fever. . . ?"[66]

But Harlan's main contribution to his new party was to serve as its candidate for governor in 1871 and 1875. On May 17, 1871, the party held its largest state convention in Frankfort. There, amid lusty cheers from the crowd, the delegates confirmed Harlan's nomination by acclamation. In a stirring address, Benjamin Bristow applauded the party's "boast . . . that every man, born in this country, or naturalized, no matter what his condition in life, his race or his color, is an American citizen . . . entitled to equal rights before the law, and to a participation in the elective franchise."[67]

The platform adopted that day was equally egalitarian. It encouraged immigration to assure development of Kentucky's "vast agricultural, mineral and manufacturing resources." It scorned the "so-called Democratic Party" for its failure to suppress "KuKluxism," opposition to black testimony in judicial proceedings, refusal to extend to blacks the exemption from the sale of homesteads for debt already enjoyed by whites, and unwillingness to make "adequate provision for the adequate education of all the children of the State." It supported the Reconstruction amendments and their vigorous enforcement. And, in a nod to former Confederates, the delegates favored "complete amnesty" to all citizens "laboring under disabilities by reason of their participation in the late rebellion." The yard of the state capitol, the *Louisville Commercial* also noted, "was plentifully provided with tables covered with food, sold by colored people, and they were generously patronized."[68]

At one time or another in his political career, Harlan had rejected virtually every plank in the platform he was now pledged to defend. In appearance after appearance with his Democratic opponent, incumbent Governor Preston Leslie, Harlan now vigorously defended Reconstruction, the civil rights amendments, and his new party's egalitarian posture. An early June debate with Leslie at Vanceburg is a case in point. Harlan's opponent was in fine form. White girls and boys in Kentucky's common schools were taught together, Leslie exclaimed. "Their happy groups in the schoolhouse are not marred by the scent of a nigger being put in with them. That is not allowed by law." In southern states dominated by the "Radical party," asserted Leslie, "little bright-eyed [white] girls and boys" could not "go to school without mingling with nigger children." Leslie wanted no part of such a scheme or the tax burdens the education of blacks would impose on "the white people of Kentucky." If Kentuckians accepted the doctrine of "perfect equality," they must also be prepared "to repeal the statutes which prohibit marriage between negroes and whites."[69]

Harlan's own remarks were not entirely free of race-baiting. The convention that nominated Leslie, he observed (to "great laughter," according to the press account), had included "three of the blackest and ugliest darkies in the Commonwealth." Nor was Harlan willing to approve integrated schooling. In the main, however, his voice rang with the moral indignation that was to characterize his later judicial opinions. Whereas his opponent's entire speech was "directed to arouse in the minds of the people of this State a war of races," the Republican candidate declared he had no patience for such demagoguery: "What is to be made toward the peace and happiness of this State by arousing the feeling of bitterness which the gentleman would desire to arouse between the white and colored people of this Commonwealth?" he wearily asked. "Here they are, mortal beings, with immortal souls like ours, fashioned in the image of their Maker. I would feel myself a dishonored man if, for the sake of obtaining votes in this or any other part of the State, I would be willing to foster a sentiment which every noble and generous man would spurn." Kentuckians surely could not now propose to banish their black neighbors. "This land would roll in blood before [such a] great wrong would be tolerated, and this I say to you as a Southern man. They have sympathies, love their wives and children and the spot of their nativity as we do; and I put it to you, does it accord with your feelings of justice that politicians should try to keep up in this Commonwealth of Kentucky a feeling of bitterness and hate for all time to come?"

Democratic leaders and newspapers again scorned Harlan as a "political weathercock" and gleefully quoted excerpts from his own anti-Republican speeches of the recent past.[70] At Vanceburg and other encounters, Preston Leslie pursued the same strategy. But Harlan met such charges head-on, most eloquently perhaps in a July 28 rally at Livermore, in which he made no apologies for breaking with his past but, instead, enthusiastically embraced the Reconstruction amendments and racial equality:

> It is true fellow-citizens that almost the entire people of Kentucky, at one period in their history, were opposed to freedom, citizenship and suffrage [for] the colored race. It is true that I was at one time in my life opposed to conferring these privileges upon them, but I have lived long enough to feel and declare, as I do this night, that the most perfect despotism that ever existed on this earth was the institution of African slavery. It was an enemy of free speech; it was an enemy of good government; it was an enemy to a free press.
>
> The time was, and not long ago in Kentucky, when any declaration, such as I now make, against the institution of slavery, would have imperilled my life in many portions of the State. With slavery it was death or tribute. It knew no compromise, it tolerated no middle course. I rejoice that it is gone; I rejoice that the Sun of Liberty does not this day shine upon a single human slave upon this continent; I rejoice that these human beings are now in possession of freedom, and that that freedom is secured to them in the fundamental law of the land, beyond the control of any state.[71]

For his detractors, who questioned his sincerity and charged that he was motivated principally by a desire for patronage and influence in Washington, Harlan had a ready response: "Let it be said that I am right rather than consistent."[72]

Harlan was particularly harsh in his denunciation of the Ku Klux Klan and other terrorist groups, branding them a "band of murderers and assassins." Asked at one rally about the anti-Klan provisions of the 1871 Civil Rights Act, which Congress had recently adopted, he conceded doubts about the constitutionality of one of its provisions but saw "nothing in it to create any serious alarm among the law-abiding citizens of Kentucky,"[73] particularly given the supremacy of the Constitution and national laws over state and local enactments.[74]

If for no other reason than to try to placate his audiences, the candidate emphasized that he was in no way promoting social as distinct from political or legal equality between the races. "What do you mean by this cry of Negro equality?" he asked of his critics. "Do you suppose that any law of the State can regulate social intercourse of the citizen? . . . We do not declare, as the Democratic orators well know, in favor of social equality. No law ever can or will regulate such relations. Social equality can never exist between the two races in Kentucky."[75] It was only "right and proper," he gave as an example, to keep "whites and blacks separate" in the public schools.[76]

Sensing the volatile nature of the civil rights planks in his adopted party's platform, Harlan gave heavy emphasis to nonracial issues in his stump speeches and attempted to couch egalitarian issues in terms of caste or class rather than color. In numerous appearances, he blamed Leslie for the large deficit in the state treasury and scorned his opponent's extravagant purchases for the governor's mansion. Harlan described for his listeners a "palace" of "oriental magnificence," which included among its accouterments two dozen whiskey tumblers and a euchre stand for that popular card game.[77] He attacked, too, the Democrats' proposal for financing Kentucky's common schools. In the past, revenue had been derived from property taxes. Now the Leslie administration favored additional funding through a head tax on every adult male. In addition, Leslie recently had signed a bill requiring the parents of school age children to pay supplemental revenue taxes based on family size and the extent of their use of the common schools, rather than their ability to pay. Under such an arrangement, Harlan sneered, "a poor man blessed in the number of his children, but unprovided with this world's goods, is taxed, while the rich, who are able to educate their children in private schools, are exempt from taxation to meet this deficit. The poor man, with six children . . . is assessed six times more than a man with one child, worth a hundred thousand dollars, and an old bachelor with unlimited resources, and with no children, is exempt altogether." Citing numerous instances of "the blessings of education given to children of poverty," Harlan declared that "[t]he poorest boy in the humblest cabin on some mountain-side of Kentucky, may, under our blessed form of government, aspire to the highest office in the gift of the American people."[78]

Economic development was another major theme of Harlan's campaign. Democratic policies had so inhibited immigration to the state, he charged, that Illinois and Ohio were now exceeding Kentucky in population growth and thus in the development of agricultural, mineral, and manufacturing resources. The virtual monopoly which the Louisville & Nashville Railroad had long enjoyed was a related target of his wrath. The state legislature's refusal to grant charters to other lines, like restrictive immigration policies, was inhibiting economic expansion. Scorning the L & N and monopolies generally, Harlan repeatedly declared from the stump, in language foreshadowing his later antitrust dissents, that monopolistic privilege should be forbidden to "stifle the powers of industry and national wealth."[79]

As election day neared, the Republicans had considerable cause for optimism. As in the past, Harlan made an impressive campaigner. He and the Republican press were also reasonably effective in countering the charges of his detractors. When his encouragement of increased immigration prompted Democratic newspapers to remind their readers of his Know-Nothing connections, the *Commercial* and other Republican organs quickly retaliated with convincing evidence that many prominent Democrats, including Governor Leslie, had also been associated with that antiforeign movement.[80] At least one Harlan supporter sent the *Commercial* a lengthy letter detailing unflattering elements of Leslie's political background, portions of which were later published.[81]

W. A. Meriwether, chairman of the state Republican committee, circulated to all county committees a glowing assessment from Harlan regarding the party's election chances. While not predicting victory, Harlan expressed confidence that "with proper organization and work," the Republicans could poll 80,000 to 95,000 votes.[82] Even the normally pessimistic Bristow was cautiously optimistic. "I cannot but think that the vote for you will fall short of the expectations of your more sanguine friends," he wrote in late July, "but you will increase the vote largely this year and you have made success hereafter attainable." Certainly, Bristow added, Harlan's candidacy had attracted "lively interest" in Washington and the North, so much so, in fact, that Bristow "fear[ed] it [had] excited the *jealousy* of some of your *personal* and *political friends*."[83] In a later letter, the solicitor general was even more enthusiastic: "I hear good reports from your canvass at every point. *Such* a canvass in any *civilized* state would surely win; and, indeed, you have won a great moral victory for our party in Ky. which makes absolute success attainable at no very distant day."[84]

But postwar Kentucky obviously did not fit Bristow's conception of a "*civilized* state." In late July, armed Klansmen entered the home of a black farmer. The farmer and several neighbors fired on the nightriders as they left his house, but not before the vigilantes had robbed and severely beaten his wife and threatened to burn their home if the couple refused to leave the area.[85] Such acts, it can be hoped, appalled decent citizens of both races, but emancipation, martial law, and Reconstruction had embittered white Kentuckians. They vented their frustrations on the candidate of the political party that was mainly responsible for the social upheaval they so bitterly resented. The Louisville *Courier-Journal* labeled Harlan "the beacon-light of Black Republicanism,"[86] and most white Kentuckians took their cue from such characterizations. On election day, August 8, Leslie beat Harlan 126,455 to 89,299; other Democratic candidates for state office won by similar majorities.[87]

Harlan had secured nearly twice as many votes as any previous Republican candidate in Kentucky, but the Republican electorate was becoming increasingly black. While new black voters had increased the party's constituency by 45,000 votes, nearly 15,000 disgruntled whites, a New York newspaper speculated, had deserted the Republicans for the Democratic Party.[88]

Even so, many Republicans found the returns invigorating. "Yesterday was a glorious day for the republicans of Kentucky," the *Cincinnati Gazette* exclaimed. "The election of the entire republican ticket in almost any other state in the union would have been no greater victory than was seen in Kentucky yesterday." The party's success was achieved, the Republican organ added, despite insults hurled by election clerks ("I didn't believe you would vote with the niggers") at Republican voters.[89]

John Harlan was especially proud. In a letter to his friend, John Bruner, he speculated that the vote would have been closer had not "the Democrats voted early and often." He predicted, moreover, that the Republicans could carry Kentucky in the 1872 presidential contest "if we will keep up our organization."[90]

Harlan was not only confident of the party's 1872 chances; he worked hard for its candidates. As early as August of 1871, the *Cincinnati Gazette*, applauding his "spirit, pluck, and tact," recommended him as the next Republican vice-presidential nominee and contended that his selection would put Kentucky in the party fold in 1872.[91] At its state convention that year, the party unanimously chose Harlan as Kentucky's favorite-son candidate for the vice-presidency—a compliment Harlan found most gratifying[92] despite Benjamin Bristow's warning that "there would be great opposition in the North to the nomination of a Southern man."[93] At the convention, Kentucky's delegation ultimately cast their votes for incumbent vice-president Schuyler Colfax over victorious Massachusetts Senator Henry Wilson, despite the efforts of Harlan and Bristow in Wilson's behalf—an embarrassment that prompted Bristow to wonder whether Wilson and other national Republicans might now "have some misgivings as to our efficiency with our own people."[94]

Harlan's efforts in behalf of the Grant–Wilson ticket surely dispelled doubts anyone might have had regarding his growing influence and commitment to the party. During the campaign, he traveled through Kentucky and the surrounding states, making speeches in behalf of Republican candidates. One rally at New Albany, Indiana, attracted a crowd of 4,000. The *Commercial* described in partisan terms Harlan's "full, concise, and clear exposition" of the positions of the parties "if we may judge from the earnest attention of the great multitude who heard it, and their emphatic and earnest applause. . . . General Harlan struck a responsive chord in the hearts of the people."[95]

At one point, Harlan received a telegram from Maine Congressman James Gillespie Blaine, inviting the Kentuckian to join 15 or 20 speakers from various states for a "whirlwind campaign" of Maine in behalf of the ticket. Harlan, who first met Blaine in 1851, when the future justice was Kentucky's adjutant general and Blaine was teaching at one of the state's military institutes,[96] readily complied. Before the speakers began their tour, they dined with Blaine at his residence in Augusta. Harlan would later recall:

> I was assigned to a seat between Frederick Douglass [the best-known black orator and writer of the day] and Benjamin F. Butler [radical military governor of New Orleans]. No two men were more cordially hated by the Southern Democracy than were Douglass and Butler, the latter especially. Of course, I made no objection to the place of my arrangement at Blaine's table. In fact, I rather liked it, for Douglass and Butler were both very remarkable, interesting men. Douglass and I spoke together several times during my Maine campaign. In my judgment, he had no superior as a public speaker. He would have made a great Senator.97

During his Maine visit, Harlan shared the platform several times with Henry Wilson, giving the future justice an opportunity for any political fence-mending he might have deemed necessary. The following year, when Wilson visited Kentucky, Harlan hosted a huge reception in the new vice-president's honor and arranged a deathbed visit with John C. Breckinridge. "The latter—then under a cloud by reason of his connection with the rebellion—was deeply touched by Wilson's visit," Harlan later remembered.[98]

The 1875 Contest

Following the 1872 election, Harlan continued his efforts in behalf of Republican candidates—on at least one occasion, at great personal risk. During a train ride to a speaking engagement, the sleeper in which Harlan was riding and a connecting passenger car suddenly "were both violently thrown from the track down an embankment fifteen or twenty feet high. Nothing but the gradual descent of the embankment saved me," Harlan wrote his brother-in-law, Dr. J. G. Hatchitt. "As it was I was much bruised being knocked about in the car as it rolled down. I was [able] to crawl out of one of the windows . . . with very great difficulty. There were twenty or thirty persons on the train, six of whom were quite seriously injured, and two very badly. All on the train were more or less bruised in the fall. . . . My escape from death was miraculous."[99]

Harlan's increasing involvement in Kentucky patronage matters at times created difficulties of a different sort. Several persons, he wrote one Republican in 1873, "advised" him that he "had no business bothering" himself with "local appointments."[100] But by now he had become an important patronage link with the Grant Administration and also communicated with the president on other matters, including an effort to secure a pardon for a friend.[101] At a close friend's request, moreover, he apparently intervened in a campaign to prevent the ouster of Republican John B. Bowman as president of Kentucky University.[102]

But Harlan was by no means enthusiastic about his new party's next election plans for him. On May 13, 1875, the Republicans held their state convention in Louisville. A Louisville *Courier-Journal* article announcing the meeting indicated that it was "generally understood" that Harlan's friend William Cassius Goodloe of Lexington would be nominated for governor.[103] By the convention's end, however, Goodloe was the Republicans' candidate for attorney general and Harlan their gubernatorial nominee.

The future justice accepted the party's decision reluctantly and with considerable concern about the impact of another campaign on his law practice and finances. "I am up for another race for Governor, very much against my wishes . . . [and] consented to do [so] only on the condition that I would not be required to make a canvass until after the Courts here adjourned. The Convention would take no denial," he wrote family friend O. S. Poston, among many others.[104] "I regret very much that you were not at the State Convention to aid in preventing my nomination," he good-naturedly complained to another associate. "I was very much averse to being in politics at this time in view of my business engagements, but it was impossible to avoid an acceptance of the nomination, and I am in for it." To supporters and potential donors, however, the candidate exuded confidence. "The contest is by no means hopeless," he declared. "With proper backing and a thorough organization we can largely increase the vote of 1871, and make such a showing as will encourage our friends everywhere and give us reasonable hope that we can carry the State in [the] 1876 [presidential contest]."[105]

Characteristically, Harlan threw himself vigorously into the canvass. In numerous letters to political allies within and outside the state, he sought funds and campaign volunteers. He enlisted the assistance of Benjamin Bristow and other national Republicans in the money hunt as well.[106] He made many stump appearances with his opponent, James Bennett McCreary, speaker of the Kentucky house of representatives. He even secured through Bristow three sets of a political manual as well as speeches and other documents relating to governmental finance, particularly conditions in the southern states.[107]

But Kentucky's postwar drift into the Democratic fold was now irreversible. Benjamin Bristow and others had some early success in securing campaign funds. In a letter to Harlan's brother, James, written less than a month after his friend's nomination, the treasury secretary announced that "a party" had secured $10,000 during a recent visit to New York, "with a promise of . . . more."[108] In a later letter, he predicted that "nearly $50,000" would be raised outside Kentucky, and "not a cent . . . by . . . questionable means."[109] Bristow was also decidedly more sanguine about Harlan's chances than he had been in 1871. In a letter to their mutual friend, W. A. Meriwether, he even declared, "I am not without hope that we may be able to elect Harlan by united effort and hard work," adding, "the disparity between him and [McCreary] will be so striking that many who have been voting the Democratic ticket heretofore will be disposed to fall into line with us."[110]

For once, the usually pessimistic Bristow was unduly optimistic. When E. F. Winslow, a Harlan supporter in St. Louis, wrote to Illinois State Treasurer Thomas S. Ridgeway, seeking contributions for the campaign, Ridgeway praised the candidate as an "able and talented man" and "gallant soldier," but added, "there is hardly the ghost of a chance of his success: too many men in Kentucky . . . will never vote for a Union officer or soldier [and] [t]he democratic majority in that state is entirely too great to hope for a possibility of success, now, or in 1876."[111]

Winslow promptly wrote Harlan, urging him to "refute" Ridgeway's "slanders on the *Ky* majority."[112] But by early July, Bristow was also encountering difficulty in his bid for funds. "I have felt my way cautiously with reference to getting further assistance here," he wrote Harlan from New York, "and am satisfied it is not [feasible] to rely on any further assistance from this quarter. . . . They complain of our wasting money on Ky., as they call it." Were Harlan able to carry the state, Bristow predicted that "you will silence all growling and can have matters pretty much your own way."[113]

The issues—or rather, *the issue*—hardly helped. Harlan more than held his own in debates with McCreary over the relative financial success of Democratic and Republican regimes in the South and nationally, on economic development questions, the common schools, and other important yet relatively uncontroversial matters. But on the question of race, the Republican candidate was now permanently on the defensive. Ironically, only a week after his nomination, a supporter wrote to Harlan noting that when the convention had moved to approve his selection by a standing vote, "not one" of several "colored delegates arose when the . . . vote was taken." The letter-writer speculated that they were "apparently showing that they did not [concur] with the action of the convention." He then asserted, "This element of the Republican party in my opinion has got to be looked to. It is useless to talk of what has been done. They are not sufficiently educated to appreciate their position—one of their number must appear in a prominent place, said person to be placed there by their action, or there will be jealousy."[114]

In his reply, Harlan predicted that he would not lose any of the black vote and expressed doubt "that any of the colored delegates of the Convention were opposed to my nomination."[115] On at least one other occasion, however, he was obliged to assure a supporter of his opposition to slavery, stating that the "Union soldiers of Kentucky ought to have no fear of my being Governor of the State."[116] Opposition newspapers delighted in once again pointing up inconsistencies in his current support for Reconstruction and earlier statements and positions. The *Courier-Journal* observed at one point of the Republican candidate that "no one can laugh off inconsistency better than he, for his youth, the passions of the time, for which he was not responsible, are always at hand to excuse forever positions that to his present view are incorrect."[117]

He was most effectively attacked, however, for his growing ties to "nigger Republicanism." Harlan was more than McCreary's match on the stump and effectively deflected a number of his opponent's charges. McCreary repeatedly claimed that the Civil Rights Act of 1875, which Congress had recently adopted, conferred on blacks rights superior to those enjoyed by whites. The Democratic candidate declared, for example, that the new law gave "the negro the right to enter any car on a railroad, and take a seat by the side of your wife and sister, while a white man, unaccompanied by a lady, can not enter that car."[118] Harlan ridiculed such absurdities, establishing that "[t]he clear and manifest purpose of the act was to secure equal, not superior, privileges to the colored race."[119]

When McCreary scorned the 1866 Civil Rights Act, which, among other things, granted blacks equal rights with whites to testify in the courts, Harlan, who had vehemently opposed such testimony in the past, readily conceded his support for the current legislation and exposed the gross unfairness of the previous ban. "As late as 1870," he told an Elizabethtown audience, "a ruffian could have entered a church in which colored people were worshipping, marched up to the pulpit and shot down the minister in cold blood in the presence of his people, and yet there was no punishment for him under Democratic rule in Kentucky, unless some white man happened to see him commit the crime. . . . To-day the colored people of Kentucky are admitted to testify upon equality with the whites, and I believe to the entire satisfaction of the great mass of the people of every political party. Popular prejudice on that subject has given way before the demands of civilization." Moreover, he repeatedly ridiculed the Democrats' "continual war on [the black] race" and vowed never again to indulge in such race-baiting himself.[120]

By his account, Harlan also deflated a number of Democratic campaign ploys designed to accentuate his image as a "nigger Republican." During the 1872 presidential campaign, it will be recalled, Harlan had been seated next to prominent black leader Frederick Douglass during a dinner at the home of James G. Blaine, the Maine congressman. During one of Harlan's gubernatorial campaign speeches, a member of his audience—"with much apparent kindness of manner [but] . . . sinister motives," Harlan later wrote—interrupted to ask whether the candidate had indeed "sat by the side of a negro at a dinner table in Maine a few years ago." Harlan promptly recounted details of the incident, emphasized that the seating had been "wholly the result of Mr. Blaine's arrangement at his own private table," not Harlan's personal choice, and expressed doubt whether "Kentuckians . . . [would] have expected me to rise from my seat and lecture Mr. Blaine at his own table." He then continued:

[F]ellow-citizens, I not only ate by the side of Douglass at Blaine's house, but during the campaign sat at the same table with him in public hotels and spoke from the same platform with him. And here let me say that there is no man of any party in Kentucky who can make an abler address before a public audience than can Frederick Douglass. And now, fellow-citizens, you know all the facts. I not only do not apologize for what I did, but frankly say that I would rather eat dinner any day by the side of Douglass than to eat with the fellow across the way who sought to entrap me by a question that has nothing to do with this contest.

According to Harlan, "[t]he audience felt that the interruption was needless and unmannerly, and they rapturously applauded what I said."[121]

Another "unmannerly" tactic met a similar fate. At one point in the campaign, the McCreary people brought in Dr. Mitchell, the Alabama minister whom Harlan had arrested during the war, thinking that the Republican candidate's treatment of the elderly cleric, as Harlan later put it, "would arouse great indignation against me and lose me many votes." But Harlan stood his ground. "Fellow citizens," he announced at a stump engagement after the Democratic press had fully covered the incident, "I admit that Gen. Thomas erred—that instead of simply arresting Dr. Mitchell and sending him north, he should have ordered him to be put in prison." Harlan later wrote that he did not really believe that the clergyman should have been jailed, but added that "the crowd applauded what I said, and I lost no votes that otherwise would have been cast for me."[122]

Harlan was plagued throughout the campaign with the race issue and sought repeatedly to minimize its significance or cast it in the most favorable light for his campaign and party. He admitted that the South had been "deeply wronged" by the war but laid responsibility at the feet of secessionist politicians. He scorned the notion that he either sought or envisioned superiority for the black race. According to a newspaper description of one of his speeches, he declared that he "liked his race better than the black race. The black race liked their own better than the white. . . . They asked only the same rights as other men—to live, and support, and protect their families." Nor should whites fear a future society dominated by blacks. "What man was afraid," he asked, that "the black man would rise above the white man [?] Fifteen years ago if any one had said the negroes would be free, they would have predicted a reign of violence, rapine, and blood. But . . . the black [man] in this State had . . . behaved well—had . . . been peaceable, tractable, and industrious, and desirous of bettering his condition by his own industry."[123]

Somewhat ironically, given the dissent he was to register in the *Civil Rights Cases* (1883), Harlan also stated his opposition to the 1875 Civil Rights Act's ban on racial discrimination in places of public accommodation. "I do not believe," he declared, "that the amendments to the Constitution authorize the Federal Government to interfere with the internal regulations of theater managers, hotel-keepers, or common carriers within the States in reference to the colored man any more than it does in regard to white people." Attempting to limit the new law's impact on the campaign, he pointed out that Halmer Hull Emmons, the federal circuit judge sitting at Memphis, had declared the regulation unconstitutional and that he "concur[red]" in the decision reached by "that distinguished Republican jurist." Judge Emmons's ruling, he asserted meaningfully if inaccurately, meant that the Civil Rights Act had "ceased to have a practical importance" to Kentuckians. "These are matters of local concern, to be determined and regulated by local authority."[124]

But no amount of soothing logic was to avail. Early in the campaign, Harlan had questioned whether his more youthful opponent met the minimum legal age for service as governor. McCreary, who clearly satisfied Kentucky's age requirement, quickly silenced Harlan by asserting that he would immediately withdraw from the race if three prominent Republicans found him ineligible, were Harlan to withdraw if they found the Democratic candidate eligible to serve. The affable Harlan took the rebuff in good humor, and the two candidates became jovial companions for the balance of the campaign, traveling together and even sharing the same bed. Each night, McCreary later recalled, it was Harlan's custom to spring into bed and exclaim, "McCreary, there's one thing certain. This bed will to-night hold the next Governor of Kentucky." One night the farmhouse bed the two were sharing collapsed beneath Harlan's considerable weight, rolling the future justice unceremoniously onto the floor. "You're right," called McCreary snug under the sheets, "the next Governor is still in bed."[125]

Harlan privately denied the incident ever occurred.[126] But apocryphal or not, McCreary's story forecast the election results accurately. Harlan lost the race by about the same margin that had accounted for his 1871 defeat.

By now, it must have been entirely clear to the future justice that the only hope for his political future lay not with electoral bids in increasingly Democratic, anti-Reconstruction Kentucky, but with whatever good will his candidacies had garnered with national Republicans, with his ties to the Grant Administration, and with Benjamin Bristow's national prospects. Throughout his years in Washington, Bristow had constantly complained to Harlan and others of intrigues against him, his disdain for various members of the Grant cabinet, and his growing disillusionment with the president himself.[127] Shortly after his appointment as Grant's treasury secretary, for example, he wrote, "I am strongly impressed with the belief that I made a mistake in accepting the office and that my best interest requires me to retire very soon. It is certain that I will be beset by conspiracies and intrigues if I remain."[128]

In his replies to such complaints, Harlan repeatedly urged his former law partner to delay any resignation until the most politically expedient time, while constantly feeding Bristow's ego and suggesting that a Supreme Court appointment, even the presidency, lay within his grasp were the treasury secretary to be sufficiently patient.[129] But Harlan clearly had an agenda of his own. As early as 1870, in a letter to Bristow, he speculated that "some lawyer in the late slave-holding states" might be tabbed for a prospective Supreme Court vacancy and "[i]t may be that you will be the man." Harlan, however, could hardly conceal his own desire for that coveted post, as well as the motives, both crass and noble, underlying his ambition: "I know of no more desirable position," he wrote, "than that of a Judge of the Supreme Court especially if the salary should be increased to $10,000. It lifts a man high above the atmosphere in which most public men move and enables him to become, in every sense, an independent man, with an opportunity to make a *record* that will be remembered long after he is gone."[130]

Reward

In the eyes of Kentuckians, John Harlan's vigorous gubernatorial bids and related efforts in his party's behalf made him a key patronage link to the Grant Administration. Aspiring office-seekers regularly sought his aid, and the future justice readily obliged.[1] Similar requests frequently came to his desk as well. In January, 1876, for example, he wrote Marshall Jewell, President Grant's postmaster general, in behalf of a man who was fearful that the post office in the village of Summer Shades would be moved from his business "to the store of some one who is not friendly to the Republican cause." Praising this "first class man and . . . good Republican," Harlan recommended that the post office stay in its original location.[2]

On at least one occasion, the tactics of a would-be public servant breached Harlan's ethical code. One Thomas E. Cooke, hoping to enlist Harlan in his campaign for the position of federal storekeeper at a liquor distillery, wrote, "If I should be successful, I will give you fifty dollars for your services."[3] Harlan was not impressed. In a letter marked "Private," he returned Cooke's letter, and a petition signed by a number of his supporters, to one of the signers, along with a message for Cooke. "Say to him for me," Harlan pointedly observed, "that while I would be glad to approve any recommendation, signed by yourself and others, the offer to pay me for my services precludes me from joining in the recommendation. I am satisfied that he meant no harm by the suggestion, but I am unwilling now to sign his papers. There are some lawyers who may accept fees for the performance of such services, but I am not one of them. . . . I have never accepted a fee for the performance of a public duty, and never expect to."[4]

Unscrupulous patronage seekers were not, however, the only irritant Harlan encountered in his relations with the administration in Washington. As Benjamin Bristow became an increasingly controversial treasury secretary, as well as more outspoken in his criticism of other members of the president's official family, his former law partner's relations with the administration also deteriorated. In the early summer of 1876, for example, Harlan learned from Marshall Jewell that the postmaster general intended to remove Captain S. D. Brown, a Kentuckian Harlan had sponsored for a post in Jewell's department. In a letter to Harlan, Jewell suggested that Brown "had dabbled too much in politics" and that he planned to replace him with "some one who has no 'political backing.'"[5]

Harlan's rejoinder was biting. Brown, he declared, had assured him "that he has not allowed his zeal for his party to interfere with the proper discharge of his official duties," adding: "What foundation there may be for this charge, I do not know, but my observation of Mr. Brown's conduct does not indicate that this charge is just." Harlan found Jewell's implication that his support of Brown's appointment had been politically motivated equally objectionable. "My recommendation of him," declared Harlan, "was based upon the ground chiefly that he was honest and capable. For my own part, I wish that I had never heard of a Federal office in this State. I have been credited in some quarters with the ability to control Federal patronage in this State when nothing is further from the truth or my wishes. . . . Federal patronage has been so managed in the State as to do our party very great harm."[6]

The Push for "Big Ben"

In the letter regarding Brown and his other correspondence with Jewell,[7] as well as in letters to the president and Jewell's cabinet colleagues, Harlan was invariably civil and cordial. At the same time, he must have been aware that his ties to Benjamin Bristow limited his influence with the administration and any future Republican president close to the Grant wing of the party. Propelled no doubt by such concerns and by a high regard for his former law partner, Harlan became a major figure in a campaign to secure Bristow's nomination as the Republicans' 1876 presidential candidate. To maintain a close watch on developments in Washington generally, and on his unpredictable presidential choice in particular, he also urged Augustus Everett Willson, his young law partner, to accept Bristow's invitation to become chief clerk of the Treasury Department.[8]

Gus Willson, as he was generally known, was born in Maysville, Kentucky, into a family that had recently migrated to the state from New York. A graduate of Harvard, where he briefly studied law before completing his legal studies with a Boston firm, Willson was later elected to a single term as Kentucky's governor in 1907. But by 1869, he was working in Harlan's Louisville law office[9]; and in 1870, he became a junior partner in the firm with Harlan and Judge Newman.

Newman died in the spring of 1873. Benjamin Bristow, who had maintained close ties with both Harlan and Newman, wrote Harlan at the time of their friend's death to inquire whether the old man's estate would be adequate to support his family and to assure Harlan that he stood "ready to do my part" should additional funds be required.[10] After Bristow left the office of solicitor general, he briefly assumed a position as railroad counsel, but he quit this post to join Harlan and Willson in forming a practice in Harlan's old law office at 508 W. Jefferson Street. Bristow's return to Washington in 1874 as Grant's treasury secretary ended that partnership before it ever actually materialized, but Harlan and Willson continued their practice. When Bristow invited Willson to become his chief clerk in 1875, he "very reluctantly and partly on [Harlan's] wish" agreed. "[Y]our father," Willson later explained to the justice's son, Richard, "sent me to Washington to keep him advised of all the developments, and I was more useful in that than I ever hoped to be."[11]

Harlan was particularly interested in having his young partner provide regular intelligence regarding the treasury secretary's state of mind, especially any indication that he might act on his repeated threats to resign—a move Harlan believed would harm Bristow's presidential chances. As the 1876 presidential season approached, Bristow continued to complain of his disillusionment with the administration, his desire to leave Washington, and his opposition to any presidential bid mounted in his behalf. In a December, 1875, letter to Harlan, for example, Bristow noted that people from all parts of the nation were approaching him daily about his interest in the presidency. "The whole matter," he declared, "is distasteful to me and I have contented myself with saying that I am not and will not be a candidate. In spite of my declarations however I am constantly spoken of and treated as a candidate, and urged by friends to begin to organize. It really seems to me that I ought to take some decided step to get myself out of the contest."[12]

Harlan may well have believed that Bristow was not really as opposed to a presidential bid, or inclined toward leaving his cabinet post, as such correspondence indicated. Even so, he wanted Willson to alert him to any possibility that Bristow might move precipitously in that direction, as well as about the treasury secretary's mental state; and Willson was entirely faithful to his task. "[O]n Sunday," he wrote Harlan in early February, 1876, "Col. Bristow's illness, which has an apoplectic tendency and is the result of the nervous strain and excitement of the past ten days, became almost alarming. He was discouraged, disheartened and, as he expressed it, unmourned completely, feeling terribly the need of some true strong friend." That evening, William Dennison, former Ohio governor, prominent businessman, and influential political power broker, had called at Bristow's Washington home. "Bristow almost leaned on him," Willson reported. "Asked [Dennison] if he knew any honorable way for him to just quietly leave the cabinet, said he was completely down, etc. I think Governor Dennison comforted him a good deal." Most distressing of all to Bristow, Willson added, was his "final conviction that Grant himself is in the [Whiskey] Ring and knows all about it."[13]

While undoubtedly finding such reports disconcerting, Harlan joined General James H. Wilson of New York, the noted engineer and soldier, and other Bristow partisans in promoting the treasury secretary's presidential nomination and urging him to remain at his post until the most politically expedient opportunity to separate himself from the administration. In a mid-December, 1875, letter to a prominent Kentucky Republican, Harlan expressed hope that their party's upcoming state convention would be "a rousing one composed of the best men which can be assembled from different parts of the State and all animated with a determined purpose to make Bristow our next candidate for President." The treasury secretary, he predicted, would "come out of his present war upon thieves and plunderers with more reputation than has been won by any public man in this country for years past." Harlan was convinced that Bristow was "the strongest man today that the Republicans can run, and [that] his chances for the nomination [were] better than those of any one who has been named in connection with the office."[14]

Harlan sent similar letters to numerous other Bristow supporters and prominent Republicans throughout the country, to generally enthusiastic response. Kentucky State Senator William Cassius Goodloe assured the future justice, "I feel it in my bones that Bristow will be the next President."[15] General Wilson wrote from New York that "every friend of good government, and of Bristow should henceforth do all in his power to secure friends for *our* candidate in the National Convention of our party and to manufacture friends for him among the people." Bristow's New York friends, he reported, were considering formation of a "Reform club" carrying a name "which will bring in Independents and regular Republicans, [yet] not reveal the fact for the present that our fundamental plank is 'Big Ben,' and good government."[16]

Other letters were to like effect. Henry V. N. Boynton of the *Cincinnati Gazette*, perhaps Bristow's most devoted follower, sought from Harlan any politically damaging statements James G. Blaine, another Republican presidential hopeful that year, might have made years before during his tenure as a professor at Kentucky's Drennon Springs military institute.[17] Replying to Harlan's concern that their party might not accept a candidate from the South, a Worcester, Massachusetts, Republican leader assured the future justice that "No such objection is expressed or felt here," adding: "One of my many reasons for preferring Secretary Bristow is . . . that he, as our candidate for the presidency, would greatly strengthen the republican party among the white voters [of] the South."[18] The Kentuckian who expressed doubt that Bristow "stands much if any chance for the nomination" was exceptional.[19]

Elements of the Republican press also seemed optimistic about Bristow's chances. In early March, the *New York Times* reported approvingly that "The Democrats seem to be getting alarmed at the growing strength of Secretary Bristow." A recent attempt by a Democratic paper in Cincinnati to discredit him, the *Times* added, had been "a very ridiculous failure."[20] H. V. Boynton, who represented not only the *Cincinnati Gazette*, but the *Chicago Tribune* and other leading members of the Western Republican Press Association as well, and was one of the most influential correspondents along Washington's "Newspaper Row," was Bristow's most ardent journalistic backer. By the time of the Republican convention, however, Richard Smith and Murat Halstead of the Cincinnati *Gazette* and *Commercial*, respectively, had joined his ranks, too; and the editors of the *New York Times*, *Boston Transcript*, *Worcester Spy*, *Hartford Courant*, *Cleveland Herald*, and *Harper's Weekly*, along with a number of minor journals, were flying the Bristow banner.[21]

Nor were John Harlan and General Wilson the only prominent politicians pushing Bristow's candidacy. Wilson's younger brother, Bluford, formerly a reformist U.S. attorney for southern Illinois, currently solicitor of the treasury, and Bristow's chief assistant in the breakup of the Whiskey Ring, was a key figure in the campaign. Walter Quintin Gresham of Indiana, a Grant appointee to a district judgeship but a fierce opponent of the spoils system and other features of the Old Politics, was another supporter, as was Carl Schurz of Missouri, perhaps the key figure in the anti-Grant liberal Republican movement of the period.[22]

Although lacking in personal magnetism, Bristow enjoyed mass popular appeal, which a student of the 1876 campaign has colorfully and succinctly captured:

[A]s Grant's third Secretary of the Treasury [Bristow] had waged such a spectacular warfare against the forces of corruption entrenched within his department that he had become in the popular mind a veritable symbol of reform. With dramatic suddenness and refreshing vigor he had decapitated the supernumeraries who cluttered his office, purged the fetid revenue service of political henchmen, snubbed the financial moguls of Wall Street, and, in the face of formidable opposition from powerful political bosses, routed the notorious whiskey rings which had infested the leading distilling centers of the South and West since the days of Andrew Johnson. As chief of the ring smashers, he had ridden the wave of reform into the front rank of presidential possibilities.[23]

Southerners of various political leanings seemed especially hopeful of a Bristow candidacy. Sharing his "private, *inside* view," South Carolina's carpetbag governor, D. H. Chamberlain, agreed with Harlan's assertion "that the nomination and election of Bristow will bring us peace and political success,—as well as success of every other kind,—here in the South."[24] An elderly black delegate to the Republican national convention that was to be held in Cincinnati in June assured Bristow "that we colored people of the South, constituting as we do the great body of the Republican party in the South, are not in favor of still [waving] the bloody flag in the faces of people with whom we live and with whom we hope to die." He and other blacks, he declared, considered Bristow "a genuine Republican, in whose garments the smell of carpet-baggery is not found."[25] Many Southerners, Democrats and Republicans alike, saw in the treasury secretary, moreover, a chance for the restoration of normal commercial relations between the North and South.[26]

Bristow and his supporters were reasonably effective in countering numerous rumors and charges circulated by his opponents to discredit his standing with the voters. Few if any presidential contenders have been subjected to a more extensive campaign of scandal-mongering. A Democratic Milwaukee newspaper charged that Bristow had accepted an enormous bribe to rescind forfeiture of the *Mary Merritt*, a sailing vessel federal officers had seized for violation of the revenue laws. Another opponent charged that the treasury secretary, while U.S. attorney in Kentucky in 1869, had ordered the seizure of a shipment of whiskey and then, after resigning as prosecutor the following year, had accepted a bribe equal to half the shipment's worth in return for interceding with Judge Ballard to secure its release from federal custody. According to one newspaper version, Bristow thought it inappropriate to formally represent the distillers in their attempt to recover the liquor, but had advised one of them "to place the matter in the hands of Gen. Harlan, his partner, promising that he (Bristow) would render all the assistance in his power."[27] Earlier, the New York *Herald* had declared in a front-page article that Bristow, while solicitor general, had accepted $50,000 for prosecuting a "fraudulent mule claim."[28]

Other reports charged Bristow with bribe-taking in other liquor suits, leaking secret cabinet information for speculative purposes, consorting with a "scarlet woman,"[29] and even once robbing a store.[30] In early June, as the Republican national convention approached, an agitated Bristow wrote Harlan that a "greatly exaggerated" account of a night of "sight seeing" in New York, based on the "affidavits of lewd women," had been prepared and would soon appear in the Chicago *Inter-Ocean*, a vehemently anti-Bristow paper. The article, the treasury secretary understood, would include "letters or notes from me making assignations with certain women [which were] [o]f course . . . forgeries."[31]

Articles and fliers carrying such allegations, among others, were widely circulated. In a letter to Harlan written on March 14, 1876, shortly after the most potentially damaging stories began to appear, his future Supreme Court colleague, Stanley Matthews, cautioned against a libel action in Bristow's behalf. "My advice, whatever be [a story's] character," wrote Matthews, "is most distinctly and decidedly against an action for libel. Genl Bristow is being tried daily by a tribunal that will do him justice. He need have no fear of the result. His character will not suffer."[32]

Bristow, Harlan, and their allies heeded Matthew's counsel but aggressively met each charge head-on. When the committee on expenditures of the U.S. House of Representatives began an investigation into the *Mary Merritt* affair, Harlan wrote the treasury secretary from Louisville, urging Bristow "not to wait for the Committee to call you, but go promptly yourself before the Committee and make your statement." Since the House investigation smacked of "a prosecution," added Harlan, Bristow "should be present when witnesses [were] examined, and cross-examine them, and show up the conspiracy to injure you. If [one of your accusers] is examined you ought to cross-examine them mercilessly and have the result of your cross-examination sent to the country every day. In brief, let the country see that you are striking right and left at the scoundrels who seek to break you down for corrupt ends of their own."[33] Bristow pursued precisely the strategy Harlan had recommended with excellent results, putting the "narrow minded and stupid asses" of the committee on expenditures, as the treasury secretary derisively branded them, completely on the defensive.[34]

In a letter to the editor of the Madison, Wisconsin, *Courier*, Bristow conceded that he may have referred one of the distillers from whom he was alleged to have taken a bribe to Harlan and Judge Newman, and may also have "rendered . . . some assistance in procuring the release of the whiskey." But he emphasized that he and Harlan were not partners at the time and labelled "utterly untrue" the contention that he "ever conferred with . . . Judge [Ballard] about the case."[35] An investigation conducted by the committee on expenditures favored Bristow.[36] Other gossip met a similar fate, and none of it apparently damaged Bristow's standing among the voters as the season's reform candidate.

Bristow, however, remained a reluctant candidate. Kentucky's state Republican convention was scheduled for May 18. As that date approached, it became increasingly apparent that many of the delegates being selected at county party gatherings to attend the state meeting were Bristow loyalists. John W. Finnell—prominent Kentucky politician, former editor of the *Louisville Commercial*, and close personal friend of both Harlan and Bristow—wrote Harlan from his home in Covington that "The 'last d—n man of 'em' " in his district was "for the 'homely youth from Elkton.' "[37] Harlan's brother-in-law, J. G. Hatchitt, reported in early May that Frankfort Republicans had met and "instructed for Bristow," adding: "I disposed of [the one dissenter from the gathering's decision] by getting him read out of the party."[38] Several days later, Harlan informed Carl Schurz that the Kentucky delegation to the Cincinnati convention would be unanimous for Bristow.[39]

But as Kentucky support for Bristow mounted, the treasury secretary decided to make public what Harlan and other Bristow intimates had hoped to keep secret— that their candidate professed not to want the position. In mid-April, when county conventions were beginning to pick overwhelmingly Bristow delegations to the state convention, Bristow sent the delegates, via his former law partner, an expression of his "earnest hope that the State Convention will not require or instruct its delegates to present my name" to the national convention. "You, who know so well my earnest desire and purpose to retire from public life at the earliest practicable day," he added, "do not need to be assured of the perfect sincerity of this declaration. I have rendered no such service to the country as entitles me to be even favorably considered in connection with the Presidency."[40]

When Kentucky Republicans made Bristow their "favorite son" presidential choice, he promptly wrote Harlan "to express the profound gratitude I feel to the republicans of Ky.," adding: "I am fully aware that I owe *you all* for what was done. It is peculiarly [gratifying] to me just now to have such an expression of confidence from my friends at home." Even so, he could not resist noting that there was "not the least possibility that I will be nominated."[41] He continued to maintain, moreover, that he was not a candidate. On the same day that he wrote to Harlan, for example, he responded to an inquiry whether he would be willing to join a James G. Blaine ticket with the assertion that he had "not contributed in any way, directly or indirectly," to the campaign being waged in his behalf and thus could not "with propriety enter into a combination, or friendly understanding, to secure the second" place on the ticket.[42]

Their candidate's reticence naturally made it difficult for Harlan, General Wilson, and other Bristow partisans to muster support in his favor—or even to enlarge his visibility to the voters. On the very day that the Kentucky convention convened, Wilson wrote Harlan that he hoped to be more successful in securing desperately needed Bristow biographical (i.e., publicity) material from his brother, Bluford, and H.V. Boynton than he had been by working through the treasury secretary's chief clerk, Gus Willson: "Willson . . . went to Bristow about it and that exalted patriot shut down on it, on the ground that he had more to fear from his friends than his enemies." General Wilson "beseech[ed]" Harlan for help, declaring that "the people and especially the [Cincinnati convention] delegates want information about Bristow's *past* in order to assure themselves that they can depend upon his future."[43] Eventually, background material was developed and circulated but with little assistance from the determined "non-candidate."

Bristow's backers also faced a growing array of competing candidates, some of whom drained delegate support from what might otherwise have been relatively safe Bristow territory. Harlan was particularly concerned about Senator Oliver P. Morton of neighboring Indiana, a Civil War governor with impeccable Republican credentials. Delegate selections at state conventions held on May 24 had placed James G. Blaine ahead in the delegate county. The following day, Harlan wrote Judge Walter Gresham at Indianapolis, praising Blaine's "great pluck and energy" and conceding his status "as the contending man." But the predicament Morton's candidacy posed for Bristow's chances was the future justice's primary concern. "Of course," he wrote Gresham, "Morton's nomination is out of the question. There is no possible chance for him. He has it in his power to nominate Bristow, but Bristow cannot nominate him. I wish he could see that it is in his interest and duty to make terms with Bristow's friends, and bring about the nomination of Bristow. I confess that I feel a little blue this morning at the prospect."[44] Nor could Bristow expect support from the champions of antireform Republican stalwarts such as Senator Roscoe Conkling of New York, the Grant Administration's choice for the nomination.

Harlan was hopeful that "good relations" could be established "between the Republicans of Kentucky and Indiana." No Kentucky delegate would abandon Bristow for Morton, he was certain. It thus seemed only logical, he wrote Gresham, that "we should prepare ourselves to have the Indiana delegation feel in good humor towards Bristow." An article was to appear in that day's *Louisville Commercial*, he added, "which I think is in the right direction."[45]

Presumably without Harlan's knowledge, however, Gresham, in concert with General Wilson and H.V. Boynton, had already embarked on a campaign to discredit Blaine and exacerbate relations between the Blaine and Morton forces. The most potentially damaging charge against the Maine front-runner was that he had received from Union Pacific Railroad President Thomas Scott a "loan" of $64,000, which was never repaid and backed only by practically worthless bonds as collateral. Morton knew of the arrangement, Blaine was aware Morton knew, and Gresham and company hoped that Blaine would leap to the desired inference.[46]

Bristow knew nothing of such machinations. While the campaign against Blaine and Morton was under way, he wrote Harlan that he had "no sympathy with the attacks on either of these men" and would "do all in my power to discourage them."[47] When Blaine delivered a stunningly cunning, well-received rebuttal to the Union Pacific charge before a packed House of Representatives, moreover, the treasury secretary promptly congratulated the ex-speaker for having "macerated these scamps"—thus "[u]nknowingly . . . arraign[ing]," as a student of the 1876 campaign would later note, "his closest friends."[48]

The Blaine campaign blamed Bristow for the attacks on the ex-speaker. The treasury secretary also learned through General Wilson that Blaine considered the Bristow forces the source for an article in an obscure Kentucky newspaper that reflected on Mrs. Blaine's virtue, despite the fact that the paper in question, as Bristow put it, was "a vile rebel sheet" that "indulges in the coarsest abuse of me."[49] Unwilling to tolerate this "unjust imputation for a day," particularly since it "related to a lady," Bristow went immediately to Blaine, denying all connection with the story. To Bristow's relief, Blaine "professed great surprise," assured the treasury secretary that he had never heard his name associated with the article, and stated that he knew Wilson's informant only slightly. ("Lord how this world is given to lying!" Bristow rather enigmatically wrote Wilson.)[50]

But whatever Blaine's feelings, his wife remained suspicious that Bristow was the source of the attacks on her and her husband. On June 4, she wrote to a friend that her "intensest feeling" regarding the Cincinnati convention was that the nomination "should not go to Bristow. . . . I hate to hate but I am in danger of that feeling now."[51] Then, on June 11, the day following Bristow's meeting with Blaine, the ex-speaker suffered a sunstroke and the treasury secretary rushed to Blaine's Washington home to offer assistance. A frantic Mrs. Blaine blocked his entry and ordered him to leave, vehemently exclaiming, "Mr. Bristow, you've got your will now; don't come in here!"[52]

Thoroughly demoralized, Bristow returned to his home and wrote General Wilson, "My God, what mortification I felt. . . . I cannot feel it in my heart to censure the poor distressed wife, for no doubt she has been told by the lying mischief-makers that I have had something to do with these dirty stories on them."[53]

The most immediate concern of Bristow's followers, if not the secretary himself, however, was the impact the incident might have on the convention then under way at Cincinnati. The day after Blaine's collapse, a Bristow supporter in Louisville telegraphed Harlan, the leader of the Kentucky delegation, that "a circular intended to injure Mr. Bristow before the Convention [was] about to be mailed from this city to each delegate."[54] An associate of Murat Halstead sent Harlan a similar telegram and letter indicating that the delegate book, from which names and addresses had been obtained for the mailing, was marked "Compliments of [Senator Morton's] Indiana delegation" and that the circular's contents, according to one source, "would kill Bristow."[55] Unfavorable reports from the Blaine camp regarding the incident at the candidate's home and Bristow's alleged connections with the gossip about Mrs. Blaine now also seemed likely to surface.

No doubt with encouragement from Harlan and other Bristow partisans at Cincinnati, the treasury secretary and Governor Dennison, who had attended Bristow's meeting with Blaine the evening of June 10, decided to write accounts of their versions of events for circulation at the convention. Bristow stressed Blaine's "cordial and friendly manner" toward him and disclaimed any responsibility for "the publication of a dirty scandal in a Western paper," while Dennison confirmed Bristow's account in every detail.[56]

The Bristow-Dennison efforts probably worked to the treasury secretary's advantage. Robert J. Ingersoll's "Plumed Knight" speech nominating Blaine that year would become one of the classics of national convention history. But John Harlan's call to the podium to place Bristow's name in nomination was greeted, according to the *New York Times*, with "one of the most enthusiastic popular demonstrations ever witnessed in this country"; and his stirring address in Bristow's behalf was regularly interrupted with tumultuous cheers.[57] His remarks, as Bristow's biographer has suggested, may have been unduly biographical;[58] but they clearly established the candidate's commitment to Republicanism, racial equality, and reform.

Malicious gossip, the antipathy of Republican stalwarts toward one of the party's most zealous reformers, continuing strained relations with the Blaine and Morton camps, Blaine's quick recovery from his collapse (which opponents suspected he feigned to win sympathy with the "gullible masses"[59]), and the temperamental Bristow's own distaste for the campaign arena had taken their toll, however. On the first convention ballot, Blaine, Morton, and Bristow—with 285, 124, and 113 votes, respectively—were the leading contenders. Bristow held his own for the next three ballots, increasing his vote to 126, while Morton's total dropped by 16 votes.

Had Indiana withdrawn Morton's name at that point and cast its 30 votes for Bristow, one contemporary observer later speculated, the Michigan delegation would have followed Indiana's lead, and Bristow's "vote would have increased so rapidly that he would undoubtedly have combined all straggling votes and been nominated on the next ballot." But when Indiana held firm and Bristow gained no new strength from any other source, Michigan took 11 votes from Bristow and threw all its 22 votes to Ohio's nominee, Rutherford B. Hayes. On the fifth and sixth ballots, Hayes's vote grew significantly, but Blaine's jumped to 308. It was now clear that "a big push would be made on the next ballot to nominate Blaine and that the [anti-Blaine] opposition must combine now or never."[60]

By the time Indiana's name was called during the seventh ballot, Blaine had advanced his total by 32 votes, and his forces were exuberant. At that point, however, Indiana's delegation withdrew Senator Morton's name and threw its vote to Hayes. Iowa held firm for Blaine. Then, Kentucky's name was called:

> Gen. Harlan rose from his place & walked toward the stand, and, the people divining his purpose, at once set up a great cheer, and it was some time before he could be heard. He stood there, his lips trembling with emotion, waiting for the storm of applause to be hushed, and then he spoke, grandly. He thanked the convention for the support they had given [Bristow, especially] . . . those men of Massachusetts and Vermont, who when it was whispered throughout the length and breadth of this land that Benj. H. Bristow was not to be President because he was born and reared in the South, had come forth, and said they were satisfied that a Kentuckian could be loyal, that Benjamin H. Bristow was a man to be trusted (great and prolonged applause). "Without detaining you further [Harlan then announced] Kentucky unanimously instructs me to withdraw the name of Benj. H. Bristow from this convention, and in withdrawing his name to cast her entire vote for Rutherford B. Hayes of Ohio." The scene of wild and tumultuous applause that followed defies description.[61]

Kentucky's—and Harlan's—action sealed Blaine's fate. Hayes's vote on the seventh ballot was 384, slightly more than the 378 majority needed for victory.

Shortly after returning to Louisville from Cincinnati, Harlan wrote Bristow his version of the Kentucky delegation's shift to Hayes. The Michigan delegates had voted for the Ohio governor on the fifth ballot, the future justice explained, after Bristow supporters in the delegation learned that Michigan's Blaine delegates "would not vote for you, but would vote for Hayes . . . your friends in that State deemed it of the last importance to defeat Blaine." At that point, declared Harlan, "I felt that our case was hopeless."[62]

Harlan also expressed doubt that Bristow could have beaten Blaine in a "square fight." After all, Blaine had received 351 votes on the final ballot, and Harlan knew that at least 16 men in the Ohio delegation were Blaine voters who would have voted for the ex-speaker were Hayes's name withdrawn. Blaine probably would also have received ten more votes from Pennsylvania as well as additional support from New York, and, Harlan continued, "you might have lost some of the scalawag Republicans of the Southern delegations" to Blaine.[63]

On realizing that "we were gone," Harlan decided—"unknown outside of the Kentucky delegation"—to "retire in a becoming manner" by "so throw[ing] our votes as to make it tell upon the rings, and secure a good nominee." His decision sealed Blaine's fate and earned the gratitude of the Hayes forces. "[A] nephew of Gov. Hayes," wrote Harlan, "hunted me up and said that his uncle was indebted to us Kentucky fellows for his nomination, and he intended to let his uncle know all about it."

Harlan hoped that his former law partner could draw some satisfaction from what had transpired: "Altogether you have reason to be proud, not only of the character of the support which you received in the Convention, but of your position before the country. The failure to nominate you was a blunder in our party, but that cannot now be remedied. I have taken peculiar satisfaction in the fact that no one of the men could be nominated whose claqueurs had been hounding us."[64]

Others have attributed Harlan's convention maneuvers to darker motives. In a two-volume biography of her husband, Walter Gresham's widow, Matilda, charged years later that Harlan participated in a "midnight conference" in Cincinnati at which a "deal was made . . . to nominate Hayes." At this conference, according to Mrs. Gresham, "it is said John M. Harlan was promised a place on the Supreme Bench" in return for bringing Kentucky into the Hayes camp.[65] E. Bruce Thompson asserts in his study of the 1876 Bristow effort that "Harlan later confessed to W. Q. Gresham that he made a 'deal' with the Hayes men" and that "Hayes carried out his part of the bargain by placing Harlan on the Supreme Court."[66] But Thompson cites no source for his claim in an otherwise copiously documented work, and while he very likely drew on Mrs. Gresham's biography, she also provides no documentation for her assertion and in no way suggests that Harlan ever "confessed" his alleged deal-making to her husband. Her feelings for Harlan, moreover, were apparently not entirely sanguine.

In an appendix to her biography, Mrs. Gresham quotes at length from one of the anti-emancipation, anti-Lincoln addresses Harlan delivered during his 1864 campaign to become Kentucky's attorney general. Harlan's speech, she wrote, "shows better than anything the opposition there was in the South to the Abolitionists and how the Union pro-slavery men of Kentucky turned against Mr. Lincoln on the negro question, and is in strong contrast with the utterances of Associate Justice Harlan."[67] Mrs. Gresham's claim was probably based on the suspicions of her husband and other Bristow loyalists rather than on direct evidence. The fact that Harlan, as will be shown later in this chapter, initially expected appointment as attorney general and that Hayes came close to formally nominating him for that post conflicts, moreover, with a key detail in Mrs. Gresham's story.

Whatever the truth of Mrs. Gresham's charge, Bristow apparently harbored no suspicions immediately following the convention. In a brief letter to Harlan as head of the Kentucky delegation, he congratulated the convention on its "good work" while "rejoic[ing] that my friends have helped to do it." In a second, longer letter to his former law partner, Bristow thanked Harlan and company for their "splendid fight," adding, "I can never cease to feel grateful to you for the great and unselfish efforts you have made to secure my nomination."

For Bristow, Blaine was still the chief villain. When next he saw Harlan personally, he observed, he planned to tell his former law partner "something . . . about Blaine's illness which I think will amaze you." Scorning the ex-speaker as "the greatest dramatic actor on earth and . . . the greatest scoundrel living," he assured the future justice that Blaine's defeat was a "glorious thing" and that it gave him "great joy . . . to know that you and others of my friends had a hand in his defeat."[68]

Several days later, Bristow wrote Harlan yet another letter, again praising his "unselfish support and splendid fight . . . at Cincinnati," and also assuring him, "Your praises are in the mouths of everybody" and that "you made more reputation than any [other] man in the convention." If Hayes were elected and did not offer Harlan "the best place in the Administration," Bristow wrote that he would "feel greatly disappointed."[69]

His Fraudulency

President Grant accepted Bristow's resignation from the cabinet on June 19. On June 24, Bristow arrived in Cincinnati to give a well-received keynote address at a "ratification meeting" signaling the beginning of Hayes's campaign. Then, he returned to Louisville.[70]

Harlan was also invited to address the Cincinnati gathering.[71] On June 21, he wrote to Governor Hayes suggesting that the Republican candidate include in his acceptance letter references to "'retrenchment' [and] 'economy' as applied to the financial affairs of the nation"—and also emphasized that among Kentucky Republicans there was "not a dissenting voice as to your nomination."[72] When the acceptance letter appeared, he wrote Hayes a brief but glowing note assuring the candidate that he should "be greatly surprised if it does not meet the approval of every one likely to vote with us in the pending contest."[73] When General Edward F. Noyes, one of Hayes's closest advisers, sought Harlan's impressions of a draft of the letter,[74] the future justice responded that the governor's issue positions were "capital in every respect."[75]

To a greater extent than in the past, Harlan declined speechmaking invitations extended him during the fall campaign, citing the demands of his law practice. He probably had little difficulty turning down—albeit he did so graciously—James G. Blaine's request that he make another Maine canvass.[76] But he declined requests from friendlier quarters as well.[77] There were limits to his reticence, though, for he realized that Hayes faced an uphill battle against Samuel J. Tilden, his Democratic opponent, and that any hopes he had for national influence—and position—lay with the Ohio governor.

Certainly, Harlan had no weight with what was left of the Grant wing of the party. Repeatedly during the summer and fall, he attempted, usually without success, to prevent removal or other sanctions against federal appointees connected with the Bristow–Harlan camp. On one occasion, he wrote Republican Congressman John D. White of Kentucky to complain that his choice for a post office vacancy was being replaced. "What I suspect," he declared, "is that this is another case of . . . the pasturing of the friend of some politician in another State upon this State, when there are Republicans here able to fill the office."[78]

It was hardly surprising, then, that Harlan accepted eight speaking engagements in Indiana and a number of others in the West as well.[79] He wrote numerous letters stressing the closeness of the contest, the importance of a Republican victory to the South, and what he believed to be Grant's desire to destroy the party's chances.[80] When he learned of a rumor that Kentuckians planned to transport blacks into Indiana to vote the Democratic ticket there, he promptly alerted a friend in Indianapolis. Such a scheme might appear "strange," he noted, but Indiana Republicans should remember that there were "some very unreliable men among that race."[81]

In the final campaign gathering of Kentucky Republicans, with Benjamin Bristow presiding, Harlan gave one of his most rousing speeches ever, urging "war to the knife" for the Republican cause. Southern Democrats were charging that a Republican victory would mean ruin for their region. Seemingly mindful of Hayes's promise to pursue a noninterventionist southern policy, Harlan vehemently challenged the Democrats' assertion:

> If fidelity to the principles of the Republican Party be treason to the South, we glory in such treason. We of the Republican Party are true friends of the South. We do not seek to oppress any people of the South. We maintain the rights of all, of every race. We recognize the rights of free speech. We are enemies of the KuKlux and the White Leagues. We are for protection to all in every right secured by law. . . . We recognize the rights of the States, but we claim that paramount allegiance is due to the country. . . . We demand the persecution of Union men in the South shall cease. We demand that the work of reform shall go forward until everywhere in all the land each citizen shall be accorded any right which, under the laws and under the Constitution, belongs to every other citizen. We demand that their nation shall stamp the life out of every combination or organization which defies the power of a State and seeks to oppress the citizen because of race, color or political opinions.[82]

Fortunately for Harlan, of course, the chaotic state of southern politics was to save Hayes—and the future justice's destiny—from defeat and obscurity. As Harlan had feared, early returns before midnight on November 7 indicated that Tilden had been elected. But confusion over the electoral vote in South Carolina, Florida, and Louisiana led to creation of a special commission to decide the issue. Stacked with Republicans, that body ruled in Hayes's favor. In the early hours of March 2, 1877, Congress completed its tabulation of the votes, giving Hayes 185 electoral votes and Tilden 184. Two days later, the Ohio governor—"His fraudulency," critics would call him—was inaugurated as the nation's nineteenth president.

While the election dispute moved toward resolution, Hayes and his advisers considered prospects for the president-elect's cabinet. The names of both Harlan and Bristow appeared often in mail to the president on the subject, with Harlan generally more favorably promoted than Bristow. Following an intelligence gathering trip to Washington, Hayes's friend and longtime political ally, James M. Comly, reported, for example, that several Republicans with whom he had talked, including James A. Garfield and Ohio Congressman Charles Foster, "could not help expressing the opinion that [Bristow] would be the worst man in the country to take into a new Cabinet," but considered Harlan a "satisfactory" compromise for "Bristow's friends, and not obnoxious to his enemies."[83] During a similar visit, *Dayton Journal* editor, W.D. Bickham, reported that Kentuckians were "divided about Harlan. Some good men think him 'Shallow,' and criticize him severely for 'want of fidelity to principle' and for grave 'inconsistency.'" But Grant's friends, Bickham exclaimed, "resent the mention of Bristow as offensive!"[84]

References to Harlan were generally positive. In his recommendation of a cabinet that would guarantee Hayes a "prosperous voyage," the *Cincinnati Commer-*

cial's Murat Halstead suggested Harlan for attorney general. Although one of the rare Hayes advisers to prefer Bristow, Carl Schurz, who would become Hayes's interior secretary, emphasized that he would not wish "to say anything to the prejudice of Gen. Harlan."[85] Harlan's friend, Judge Ballard, declared that Harlan's appointment as attorney general "would give eminent satisfaction to all good republicans in this region" and offered the opinion, no doubt with coaching from the future justice, that Harlan "could not afford to accept any other position in the Cabinet."[86]

The record is clear, moreover, that Hayes fully intended to make Harlan the nation's chief law enforcement officer. Harlan, unlike Bristow, was not excluded by guidelines for cabinet selections mentioned in a Hayes diary entry as early as January 17, including a decision to appoint no "leading competitors for the Presidential nomination." In listing possible cabinet choices in that same entry, Hayes also indicated that his "thoughts rest[ed] on," among others, "General Harlan, of Kentucky, for Attorney General."[87]

About the time of Hayes's inauguration, however, Senator Morton of Indiana derailed, if temporarily, Harlan's momentum. Writing the president-elect of "rumors that you contemplate selecting Gen. Harlan of Ky. for a seat in your cabinet," Morton "in frankness" opposed such a move "for reasons too numerous and lengthy to be referred to here," then proceeded to note one basis for his opposition: that "Kentucky never cast a Republican vote and perhaps will not in our lifetime, and Kentucky Republicanism never meant much."[88]

Harlan's supporters did what they could to counter Morton's efforts. A concerned Richard Smith of the *Cincinnati Gazette* wrote the president-elect the day before his inauguration, expressing doubt that "any appointment could be made to compensate for [Harlan's] omission" from the cabinet, as well as his confidence that Harlan's selection "would satisfy what we call the Bristow sentiment more fully and more successfully . . . than any selection that might be made."[89]

But Morton had his way. Hayes's cabinet nominations, announced on March 5, included no position for Harlan. In conversations with journalist William Henry Smith years later, Hayes disputed rumors that President Grant had opposed the selection of Bristow or the former treasury secretary's friends to posts in the new administration. "Gen. Hayes had selected John M. Harlan for attorney-general," Smith recorded, "but this was abandoned at Morton's request. [Hayes] never knew why Morton objected to Harlan."[90]

The Louisiana Commission

Mutual friends of the president and Harlan attempted to cast Hayes's oversight in a favorable light to Harlan or Bristow, but not necessarily to both. Hayes's fellow Ohioan William Dennison assured the future justice that "no disrespect was intended you or any of our friends" and that the White House entertained "the most kindly feeling" toward Harlan—feelings which, Dennison hoped, would "be fully displayed within reasonable time."[91] On the day the cabinet nominations were announced, Murat Halstead suggested to Benjamin Bristow that the president's failure to choose Harlan for attorney general meant "that he intends to appoint you (or Harlan)" to the Supreme Court. "I told him," Halstead added, that "I thought you should have the place."[92]

Bristow, of course, would receive no post in the Hayes Administration; and Harlan's reward was yet to come. In April, the president did give the future justice a temporary assignment but not one anybody was likely to welcome.

Confusion over the 1876 election results were not confined to the presidential race. In South Carolina and Louisiana, each party had declared victory in the state elections and established rival state governments. In Louisiana, the situation was particularly tense. The Democratic gubernatorial choice, Francis Redding Tillou Nicholls, had served gallantly in the Confederate army, sacrificing his left arm and leg to the southern cause. He had been a popular candidate, railing against carpet-baggers and black rule and inspiring confidence in like-minded white voters. When the state's Republican-dominated election board gave the office to Nicholls's carpetbag opponent, Stephen B. Packard, Nicholls ignored its decision, establishing a de facto government of his own. By early April, the Nicholls forces clearly had the upper hand. Packard, using New Orleans's St. Louis Hotel as a statehouse, was in a state of virtual siege, surviving only via the presence of federal troops and limited in jurisdiction to his statehouse and four surrounding streets. Legislators committed to Packard occupied the same location but, lacking a senate quorum, were transacting no business. Meanwhile, Nicholls and his legislature conducted business regularly at their statehouse in New Orleans's Odd Fellows Hall. The city's government recognized Nicholls's authority, and his supreme court held daily sessions, while the court which recognized Packard's authority had been deprived of its courtroom and records since early January.[93]

Had President Grant removed the troops guarding Packard, his administration would have come to an abrupt end. But Grant took no action, and President Hayes now considered himself obliged to seek some resolution of the issue. Hayes pursued a variety of avenues, including appointment of a study commission. A bipartisan body, the Louisiana Commission was composed of Judge Charles B. Lawrence of Illinois, General Joseph R. Hawley of Connecticut, Wayne MacVeagh of Pennsylvania, ex-Governor John C. Brown of Tennessee—and John Harlan. In a letter to the commissioners, Hayes's secretary of state, William M. Evarts, conveyed the president's wishes that they use whatever "conciliatory influences" might appear most effective in moving the state toward acceptance of one government and also that they collect "accurate and trustworthy information" from officials and "prominent citizens of all political connections as to the state of public feeling and opinion in the community at large."[94]

Harlan did not have to await his arrival in New Orleans to receive the impressions of friends regarding the Louisiana question. Walter Gresham doubted whether any "good [could] come of the visit" from Harlan's perspective or that the future justice had "been treated just right" in being given the assignment, and expressed hope that "you will not commit yourself in favor of Packard."[95] John Finnell liked neither "Packard and his reprobates" nor "Nicholls and his class," but gave ultimate weight to his lack of "overweening love for a firmly 'Nigger government' in the abstract." In Finnell's view, "our colored brethren of the South have not developed a capacity for 'governing things' in a degree that would . . . enable them to carry on that line of business to the exclusion of the white people!" Republican efforts in that direction since the war, he declared, had "done infinite harm to the South and . . . brought the Republican party to the verge of ruin!" Like Gresham, Finnell could see little advantage in the venture for Harlan. "[I]t is reasonably clear that you catch the ____, no matter what comes of your mission."[96]

From Louisianians, of course, the commissioners received mixed reports and prescriptions. On April 6, the day they arrived in New Orleans, speakers at a mass gathering of citizens extolled the legitimacy of the Nicholls administration against Packard's "pretended Government," vowing never to submit to the carpetbagger's authority or pay his regime a dollar of taxes.[97] A Republican Evansville, Indiana, native and Harlan family friend, who had invested all he had in a Louisiana cotton plantation, decried the "corruption" of the state's Republican party and assured Harlan that "the better and more sensible negroes [were] disgusted" with its current "management."[98] Challenging the pro-Nicholls resolutions adopted at the April 6 demonstrations, a Packard legislator branded Nicholls's supporters as "[b]arbarians who have murdered and slay'd our white and colored Republicans," while lamenting the recent unsolved murder of his brother, a black Republican tax collector, "at noon-day in the heart of a populous town."[99] The commissioners were also privy to a report prepared by William H. Hunt of New Orleans, a Republican and staunch Civil War unionist, who favored immediate "recognition and protection" for the Packard government against "the insurrectionary organization which now confronts it," a combination based on "resistance to law, and the impurity which attends such resistance in a disorganized society."[100]

Harlan and company devoted most of their visit to interviews, the collection of documents, and strategic socializing (New Orleans' Boston Club extended to Harlan, and presumably other commissioners as well, club privileges for a period of 20 days).[101] By the end of the first week of his stay, Harlan seemed mildly disposed toward support for the Nicholls regime. Louisiana's political situation, he wrote Benjamin Bristow, was in a state of "utter confusion." He had decided, however, "that the wrongs done by our folks, in the name of Republicanism, [had] taught the opposite party to think and feel that they must deal more liberally with the colored people." He had learned much in Louisiana "which stir[s] my blood as a Union man and a Republican," but he believed that the "Democratic party here has advanced as to most matters affecting the colored race, that is to say, they talk more liberally than they would have dared to do 8 years ago upon such matters."[102]

However sanguine Harlan and his colleagues may have been regarding the racial leanings of Governor Nicholls and his supporters, they understood the ultimate political realities of the situation. Packard's regime had little support among influential whites and no chance of survival once the federal troops were withdrawn, according to the dictates of Hayes's southern policy. Gradually, members of the Packard legislature drifted over to the Nicholls government. On April 18, the commissioners sent the president a coded message. The parties were not likely to agree to any proposed settlement, they reported; "nevertheless the situation here is rapidly changing, and we have no doubt the Nicholls Legislature will very soon contain a quorum" of legislators in each chamber certified by the state election board. An order removing the troops, they assured Hayes, would not lead to violence, and it was "almost certain that such changes will soon occur as will practi-cally dispense with any excuse for National intervention."[103]

Two days later, after learning that Hayes planned to remove the troops as soon as their withdrawal could be accomplished without any outbreak of violence, the commissioners sent the president a second telegram indicating that an "immediate announcement" of the withdrawal date would be "better for the peace of the people" than delay.[104] On April 24, the troops were withdrawn and the Packard government, as Hayes's biographer later described it, "melted away as noiselessly as early frost in autumn under the rays of the rising sun."[105]

Many considered Hayes's abandonment of Packard an act of betrayal. William Lloyd Garrison branded it a "cowardly compromise" with the "incorrigible enemies of equal rights and legitimate government."[106] Elements of the press treated the commission and its tactics as equally suspect, circulating rumors that Harlan would be obliged to refute during Senate confirmation proceedings over his Supreme Court nomination. But T. De S. Tucker, a prominent black New Orleans Republican and supporter of the Packard regime wrote Harlan to criticize such attacks. He praised "the fruits [thus] far produced from this well-meant action,"[107] and offered his services and those of other Louisiana blacks as speakers in support of the com-mission's action in the North. Shortly after Harlan's return to Louisville, moreover, his wily Covington friend, John Finnell, put the assignment in proper political per-spective. "I am proud to say," wrote Finnell, that "you [survived] the trip to 'Saint Antone' and avoided both the upper and the lower road. Your trip was a success and the great good accomplished leaves surviving the five great statesmen who did the work; but who seemed to me [initially] to be on the road to certain death! You de-serve well of the country—all the more because you took the risk."[108] By the year's end, Harlan would indeed be rewarded for service to his president and party but not without painful controversy and the permanent rupture of a valued friendship.

The Appointment

A breach in Harlan's long association with Benjamin Bristow began to develop close to the time of Hayes's inauguration. According to Harlan's version of the rift—a handwritten narrative drafted on August 21 that became known as "Harlan's One-Day Diary"—Murat Halstead, on learning of Hayes's plan to nominate Harlan as attorney general, asked Bristow whether his friend's selection would be agree-able. Bristow angrily replied that, if consulted, he would have supported Harlan's nomination, but then "proceeded to utter a growl & complaint that he had not been consulted." He complained so vehemently of his treatment, in fact, that Harlan was convinced the president's advisers feared that Harlan's selection "would not satisfy all elements of the Bristow organization."[109]

Next, Bristow's close friend H. V. Boynton speculated in the *Cincinnati Gazette* that Hayes's failure to make Harlan attorney general probably meant that the presi-dent intended to appoint Bristow as successor to Justice David Davis, who was leaving the Supreme Court for one of Illinois' seats in the U.S. Senate. When Bris-tow took no steps to prevent Harlan's "sacrifice upon any such ground," Harlan's consternation grew. Nor were his feelings soothed when Bristow explained that he could not approach Hayes without an invitation, yet wrote letters supporting other friends for administration positions.[110]

When Harlan complained to mutual friends about Bristow's behavior, three of their closest associates—Eli Murray, Gabriel Wharton, and Harlan's law partner, Gus Willson—visited the former treasury secretary's Washington hotel room in an effort to reunite their friends. That day, Bristow had received a letter from former Ohio Governor Dennison, who, fresh from an interview with the president, speculated that Hayes would appoint Bristow to the Supreme Court. In his friends' presence, and without Harlan's knowledge, Bristow penned a telegram to Dennison asking him to convey to the president that he did "not desire the appointment" and recommending Harlan for the position.[111]

Harlan's diary indicates that Murray, Wharton, and Willson went promptly to Harlan's room with news of the telegram, "full of the idea that Bristow had done a manly, generous thing which ought to satisfy me that he had [not] intended to be untrue to his friendship for me." At their friends' urging, Harlan went to Bristow's room for a reconciliation, later celebrated with a night of cards. But Harlan remained suspicious that Bristow's message might never reach the president—and "perhaps . . . was not intended to reach him." And when the former treasury secretary never again alluded to it, the future justice considered his misgivings confirmed.[112]

Depending on the evidence consulted, Harlan's doubts seem either unfair or well-founded. In a March 22 letter, Governor Dennison assured Harlan that, immediately after Hayes's nomination for the presidency, Bristow had told Dennison that he would want no position in the new administration but instead was anxious that Harlan receive "a handsome recognition."[113] On the other hand, in a follow-up letter to his March 15 telegram to Dennison—a letter not shared, presumably, with Murray, Wharton, or Willson—Bristow indicated to Dennison only that he would at no time "seek" the Supreme Court position, not that he did not want, or would not accept, it. Omitted, too, was any recommendation of Harlan for the post. Instead, Bristow noted only that one of his reasons for having sent the telegram "touch[ed] my personal relations to a friend which I have reason to fear have been endangered by [certain] impressions on his mind, which I very much desire to remove."[114] One who was only mildly cynical by nature might read that passage to mean that Bristow's telegraphic message supporting Harlan was intended more to soothe his feelings than as a sincere recommendation that he be appointed to the Court.

Whatever Bristow's motives, his feelings were the next to suffer injury in the developing course of the two friends' estrangement. On April 3, correspondent H. V. Boynton, Bristow's most zealous partisan, wrote the former treasury secretary of his pleasure at learning from Bristow that he would "take Davis's place if tendered," as well as Boynton's account of a recent conversation journalist Richard Smith had with the president. "Hayes . . . said he had sent you [Bristow]," reported Boynton, "a message by Harlan to the effect that you were to be consulted about Kentucky matters and . . . that the wrongs done you and your friends . . . were now being examined with a view to rectifying them."[115] In a follow-up letter, dated April 8, Boynton asserted that Harlan had told Smith in Cincinnati in late March that

Bristow "would not take the Davis place if it was offered, and he pretended to speak *advisedly*." Repeating the story of Hayes's message to Bristow "by Harlan," Boynton added that "double dealing will go a very short way in the honest game as long as I hold a hand."[116]

Shortly after receiving Boynton's first letter, Bristow had a visit from Eli Murray. Referring to the "confidential message" the president had sent the former treasury secretary through Harlan, Murray urged Bristow to "throw off all reserve" and write Hayes "freely" regarding Kentucky appointments.[117] When Bristow responded—no doubt with characteristic agitation—that he had received no message, Murray sent a telegram to that effect to Harlan, then in New Orleans with the Louisiana Commission. Harlan and Bristow had conferred briefly at Louisville's railroad depot before Harlan's departure for New Orleans. In an April 9 letter, Harlan mentioned telling Bristow "at Louisville that I had an opportunity to have a very brief interview with the President about Kentucky affairs. He inquired whether you and I would concur on our suggestions. Upon my replying that we would, he intimated that he would dispose of Kentucky matters according to the wishes of the Bristow element."[118] Two days later, Harlan sent Bristow a telegram of his own: "I learn you have information from someone at Washington that a message was sent you by President through me. I communicated to you at Louisville all President said concerning you on Kentucky affairs."[119]

Bristow was hardly satisfied. He had "no recollection whatever," he wrote the Louisiana commissioner on April 11, of the conversation Harlan had recalled in his letter. But even if his memory, rather than Harlan's, were at fault, Harlan's version of the situation had mentioned no "message." "[S]o . . . I was both substantially and literally correct in saying that I had received no message." He intended no "complaint," added Bristow; he merely wanted to set the record straight. "I cannot afford to be otherwise than frank with you, and I hope the time will never come when it will be either necessary or desirable to be less frank than we have always been with each other."[120]

But Harlan held his ground. He conceded that Richard Smith could honestly have construed the president's remarks as a "*message*." And he realized that Hayes "expected" Bristow to know what had been said; thus, he had "determined" to tell Bristow "of it as soon as I saw you." But Harlan was confident that he had told Bristow in Louisville substantially what his earlier letter recounted, although "[o]ur conversation was . . . a very hurried one, and I am not surprised that you failed to gather what I supposed I was communicating."[121]

On Harlan's return from New Orleans, the two resumed outwardly cordial relations; but their feelings for each other continued to fester. H. V. Boynton's growing outrage at what he considered Harlan's "betrayal" of Bristow did not help either. After Bristow shared one of Harlan's letters with the loyal but volatile correspondent, Boynton offered his own theory of Harlan's conduct. Withholding the president's "friendly message" from Bristow at a time when the former treasury secretary's frustrations over "deliberate neglect" by the president were most intense might have led Bristow to "openly say or do something which would make it certain that you would not be appointed to the bench." Such a tactic "would have been a good ploy in a *sharp* game for Davis' place." For Boynton, there was no other "rational solution" to the puzzle.[122] Nor was this an isolated instance. In the coming months, Boynton repeatedly fueled Bristow's growing resentment of Harlan's "treachery," exacerbating an already unfortunate situation.[123]

While the Harlan–Bristow relationship deteriorated, President Hayes considered prospects for the Davis vacancy on the Supreme Court. Justice Samuel Miller had long coveted a judgeship for his brother-in-law, William Pitt Ballinger, a Galveston lawyer with a large federal practice. In March, Miller learned that Hayes was "hesitating between Harlan of Kentucky or possibly Bristow their interest being one, and a *real* southern man" for Davis's seat.[124] In early May, Miller met with the president to press Ballinger's case. During their conversation, Hayes again mentioned Harlan and Bristow, suggested that Harlan probably possessed the "most vigorous intellect" and Bristow the "soundest judgment," and expressed "fear" of Bristow's presidential aspirations—a concern in which Miller readily concurred, making "some very forcible remarks on the evils of presidential hopes in our court."[125]

Shortly after his meeting with Hayes, Miller discussed Ballinger and the Kentuckians, as well as New Orleans' William Hunt, another Court possibility, with Chief Justice Morrison R. Waite. Waite thought Hunt's ability inadequate, Bristow "too much aspiring," and the selection of either Harlan or Bristow inappropriate given the presence already on the Court of two members (Waite and Noah H. Swayne, both Ohioans) from the same federal circuit as Kentucky.[126]

Whatever Harlan's interest in the Court vacancy, or his chances at that point of acquiring it, he obviously was not inhibited from complaining when the administration's patronage decisions went against his preferences. In late May, he learned that the widow of a Democratic lawyer, rather than the choice he and Bristow had supported, was to become Louisville's postmistress. He immediately telegraphed W. K. Rogers, Hayes's personal secretary and former law partner, seeking a delay in the appointment,[127] and then wrote Stanley Matthews a lengthy request that he intervene in behalf of Louisville's Republicans. "No female," he chauvinistically declared, could "manage so large a Post Office as the one here"; and selection of a Democrat ignored "the brave men who, under the most adverse circumstances, have breasted the storm of Sectional hate, and remained true to the country."[128] Matthews forwarded Harlan's letter to Rogers for the president's "personal perusal."[129] Harlan also contacted Ohio Senator John Sherman, brother of the general, about the slight; and when informed by Sherman that the appointment was firm, he responded that the action was "a very severe . . . undeserved blow at the friends of the President" in Kentucky.[130]

But such complaints were a normal part of politics and apparently in no way dampened the president's interest in Harlan. Hayes had indicated to Justice Miller in early May that he would not fill Davis's seat until fall,[131] and for a time it appeared that he preferred Harlan for a diplomatic rather than judicial post. In July, Harlan, Eli Murray, and others went to Washington to invite the president and his cabinet to visit the Louisville Industrial Exposition on September 17, the centennial of the adoption of the Constitution by the Philadelphia convention. During their stay, Harlan spoke privately with Hayes's close adviser, Edward F. Noyes, the president's recent appointee as minister to France, who told him that Hayes had recently inquired whether Harlan would accept an appointment to the English mission. Harlan "promptly" replied, according to his account, that he would accept no diplomatic post.[132]

The next day, Harlan visited President Hayes to urge Bland Ballard's appointment to a circuit judgeship and Eli Murray's assignment to a second-class European mission. "We have not said anything," Hayes remarked at one point, "as to your wishes as to yourself." "I am not surprised, Mr. President," Harlan would recall responding, "as I have not been a *candidate* for any position." Hayes then asked, "Would a first class mission tempt your ambition?" Harlan gave the president the same response he had given Noyes: "I think not, Mr. President. My ambition has not led me in that direction—I do not see how a man of my limited fortune and large family, could afford to live abroad in official position, and abandon his profession for four years. To be entirely frank, Mr. President, I have never cared for any public position, which was not in the line of my profession."

Out of courtesy to the president, Harlan declined a definite immediate answer, asking instead for three weeks to consider Hayes's offer, an allowance the president readily granted. Following a week with his family at Block Island, Rhode Island, a favorite Harlan vacation spot, he returned to Washington and declined the appointment. "I hope you understand me," Hayes pressed, "as including in my suggestion the very best Mission we have—the English Mission." Harlan responded that the obstacles to his acceptance were the same, whatever the post involved. "We then talked," he later wrote, "about other matters."

At that point, Harlan may well have wondered whether Hayes was seriously considering him for the bench. In less than a month, however, he seemed convinced that Justice Davis's seat was to be his. On August 21, he wrote his "One-Day Diary," recounting his numerous efforts to promote Benjamin Bristow's career and what he believed to be Bristow's recent betrayal of their friendship.

> [F]ar from suggesting any method to aid me [in securing nomination to the Court], his immediate friends have been, with his knowledge and approval, pressing his name upon the President—And no one now doubts that he has, from the outset, been anxious to be Davis' successor. . . . He was unwilling to make any sacrifices for one whom he had professed to regard as his most intimate, confidential, valued friend. . . . When the time came for me to secure what my ambition coveted, he, by his actions said, stand back until I am satisfied with additional official station, and then you may come forward—not before.

Harlan seemed optimistic, however, about the ultimate outcome of their rivalry: "[T]he willingness of Col. Bristow to sacrifice a friend will not be rewarded. It is quite certain that he will not reach the Bench. There is a greater probability that I will be appointed."

Harlan's supporters left nothing to chance. Several days after the future justice vented his feelings in his "diary," his young law partner, Gus Willson, then on an extended wedding trip, wrote to express interest "in the progress of your friends' movement in your behalf" and to praise Harlan's approach to the judgeship contest. "The course you have adopted seems as it always has the best, to let it take its own course so far as you are concerned."[133] With the campaign his friends had orchestrated, any direct effort on Harlan's part would have appeared redundant. From mid-August to mid-October, the flow of letters and petitions to the Hayes White House was constant and voluminous. Kentuckians of both parties, including the father-in-law of future Justice Louis D. Brandeis[134] and virtually every politician with whom Harlan had been associated, extolled his virtues as a fine lawyer, staunch unionist, and true Republican.[135] State officers and members of the Kentucky court of appeals submitted petitions in his behalf.[136] Governor McCreary, Harlan's victorious 1875 campaign opponent and bed partner, wrote to the future justice that in "laborious service for your party you have surpassed any Republican in Kentucky,"[137] and later professed to have given Hayes the same assessment during a personal meeting.[138] A. H. Siegfried, current publisher of the *Louisville Commercial*, expressed doubt whether "the republican faith would have retained an organized life in Kentucky without" Harlan, as well as certitude that he was "the representative exponent of the best and purest phases of Southern republicanism."[139] An Indianapolis lawyer, fearful that Hayes might appoint a "real southerner" (i.e., a former rebel), endorsed Harlan and charged that "the appointment of one who took part in the rebellion to the Supreme Bench, would be a destructive blow to Republicanism."[140] Wayne MacVeagh of Philadelphia, Harlan's Louisiana Commission colleague, wrote several enthusiastic letters in the future justice's behalf,[141] as did numerous Democrats, including one former Whig who vouched for the candidate's "high moral worth and ability."[142]

Not all of the president's correspondence relative to Harlan was favorable, of course. Hayes's nephew, Charles W. Fairbanks, who had promised at Cincinnati to remind his uncle of Harlan's role in Hayes's nomination, favored a choice from the seventh circuit, Davis's home district, rather than Harlan's sixth circuit, which, as noted earlier, already held two seats on the Court.[143] Others, especially Indiana and Illinois residents, raised the same concern. Indeed, even after Harlan's selection, his fellow Louisiana commissioner, Charles B. Lawrence, would write the nominee to praise his appointment as "the one I most desired," but also to brand it "rather . . . an affront on the bar of our circuit."[144]

H. V. Boynton's anger had not abated. In an August letter to Bristow, he agreed that Harlan was "hard at work for the judgeship" and boasted that he had recently "put in one stroke against" that effort. According to Boynton, Harlan, or his partisans, had been trying to create the impression that his appointment would actually be a compliment to Bristow, given their long relationship. Boynton had ridiculed such reasoning in a conversation with one of the president's friends, remarking that Harlan's appointment "would be regarded by all your true friends as the success of as contemptible intrigue and trickery as ever attended obtaining public position."[145] Boynton was principally responsible, moreover, for newspaper pieces questioning Harlan's Republicanism and support for the war amendments and Reconstruction.

But Harlan's partisans also continued their campaign, gradually building a momentum for his selection. When one of Boynton's dispatches appeared, John Finnell expressed "amaze[ment]" at the correspondent's recklessness and vowed to "go to Washington or to the devil if I can help you."[146] Finnell and other supporters made numerous trips to the nation's capital in their friend's behalf.[147]

Gradually, the lobbying had the desired effect. "Confidentially and on the whole is not Harlan the man?" President Hayes wrote his friend William Henry Smith on September 29. "Of the right age—able—of whole character—industrious—fine manners, temper and appearance. Who leads him?"[148] Smith agreed, terming Harlan a "very much better man every way than Bristow."[149]

Others sensed Hayes's movement toward Harlan. Numerous candidates, including W. B. Woods, federal circuit judge of Alabama; Henry Clay Caldwell, an Arkansas federal district judge; Judge Thomas Drummond of Illinois; Samuel Breckinridge of Missouri; and Justice Miller's brother-in-law, William Pitt Ballinger, among others, had been pressed on the president. In an October 8 letter to Ballinger, however, Miller speculated that Hayes's "personal preferences lay between Harlan and yourself."[150] Wayne MacVeagh wrote Harlan on October 3 that he had just returned from Washington "with a profound conviction that matters were going well" and reported a week later his belief that "we are 'out of the woods.'"[151]

MacVeagh's optimism was well-founded. On October 10 and 11, various newspapers reported that the president's intention to nominate Harlan had been announced in his October 9 cabinet meeting.[152] Such reports were undoubtedly accurate. On seeing one such item, an unidentified member of the administration penned the president a note assuring Hayes "that I have scrupulously regarded your injunction concerning giving publicity to the announcement."[153]

The day after the cabinet session, William Henry Smith asked Hayes to delay the appointment. "I am troubled about that Supreme Court business," wrote Smith from Chicago. "The offense to the people of this District, if an appointment is made out of it, *is going to strike deeper than I at first thought.* . . . To appoint Harlan will be to give the Ohio Dist. three members, and deprive this strongly Republican one of any. Then the appointment of Harlan would be less acceptable here than a man from the Gulf States."[154] In his reply to a telegram Smith also sent, the president's secretary, W. K. Rogers, confirmed that Hayes's choice was "still" Harlan, but that he was inclined "to postpone a determination upon the matter a few weeks longer," despite "considerable pressure" for an earlier decision.[155]

But the delay was to be less than a week. On October 13, Wayne MacVeagh assured Harlan that his "advices of yesterday [left] no shadow of doubt as to the result."[156] Even the tenacious Justice Miller threw in the towel, sharing with his brother-in-law the judgment of a Hayes cabinet officer that, after a Democratic sweep in the Ohio state elections of October 9, "the President will not have the courage to appoint any one but a recognized Republican to the place and . . . that Harlan's name will be sent in early next week."[157] Miller's source was correct. On October 16, one day after Congress convened in a special session called by Hayes, the president submitted Harlan's nomination to the Senate for its "advice and consent."

When Hayes notified Harlan of his action, the grateful Kentuckian assured the president of his "very great satisfaction . . . , not only for the honor and dignity of the office, but for the evidence it affords of your confidence." Although "distrustful," he wrote, of his fitness for "a position so exalted," he promised to undertake the duties of the office "at once," should it "be the pleasure of the Senate to confirm the nomination."[158]

Initially, Harlan's partisans assumed that the Senate's approval would be speedy and uneventful. Robert M. Kelley of the *Louisville Commercial*, a longtime ally, wired his congratulations and a message from Kentucky Senate Democrat James Beck that there would "not [be the] least trouble about confirmation [from] his side" of the aisle.[159] Senator Lucius Quintus Cincinnatus Lamar of Mississippi, the Confederate general and statesman who would follow Harlan to the Court in 1887, advised Louisville *Courier-Journal* editor Henry Watterson that the nominee would have no trouble "from any of our people."[160] And Watterson—whose advocacy of a "New South" accepting Reconstruction amendments, black suffrage, and industrialization had once prompted Harlan to remark, "A residence in Kentucky may yet be very desirable"[161]—shared Lamar's message with the nominee. William Cassius Goodloe reported the belief of "some" that the nomination might have "trouble" in the Senate, but John Finnell suspected that there were "*some* with whom the wish is father to the thought."[162] Numerous letters to the president and to Harlan praised the nomination and predicted little Senate opposition.[163] Some took confirmation for granted. Justice Stephen Field's nephew, Frederick T. Stone of New York, whose wife and sick baby the Harlans had assisted during a recent visit to Block Island, took pleasure, for example, in the president's selection of the Kentucky Republican rather than an "extreme ultra Southern Democrat" and predicted that Harlan would find his uncle "very pleasant on all subjects except politics,—he is a Rabid Tilden Democrat."[164]

Harlan's fate in the Senate was to hang in the balance for 45 days, which was not surprising, given his checkered political record, ties to the reformist Bristow, and recent estrangement from the same controversial figure. Further clouding his course, moreover, were the charges of seventh circuit Republicans that they were being robbed of "their" seat on the bench and the concerns of liberal party members generally about President Hayes's southern program—policies with which the nominee, after all, was in part directly connected via his service on the Louisiana Commission.[165]

Typical of that period, the Senate judiciary committee, which would initially review Harlan's credentials and make its report to the full Senate, would hold no hearings on the nomination; nor would Harlan attend its proceedings. But the Senate included in its membership many of the president's bitterest enemies, most notably New York's Roscoe Conkling. Conkling detested Hayes, believed he had stolen the presidency and destroyed the Grant machine in which Conkling had enjoyed substantial influence, and vehemently resented the president's selection of William Evarts, whom Conkling also hated, as secretary of state. Conkling could be counted on to seek to embarrass both Hayes and his nominee.[166] While apparently harboring no personal animosity toward Harlan or the president, the Senate Judiciary Committee Chairman, George F. Edmunds of Vermont, was a staunch radical Reconstructionist who was suspicious of Harlan's Republicanism and had also been recommended for the post to which Harlan was nominated.[167] Edmunds would seem unusually persistent in probing Harlan's background, and not necessarily with the most objective sources. He wrote Benjamin Bristow a confidential letter, for example, to ask whether the nominee had opposed the Emancipation Proclamation "in the time of it," repudiated Lincoln and supported McClellan, condemned the Thirteenth and Fourteenth Amendments, and considered the 1866 Civil Rights Act unconstitutional—in short, whether Harlan's "opinions were substantially those of the Democratic party."[168]

Whether on their own or prompted by Senate opponents of the nomination, critics of the nominee, the president, or both, soon supplied Edmunds and other senators with negative correspondence. Chicago lawyer Melville W. Fuller, with whom Harlan would serve on the Supreme Court and his son, James, would study law, lamented the president's failure to select a justice from his circuit and branded the nomination a "disagreeable surprise" that "accomplishe[d] nothing except to reward a Louisiana commissioner, a personal and secondary consideration."[169]

Others attacked the nominee's professional and Republican credentials. Charging that he was "not in full sympathy with the Republican Party and never was," one Iowan asserted that Harlan wanted only the sort of minimal change in the nation's civil rights policies that would "suit Kentucky Rebels," adding: "He is in fact a milk and water politician, a political demagogue who all his life has been after office."[170] Complained another:

> Harlan is deficient in legal and professional education, such as ought to be had by any one on the Supreme Bench. As for general scholarship or literary attainments he has *none*. I defy any one to prove from any oral or written or printed utterance, he has ever made that a literature, ancient or modern, ever existed; and as sure as you and I live, we will both see the hour when he will be the sycophantic friend and supplicant tool of the Democratic party. He *was that* when he thought it was to his interest to be so. He *will be so again* when he believes his interests require it.[171]

But the allegations of Speed Fry were potentially most damaging. The nominee and General Fry, who was reputed to have killed Confederate General Felix K. Zollicoffer, had served together in the Union army. In one of his reports, in fact, Fry had praised Harlan for "energy, promptness, and success in pursuing and driving rebel forces from [Kentucky] railroad" lines.[172] Following the war, the two were close political allies. But in recent years Fry had become increasingly bitter over his failure to secure a federal patronage post through Harlan and Benjamin Bristow. In 1874, Bristow had written Harlan of his "chagrin" at being unable to place Fry in the Treasury Department. "Fry," a member of Bristow's staff had insisted, was simply "too much of a gentleman for a quasi-detective and every body in the Commissioner's office laughs at the idea of appointing Fry supervisor. . . . [T]he Pres[ident] has the same notion . . . and *would not* appoint him. . . . Can't you set me right with him [?]"[173] More recently, Fry had sought Harlan's assistance in an unsuccessful campaign to secure a position as collector of internal revenue;[174] and two days after Hayes's inauguration, he had written the future justice and others to complain of their failure to aid him in his efforts to become federal marshal for Kentucky[175]—a post Harlan was seeking for another friend. Later, he complained vehemently that President Hayes had snubbed him during the president's Industrial Exposition visit to the state.[176] In his letter regarding the marshal's post, moreover, he had assured Harlan that he did "not intend to resort to any unfair means to secure the place," but warned that "when . . . convinced" such tactics were used to bring about his "defeat," he would consider it "but just to himself" to employ them "with all their force upon those . . . responsible for" his troubles.[177]

With Harlan and Hayes, the confirmation proceedings offered Fry his opportunity. In a letter to another of the nominee's critics, which was transmitted to the judiciary committee, Fry related his version of an 1866 conversation with Harlan on the slavery issue. The nominee, he reported, had been "very bitter in his denunciation of the Emancipation Proclamation issued by Mr. Lincoln and . . . remarked that 'he had no more . . . scruples in buying and selling a negro than he had in buying and selling a horse, that the right of property in a negro was identical with that of the property in a horse, and that the liberation of slaves by our general government was a direct violation of the Constitution of the United States.'" He conceded that the views Harlan had expressed that day were "directly opposite to those expressed by him while with me in the army," and thus had "surprised [him] beyond reason." Fry also acknowledged having heard the nominee more recently "give utterance to very opposite sentiments," claiming "to be a thorough Republican on all issues growing out of the Amendments to the Constitution affecting the rights of colored people." He even admitted suspecting that Harlan's influence had gone "very far to defeat me" in his bid to become marshal for Kentucky.[178] Even so, on its face Fry's letter, particularly his charge that Harlan had compared commerce in blacks to trade in livestock, would hardly help the nominee's prospects among radical Reconstructionists.

Fortunately for the nominee, Fry's credibility, not to mention his objectivity, was debatable. In a letter to his cousin regarding the charges, Wellington Harlan scorned both their source ("'Fry who killed Zollicoffer' about as much as I did") and the "ancient history" they contained. From conversations with others, Wellington had concluded that the president's alleged snubbing of Fry, exacerbated by the goading of Harlan and Hayes's enemies, was the immediate catalyst for the general's behavior. Wellington doubted the charges would carry much weight. Fry, he claimed, was a "fool and the greatest liar in the state," who could "be used as a tool by any knave who flatters him a little. . . . He seems to have neither sense nor conscience. I said long ago that he was the best man to his enemies and the worst one to his friends in the world."[179]

A charge that Harlan and other members of the Louisiana Commission had been involved in a bribery scheme to bring about the collapse of the Packard government proved equally suspect. In a letter to Senator Edmunds, one W. H. Painter asserted that some $40,000 raised by the friends of Governor Nicholls had been used, with the commissioners' knowledge, to buy the support of Packard legislators for the Nicholls regime. Painter claimed that H. V. Boynton knew the facts and urged Edmunds to investigate "the venality at New Orleans" and thus make "some little effort . . . to save the Supreme Court from passing into the hands of the late enemies of the gov't and their allies."[180]

Senator Edmunds approached Boynton regarding Painter's letter and similar charges. In his statement to the committee, however, the correspondent quoted Harlan as saying only that some money could have been raised to pay the back salaries of government employees and get the Nicholls government "on its feet. . . . Nothing was ever said by Harlan," added Boynton, somewhat testily, "in reference to the use of money to break up the Packard Legislature—nothing whatever."[181]

The allegations of the nominee's critics were substantially offset by the praise of supporters. Lincoln's attorney general, James Speed, for example, telegraphed the judiciary committee's chairman that Harlan "never was a Democrat," and that he had "been for eight or ten years and is now a true Republican, a hard worker for and in full fellowship with the party; he is qualified and faithful and ought to be confirmed."[182] "It is due to Gen'l Harlan," asserted Speed in a later letter, "to say that eight or ten years ago, he sloughed his old pro-slavery skin and has since then been an earnest, open and able advocate of what he had [formerly] thought wrong or inexpedient." Even before Harlan became anti-slavery, Speed added, "the idea that ruled his course was the integrity of the country. For that he was ready to sacrifice everything."[183]

Nor was James Speed alone. Bluford Wilson sent a telegram to Senator Davis, assuring the former justice that "friends" in Louisville and Illinois, "without a single exception in my knowledge earnestly desire to see Gen'l Harlan's appointment promptly confirmed as one every way fit and worthy."[184] Bland Ballard praised his friend as "a good lawyer" with a "fine capacity."[185] And an 1872 letter from Senator Oliver Morton to Harlan, praising the Kentuckian's efforts in behalf of Indiana Republicans,[186] also somehow made it into the confirmation records, even though Morton, it will be recalled, had opposed President Hayes's plan to make the future justice attorney general.

A number of Harlan's friends also made frequent trips to Washington in Harlan's behalf; some remained there throughout the confirmation process. Gus Willson would later recall to the justice's son, Richard, that he "was in Washington for your father during the several months Senator Edmunds held up the nomination and was useful."[187] John W. Finnell was frequently encamped at Washington's Willard Hotel, writing the nominee on one occasion, "I think now, I will stay and see it out, though I am getting very tired."[188] And other friends proved equally dedicated.

In a more indirect lobbying effort, the *Louisville Commercial* published a lengthy article, entitled "General Harlan's Republicanism," which presented the nominee's checkered political record and conversion to the Republican Party in a highly favorable light.[189] Copies of the piece were widely circulated, and one was included in the Senate records.

Harlan's battle, however, was not waged through surrogates alone. Kentucky's James Beck and other Senate Democrats seemed generally supportive of the nomination, lending weight to the charge, as one critic put it, that Harlan had struck a deal with "the Democrats or they would not be so anxious to have him confirmed."[190] At Beck's request, Harlan wrote a lengthy letter outlining, with considerable candor for such a document, his political career. In it, he forcefully challenged, among other assertions, allegations that emancipation rather than his father's death had prompted his resignation from the army and that his professed support for Republicanism, the war amendments, and Reconstruction was a calculated exercise in expediency rather than a reflection of principle. He branded as "utterly false," moreover, the charge that, as a Louisiana commissioner, he had "offered pay and mileage to members of the Packard Legislature to induce them to gain the Nichols [sic] Legislature. . . . The record of the Commission and of each individual member of it, is clean and clear of all impropriety," he declared. "[N]othing was said, done or written by the Commission or by any member of it which all the world might not know, and which all the world may know so far as I am concerned. Any imputation of improper methods to the Commission or to any member of it . . . is unjust, and without the slightest foundation upon which to rest."[191]

Harlan's partisans regularly assured him that, as one put it, there was "no doubt about confirmation."[192] Within two weeks of the submission of his name to the Senate, however, he became frustrated at the continuing delay in the completion of the process. On October 31, the same day that he wrote Senator Beck, he speculated in a letter to the president that his participation on the Louisiana Commission, not doubts about his Republicanism, represented the principal obstacle to his confirmation and that he was dispatching Eli Murray to Washington to "take such steps as he

John Marshall Harlan I (1833–1911).
(Courtesy Edith Harlan Powell.)

(left) Justice Harlan's mother, Eliza Shannon Davenport Harlan (1805–1870). (Courtesy Kentucky Historical Society.) *(right)* Justice Harlan's father, James Harlan (1800–1863), was a member of Congress and prominent figure in Kentucky politics. (Courtesy Kentucky Historical Society.)

The "Old Stone House," the Harlan ancestral home near Danville, Kentucky, where Justice Harlan was born on June 1, 1833. (Courtesy John Marshall Harlan Papers, Library of Congress.)

(left) A photograph of Harlan taken in 1856. In physical appearance, the Harlan men and women fell generally into one of two groups, the "Big Reds" and "Little Blacks." There was never any doubt into which group the strapping Harlan fell. (Courtesy Edith Harlan Powell.) *(right)* A rare youthful photograph of Malvina French Shanklin Harlan (1839–1916), whom Harlan married on December 23, 1856. By all accounts, it was a strong, happy union. (Courtesy John Marshall Harlan Papers, Library of Congress.)

Robert Harlan (1818–1897), Harlan's mulatto half-brother. While John Harlan apparently never formally acknowledged their relationship, he and Robert maintained regular contact. On one occasion, Robert Harlan intervened in behalf of a white Harlan relation jailed for assaulting a prominent Washington, D.C., black. Unfortunately, no photographs survive of Harlan's other siblings. (Courtesy Roberta Harlan Nabrit.)

As a Union army officer during the Civil War, the usually clean-shavened Harlan sported an impressive beard. When Harlan arrested an elderly Presbyterian minister who had prayed for a Confederate victory from the pulpit of his Florence, Alabama, church a beautiful young belle scornfully reproached the "red-whiskered Yankee." (Courtesy Edith Harlan Powell.)

Benjamin Helm Bristow (1832–1896). The controversial Republican politician was Harlan's closest political ally until mutual ambitions for a Supreme Court seat led to a permanent break in relations. (Courtesy Kentucky Historical Society.)

Harlan in 1877, at the time of his appointment as an associate justice of the Supreme Court. (Photograph by Handy Studios/Collection of the Supreme Court of the United States.)

The Supreme Court in 1882, the year before Harlan's dissent in the *Civil Rights Cases*. Seated left to right, Horace Gray, Samuel F. Miller, Chief Justice Morrison R. Waite, Stephen J. Field, and Harlan; standing left to right, William B. Woods, Joseph P. Bradley, Thomas S. Matthews, and Samuel Blatchford. (Photograph by George Prince/Collection of the Supreme Court of the United States.)

The Supreme Court in 1894, a year and two years, respectively, before Harlan's dissents in the *Income Tax Cases* and *Plessy* v. *Ferguson*. Seated left to right, Gray, Field, Chief Justice Melville W. Fuller, Harlan, and David J. Brewer; standing left to right, Howell E. Jackson, Henry B. Brown, George Shiras, and Edward D. White. (Photograph by C. M. Bell/Collection of the Supreme Court of the United States.)

In 1908, Justice Harlan made a nostalgic visit to Kentucky and Transylvania University, his law school alma mater. Pictured at his right is Augustus E. Willson, then Kentucky's governor. Willson began law practice with Harlan and remained one of the Justice's closest friends and confidants. (Courtesy John Marshall Harlan Papers, Library of Congress.)

(facing page) The Supreme Court in 1911, the year of Harlan's death. Seated left to right, Oliver Wendell Holmes, Harlan, Chief Justice White, Joseph McKenna, and William Rufus Day; standing left to right, Willis Van Devanter, Horace H. Lurton, Charles Evans Hughes, and Joseph R. Lamar. President William Howard Taft's selection of White over Harlan as Chief Justice was a bitter disappointment to the aging jurist. (Photograph by Clinedinst/ Collection of the Supreme Court of the United States.)

Harlan spent most of the last summers of his life at the family's Murray Bay, Quebec, house, honing his skills as "the golfer," which his brethren quickly dubbed him in private correspondence. Painting by Roger Alden Derby, husband of the Justice's eldest grandchild Elizabeth, from a photograph. (Courtesy Roger A. Derby, Jr.)

A Harlan family photograph made at Murray Bay around the turn of the century. Standing left to right are the Harlans's son James and his wife Maude, son Richard, the Justice, and Elizabeth and John Maynard Harlan, the parents of the second Justice Harlan. Justice Harlan's wife Malvina is seated in the second row in front of the Justice, and Richard Harlan's wife Margaret is seated in front of Richard. At the end of the second row on the right is one of the Harlans's three daughters, Ruth. Family members were unable to identify others in the photograph. (Courtesy Edith Harlan Powell.)

may deem proper for the protection of my good name."[193] Harlan also shared his growing consternation with others, prompting several to caution him against any reaction to the delay that might damage his cause. In one letter, for example, Stewart L. Woodford, who had nominated Roscoe Conkling at Cincinnati but supported Harlan's appointment, advised the nominee to "not let your warm nature and keen sense of the wrong done you by delay betray you into any hasty word or impatient act."[194] And his fellow Louisiana commissioner, Wayne MacVeagh, concluded that he was "borrowing trouble and that the delay [was] only owing to the general ill feeling which seems to prevail in the Senate."[195]

MacVeagh ultimately had cause for his optimism. On November 21, 1877, Missouri Democratic congressman and close Harlan friend, Thomas L. Crittenden, assured the nominee, "There is a fight against you, but you can't be beat. Keep quiet and. . . . I believe the case will be taken from the Committee if necessary, but hope it will not be necessary."[196] Four days later, the *New York Times* reported that the judiciary committee, with one member absent, was equally divided on Harlan's fate, three Republicans opposing, and three Democrats favoring, his confirmation.[197] But the reported absence turned out to be an error in Harlan's favor,[198] and Senator Beck soon confided to Harlan, "I know, don't ask how, that you are to be reported favorably."[199] He was confirmed, albeit without a recorded vote, and on November 29, a jubilant Gus Willson sent his law partner the following telegram: "Senator McCreary informs me at half past four o'clock that Senate has just confirmed you as Associate Justice of the Supreme Court."[200] At about the same time, Beck and Senator Daniel W. Voorhees wired him that the "confirmation was unanimous."[201]

Years later, Mallie Harlan would recall the occasion vividly, if not entirely accurately. By that point, the Harlans had five children. Edith, Richard, and James now had three younger siblings: John Maynard, Laura Cleveland, and Ruth, born in 1864, 1871, and 1874, respectively. Following Thanksgiving services at Louisville's College Street Presbyterian Church and lunch at home, Harlan's sons persuaded their father to join them in a game of football on the outskirts of the city. Mallie Harlan recalled,

> With great glee they afterwards described to me the way in which their father had played "full-back" on their side, and how everyone had "stood from under" when he advanced, with great deliberation and dignity, to kick away the ball whenever it threatened their goal.
>
> When my *four* "Boys" (for my husband was always a boy with his three sons) returned, late that afternoon, to our Broadway home—tired and happy, and hungry for their Thanksgiving Dinner—a telegram was waiting for him, informing him that on that very morning "the Senate had confirmed his nomination as an Associate Justice of the Supreme Court of the United States."
>
> The head-line in one of the Cincinnati papers of the next morning ("Harlan's Thanksgiving") was an accurate description of the mingled happiness and pride with which we sat down to our family dinner that night.[202]

Harlan was not yet able, however, to savor fully the taste of victory. Following the affirmative Senate vote of November 29 on Harlan's nomination and 17 other presidential appointments, the tenacious Roscoe Conkling, citing the absence of several key senators, immediately moved to reconsider the vote at a later date. Conkling's motion naturally caused Harlan further grief and confusion. But the letter of a friend, dated Monday, December 3, provided welcome news. "No action having been taken on the motion to reconsider, before the Senate adjourned at noon today," the friend assured him, "you stand confirmed under the Rules. . . . [N]otice of your confirmation has been sent to the President for a Commission to issue."[203] By now, Harlan's competitors had accepted the inevitable. On December 4, Samuel Breckinridge wrote a relative that "Harlan seems to be in at last"—the result, he added, of a "shuffle of the cards."[204]

In early January, H. V. Boynton would write Benjamin Bristow that he was "losing . . . hope that we can be in hearty accord with the present Administration," but assured his friend that President Hayes's secretary, W. K. Rogers, would "never see Harlan again . . . without recalling the disgraceful history I gave him."[205] At Boynton's urging and Hayes's invitation, Bristow had a meeting with the president, but to no avail.[206] Shortly thereafter, Bristow left Louisville for New York, where he established a thriving practice and, in 1879, became the second president of the American Bar Association. Prior to his death in 1896, Bristow would argue many cases before the Supreme Court. But he and Harlan were apparently never again to have any personal contact.

For his part, Harlan moved speedily to assume his place on the Court. On December 3, the day the Senate adjourned and his confirmation became final, he wired Chief Justice Waite that he planned to leave for Washington the following Saturday evening.[207] By Thursday, December 6, he had apparently advanced his date of departure; for that day he declined an invitation to join Bland Ballard and other old friends for a dinner in his honor, explaining that he was scheduled to leave for Washington in a few hours.[208] In succeeding days, he severed relations with his clients. His brother James, he informed one, planned to resign his position as vice-chancellor of Louisville's chancery court in several days to establish a partnership with Gus Willson. "My brother's standing at the bar," he generously added, "is such that I can say, without being considered partial in my judgment that his aid will be of more consequence . . . than any I have been able to render."[209]

On Monday, December 10, Lucy Hayes, the president's wife, called for Mrs. Harlan in her carriage for a short ride to the capitol.[210] There, between eleven o'-clock and noon, the Court's newest justice met his brethren in their robing room, where Chief Justice Waite administered his colleague the oath, known as the "iron-clad," to support country and Constitution, never giving aid to their enemies.

Then the justices filed into the courtroom, with Harlan following in the rear and halting at the clerk's desk. Following the clerk's reading of Harlan's commission, the chief justice announced, "The oath will now be taken"; and Harlan, speaking forcefully, swore to "administer justice without respect to persons and do equal right to the poor and to the rich." For Harlan, those words were to possess a special meaning and, given his checkered background and elements of his future, a certain irony.

Washington

A little over a year after their arrival in Washington—or Washington City as it was more commonly known in those days—the Harlans's son, Jim, offered his Uncle James a frank assessment of the nation's capital. The city, he conceded, did have "its many beautiful buildings, parks, and streets." But it also presented "many eyesores," most notably "wooden shanties stretching out block after block on some of the principle [sic] streets." Nor was young Jim impressed by the officeholders who dominated Washington's streets and sidewalks. "They have, as a rule, a certain rooster-like stride and self-important air, which must be aggravating to those without office."

The sons of senators, congressmen, and cabinet officers were equally arrogant; but Jim was quickly cured of that failing (with which, he assured his uncle, he had not been afflicted "very bad" anyway). A budding stamp collector, Jim had joined a long line at the post office early one morning. "One of the boys told me to tell . . . who I was and they would give *me first* choice. I went to the proper place, knocked on the door and went in. The clerk was a negro (they employ a good many negroes here as clerks). I told him what I wanted and *who* I was . . . he answered; 'you would stand a better chance if you were a boot-black.'" Jim had not opened his stamp book since, nor "ever intimated to anyone that [he] was the son of a Judge of the Supreme Court."[1]

Mallie Harlan's impressions of life in their newly adopted city were decidedly more favorable than her son's. On their arrival in Washington, Mrs. Harlan later recorded in her memoirs, the family took a suite of rooms in a Twelfth Street boarding house—"a well-ordered establishment that for years had been patronized by many well-known Senators and Congressmen with their families." And soon they were caught up in the city's social whirl. By custom, friends had long called on the wives of justices on Monday afternoons, when they were said to be "at home." During the Harlans's first years in Washington, Mrs. Harlan and their eldest daughter, Edith, were ready to receive guests by two o'clock and often entertained 200 to 300 in a single afternoon.[2]

The Harlans not only regularly hosted gay social gatherings; they were also regular guests at the Hayes White House and the homes of cabinet members, justices, diplomats, and other prominent figures.[3] Although a strict disciple of temperance, "Lemonade Lucy" Hayes was an extremely popular hostess and even provided some solace to those of strong thirst. Midway through White House dinners, she served a rum-laced frozen "Roman Punch" (the "Life-Saving Station," imbibers dubbed it) "of which," Mrs. Harlan later wrote, "dear Mrs. Hayes always partook; [prompting] some good-natured comment . . . as to the distinction which she seemed to draw between 'eating' intoxicants and 'drinking' them."[4]

Mrs. Harlan and her affable husband genuinely enjoyed the Washington scene, but only to the extent that it did not interfere with their loyalty to their church. As in Kentucky, the Harlans remained devout Presbyterians. On moving to Washington, they became regular communicants at the New York Avenue Presbyterian Church, where the justice taught a Bible class. Over the years, he also served as vice-moderator at the annual meetings of the Presbyterian general assembly. Not that Harlan always took church policy seriously. When the general assembly adopted a resolution enjoining deacons, elders, and clerics from partaking of tobacco products, he and another delegate promptly adjourned to the rear of the hall and puffed vigorously on cigars—"the solemn act," his cohort later wrote, "of 'vindicating' the Right of Private Judgment."[5] In general, though, religion was for the Harlans an extremely serious matter. When a Kentuckian charged in 1891 that every Supreme Court Justice was "either an atheist or infidel [and] den[ied] the truth of the Christian religion,"[6] Justice Harlan promptly responded that while he might be "mistaken in saying that *all* [his brethren] are communicants," he was entirely accurate in asserting "that all believe the truths that are commonly regarded as fundamental in the Christian religion."[7] And while he once accepted a cabinet member's invitation for Sunday evening dinner, he later declined such offers, explaining to one would-be host, as Mallie later put it, that he had a "standing engagement" for Sunday evening church services.[8]

The Twelfth Street boarding house was not to be the Harlans's permanent dwelling. Early in 1881, they moved into a house at 1623 Massachusetts Avenue. In 1882, financial pressures created by the simultaneous enrollment of their three sons at Princeton required additional economies; and the Harlans left Washington for Rockville, Maryland, 16 miles from the capital, where they found less expensive lodging in the home of a southern gentlewoman. For two years, the justice was a commuter, making the 32-mile round trip six times each week. To help supplement his salary as a justice, moreover, he had by this point begun an immensely satisfying career teaching in the law department of Columbian University, which later became George Washington University. Three days each week, he was obliged to remain in Washington until the mid-evening train in order to teach his law classes.[9]

In 1883, however, the Harlans' sons "engineered," to use their mother's term,[10] arrangements by which they and their father financed the construction of a large, new home at 1401 Euclid Place, near the Columbian campus. Situated at the intersection of Euclid and Fourteenth Street on a hill overlooking the city, the property covered nearly a block and was located near both the Chinese legation and several of Washington's more impressive mansions. Of Queen Anne design, with wide porches, cozy nooks, and a backyard garden, the house soon became a center of what one reporter called "cordial, old-fashioned hospitality."[11] The justice, his wife later wrote, "came to be very fond of the place, greatly enjoying the work of improving it, by planting trees and shrubs from time to time; and I can remember with what great joy, on our return from [trips] . . . , he would always look up at our house on the hill . . . as we neared it, saying, 'Oh, it is *good* to be home again.'"[12]

The Harlan Siblings

At the time of his appointment to the bench, Harlan's youngest daughters, Laura and Ruth, were only six and three, respectively. The four other Harlan siblings were reaching adulthood and were a source of joy and sorrow, pride and disappointment, to their parents. Edith Shanklin Harlan, the eldest, was 20 when the family moved to Washington. A favorite at the White House,[13] Edith often assisted President and Mrs. Hayes with receptions and dinners. On Sunday evenings after church services, the Harlans typically joined the president, his family, and selected friends in the White House's second-floor Green Room for hymn singing. Edith provided piano accompaniment at such gatherings[14] and also taught at the Bethel Industrial School, an institution, apparently, for pauper black children.[15]

In October of 1881, Edith married Frank Linus Child, a wealthy Worcester, Massachusetts, manufacturer;[16] the following August, she presented her husband with a daughter, also named Edith.[17] Before the year's end, however, Edith Shanklin was dead, the victim of typhoid fever. On November 9, Harlan wrote his sons from Chicago, where Edith and her husband had recently moved, that their sister's life "seems to be hanging by a thread."[18] For a time she rallied. But on November 12, the justice sent his son, Richard, two telegrams, first reporting that "[t]he situation [had] changed suddenly for the worse [and] could not be more critical," and later in the day that she had died.[19] "It seems a hard providence, indeed," Wellington Harlan wrote the justice, that "one so happy as she, and so capable of giving happiness to others, should be taken. I can well understand how loth [sic] you are to give up little Edith, representative as she is of so much worth and sweetness."[20]

Edith's death was devastating to her parents. "I find it difficult to realize," the justice wrote one of his sons, "that we are to see Edith no more in this life. The blow was so sudden & unexpected that I can scarcely recognize that she is gone. I do not expect to be able ever to feel that she is away from us. Wherever I go, & whatever I may be doing, her presence will be recognized in its influence upon me. She was to me not simply child, but companion. I am quite sure no character more noble & elevated ever appeared on this earth."[21] Unwilling to be separated from their daughter's only child, the Harlans convinced little Edith's father to permit her to live in Washington with her grandparents. Frank Child would occasionally visit and correspond with his daughter,[22] but little Edith became, in effect, her grandparents' daughter, raised, educated, and presented to society in Washington.

The responsibility for raising Laura, Ruth, and little Edith was daunting, especially for Mrs. Harlan. But the Harlans's sons, who at this point were all students at Princeton, posed challenges as well. Mrs. Harlan corresponded regularly with her sons, taking a deep interest in their education, romances, and problems.[23] But Justice Harlan devoted considerable time to them as well, despite the press of his judicial duties. Richard, the eldest son, earned bachelor's, master's, and divinity degrees at Princeton and was an exemplary student. James and John Maynard would receive baccalaureate degrees there also,[24] but with somewhat greater difficulty and prodding from their father. In one letter to James, the justice urged greater academic diligence, recommended a regimen of reading, and warned that most young college men "*waste* a great deal of time in the expectation that they will have abundant opportunity, after they reach manhood, for study," adding, "The mischief of such a course lies in the inevitable results of postponing present duty."[25] "[A] drone," he wrote on another occasion, "is a mere pretender. Labor, unremitting labor, study, serious, constant study, is essential to great success."[26] In yet another letter, he shared with James his doubts that "either you or John [is] putting forth your best efforts; while you stand well, you should hold a higher rank in your class. What is more important than mere rank in the class is serious, sober, constant work towards the development of the mind. You are now 19 years of age, and there is no time to lose."[27]

Not surprisingly, given their interest in pursuing careers in the law, the justice also urged James and John to participate in debate and even helped them prepare for such events. Mallie's brother, George W. Shanklin, long associated with another brother, John Gilbert, in the editorship of a leading Democratic paper in Indiana, was then living in Washington during an unsuccessful venture as correspondent for the *Cincinnati News.*[28] When James prepared to enter a debate on co-education of the sexes, the justice wrote his son that "Uncle George will write his own views on the side of co-education," while Harlan would send his son "something on the other side," so that James could "have for what they are worth our crude views." The justice also sent James a book on the "Calling of Christian Women," a chapter of which, he wrote, defended "one side of the woman question,"[29] and even enlisted the assistance of the congressional librarian in James's behalf.[30]

Harlan's advice, encouragement, and cajoling were not limited to his sons' purely academic pursuits. He promoted their interest in a legal career, writing James on one occasion, for example, that the law was "next to . . . the ministry, *the* profession in this country. Wherever you settle, social position comes at once from the fact that you are a lawyer, provided your habits are good. It is the gate-way to public life."[31] Next to the law, Harlan favored journalism, but as an owner, not an editor. When James suffered mild depression, his father, in typical, if unrealistic, old-school fashion, recommended, "grit your teeth, and determine that you will not have [the blues]." He also offered a variety of home remedies (brisk towel rubs before sleeping, a glass of "hot . . . not warm" water before every meal) designed to promote general good health.[32] When his sons complained of "annoy[ance] for the want of money," Harlan assured them that he understood their concern, but stressed that "what cannot be helped must be borne," and promised that they would not be required "to abandon college because of [their father's] poverty," adding, "let what may come, I shall take you and John through college . . . [and] find employment for you [in Washington] while you are studying your profession."[33]

Not surprisingly, given his devoutness, Harlan readily offered religious treatises. When James expressed concern about eternal punishment in a letter to his mother, the justice asserted his "certain" belief in the existence of "two distinct places or localities in the next life . . . [one] peopled by those who are 'comforted,' the other by those who are 'tormented.'" Harlan would not "bother [his] brain with . . . subtle inquiries" into the nature of either state. But he hoped that James would "not fall into the habit too common among young collegians of calling into question the fundamental ideas upon which all religion rests." James was in no way obliged to accept traditional religious doctrine "blindly," but he should also be "slow in striking down the old landmarks, or ploughing up the old ways."[34]

If James seemed most concerned about religious and moral questions, his brother, John Maynard, perhaps should have been most fearful of a grim eternity. At Princeton, John excelled in sports and disciplinary infractions, to his father's extreme disappointment. Following readmission after an initial suspension for hazing, John was again expelled for the same infraction. His father was mortified. John's dismissal "for repeated acts of Hazing," the justice wrote James, "causes me very great pain. . . . My faith in his future usefulness is greatly shaken. In the first place he knows my abhorrence of Hazing. . . . Then, he knew that he was violating a rule of the college—one essential to its existence. But I am still more horrified that his own sense of propriety did not restrain him. If a freshman happens to be a weak-spirited fellow, it is mean and cowardly to impose upon him. There is an element of brutality in the spectacle of a crowd of boys making one boy a subject of ridicule and indignity. . . . The spirit out of which Hazing comes is that kind of low brutality which crops out finally in robbery, burglary and murder. I cannot think of hazing without abhorrence of its innate wickedness."[35]

The justice hoped that his son had simply been led on by others, lacking "the nerve to put his foot down and say that he would not join in insulting others or making others the subject of ridicule." Were he to find that John had been the "controlling spirit" behind such acts, he would "despair of his being useful to himself, to his family or to his country." The atmosphere of the elite college itself concerned Harlan. "[M]any things in the college usages of these days," he wrote, "make me doubt whether any body ought ever to go there. The idea that a young man is to merge his sense of right and justice and his manliness in the usages of his class is to my mind very disgraceful. You may rely on it that if you find any boy in your class who is continually and *deliberately* pulling indignities upon others, he is a mean cowardly fellow who will turn pale and cower when confronted by a brave, self-respecting, justice-loving comrade who has the courage to resent personal insult."[36] The entire affair, he concluded, was "a sorry business altogether."[37]

John Maynard expressed remorse at his "thoughtlessness." But his initial dismissal had also been for hazing, and his father had warned him repeatedly about such behavior. The justice thus assumed that his son's banishment from Princeton on this occasion would be lengthy, perhaps permanent.[38] But privilege has its privileges. The incident had occurred early in the fall term of 1881; John returned to campus for the winter term. The Harlans were relieved and pleased. "I am glad," the justice wrote James in February, "that you boys are again together. It will not be many years before your paths in life will separate and your intercourse will then be very limited or only occasional. One may locate in Chicago, one in some other western city while Richard may locate in the East."[39]

The justice was partially correct. Richard, who was valedictorian of his Princeton class, would serve as minister of Presbyterian congregations in Rochester and

New York, then as president of Illinois's Lake Forest College, and finally in an administrative post at George Washington University. James, as noted earlier, read law with Melville Fuller before establishing a Chicago law practice; and following graduate and law study at the University of Berlin and George Washington, as well as a stint as his father's legal secretary, John Maynard moved to Chicago and began law practice there with a series of partners, including his brother.[40]

Justice Harlan was also particularly attentive to two nephews. James Harlan Cleveland, the son of Harlan's sister, Laura, who died in 1870, attended Princeton and the University of Berlin, studied with his uncle at George Washington, and served briefly as an assistant U.S. attorney in Cincinnati before establishing a successful law practice there. Cleveland was a regular visitor in the Harlans's home, and his professional success was a source of satisfaction to them.[41]

The justice's experience with another relative was not so sanguine. Harlan's sister, Sallie, died in 1887 and her husband, David P. Hiter, in 1895. Shortly after David Hiter's death, their daughter, Laura, asked the justice in effect to assume responsibility for the education and career development of her brother, Harlan Hiter. "[Y]ou know," she wrote, "he is just the age, he needs a very strict man."[42]

The justice secured his nephew's admission to Washington and Lee University's law department and provided financial support. But Harlan Hiter proved to be an undistinguished student, and his university tenure was brief. "Your nephew," wrote the justice's friend, Henry St. George Tucker, dean of the law faculty, "is a fine young man, with fine talent, I'm told, but he did not study." Tucker thought that "with some admonition from" Harlan, Hiter's work would improve; and he hoped that the justice would give his nephew another year of study.[43] Near the end of the academic year, however, Washington and Lee's president conveyed to the justice the faculty's wish that Hiter withdraw from the university, "quietly and without any public or announced imputation upon him."[44] By that point, Justice Harlan may have been at the end of his patience with his charge. "No word have I yet received from you," his nephew wrote him in early June, "but I hope you are not dour and disgusted with me."[45] Hiter pressed his uncle for money, but the justice's generosity was apparently exhausted. "Please write me," Hiter pleaded in another letter. "I have only fifteen dollars, and I do not know where I can get any more . . . please send me fifteen dollars to go home."[46]

Politics, Pork, and Patronage

Relatives were not the only ones seeking the justice's assistance during his years on the bench. Within two years of his appointment, Harlan was widely considered to enjoy unusual influence with the Hayes White House. In 1880, for example, Justice Miller wrote his brother-in-law, William Pitt Ballinger, that he was enlisting Harlan's aid in yet another unsuccessful campaign to obtain a federal judgeship for Ballinger. Harlan, Miller explained, "has secured more favors at the hands of the President than any man I know, and . . . is skilled in such matters."[47]

The justice often attempted to minimize his political clout and underscore his distaste for the spoils system. In a letter to Benjamin Harrison detailing his strategic recommendations for the 1888 presidential campaign, for example, he stressed that he had no connection with political management and assured his party's nominee that he wrote only out of love for "my country."[48] As the nation moved toward the beginnings of federal civil service reform, moreover, he wrote his son, James, at Princeton that the country "must take the distribution of offices out of politics and away from congressmen, else our government will become rotten and corrupted by the Spoils System."[49] Kentuckians and others regularly joined Justice Miller, however, in appealing for Harlan's intervention; and the justice readily obliged.

The requests varied in nature and importance. Most involved government posts, from cabinet appointments and federal judgeships to relatively lowly post office positions and assignments as federal storekeepers at liquor warehouses. Others related to government largesse. A Frankfort lawyer expressed dismay at the delay in the allocation by Congress of $100,000 in federal funds for a Kentucky River project, urging Harlan to see the secretary of war "at once . . . and find out what is the matter."[50] An official of Louisville's Third National Bank sought a share of federal deposits there, citing as justification for his request "the facts that more than four-fifths of our stockholders, and all but one of our directors are republicans, and that I am one of the few Louisvillians, who voted for Mr. Lincoln in 1860, almost at the peril of their lives."[51] There is considerable evidence that Harlan acted on such entreaties. In May of 1879, for example, a Treasury Department official promised "favorable action . . . at an early day" on the justice's request that a Covington bank be designated a public depository.[52]

Those seeking Harlan's assistance were as varied as their requests. Many were total strangers. Some were acquaintances, slight and close, whom Harlan had offered to help.[53] He seemed especially solicitous of those with whom he had served in the war and their families, writing the son of one veteran of his "deep interest in the prosperity of the children of my old comrades of the 10th Ky. Infantry," and promising, "Whenever I can serve any of them I will be glad to do so."[54] He understandably put forth his most vigorous efforts in behalf of his closest friends. He was significantly involved, for example, in the nomination and confirmation as governor of Utah of his friend Eli Murray,[55] who, on arriving there, promptly shared with the justice his judgment that the territory's controversial Mormon Church "seems to be a great big money making institution—making slaves of human being[s], in the name of the Lord"; he then asked Harlan to speak with Kentucky Senator Beck and other members of Congress about a raise in his salary and expense allowance!"[56] Nor was Murray the only friend Harlan sponsored. He recommended his fellow Louisiana commissioner, Wayne MacVeagh, for the English mission;[57] and although that campaign was unsuccessful, MacVeagh's appointment as attorney general by President Garfield probably bore the Harlan imprint.

Particularly when his efforts bore fruit, Harlan's beneficiaries were generally grateful. The death of his friend, Bland Ballard, led to a mad scramble for Ballard's judgeship. Press reports indicated that Harlan was taking no part in the process, but this in no way deterred hopefuls, their partisans, and detractors from approaching the justice.[58] Harlan himself recommended to President Hayes, based on his "knowledge of the persons whose names are likely to be presented," that the administration proceed "slowly" in picking a nominee,[59] and later offered to confer with the president "upon the subject."[60] When Hayes sought the justice's impressions of one candidate, John W. Barr, Harlan vigorously defended both his Republicanism ("of the best type")[61] and professional competence.[62] And when Hayes appeared to falter in his support of Barr, Harlan quickly urged him to "adhere to [his] first impressions" and rated Barr, "confidential[ly]" as the "very best appointment for the country, for the Administration and for the Republican party."[63] Harlan's efforts were not lost on Barr. Following his nomination, he wrote the justice that his selection had been "most unexpected," adding, "I must have had kind and partial friends in Washington to whom I shall always be under the deepest obligation."[64]

Harlan's efforts, of course, were not always successful or appreciated. In the summer following his appointment, Theodore B. Tracie, a former editor of the *Louisville Commercial*, wrote the justice a ten-page letter dripping with venom and self-pity. According to Tracie, a mutual friend reported being told by Harlan that he "knew who were [his] friends in Louisville, and that the strangest thing was Tracie's treatment of [him]." Tracie assured Harlan that he had remained "silent," but clearly had reason "to feel aggrieved" at a "gentleman who had demonstrated to me the existence of the most reprehensible of vices—that of ingratitude." As journalist and political ally, Tracie had "obeyed [Harlan's] slightest wish," promoted his interests, and suppressed unfavorable news dispatches. He had thus assumed that he had a "legitimate" claim on Harlan. But the justice instead subjected him only to "marked indifference," promising to promote him for the post of collector of customs, yet offering only "the place of temporary deputy, at four dollars a day!" Thus "humiliated and embittered," Tracie had "abandoned further efforts, and simply ignored" his ungrateful former friend. He hoped, however, that Harlan would support a friend for a post office position.[65]

Tracie was not alone. A Grant appointee replaced by a Harlan choice as collector of internal revenue in Louisville wrote President Hayes shortly after he left the White House, vehemently complaining of Harlan's "intermeddling with appointments" and questioning, as others had done so often before, his Republicanism.[66] As Benjamin Harrison's 1889 inauguration approached, even Harlan's former law partner, Gus Willson, was briefly annoyed that the justice was not promoting him sufficiently for a place with the new administration. On the understanding that what he wrote was to be treated as "thoroughly" confidential and that he could not "afford to have it understood that I will have anything whatever to do with solicitation for office, except so far as it may be necessary to aid you, and a few close friends," Harlan assured his friend of his efforts in Willson's behalf. That very day, he declared, he had written Harrison to urge his former law partner's selection as U.S. attorney in Kentucky.[67] Fortunately, their friendship was in no way permanently damaged; and Harlan's patronage efforts were generally appreciated rather than suspected.

Partly out of a continuing desire to promote his friends' political ambitions and a genuine interest in the fortunes of his party and "Old Kentucky Home," Harlan assiduously cultivated close relations with Republican presidents and their lieutenants throughout his years on the bench. The justice and his family, as noted previously, enjoyed especially close relations with President and Mrs. Hayes. The president no doubt realized the role Harlan had played in his nomination, and the two embraced similar positions regarding the South as well as other issues of national importance. In fact, when Harlan shared his policy judgments with Hayes shortly after the Cincinnati convention, the new presidential nominee quickly saw that Harlan's "views are mine, through and through."[68]

The Harlans were not only regular social guests at the Hayes White House. Harlan was often included in more intimate—and no doubt politically oriented—gatherings with the president, Carl Schurz, and other prominent members of the administration.[69] He frequently offered both solicited and unsolicited advice regarding patronage matters[70] and substantive political issues. In an 1880 letter, for example, the justice complained that a pending rivers and harbors bill included pork barrel "appropriations for purposes with which the national government can have no rightful concern." He declared, "you would do the country a service, and strengthen your administration, if you will, by a ringing veto, call public attention to the scandalous combination[s] which are made, by such bills, for the purpose of emptying the public treasury."[71]

President Hayes honored his pledge not to seek a second term. But Harlan was on intimate terms with Hayes's successor, James A. Garfield, well before Garfield's nomination and election, both as whist partner[72] and political ally. Both before and after his election, Harlan wrote Garfield lengthy letters on the importance of including Southerners generally, and Kentuckians in particular, in the new cabinet. Beginning in 1868, Harlan declared in one letter, the "managers" of the Republican party had apparently concluded that native white Republicans were "*prima facie*, either unfit for high public station, or . . . not to be trusted." The consequences had been disastrous:

> [O]ffices in the South . . . were very largely filled by mere adventurers, who could not be supplied with position elsewhere and who had no part or lot with the people over whom they were placed. They cared nothing for Republican principles, and were not at all anxious to extend the lines of the party. Instead of commending their party to the people, by every proper means, they engaged, many of them, in jobs and plundering. Such men made Republicanism odious with a very large number who might have been drawn into our ranks. The result was that in many Southern states, the whites were driven out of the [Republican] party, and the people became divided upon the color line.[73]

Garfield could extend "a helping-hand" to southern Republicans, and ultimately to the party nationally, by placing more of them into the cabinet. Such steps, the justice was certain, would go far to break the Democrats' hold on the "Solid South."

The justice and Garfield maintained a close association. It was thus not surprising that Harlan provided Chief Justice Waite reports from the White House on the president's condition in the weeks between Garfield's shooting by a disappointed office-seeker and his death on September 19, 1881.[74]

Harlan enjoyed similar relations with later Republican presidents and also continued to push for greater southern representation in their cabinets. When, for example, President-elect Harrison sought his impressions regarding the leading Republicans of the South, the justice readily obliged, providing Harrison on Christmas Day, 1888, with a letter more than 15 pages in length on the subject.[75] While his prowess in securing patronage probably dimmed with the years, he remained one of the more politically influential justices in presidential circles.

The Brethren

The center of Harlan's life in Washington was necessarily the Court itself. Long relegated to cramped, poorly ventilated quarters in the basement of the Capitol, the justices had moved in 1860 into the Senate's original chamber when Congress' upper house took over one of the wings added to the Capitol the previous year. The Court occupied those accommodations throughout Harlan's tenure. They were spacious, consisting not only of the new courtroom but 12 other rooms as well, including the old courtroom, which was converted into a library. Even so, the justices enjoyed no private offices; instead, they established libraries or studies at home, funded through a modest congressional appropriation.[76]

Situated at the top of a spiral stairway in his Euclid Avenue home, Harlan's impressive study was finished in antique oak and lined with bookcases. On its walls were the portraits of prominent figures in Kentucky judicial history, including the justice's mentors, Thomas Marshall and George Robertson. Dominating the room were two large work tables, one for reading and writing, the other for revising and preserving completed opinions and related work. Over the years, Harlan often worked in his study until late at night, drafting and refining opinions. Typically for one or two hours each morning, he conferred there with his secretary before leaving for the Court. Although he generally took the trolley to the Capitol, he often walked, even the three-mile trek from Euclid Place to the Court.[77] On at least one occasion when the Fourteenth Street trolley cars were down, he rode home in an open grocery wagon, an experience that brought on severe chills and cost him a day at Court ("My wife says I must keep in my room all day, and I will obey her," he wrote Chief Justice Fuller), but did not prevent him from sending the brethren by messenger his impressions of several cases.[78]

When Harlan first joined the Court, he quickly realized that the date by which he had originally planned to settle his affairs in Louisville would be impossible to honor "without serious pecuniary loss," and so wrote Chief Justice Waite.[79] But Harlan had participated in several cases in the week following his December 10 swearing-in—the first was *United States* v. *Fox*,[80] heard on December 17, 1877— and by late January, 1878, he was fully immersed in the Court's work. He wrote his first opinion for the Court, announced on January 21, in an obscure case involving the liability of an insurance company under a fire policy.[81] But his first dissenting opinion, delivered on February 25, involved the sort of issue on which his judicial reputation was to be forged—the meaning of a statute forbidding the exclusion of witnesses from judicial proceedings on account of race—although the decision in the case was based on a more narrow question.[82] During the 33 years, ten months, and three days he was to serve, Harlan would establish a formidable record, participating, by one count, in 16,826 cases and registering 850 opinions for the Court, 27 concurrences, 127 dissenting opinions, and 160 dissents without opinion.[83]

When Harlan first went on the Court, he no doubt shared misgivings common to many novice justices regarding his fitness for the position. In an early note to Chief

Justice Waite, he suggested that "one of the older members of the Court" be assigned the opinion in one case, "in view of the importance of the questions [it] involved."[84] On another occasion, he suggested that assignment of a case to him rather than a more seasoned colleague be contingent on whether a dissent were filed in the case.[85] With the passing of years, as the certitude and force of his opinions would suggest, he gained confidence in both his skill as a jurist and the legal positions he embraced. In fact, there is some evidence that he was reluctant to write opinions for the Court that did not entirely square with his personal views, even though such opinions are obviously considered collegial efforts rather than the products of their named authors alone. In a note to Chief Justice Fuller, for example, Harlan indicated that he preferred not to write for the Court in a case Fuller had assigned him. "I would say some things about a part of the case," he explained, "that would not be acceptable to the majority. If I did not say what I would like to say, it would be taken, by implication at least, that I believed some things that I do not believe."[86]

It seems equally probable, however, that Harlan was plagued with self-doubt throughout his career, despite the confidence his opinions exuded and that he to a considerable degree undoubtedly possessed. While his sons were at Princeton, he applauded the "great care" evident in a letter James had written his mother, and, in a display of father–son candor remarkable for the period in which he wrote, unburdened himself of his frustrations at his own perceived shortcomings:

> My whole life has been characterized by too much hurry, and too little method and order in business. The best rule is to do *well* everything that is to be done. If a letter is to be written let it be prepared with the utmost care and neatness. . . . My opinions are often re-written several [times]. It is because my habit is not to prepare, at the beginning, with care. In other words I am the victim of a bad habit. We are all bundles of habits. It would have been worth a good deal to me had I started in life with the determination to put in the neatest possible shape everything that I was required to write.[87]

While such spontaneity may have contributed significantly to the moral fervor and power that earmarked Harlan's opinions, the unorthodox constitutional philosophy they reflected may have convinced many of his brethren that they were the product of a hurried, careless approach in substance as well as form. In general, however, the justice enjoyed his colleagues' affection and, albeit less commonly, their respect. Chief Justice Waite, it will be recalled, had opposed Harlan's appointment to the bench. But the two apparently developed a cordial relationship during their decade together on the Court. When during the Court's 1883 summer recess the newspapers reported that the chief justice had been thrown from his horse and severely injured, Harlan was immediately solicitous, writing Mrs. Waite to inquire of her husband's "exact condition."[88] On learning of Waite's recovery, he offered expressions of relief and a note of caution. "The older I get," he wrote, "the better satisfied I am that . . . violent modes of exercise are not of real service to men leading sedentary lives, who have passed middle life."[89]

Harlan enjoyed the close friendship of other justices as well. His nephew, Harlan Cleveland, married a daughter of Stanley Matthews, an associate justice 1881–1889. Harlan and Matthews enjoyed a pleasant association; and Harlan's funeral eulogy for his colleague touched their mutual friend, ex-President Hayes.[90] The justice also maintained relations with former members of the Court, including those with whom he had not served. In 1881, for example, he exchanged correspondence with John Archibald Campbell, the Alabamian who served on the Court 1853–1861, about what the two perceived to be efficiency problems confronting their institution.[91]

Of all the justices with whom Harlan served, however, he probably enjoyed the warmest relationship with Chief Justice Waite's successor, Melville Weston Fuller, who became chief justice in 1888. As noted earlier, Fuller, like Waite, had opposed Harlan's appointment—in fact, had scorned it as little more than President Hayes's pay-off to a Louisiana commissioner. But Harlan's son, James, had read law with Fuller, accompanied him to Washington as his secretary during the early weeks of Fuller's tenure as chief justice, and became a founding member of Gregory, Booth, and Harlan, the Chicago firm that took over Fuller's lucrative practice following his elevation to the supreme bench and that served as Fuller's headquarters during summer visits to the city.[92]

Even more important, perhaps, to their judicial relationship was the interest Harlan had shown in Fuller's elevation to the Court's center seat. Prior to Fuller's nomination, Harlan visited President Cleveland and praised the Chicagoan's standing as a lawyer. He also warned Fuller, who regularly argued cases before the Supreme Court, against visiting Washington in connection with a pending suit, suggesting that the public might misinterpret his presence there as evidence that he was actively seeking the judgeship.[93] When Fuller's nomination was announced, Harlan promptly telegraphed his congratulations, polled a number of senators on Fuller's chances for confirmation, predicted opposition only from the partisans of other aspirants, and exclaimed, "All hail to the Chief!"[94] Then, when Fuller's nomination fell victim to more than two months' delay in the Senate, Harlan lobbied senators in the nominee's behalf, urged Fuller to respond aggressively to charges raised against his confirmation, and proposed strategies for disarming his critics. After opposition newspapers complained, for example, that as a member of the Illinois legislature at the beginning of the Civil War, Fuller—like President Cleveland, a Democrat—had opposed military action against the rebellious states, Harlan urged the nominee to share with the press every statement he had ever made "in support of the Union case," adding: "This is not an occasion for too much dignity. You and your friends should not stand still, and allow you to be put down or hurt by misrepresentation." When the Court adjourned the following week, Harlan promised to "take the matter in hand."[95] He was true to his word.

Not all his associates appreciated Harlan, of course. Oliver Wendell Holmes, Jr., who served with him from his appointment in 1902 until Harlan's death in 1911, was perhaps the most caustic in his assessment of the justice. In one of his letters to Sir Frederick Pollock, Holmes concluded that Harlan, "although a man of real power, did not shine either in analysis or generalization." Ridiculing his by then deceased colleague as "that sage," Holmes compared Harlan's mind to "a powerful vise the jaws of which couldn't be got nearer than two inches of each other."[96] Harlan and Edward Douglass White, who served first as an associate justice (1894–1910), then as the Court's chief (1910–1921), were hardly close either.

Charles Evans Hughes, who served with Harlan, Holmes, and White at the beginning of his 1910–1916 tenure as an associate justice, later recalled,

> I confess that at the outset I found the atmosphere of the Court somewhat less agreeable than I had expected it to be. It was apparent that Justice Harlan and Justice White did not like each other. Justice Harlan was antipathetic to Justice Holmes, and Holmes to Harlan, though each respected the soldierly qualities of the other. When in conference Justice Harlan would express himself rather sharply in answer to what Justice Holmes would say, the latter, always urbane, would refer to Justice Harlan as "my lion-hearted friend."[97]

One day at luncheon, with Hughes present, Harlan and White discussed their first meeting in Louisiana, where Harlan had been sent as a member of the Louisiana Commission and White headed a delegation of Democrats supporting Governor Nicholls's claim to the statehouse. When White completed his version of the state's situation for the commissioners, Harlan had arisen from his seat, approached his future colleague, and declared, "Well, you are damned frank."[98] Some have traced the friction between the two justices to that incident.[99] But their strained relations probably grew out of a combination of political and philosophical differences.

Harlan's personality at times undoubtedly exacerbated his relations with White and other colleagues as well. His opinions were to ring with a certitude and righteous indignation the brethren at times surely resented. He could also be overbearing. Once, the justices decided to cancel a conference when they learned that Chief Justice Fuller would be unable to attend. Apparently peeved at his colleagues' action, Fuller decided that he would also absent himself from the justices' next scheduled conference and so informed Harlan in a caustic note. Harlan agreed that it obviously would be appropriate for the chief justice to miss a conference for reasons of health. "[I]f the condition of your health is such that it is best for you to stay in the house," Harlan advised, "*that* should be given as the reason, and I should be authorized to so state." But the tone of Fuller's note led him to suspect that Fuller was simply irritated, and he promptly scolded his friend. "It is not like you," he wrote Fuller, "to arraign your brethren for what they had the right to do. You must have had a pain in your back when you wrote that note. The thing is not worth a moment's thought, except to see to it that matters do not go on a wrong basis."[100]

In general, however, Harlan's personal qualities were more likely to enhance than impair his relations with other justices. He seemed unable to develop the bitter resentments that at times afflicted members of the Court in their interpersonal relations. When early in his tenure, for example, Gus Willson reported that Justice Miller had been critical of Harlan, the justice merely dismissed the matter as "curious in view of our past relations, which have been very pleasant."[101] He was also exceptionally solicitous of his colleagues, keeping them posted about developments in Washington when they were out of the city, writing them regularly during summer recesses with news of his activities and those of colleagues, sympathizing with their misfortunes, and boosting their egos.[102] On one occasion, for example, he wrote Justice Joseph P. Bradley, "I greatly rely upon you, while you are on the Bench (and I hope your departure from it is far in the future) to keep me *straight*."[103]

At times, Harlan would go out of his way to assist a colleague, even when the two were on opposite sides of a case. When, for example, J. C. Bancroft Davis, the Court's increasingly eccentric reporter of decisions (1883–1902), botched the head-notes for an opinion from which Harlan had dissented, the justice wrote Chief Justice Fuller, the majority's spokesman, that the headnotes were "awful and are enough to make you and not me sick," but assured the chief justice that "[t]here [was] time to correct them."[104] Had Fuller contacted the publisher directly, as Harlan suggested, the errors could indeed have been corrected. But perhaps out of regard for the Court's reporter, a Fuller relation, the chief justice attempted instead to work through Davis; and the revisions were never made.[105]

Even Harlan's jabs at his brethren seemed relatively mild. He characterized many of Justice Holmes's constitutional views as "unsound" and his opinions cluttered with "obscure phrases."[106] And he gently mocked Justice Field's ardent defense of economic privilege as a noble quest for "eternal principles of right and justice."[107] But he was generally too much the Kentucky gentleman to stoop to stinging personal harangues or withering sarcasm.[108]

Whatever his relations with his brethren, Harlan became a popular Washington figure, widely sought after as an after-dinner speaker[109] and a frequent guest, as noted earlier, at White House, diplomatic, and related official functions, as well as more intimate gatherings of Washington elites. A great storyteller, he became a favorite with reporters. Late in the justice's career, the journalist Louis Brownlow was covering Washington for Louisville papers. Brownlow was in Court one day when Harlan summarized an "extraordinarily legalistic and technical" opinion in a case of interest to the reporter's editors. In a note passed up to the justice, Brownlow explained that he was to telegraph a dispatch on the case to Louisville and lacked sufficient legal knowledge even to know which side had won.

Harlan was willing to assist Brownlow if the journalist could be of assistance to him. "You came to court forgetting your legal lore," read a note penned to Brownlow. "I came to court forgetting my chewing tobacco. If you will go down to Engle's at New Jersey Avenue and C Street, N.W., and buy me a ten-cent cut of Graveley's Natural Leaf chewing tobacco, I will endeavor to have your dispatch written by the time you get back. J.M.H."

Brownlow promptly obliged, and the justice did, too. When a page handed Harlan the prized package of tobacco, the justice gave the page several sheets of paper—a readable account of the case Brownlow had found so confusing. "All I had to do," the journalist later recalled, "was take it out, rush down the hall to the Western Union desk, and file the dispatch. I didn't even read it."[110]

Nor was that the journalist's only experience with Harlan. When a Tennessee sheriff refused to serve writs issued by a master appointed by the Supreme Court to investigate a suit brought by Georgia against Tennessee, an assistant clerk of the Court jokingly suggested that Brownlow, then a correspondent for a Chattanooga paper, be taken "hostage." Harlan told the journalist that the brethren were considering his case but were uncertain "whether to have you hanged, drawn and quartered, or merely boiled in oil." Later, when Brownlow encountered Harlan and Justice White leaving the capitol, Harlan announced the Court's "decision." "[W]e will punish you as was the Duke of Clarence, who, you will recall, was drowned in a butt of malmsey. Malmsey is hard to come by here in sufficient quantity; but, if you will come along, my Brother White and I will drown you in a butt of bourbon." The three then repaired to the Mades' Hotel, where the sentence was "duly executed."[111]

Harlan was popular with the Washington legal establishment. For years he was to be "the regular and favorite guest" of the District of Columbia bar association at its annual Shad Bake River Excursion to Marshall Hall, along the Potomac River. "From the time when he got on the steamer at the Seventh Street wharf," by one account, "until he said good-bye on his return he was always the center of interest and admiration. He entered with youthful zest into the enjoyment of the day, told stories and exchanged repartee, took part in the athletic sports, especially baseball, shot at the mark in the shooting gallery, bowled in the bowling alley, ate the planked shad dinner with obvious pleasure, led in the singing of the college songs, and generally was the jolliest and apparently the youngest member of the party." An expert marksman, he regularly hit the bull's eye at the shooting gallery; and while his competitors sought to select the most accurate rifles and finely adjust the sight on the one selected, "Judge Harlan took any rifle that was handed him, . . . took a careless squint through the sights, promptly fired and rang the bell." Typically on the trip to and from Marshall Hall, he regaled listeners with stories of the Civil War and his early days. His father, he reported on one such occasion, detested tobacco and said that no gentleman would use it in any way. Harlan never thought of using it himself until his schoolmaster caught an anemic youth with tobacco in his mouth and "rated him soundly" about its evils. Then, however, the teacher had turned to young Harlan. "Now if you were as strong and tough as John Harlan, you might chew with impunity, but as it is you are preparing for an early grave." With what he assumed was his schoolmaster's blessings, Harlan told his gleeful audience, he had begun chewing tobacco that very day and never stopped.

But Harlan was generally well-liked not merely by Washington political elites and the bar. Not surprisingly given his frontier background, he never lost the common touch. He was a familiar sight walking to and from Court or riding the streetcars, chatting with the conductor and other passengers and occasionally munching on a sandwich or pie. While researching an intended biography of his father in the 1930s, the justice's son, Richard, sought affecting anecdotes from a variety of sources. The response was impressive. One writer recalled the day he and his wife were riding a Connecticut Avenue streetcar, sitting opposite Harlan and Justice Joseph McKenna, a member of the Court, 1898–1925. "Suddenly, Mr. Justice Harlan drew from his pocket a knife, cut out a generous quarter [of an apple] which he offered to Mr. Justice McKenna on the end of the knife blade." The reserved McKenna "accepted the proferred fruit dutifully but reluctantly." The writer had "never . . . forgotten the incident which, though trivial, was entirely typical of the Democracy of an outstanding American to say nothing of the Democracy of the American Commonwealth."[112]

A student of the justice's at George Washington University was impressed with Harlan's willingness to admit to "a class of greenhorns" that he was unable to answer a question raised by one of his students, but "would look into the subject and reply definitely at the next session." The same student found the justice's sense of humor "always entertaining"—especially his habit of outlining one of his dissenting opinions, pausing meaningfully, then noting, "But of course I was wrong." Nor had the student forgotten the refreshing "simplicity" of the justice's character. Harlan once remarked, the student reported, "that he liked to stand on the outside platform of the streetcar on his way home from court, as he never found a streetcar conductor from whom he could not gain some information."[113]

Others shared stories about the justice with John Maynard Harlan. One Samuel Hill wrote that on hearing his name called when he made his first appearance at the Court, Justice Harlan invited him behind the "high-backed chairs." Vigorously shaking the young man's hand and recalling the old saying, "What in the Sam Hill!" the justice had laughingly remarked, "I always wondered if there was a real Sam Hill and I wanted to meet him." "Just fancy," declared Hill, "how that kindness made a young attorney feel. . . . [T]he respect I had always had for him deepened into an affection from that incident."[114]

A Chicago lawyer recalled the time that the justice had slipped quietly off the bench for a sandwich and drink while Solicitor General Holmes Conrad was arguing a case. On returning to his chair, Harlan interrupted Conrad with a question on a point the solicitor general had covered during his absence. When Conrad expressed displeasure at the justice's inattention, Harlan's face "got very red and he manifestly was irritated." Afterwards, however, he was friendly and cordial, "speaking of Conrad in such a way that it brought him employment in the greatest case" he was ever to litigate. Such, asserted the writer, was the justice's "greatness of character."[115]

Riding Circuit

Given the controversies surrounding his appointment, one might assume that Harlan could not have enjoyed the same popularity in the circuit to which he was assigned as he apparently did in Washington. Traditionally justices periodically sat on one of the circuit courts that, along with the district courts, served as lower tribunals in the federal judiciary. Harlan was assigned to the seventh circuit, comprising Illinois, Indiana, and Wisconsin, which had lost representation on the Supreme Court when Justice Davis's seat went to Harlan rather than to one of the circuit's residents. The justice was obviously aware of the resentments his Supreme Court appointment had created in the circuit. In fact, shortly after his assignment there he wrote Judge Thomas Drummond, one of the circuit's prime contenders for the seat Harlan had won, that he "frankly" would have preferred assignment to one of the southern circuits and realized that seventh-circuit lawyers would "quite natural[ly]" favor assignment of an older, more experienced justice.[116]

Whether out of prudence or genuine cordiality, the circuit's bench and bar gave Harlan an enthusiastic welcome, including a dinner with leading lawyers and a reception hosted by the Chicago bar association. "Already I am at home and have been captured by the kindness shown on all hands," the grateful justice wrote to Chief Justice Waite shortly after his arrival in Chicago in early June of 1878.[117]

Building on that hopeful beginning, Harlan attempted to cultivate favorable relations with the circuit bar and his fellow judges. Once, for example, when Rutherford Hayes was still president the justice stood by while the local federal judges passed over a candidate Hayes and Harlan supported for appointment as a master to represent the court in certain cases. "Without reference . . . to the question of power," Harlan later explained to the president, "I reached the conclusion . . . that I would leave to them to determine how many additional Masters were needed, and that unless I knew of objections to the person or persons they might designate, I would approve any appointment they concurred in making. This course I deemed proper in view of the fact that I passed very little time in the District and that it was important there should be entire harmony between the Court and District Judges and the Masters in Chancery."[118]

But Harlan's misgivings about his circuit assignment persisted; in 1880, on the occasion of W. B. Woods's appointment to the Supreme Court and a potential reshuffling of assignments, he apparently considered seeking a different circuit. In December of that year, his brother, James, wrote him two letters urging him to "[b]y all means stick to your present Circuit. Independent of the fact of Chicago being the place above all others for the advantages it will afford to the boys [Harlan's sons]," he declared in the first, "it is a field where more reputation is to be gained. Chicago is one of the Centers of the world, and a Chicago reputation is for a wider scope."[119] The justice's Chicago connections would be especially advantageous, James added in the second letter, should his brother leave the bench and return to private practice. "For some years to come you would have no one to fear from comparison [in Chicago]." Kentucky's circuit, on the other hand, was "not worth having."[120]

Harlan's sons, as noted earlier, did establish Chicago law practices. The justice's commitment to the circuit deepened, as became evident on Melville Fuller's appointment as Chief Justice in 1888. Since the days of John Marshall, the chief justice had been assigned to the fourth circuit in Richmond. Fuller had family ties as well as extensive real estate holdings in Chicago that he expected would supplement his $10,500 annual salary (a mere $500 more than associate justices received) as chief justice. He made no secret of his desire for the seventh circuit. In fact, before accepting nomination to the Court, he asked Harlan whether he would be willing to give it up.[121]

In a decidedly equivocal reply, Harlan reminded Fuller of the traditional assignment of the chief justice to the fourth circuit and that "my boys are to be at Chicago," while stressing that his present assignment was "agreeable." He assured Fuller, however, that "if your comfort as Chief Justice is to depend *in any degree* upon your having the Chicago Circuit, you shall have no difficulty about it so far as I am concerned."[122]

Harlan's sons were hardly as cooperative. Although only portions of the pertinent correspondence survive, James and John Maynard apparently urged the justice to resist a change. In his responses to their entreaties, Harlan emphasized that while it was "of no consequence . . . judicially" what circuit he had, his personal preference was for the seventh circuit since he wished to "consider your home my home." He was concerned, though, that by remaining in the circuit he might harm rather than benefit their interests. Harlan was to sit on Supreme Court cases in which his sons were counsel, although on none apparently where he cast a deciding vote.[123] But he questioned whether he could properly hear circuit cases which his sons argued and wondered "what effect . . . my refusal to do so" would have on their law practices. "Suppose," he wrote John, "that I do not hear the cases in which you or he are involved as attorneys, do you still think that it is best for me to take the Ill. Circuit?" If they agreed, he would "try to undo what [had] been done, or rather recall my promise to . . . Fuller."[124]

James and John persisted, and their father retained the circuit. Whether Harlan personally pressed his claim with his colleagues is not known. In one letter to John, however, the justice noted that "even if we agree [to give up the circuit], our brethren may insist upon the Chief Justice taking the Va. Circuit. Some of them, I am sure, think that way."[125]

Relatively little is known of Harlan's circuit court routine beyond the caseload he confronted. Justices were expected to visit their circuit at least once a year, but smaller cities in a circuit were given less frequent attention. A Madison, Wisconsin, attorney wrote Harlan shortly after his assignment to the circuit, for example, that Justice Davis had last visited his community two years before.[126] Harlan's correspondence suggests that he was reasonably faithful to his circuit obligations, typically making one or more visits in the spring and summer and at times during the Court's February recess as well. While holding court most regularly in the circuit's major cities of Chicago, Indianapolis, and Milwaukee, he also sat fairly often in Madison and other smaller communities of the circuit. Once his sons were settled in Chicago, he and Mrs. Harlan probably visited often with them during his circuit tours. Early in his tenure, however, he lodged in Room 61 on the third floor of Chicago's federal building and may have had similar arrangements in other cities of the circuit as well.[127] On at least one occasion, he supplemented his income by participating in a relatively lucrative arbitration with which his son, John Maynard, was also connected.[128] And, as elsewhere, he was a popular after-dinner speaker.

On the circuit, as in Washington, the justice was the frequent subject of colorful newspaper copy. One 1887 account described Harlan as "a large, smooth-faced gentleman, bald, with a heavy fringe of auburn hair at the back of his head (a magnificent dome of thought), [who] wears a wide standing collar which is seen in portraits of statesmen of Henry Clay's time." The justice, the same journalist added rather indelicately, "uses plug tobacco and does not allow dignity to interfere with expectoration while on the bench."[129]

Harlan's circuit caseload revolved largely around railroad bankruptcies, patent disputes (which the justice found largely incomprehensible and avoided with a passion, both on the circuit and in Washington), and similar mundane, often highly technical matters. Two cases with which he became involved, however, developed into hotbeds of political controversy. The first concerned one Simeon Coy, an uneducated Indianapolis saloon keeper and bail bondsman who in 1884 became chairman of the county Democratic organization over the protests of party reform elements. Two federal indictments charged Coy with ballot tampering in connection with the November, 1886, elections. The contests of that year included congressional as well as local races, and the indictments did not specify the election Coy was alleged to have obstructed. But the defendant's target was apparently a race for county criminal court judge, rather than the congressional contest. While naturally making no admissions along those lines, Coy argued that the indictments did not specifically claim interference with a federal election and that his case thus lay beyond the jurisdiction of the federal courts.

Sitting on the circuit bench, Justice Harlan rejected Coy's claim and held that the applicable federal statutes encompassed election fraud relating to elections in which federal officers were selected, whether or not the defendant had any intent to interfere with a federal race.[130] The Supreme Court, speaking through Justice

Miller, agreed. Freeing Coy on the basis of the defendant's logic, declared Miller, would be roughly analogous to releasing a culprit in a homicide case who fired into a crowd but killed someone other than his intended victim.[131] Justice Field argued convincingly in a lone dissent, however, that the majority's—and Harlan's—expansive construction of federal law conflicted with earlier precedents, as well as basic principles of federalism.[132] Infuriated Indiana Democrats charged Harlan and company with playing politics.[133]

If the *Coy* case made Democrats suspicious, Harlan's involvement in a later and similar election dispute focusing on Republican culprits convinced them that the justice's partisan leanings were influencing his constructions of federal law. Fearful that his party would fail to carry Indiana in the 1888 elections, Republican National Treasurer W. W. Dudley mailed the infamous "blocks-of-five" circular to the state's Republican leaders. Writing on Republican National Committee stationery, Dudley urged his fellow Republicans to hold enough "floaters" and doubtful voters to give Benjamin Harrison a 10,000-vote plurality and promised that the party national chairman would provide "the assistance necessary" to the task. Local leaders, Dudley instructed, were to "[d]ivide the floaters into blocks of five and put a trusted man with necessary funds in charge of these five and make him responsible that none get away and that all vote our ticket."[134]

An alert Democratic mail agent on the Ohio & Mississippi Railroad, whose suspicions were aroused by the large number of Republican letters that were suddenly being sent to Indiana addresses, opened one, then alerted Democratic leaders, who quickly shared Dudley's "incitement to wholesale bribery," as the historian Allan Nevins termed it,[135] with the press. The Republican treasurer denounced the letter as a forgery, threatened criminal charges against the mail agent, and initiated suits, later dropped, against several of the many newspapers that gave the incident extensive play. Such bluster saved Indiana for the Republicans, but irate Democrats and the party's press organs demanded criminal action against Dudley and culpable Indianians.

Solomon Claypool, a Democrat and assistant U.S. attorney in Indianapolis, was anxious to oblige. On the day of the election, by one account, he discussed the Dudley case with U.S. District Judge William A. Woods, a Republican, in Woods's chambers. The two agreed that Dudley could be prosecuted under Section 5511 of the Revised Statutes, one of the laws Coy was convicted of violating. When the federal grand jury assembled on November 13 to consider charges against Dudley, Judge Woods issued the jurors instructions to the same effect.[136]

Later Woods began to have second thoughts. In a Christmas Day letter to Justice Harlan, he asked whether an offense under Section 5511 "consist[ed]—is it complete—in the mere giving of the counsel or advice, whether acted upon or not, or can the adviser [Dudley's name was never mentioned] be punished only when the act which he advised was committed?" Woods indicated that he was now "strongly inclined to the latter view," but that Solomon Claypool and another assistant U.S. attorney were insisting that "the mere giving of the forbidden counsel or advice, though not acted upon, is a punishable offense."[137]

Initially, Harlan sided with Claypool, concluding that the offense could "become complete, without the counsel or advice being acted on." Even at that point, however, the justice advised Woods not to "allow what I have written to embarrass you." The issue had not been settled by earlier cases, he declared, "and as it involves human liberty, you should, in the trial of any criminal case, give effect to your own views, placing upon others the responsibility of overruling you when they are *required* to act."[138] Later, moreover, Harlan informed his colleague that he had "reluctantly" concluded that Woods's interpretation was correct, adding, "I say, reluctantly, because there ought to be a statute making it an offense against the United States for one person to *advise* another *to do* any act, or to *attempt to do* any act, that would prevent the free exercise of the elective franchise at an election for a Federal officer, *whether such advice is acted on or not.*"[139]

Bolstered by Harlan's concurrence, Judge Woods convened the grand jurors and instructed them that the "mere sending . . . of a letter or document containing advice to bribe a voter, or setting forth a scheme for such bribery, however bold and reprehensible, is not indictable."[140] Dudley was thus not indicted. Two hundred other Republicans were indicted but never convicted.

Indiana Democrats and their press organs were again enraged. The *Indianapolis Sentinel* scorned the "spectacle of a judge deliberately and unblushingly prostituting his office to the service of a notorious scoundrel."[141] A packed meeting of the Hendricks Club, an Indianapolis Democratic group named for Samuel Tilden's 1876 running mate, unanimously adopted a report denouncing "a debauched judiciary and a corrupt, unjust, partisan judge."[142] When Judge Woods defended himself by asserting that Justice Harlan had agreed, albeit reluctantly, with his instructions to the grand jury, the *Sentinel* attacked Harlan, too, for allowing partisanship to affect his judicial duty.[143]

Nor were the *Sentinel* and Hendricks clubbers alone. Solomon Claypool, who had become acting U.S. attorney while the Dudley affair raged and would resign in March in protest against Judge Woods's handling of the case, was so critical of Woods that the judge threatened him with a contempt citation. When Woods shared Harlan's letters with Claypool, moreover, the prosecutor wrote the justice, complaining that they should be opened to the public and that his "treatment *here* ha[d] not been altogether what I had a right to expect."[144]

The entire mess was naturally embarrassing to Republicans generally and particularly to President Harrison, who after all was an Indianapolis attorney. Democrats could understandably suspect the motives of Republican judges whose shifting constructions of federal law seemed to parallel a growing perception of the damage the scandal might cause the party and its new president. The contrast between the narrow reading given the law in the case of Dudley, a Republican, and the broad constructions used to send Coy, a Democrat, to prison was also painfully evident.

It is likely that both Harlan and Woods acted out of sincere conviction rather than partisan leanings. Judge Woods's confidential letters to the justice suggest a man genuinely hurt and indignant that anyone could question his integrity.[145] Woods's vigorous defense of his honor is equally compelling. Over a period of months, he painstakingly compiled and secured publication of all correspondence and other materials connected with the incident, including the letters he and Harlan had exchanged. That collection indicates that Woods's changing stance in the case resulted from an extensive review of legal precedents rather than partisan considerations.[146] In time, apparently he won back the confidence of his fellow citizens. In

October of 1890, he wrote Harlan that the "clamor" against him had "practically ceased," adding: "I have received many individual responses personally and by letter from judges, lawyers, preachers and laymen, which have been in the highest degree gratifying. The essence of their expressions is that they always had confidence but now *they know* I was right and consistent."[147]

Evidence tending to vindicate Justice Harlan seems even more persuasive. First, he had supported Solomon Claypool's selection as acting U.S. attorney even after Claypool's zealous pursuit of Dudley was apparent. In a December 24, 1888, letter, the justice informed Judge Woods that he considered it his "duty" to appoint a Democrat to the post, both because the party then controlled the White House and to avoid any appearance of impropriety:

[I]f I were to appoint a Republican," he asserted, "it would be said at once that my purpose, in so doing, was to suppress investigation as to alleged offenses by Republicans. I must avoid doing anything that will impair or lessen the respect which is due to the Judiciary from all the people. I must appoint some Democrat of acknowledged integrity, who will do justice though the heavens fall; who, in his soul, abhors frauds upon the election franchise, and will conduct the pending investigation entirely with reference to the public interests, and without any regard to the political relations of the persons who may appear to have violated the laws.

He believed that Claypool was "a Democrat [who would] meet these requirements."[148] Nor was Judge Woods the only person with whom Harlan shared such impressions. In January of 1889, Senator George F. Edmunds informed Benjamin Harrison that Harlan considered Claypool "a gentleman of high character, commanding the confidence of everybody."[149]

Even more convincing is a letter Washington attorney W. Hallett Phillips wrote Harlan. The justice had sought Phillips's interpretation of the regulation at issue in the Dudley case. "I do not think," Phillips responded, that "it prescribes a crime except where there is an act done, omitted or attempted by a principal. . . . The words 'counsel and advise' must, as it seems to me, be taken in connection with the other words in the same context, and do not in themselves import a specific crime."[150] Phillips's letter, although undated, is included in the justice's papers with other material relating to the Dudley affair; Harlan's construction of the law largely tracked Phillips's analysis. Had Harlan's reversal of his position on the law's meaning been politically motivated, it is unlikely that he would have sought the opinions of others—viewpoints that might have supported Dudley's indictment.

The Dudley incident probably did little to impair Harlan's standing in the seventh circuit, certainly not among most Republicans. Shortly thereafter, however, a major restructuring of the federal judiciary led to the justice's departure from the circuit. In 1891, Congress created the circuit courts of appeals as an intermediate set of appellate tribunals to review decisions of district judges and, until their dismantling in 1911, the circuit courts. Although the reasons are now unclear, Harlan had grown increasingly ambivalent about his circuit assignment. In 1892, for example, he wrote Chief Justice Fuller that he "preferred *any* circuit in the West or South to the Chicago Circuit," enigmatically adding, "the reasons for which you understand. They are not all personal to the Chicago Circuit. The truth is, I ought at the outset to have acceded to your wishes for the Chicago Circuit."[151] Creation of the appeals courts offered the justice an opportunity for assignment to the new Court of Appeals for the Sixth Circuit, encompassing Kentucky, Michigan, Ohio, and Tennessee—a move Harlan eventually accepted.

Harlan's sixth circuit tenure enabled him to develop closer associations with political and judicial friends, including William Howard Taft, appointed to the circuit by President Harrison in 1892, and Horace Lurton, who followed Taft to the circuit the following year and later joined Harlan on the Supreme Court, courtesy of an appointment by President Taft. On at least one occasion, moreover, Harlan was obliged to put his considerable interpersonal skills to work in attempting to resolve growing complaints against one of the circuit's district judges.

In April of 1900, Judge Lurton wrote Harlan that a "very ugly and ominous state of feeling [had developed] at Cleveland and Toledo against our dear friend Judge [E. S.] Hammond." A Memphis judge assigned to the area to relieve its resident district judge, Hammond had taken over 11 cases, about half involving motions for new trials. Several of those motions had remained on his desk for over two years. He had refused to answer the letters of increasingly frustrated counsel, and litigants were now "clamorous" for relief. Before resigning as the circuit's chief judge to become chairman of the Philippine Commission, Judge Taft had tried to persuade Hammond to act on the motions, but to no avail. Nor had the judge answered three letters Judge Lurton wrote to him. Lurton hoped that Harlan could intervene to spare their friend the "humiliation" of formal disciplinary measures.[152]

Harlan decided to approach Judge Hammond directly via a confidential letter written "in the utmost kindness" and to encourage his colleague to "avoid any pretext for movements or demonstrations" against him. The justice was certain "that no apparently unnecessary delay [had] occurred without some reasonable grounds for it on [Hammond's] part." He well knew, he added, that considerations influencing a judge's actions were "not always known to others." He assured Hammond, moreover, that he "would, so far as in me lies, prevent any movement or demonstration that would wound your feelings." But Harlan also gently warned Hammond that any movement against him "could only work harm to yourself, even though your explanation of the matter were, I doubt not it would be, entirely satisfactory to the public," and urged Hammond to write to him at once.[153] Presumably, the difficulty was settled; Judge Hammond remained on the bench until his death in late 1904.

No case aroused as much enmity against the justice as the Dudley affair provoked, but Harlan was never immune from the slings and arrows of Democratic newspapers. While presiding over the opening session of the Court of Appeals for the Seventh Circuit before his transfer to the sixth circuit, Harlan announced that members of the new court would preside in judicial robes. Earlier, a large delegation of the Chicago bar had petitioned the judges to clothe themselves in the "time-honored garb of judicial authority,"[154] and the second circuit had already adopted the practice; but not everyone was happy with the new rule. While professing no objection to the new arrangement, Judge Gresham could not resist noting the logistical problems it might create, advising Harlan at one point, "I do not think that a gown that would fit you would fit me. There is a difference between a man who

weighs nearly three hundred and one who weighs one hundred and eighty-five."[155]
A Democratic paper was unmerciful in its scorn:

> This will not be the first attempt at flummery in the West, but it will be the first successful venture in that line. The dignity that doth hedge about a judge and the power that he possesses to commit to jail for contempt persons who render themselves personally offensive will make the scheme a success whether the North Americans who live hereabouts and pay taxes like it or not. Any official other than a judge who arrayed himself in a gown would be laughed out of it in thirty minutes.
>
> In the presence of this impending evil THE HERALD, as a true disciple of Thomas Jefferson, wishes to record its solemn protest and to observe that the democratic party will take hold of the federal bench some fine day and reform the nonsense out of it.[156]

Equality

Rutherford Hayes's 1876–1877 election had ended military occupation of the South. Congressional civil rights zeal subsided during the same period, and by the turn of the century a majority of Harlan's brethren had largely completed the dismantling of Reconstruction. In the years following Harlan's elevation to the bench, the Court rejected arguments that racial discrimination, governmental or private, constituted badges of slavery that Congress could ban under its authority to enforce the Thirteenth Amendment.[1] A majority also literally construed congressional power under the Fourteenth Amendment to extend only to state rather than private interferences with equal protection of the laws;[2] the justices generally refused to look beyond the surface of ostensibly race-neutral laws to their discriminatory application.[3] In a number of racial discrimination cases, they concluded that national citizenship embodies a number of inherent privileges, including a registered voter's right to participate in federal elections, which Congress could protect against Klan violence and other private interferences, as well as state action. But the Court upheld only one exercise of such power[4] and emphasized that voter qualifications and registration were largely a state matter. In the *Plessy* case, a majority affirmed the "separate but equal" doctrine and rejected Thirteenth and Fourteenth Amendment challenges to segregation laws.[5]

The Harlans and Race

John Harlan played little part in the development of such precedents. At the time of his appointment in 1877, however, any predictions regarding the judicial record he might forge in discrimination cases would have been highly speculative at best. As a young man, it will be recalled, he had been a candidate and defender of the anti-foreign, anti-Catholic, Know-Nothing agenda. His father once chastised a brutal slave driver, yet also charged that anyone who accused him of being an abolitionist "lies in his throat."[6] John Harlan, according to his wife's memoirs, was present at his father's encounter with the slave driver and was repulsed by his brutality.[7] But as a political candidate during and immediately following the Civil War, he hotly rejected emancipation. If his onetime friend, Speed Fry, is to be believed, as late as 1866 Harlan had sneered that "he had no more scruples in buying and selling a negro than he had in buying and selling a horse."[8] Even after his conversion to Republicanism, he publicly supported segregated schools and opposed the 1875 Civil Rights Act's ban on discrimination in theaters, inns, and other places of public accommodation. Nor was Harlan above the use of crude racial humor on the stump. While campaigning for the Democratic presidential ticket in 1864, it will be remembered, he had regaled at least one audience with the story of "ze little black nigger."[9] As the Republican candidate for governor in 1871, he identified black delegates to the state Democratic convention as "three of the blackest and ugliest darkies in the Commonwealth."[10]

Evidence that Harlan shared certain racial attitudes common to those of the most unreconstructed Southerner is not confined to his stances on public issues or infrequent lapses into racial humor on the stump nor to the period prior to his conversion to Republicanism. Such Harlan intimates as John Finnell and even Benjamin Bristow, as we have seen, apparently were not reluctant to indulge in racial slurs in correspondence with their friend; even after his appointment to the Court, Harlan shared racial jokes with associates. In an 1892 letter to William Howard Taft, for example, the justice told of the black who, on regaining consciousness after being thrown from a mule, spotted the beast calmly feeding on a bag of corn also spilled in the fall, and exclaimed, "That's what's make me *shize* a mule."[11] Even after his conversion to Republicanism, moreover, Harlan continued to harbor doubts about the general integrity of blacks. Recall, for example, that on hearing rumors Kentucky blacks were to be imported into Indiana to vote the Democratic ticket in the 1876 elections, he promptly reported his concerns to an Indianapolis associate, warning that "there are some very unreliable men among that race."[12]

Numerous anecdotes in Mrs. Harlan's memoirs, completed after her husband's death, also suggest that she, and presumably the justice as well, embraced the traditional southern image of blacks as happy, simple folk devoted to the whites they served, as well as other stereotypical impressions. In Washington, she frequently hosted "race elevation" meetings in her home,[13] and she once wrote an unpublished novel on "the distractions of *caste* in America and England."[14] But the cordial relations that apparently existed between the Harlans's slaves and their masters prompted her to reconsider her earlier condemnation of the "peculiar institution"; passages from her memoirs indicate that her feelings toward blacks were not much different from those of her husband's family and friends.

Several portions of Mrs. Harlan's manuscript are particularly revealing. Her accounts of the servants' slavish devotion to their mistresses, while obviously intended as affectionate descriptions of the servant–mistress relationship, smack of condescension, as does her observation that the slaves' "quaint drollery, . . . [which] would have been gross impertinence in a white servant, often surprised and always amused the looker-on." Her stories of the "darkies' fondness for large words," and "excruciatingly funny" misuse of them, were to the same effect.[15]

In a particularly lengthy passage, Mrs. Harlan told of her husband's valiant, life-threatening efforts in the autumn of 1858 to save the young maid of one of his sisters from being burned to death. While she slept, the flame from a candle had ignited her clothes. Hearing her agonized screams, Harlan rushed into the room and found her "a veritable pillar of fire," running about the room "like a wild animal." Seizing her with one hand, Harlan quickly tore off her clothes with the other, severely burning himself in the effort. The girl lived only a few hours, and Harlan's injuries brought him wrenching pain and convulsions. Mallie's account of the incident, the girl's funeral, and "the scars ... both physical and mental" they left with her husband "throughout his life" was no doubt intended to underscore his courage as well as his empathy for the family's servants. In explaining how the girl became hopelessly engulfed in flames, however, Mrs. Harlan noted that she had been "[u]nconscious, at first, of the heat that would have quickly awakened one of another race." At the victim's funeral, a black minister led mourners in singing an improvised hymn whose verses, she added, "[o]n any other occasion ... would have been amusing to a white person."[16]

Mallie's descriptions of one of Justice Harlan's messengers are equally instructive. In Harlan's day, as now, each justice was authorized to have a messenger. Traditionally, these were black and, although formally responsible only for transmitting memoranda and performing other functions relating to the justice's official work, were generally, if not universally, treated as servants, performing personal services for the justices in chambers, at home, and on trips. Harlan was to have three messengers during his years on the Court. James Jackson, who served him for the last dozen years or so of the justice's life, made the strongest, most favorable impression on Harlan and his family. He was, Mrs. Harlan wrote, "not only a most faithful attendant, but served my husband with an affectionate loyalty that endeared him to every member of our family. He was with my husband when he died, and he shared our grief as one who was in a real sense a member of our household."[17]

If Mrs. Harlan's memoirs are any indication, however, the Harlans's feelings for their messenger were every bit as paternalistic as any kindly master's for his slaves. A man of "fine character and kindly feelings," whose "dignified and courtly manners" were acquired from "the fine old Maryland family in which he was brought up as a slave," Jackson—as all in the family called him—was on "peculiarly friendly and even affectionate terms with" the Harlans, Mallie wrote; yet he "never for one moment forgot his place, nor the respect that was due from him to all the members of the family. Unlike most of his race," she recalled, he initially had little interest in religion. When he began attending a Washington Methodist church, however, he was so "far above the level of intelligence and education of most of his people, he became at once a prominent figure in his congregation." The justice was never so busy "preparing for his own Bible Class, that he could not stop long enough to give Jackson a helping hand." After being in Harlan's service only briefly, the messenger "so thoroughly identified himself with my husband and all our family interests, that, whenever he spoke to others about my husband or addressed him personally, he always used the pronouns 'We,' 'Us' and 'Ours.'" Once, when the Harlans's son, John Maynard, won a golf tournament, "Jackson, with his kindly, ebon countenance fairly shining with affectionate pride, grasped [John's] hand in both of his and said,

'Mr. John, *when* will *these people* around here understand what kind o'stock *We* come from?'"[19]

The justice's relationship with his mulatto half-brother, Robert Harlan, also suggests that his racial attitudes were more complicated than a superficial reading of his civil rights dissents might suggest. Mrs. Harlan referred to Robert as a "quasi member" of the family; but his contacts with the Harlans, including the justice, apparently extended largely to political and related matters and to loan requests. In fact, the most extensive correspondence between the half-brothers, it will be recalled, appears to have concerned Robert's efforts to assist a white Harlan relation charged with assaulting a prominent black jurist in Washington. Robert, his son, Robert, Jr., and the justice shared mutual acquaintances, including Frederick Douglass and William Howard Taft, who was a classmate of Robert, Jr. in Cincinnati. Yet none of their correspondence hints that the half-brothers knew each other, much less that they were related. Taft, if not Douglass, was undoubtedly aware of the circumstances of Robert's birth. Robert, Jr., it will be remembered, once complained to Taft that he should not be compelled to "pay a vicarious atonement" for the "moral lapse" of his grandfather.[20]

The justice's limited contact with his half-brother may have reflected his willingness to bow to the prevailing social mores of his day, or he may have believed that any public revelation of their relationship might undermine the credibility of his civil rights opinions, or he may have found the circumstances of Robert's birth an embarrassing and uncomfortably personal reflection of the evil inherent in slavery. But he may simply have shared the prevailing attitude of his era that blacks, even blood relations, were the social inferiors of whites, irrespective of their status before the law. On Robert's return to the United States from Europe following the Civil War, it will be recalled, close family friend O. S. Poston reported to John Harlan that he had seen "Robert Harlan, late of England," recently in Chicago.[21] The tone of that observation and related portions of Poston's letter suggests a condescending attitude toward the subject. It is doubtful Poston would have used such language had he not been reasonably confident Harlan would find his remarks tolerable, if not amusing.

Whatever the nature and extent of their relationship, the justice's association with his half-brother—an intelligent, articulate, enterprising figure who achieved considerable success within the black community—probably did make Harlan more sensitive to the evils of racial prejudice and its impact on human lives, as well as more determined to champion the cause of equality before the law. To the extent that Robert Harlan's views influenced the justice's thinking, however, their impact may have been relatively conservative. Robert, Jr., after all, shared crude racial humor with William Howard Taft in the dialect of uneducated blacks and depicted the black masses as a naïve lot and easy prey for political manipulation. Presumably, the elder Robert Harlan also embraced such racially aristocratic leanings as were common to the "better" elements of blacks.

Numerous aspects of Justice Harlan's background, however, were consistent with the civil rights record he was to develop on the bench. As a Whig nationalist, he had little reason to be concerned about the war amendments' expansion of federal authority over the states. From the late 1860s until his appointment to the bench, moreover, he vigorously defended his newly adopted party and most of the goals of Reconstruction; any weaknesses in his resolve stemmed from the dictates of the political stump rather than from doubts about the principles underlying his new loyalties.

Whatever doubts some may have expressed about the sincerity of his conversion to Republicanism, black leaders generally did not share such concerns. In 1874, for example, Owensboro whites enlisted Harlan's assistance in winning black support for their interpretation of a local voting regulation. "The mayor of our city thinks," wrote one principal in the dispute, "that although they [local blacks] will not believe 'Moses and the prophets' they may believe you."[22] When Harlan won nomination to the bench, black groups praised President Hayes's judgment. One black Ohio Republican official assured Harlan, for example, "that you are well thought of by the influential colored man for what he believes to have been your interest in behalf of his oppressed race." He added, "I know . . . that you are gratefully remembered by colored men the country over for your advocacy of the justice of making the colored youth of Kentucky eligible to common school privileges. . . . It was a disappointment to some colored men who had done a full share in making the present Administration that you were not put in the Cabinet; they felt more comfortable, however, when they understood that you were to go on the bench of the Supreme Court. If that fails their disappointment will be mortif[ying]."[23]

Even before his elevation to the bench, Harlan included among his associates Frederick Douglass, the most visible black leader of their day. The two first met, it will be recalled, when they campaigned for Republican candidates in Maine. Later, when Harlan's opponents attempted to use that association to damage his gubernatorial campaign, the future justice praised Douglass as a far more worthy friend than their critics. But their association apparently was not limited to the public arena. On at least one occasion, Douglass visited Harlan's Washington home for a meeting to discuss matters about which he had written the justice.[24] When Harlan's absence from Washington prevented him from attending a reception celebrating the black leader's seventy-first birthday, the justice wrote to express regret and to assure Douglass, "It would have given me great pleasure to testify my high regard for you . . . [and] my gratification that you had been spared to reach an advanced age." He wished his friend "many [more] years of usefulness to your country."[25] Following Douglass's selection as U.S. minister to Haiti the following year, Harlan expressed confidence that the nominee's "new field of labor . . . [would] bring honor to our country and to yourself."[26] As will be seen later, Douglass often praised the justice's civil rights dissents. When the black leader died in 1895, Harlan attended his funeral.[27] Harlan's association with Douglass and, for that matter, with such white apostles of Reconstruction as Benjamin Bristow following his conversion to Republicanism may have helped to bolster and reinforce his commitment to racial equality.

The racial attitudes of members of Harlan's family probably strengthened his zeal as well. His father did oppose abolition, but he also abhorred the brutality of the slave system; permitted at least two promising slaves, including Robert Harlan, to purchase their freedom; and tried unsuccessfully, according to some accounts, to enroll Robert along with his other sons in a local school. However traditional and stereotypical her attitudes may have been, Mallie Harlan obviously found slavery offensive, hosted "race elevation" classes in her home, and probably supported fully the positions her husband developed in civil rights cases.

The Harlans no doubt had the greatest impact on their children's racial views. In letters to his sons, the justice at times shared his feelings regarding the racial problems confronting the nation and the measures necessary to improve the lot of blacks. In an 1888 letter to his son, John, regarding an upcoming Union League banquet in Chicago at which the justice might be expected to offer a toast and remarks, Harlan asserted, for example, that President Harrison must "break the Solid South—not by violent, sharp methods, but by good appointments in that section, and in other modes, turning the flank of the race problem, without marching squarely against it and keeping up antagonisms." Improved education and greater self-esteem for blacks, he added, were the key to meaningful racial reform:

> The negroes of the South must be educated and relieved from their present condition of subserviency to white political masters, otherwise their right to vote will do them no good, and will imperil our institutions. The negroes in the South are increasing rapidly in numbers and in time—perhaps in twenty-five years—will number fifteen or twenty millions. They must be so elevated by education that they will compel respect for their rights, and secure their own self-respect. That end can be accomplished by wise statesmanship.[28]

The Harlan children appear to have enthusiastically embraced their parents' racial thinking and thus may have helped to reinforce their father's own commitment. In December of 1879, while Harlan's son, James, was attending Princeton, E. S. Hammond the eccentric Memphis federal judge with whom Harlan, as noted previously, would later have trouble in his capacity as circuit justice, quashed an indictment against a Tennessee man charged with holding two young black women in slavery. The accused, who refused to recognize the abolition of slavery, claimed that he owned the women because their mother had been his slave. In dismissing the indictment, Judge Hammond took the remarkable position that the anti-slavery statute the defendant was charged with violating could not be applied to anyone holding, or pretending to hold, someone in slavery; since slavery had been abolished, Hammond reasoned, no person could be held as a slave, or charged with holding someone in slavery.[29] In a letter to his father, young James ridiculed Hammond's "poor logic" as "very peculiar and . . . contrary to the spirit of the act which liberated the slaves." Hammond, wrote James, "might as well say that since the law prohibits theft, no theft can exist."[30]

John Maynard's racial views, too, appear to have been similar to his father's. While the justice was preparing his dissent from the majority's decision in the *Civil Rights Cases*, striking down the Civil Rights Act of 1875, John wrote his father that he was glad Harlan had been "able to reach a conclusion from a legal standpoint which others unversed in constitutional interpretation are sure to come to for humanity's sake." Where "the interests of humanity demand a certain interpretation of the fundamental law," reasoned John, 'the judges, in my opinion, should give it such an interpretation if it can possibly [be done] on reasonable ground. . . . [T]he rule of constitutional construction should be to interpret in a liberal manner the language of the law and when the phraseology is inadequate to express what is well known to have been the intention of those who passed it, then to so construe it as to carry out" the framers' intentions.[31]

In John Maynard's judgment, the framers of the Fourteenth Amendment had clearly intended to confer on Congress power to intervene in instances of racial discrimination by inns, theaters, and common carriers, which the 1875 law prohibited. Such facilities operated under state charters and regulations; when they discriminated, it was thus the state itself that discriminated. The failure of states to control such practices, he added, also justified congressional intervention.

> I say that though the States may not have legislated positively against the civil rights of the negro, yet their inaction can fairly be regarded as an actual denial to the negro of the protection of the laws equal to that accorded to whites—that in reality their failure to compel corporations to respect the rights of the negro is substantially the same as legislation against the rights of the negro. . . .
>
> If the states are to be allowed thru the corporation . . . to trod upon the privileges and rights of the negro and are only to be checked by the National govt. when they directly legislate against the negro—then where is the good from the amendment contemplated by its framers.[32]

John Maynard, then a student at Princeton, stressed that he was "not egotistical enough to suppose" that any of his suggestions had "not already occurred to" his father.[33] He was probably correct. But the justice's dissent paralleled his son's remarks in a number of important respects. The letter is further evidence, moreover, that Harlan's children vigorously concurred with his ideas and may have helped to buttress them.

The racial views of Harlan's eldest son, Richard, are less clear. In a 1910 letter to President Taft supporting extension to the District of Columbia of the Morrill Act, which authorized federal appropriations for agricultural education, Richard, who was then holding an administrative position at George Washington University, noted that the government's "generous annual subsidy to Howard University" made "ample provision for the education of the colored people of the District." Extension of such assistance to the district would, he observed, "make it possible to provide similar forms of practical education for the WHITE students" of the area.[34] Presumably, however, the racial attitudes of Richard, a clergyman and college administrator, were as progressive as those of his other brothers.

Nothing is known of the opinions Laura and Ruth Harlan held regarding the racial questions their father confronted. But the Harlans's eldest child, Edith, was apparently deeply concerned about the problems of the disadvantaged and taught black pauper children in Washington's Bethel school.[35] Edith's untimely death in 1882 may have strengthened the justice's commitment to racial equality. Judge Richard T. Rives of the Court of Appeals for the Fifth Circuit was one of the "unlikely heroes" of the second Reconstruction of the 1950s and 1960s. Friends believed that Rives, a member of one of Alabama's oldest families, had broken with the racial traditions of his native state partly to perpetuate the ideals of his revered son, a racial liberal killed in an automobile accident while on holiday from law school.[36] Although Justice Harlan did not demonstrate the same degree of obsession with Edith's memory, at her death, it will be remembered, he wrote her brother, James, that he did "not expect to be able ever to feel that she is away from us" and that "[w]herever I go, and whatever I may be doing, her presence will be recognized in its influence upon me. She was to me not simply child, but companion. I am quite sure no character more noble and elevated ever appeared on this earth."[37] It may not be mere coincidence, therefore, that Harlan's fervent, indignant defense of human dignity became pronounced with his dissent in the *Civil Rights Cases*, decided a year after Edith's death. To some degree, the mounting intensity of the justice's resolve may have reflected his daughter's influence.

Finally, the controversy surrounding Harlan's appointment to the Court may itself have helped to dictate the direction of his civil rights stance. In winning confirmation, he was obliged to affirm, vehemently and repeatedly, the sincerity of his conversion to Republicanism as well as his commitment to the war amendments and the goals of Reconstruction. Had Harlan developed a judicial record markedly at odds with that image, his credibility as a justice might have been seriously damaged.

Numerous factors in Harlan's background and associations, then, were to push him toward the zealous advocacy of racial equality with which his opinions would be most closely associated. At the same time, his southern heritage, as we shall see, was to complicate his reaction to civil rights claims.

The Civil Rights Cases

The first racial cases decided by the Court following Harlan's appointment came down in 1880. In *Strauder* v. *West Virginia*,[38] the justices had no difficulty overturning a statute limiting jury service to white males. A second case also affirmed the right of blacks to be tried by juries free of racial discrimination, as well as the right to have their cases removed to a federal court when necessary to afford equal protection.[39] In a third case, the justices upheld the federal indictment of a state judge charged with excluding blacks from jury service.[40]

Harlan joined each of the 1880 rulings and, the following year, wrote the Court's opinion in another jury case, *Neal* v. *Delaware*.[41] William Neal, a black man indicted for rape, sought to remove his case into federal court on the grounds of systematic discrimination against members of his race in the selection of the grand jury that indicted him and the petit jurors summoned to try him. After a state court denied his motion, an all-white jury tried, convicted, and sentenced him to death. A provision of the Delaware constitution limited the suffrage to white males, and jury lists were drawn from voter rolls. But the state court had concluded that Delaware's voter and juror qualifications were now subject to the Fourteenth and Fifteenth Amendment bans on racial discrimination. The state judges conceded that no black person had ever been summoned for jury service in Delaware, but they attributed this to "the fact—too notorious to be ignored—that the great body of black men residing in this State are utterly unqualified by want of intelligence, experience or moral integrity, to sit on juries."[42]

Harlan and his brethren were not persuaded. Blacks, he asserted, were not entitled to have their race represented on a jury but did have a right to jury selection practices free of racial discrimination. The failure of any black person ever to have qualified for jury service in a state in which, in 1880, there were more than 26,000 blacks in a total population of less than 150,000 created for Harlan and the majority a prima faciae case of racial prejudice—a presumption the state made no attempt to rebut. "It was, we think, under all the circumstances," he declared, "a violent presumption which the State Court indulged, that such uniform exclusion of that race from juries, during a period of many years, was solely because, in the judgment of these officers, fairly exercised, the black race in Delaware were utterly disqualified" for such service.[43]

The state court had denied Neal's motion to have officers of the court called as witnesses to substantiate his claims. Harlan declined to decide whether that aspect of the state court's conduct violated the defendant's constitutional rights. But the justice could not resist remarking, "with entire respect for the court below, that the circumstances, in our judgment, warranted more indulgence . . . than was granted to a prisoner whose life was at stake, and was too poor to employ counsel of his own selection."[44]

Harlan's stance in the next racial discrimination case to come before the Court reflected more the traditional elements of his racial heritage than his later commitment to civil rights. In *Pace* v. *Alabama* (1882),[45] the Court held that a state could impose more severe punishment for interracial fornication than that committed within a single race, so long as each interracial offender received the same punishment. Harlan joined a unanimous Court. The following year he was the lone dissenter when the justices, in *United States* v. *Harris*,[46] overturned the 1871 Ku Klux Klan Act on the ground that its provisions extended to private persons seeking to interfere with Fourteenth Amendment rights, as well as state action. But he rested his objection to the majority's stance on a narrow, technical contention rather than on broad constitutional considerations.

In November of 1882, four prosecutions under the Civil Rights Act of 1875, banning discrimination in places of public accommodation, became part of the Court's docket. In two of the cases, defendants were charged with denying blacks hotel accommodations. The defendant in the third case had refused a black person a seat in the dress circle of San Francisco's Maguire's Theater; the fourth case involved discrimination at the Grand Opera House in New York. In late March, 1883, briefs relating to a fifth case were also filed with the Court. A married couple had sued the Memphis and Charleston Railroad Company for damages under Section 2 of the Civil Right Act of 1875 after a conductor refused to allow the wife to ride in a car reserved for women. The conductor claimed he had reason to suspect that the wife was an "improper person" because she was in the company of a young man he assumed to be white; thus there must have been some inappropriate connection between them. Apparently impressed by such an explanation, the jury had rendered a verdict for the railroad; the black couple thereupon sought the Supreme Court's review on a writ of error. In three of the criminal cases, trial judges divided on the issue of the statute's constitutionality. In the San Francisco case, the federal circuit court in California dismissed the charge, holding the law invalid.[47]

Apparently the *Civil Rights Cases*, as the suits would be called, immediately engaged Justice Harlan's interest. In late November, following the filing of the criminal cases with the Court, Harlan met with Senator George F. Edmunds, a chief sponsor of the 1875 act. Soon thereafter, Edmunds provided the justice with a listing of civil rights legislation Congress had enacted during Reconstruction as well as the pages of the *Congressional Globe* transcribing the debates over their constitutionality. While declining to comment on "the tendency and effect of the debates" as they related to the 1875 statute, "for reasons that your sense of delicacy will appreciate," Edmunds assured Harlan that the discussion brought "fully into question the scope of the Fourteenth Amendment."[48]

On October 15, 1883, the Court, over Harlan's lone dissent, declared the 1875 act unconstitutional.[49] The Fourteenth Amendment, declared Justice Bradley for the majority, forbade "states" to deny equal protection of the laws; Congress's authority to enforce the amendment's guarantees thus reached only state action, not the kinds of private discrimination the 1875 law covered. "If this legislation is appropriate for enforcing the prohibitions," Bradley asserted, "it is difficult to see where it is to stop. Why may not congress, with equal show of authority, enact a code of laws for the enforcement and vindication of all rights of life, liberty, and property?"[50] To Bradley, the answer was obvious, given the Fourteenth Amendment's language and the primary role of the states in the regulation of relations among private persons.

Bradley gave a Thirteenth Amendment defense of the law equally short shrift. He conceded that congressional power to enforce the constitutional ban on slavery extended to "all [its] badges and incidents,"[51] but held for the majority, "It would be running the slavery argument into the ground to make it apply to every act of discrimination which a person may see fit to make as to the guests he will entertain, or as to the people he will take into his coach or cab or car, or admit to his concert or theater, or deal with in other matters of intercourse or business."[52] Bradley also had some advice for former slaves and their descendants. They should remember, he seemingly sneered, "When a man has emerged from slavery, and by the aid of beneficent legislation has shaken off the inseparable concomitants of that state, there must be some stage in the progress of his elevation when he takes the rank of a mere citizen, and ceases to be the special favorite of the laws, and when his rights as a citizen, as a man, are to be protected in the ordinary modes by which other men's rights are protected."[53]

Following Bradley's presentation from the bench, Justice Harlan announced his lone dissent, summarized his objections to the majority's rationale, and promised to produce a written opinion of his own in the near future. Reaction to Harlan's announcement was generally favorable, especially among black leaders, sympathetic whites, prominent Republicans, and influential editors. At a meeting attended by 3,000 blacks and whites packed into Washington's Lincoln Hall, Frederick Douglass applauded Harlan for "so nobly dar[ing] to follow his convictions." While urging restraint on the part of the nation's blacks, Douglass charged that the Court's decision had "inflicted a heavy calamity upon" blacks, leaving them "naked and defenseless against the action of a malignant, vulgar, and pitiless prejudice."[54] Speaking at the same gathering, controversial lecturer Robert Ingersoll echoed Douglass's sentiments and, anticipating Harlan's *Plessy* dissent by more than a decade, proclaimed, "From the moment of the adoption of the thirteenth amendment the law became color blind."

Numerous newspapers floated the idea of a Harlan presidential candidacy. The *Baltimore American* reasoned, for example, that the Kentuckian might be just "the right man from one of the Southern States [to] do very serious damage to the solid Democracy of the South." And while several papers expressed admiration for the justice's prompt rejection of the unauthorized use of his name, such suggestions persisted. When a Frankfort, Kentucky, citizen dredged up Harlan stump speeches inconsistent with his dissent, as well as the old charge that Harlan had resigned his military commission in protest against the Emancipation Proclamation, many newspapers rushed to his defense. "[T]here is nothing in the constitution as amended, or in the revised and codified statutes," noted the *Washington Post*, "which forbids a man to change his mind."

Nor was praise of Harlan and scorn for the Court's decision and the justice's critics confined to the public arena. In a letter to the justice, a black correspondent from Ohio described Harlan as the "only hope" for those of his race and condemned the majority's "*cold, cruel*, merciless words."[55] A Washington bureaucrat took comfort in the fact that there remained on the Court one member "loyal still to the cause of the Union for which Lincoln died and Sumner suffered."[56] A Lexington, Kentucky, associate reported that "a gentleman of rebel antecedents" had asked him "with quite a triumphant glow on his face what I thought of Judge Harlan's decision. I replied I thought that Judge Harlan was right and the other eight judges all wrong."[57] An intimate of President Hayes recalled a long conversation in which Hayes explained why, earlier that day, he had picked Harlan for the Court. "He dwelt especially upon the fact of your being an earnest, loyal man—devoted to the union, the soldiers, the cause, and humanity."[58]

Several correspondents raised fears about the decision's impact similar to those Frederick Douglass voiced at Lincoln Hall. Harlan's Covington friend, John Finnell, was characteristically blunt. For Finnell, the ruling meant that whites would now "assume that the negro has [no] protection at all,—no rights that even the most degraded white man is in any measure bound to respect. The antipathy of the 'poor white trash' to the negro, will now find full license. . . . What is to become of the poor devils it is difficult to foresee." Finnell thought he knew. "[T]he Court's action will invite assaults upon the colored people from the worst class of whites in the country. As long as it was understood that the Federal government felt bound to protect the negro,—there was a healthy fear of the Federal government by the poor whites [and] the negro except in certain localities in the far South was getting along passably well. . . . [N]ow the patriotic vagabond of the South will feel called upon to vindicate the Supreme Court by 'jumping on' the poor darkey. . . . You may look for a carnival of cruelty, outrage and wrong to them, whenever and wherever it may be deemed to the interest of the democratic party in the South."[59]

As Harlan digested and responded to the letters of well-wishers, as well as editorial praise of his stance, he attempted to draft a devastating rebuttal to the majority's rationale. He was not without offers of assistance. His son, John, as noted previously, suggested several lines of argument which, coincidentally or not, would find their way into the justice's opinion. The son of Noah Swayne, an associate justice, 1862–1881, mailed Harlan a brief he had filed in a related case and a defense of a "generous [judicial] construction" for all governmental powers "essential" to individual "freedom and security."[60] For a lengthy period, Mrs. Harlan later recalled, Harlan's thoughts "refused to flow easily." His mental block may explain why his dissent was not prepared at the time the Court's decision was announced, and perhaps even why the Court's announcement was itself postponed from the previous spring to mid-October.

Mallie hit on a plan to provide her husband the necessary inspiration to fulfill the task before him. During their first years in Washington, the justice had regularly visited numerous parts of the Capitol, finding much to interest him, especially objects associated with the great men of the nation's past. One day in the marshal's office, he had spotted an old-fashioned inkstand that had belonged to Chief Justice Roger B. Taney and reportedly supplied the ink with which the chief justice penned his opinion in the infamous *Dred Scott* case,[61] which denied even free blacks U.S. citizenship and galvanized antislavery feelings in the nation. Noting Harlan's unusual interest in the inkstand, the marshal had given it to the justice, who took it home "as a great treasure." At a reception sometime later, the wife of Ohio Senator George H. Pendleton, a Taney relation, told Harlan that she "would so love to have that little inkstand." The justice's "feeling for women was so chivalric," Mrs. Harlan later wrote, "that without hesitation he promised to send her the . . . inkstand the very next day." But Mallie was not so generous; she hid the inkstand from the justice. After searching for it in vain, he wrote Mrs. Pendleton that it had been lost, but that he would send it to her as soon as he found it.[62]

The justice soon forgot about the elusive inkstand. But now, as he grappled with a response to his brethren in the *Civil Rights Cases*, Mrs. Harlan rescued it from its hiding place and placed it on her husband's writing table. Her ploy worked. "The memory of the historic part that Taney's inkstand had played in the Dred Scott decision, in temporarily tightening the shackles of slavery upon the negro race in the antebellum days, seemed, that morning, to act like magic in clarifying my husband's thoughts in regard to the law that had been intended . . . to protect the recently emancipated slaves in the enjoyment of equal 'civil rights.' His pen fairly flew on that day and, with the running start he then got, he soon finished his dissent."[63]

Harlan's opinion in the *Civil Rights Cases* was to be among his most eloquent and forceful, if not his most tightly reasoned, efforts. The central weakness in the Court's rationale, he declared, was that it "proceed[ed] . . . upon grounds entirely too narrow and artificial," sacrificing the "substance and spirit of the recent amendments" to "a subtle and ingenious verbal criticism. 'It is not the words of the law but the internal sense of it that makes the law. The letter of the law is the body; the sense and reason of the law is the soul.'"[64] In these cases, he asserted, the Court's approach had produced a tragic result: "Constitutional provisions, adopted in the interest of liberty, and for the purpose of securing, through national legislation, if need be, rights inhering in a state of freedom, and belonging to American citizenship, have been so construed as to defeat the ends the people desired to accomplish, which they attempted to accomplish, and which they supposed they had accomplished by changes in their fundamental law."[65]

Viewed against the war amendments' "substance and spirit," the Civil Rights Act of 1875 was for Harlan clearly constitutional. The Thirteenth Amendment was not intended merely "to prohibit slavery as an *institution*," but its "badges and incidents" as well, as even the majority had conceded. Harlan observed that "since slavery was the moving or principal cause of the adoption of that amendment, and since that institution rested wholly upon the inferiority, as a race, of those held in bondage, their freedom necessarily involved immunity from, and protection against, all discrimination against them, because of their race, in respect of such civil rights as belong to freemen of other races." Under its power to enforce the amendment through appropriate legislation, Congress could thus forbid all racial discrimination in the exercise "of any civil rights enjoyed by other freemen in the same state."[66] Numerous precedents, moreover, included among such civil rights freedom of access to the facilities covered by the 1875 law.

Harlan also objected to the majority's conclusion that congressional authority to enforce the Fourteenth Amendment extended only to "state action" that interferes with rights the amendment guarantees. The amendment's first sentence overruled the *Dred Scott* decision and conferred national and state citizenship on the newly freed slaves as well as all other persons born or naturalized in the United States and subject to its laws. In earlier cases, the Court had concluded that citizenship, both national and state, carried with it certain inherent rights. For Harlan, one right of state citizenship, even "if there be no others," was "exemption from race discrimination in respect of any civil right belonging to citizens of the white race in the same state. . . . And such must be their constitutional right, in their own state, unless the recent amendments be 'splendid baubles,' thrown out to delude those who desired fair and generous treatment at the hands of the nation."[67] In these cases as "always" in the past, Harlan asserted, the Court should give "a broad and liberal construction to the constitution, so as to enable congress, by legislation, to enforce rights secured by that instrument."[68] Those who drafted the Fourteenth Amendment surely knew "that the great danger to the equal enjoyment by citizens of their rights, as citizens, was to be apprehended, not altogether from unfriendly state legislation, but from the hostile action of corporations and individuals in the states." Given that likelihood, declared Harlan, it should be "presumed" that they intended to clothe Congress with the power to "meet that power."[69]

Harlan did not rest his Fourteenth Amendment defense of the 1875 law solely on his distaste for the majority's "state action" thesis. Even if the Court's interpretation of congressional power under the amendment were correct, he declared, the law was still within the reach of Congress. Transportation facilities, innkeepers, and theater operators were, he reasoned, "agents of the state, because amenable, in respect of their public duties and functions, to public regulation." Racial discrimination on their part was thus comparable to discrimination "by the state within the meaning of the fourteenth amendment."[70]

Nor, in Harlan's judgment, could support for the challenged law properly be construed as conferring on Congress power "to adjust what may be called the social, as distinguished from technically legal, rights of individuals." The 1875 law was intended, he insisted, to protect only "legal, not social, rights." If one person refused to "hold social intercourse with another," such discrimination was "no concern" of government. But Harlan was equally adamant that "no state, nor the officers of any state, nor any corporation or individual wielding power under state authority for the public benefit or the public convenience, can, consistently either with the freedom established by the fundamental law, or with that equality of civil rights which now belongs to every citizen, discriminate against freemen or citizens, in their civil rights, because of their race, or because they once labored under disabilities imposed upon them as a race."[71]

Of all the elements in the majority's rationale, the Court's assertion that the former slaves had been the beneficiaries of preferential treatment by government aroused Harlan's sense of moral outrage the most. In the most memorable and moving passage of his dissent, he gently but firmly admonished his brethren:

It is, I submit, scarcely just to say that the colored race has been the special favorite of the laws. What the nation, through congress, has sought to accomplish in reference to that race is, what had already been done in every state in the Union by the white race, to secure and protect rights belonging to them as freemen and citizens; nothing more. The one underlying principle of congressional legislation has been to enable the black race to take the rank of mere citizen. The difficulty has been to compel a recognition of their legal right to take that rank, and to secure the enjoyment of privileges belonging, under the law, to them as a component part of the people for whose welfare and happiness government is ordained. At every step in this direction the nation has been confronted with class tyranny, which a contemporary English historian says is, of all tyrannies, the most intolerable, "for it is ubiquitous in its operation, and weighs perhaps most heavily on those whose obscurity or distance would withdraw them from the notice of a single despot." To-day it is the colored race which is denied . . . rights fundamental in their freedom and citizenship. At some future time it may be some other race that will fall under the ban. If the constitutional amendments be enforced, according to the intent with which, as I conceive, they were adopted, there cannot be, in this republic, any class of human beings in practical subjection to another class, with power in the latter to dole out to the former just such privileges as they may choose to grant.[72]

Not surprisingly, given his extensive political background and reputation as an accomplished stump speaker, Justice Harlan's judicial opinions were more inspirational than tightly legalistic. His dissent in the *Civil Rights Cases* was no exception. Even before the Fourteenth Amendment's adoption, the Court had held that certain rights were indeed implicit in national citizenship;[73] but its approach to defining such guarantees was arguably less open-ended than Harlan's dissent suggested. His construction of the Thirteenth Amendment and assertion that private action subject to governmental regulation is tantamount to state action under the Fourteenth Amendment seem equally boundless. It is not surprising, therefore, that newspapers critical of his dissent focused their attention on the justice's loose readings of constitutional text. In a blunt, if respectful, assessment, for example, the New York *Daily Tribune* conceded Harlan's "sincerity and ability." Of his interpretation of the Thirteenth Amendment and conclusion that the Fourteenth reached private facilities "amenable to public regulation," however, the *Tribune* caustically observed, "This is surely straining the Constitution until it cracks. The purpose of a written Constitution is to fix the law. We must adhere to the law as written, or lose ourselves on a sea of doubt and confusion. The meaning of these amendments is plain. One abolishes slavery, abolishing what is commonly known as slavery—not giving power to punish acts which may, by a forced construction, be regarded as badges of slavery. The other prohibits any 'State' from infringing upon the rights of citizens. If their clear meaning could be distorted to Justice Harlan's view, it would only be to gain a temporary advantage in a matter of little practical moment by the sacrifice of great principles."[74]

For many, though, it had been the majority, not Harlan, who gave the war amendments a "distorted" reading inconsistent with the aspirations of their chief sponsors. Robert Ingersoll hailed the justice's opinion as "unanswerable," adding: "He has given to words their natural meaning."[75] "That the will of the people should be reversed on so narrow not to say technical ground as that put forward by the majority opinion," a congressman wrote the justice, "must lessen the respect due from the people to their court of last resort. Nothing short of the absolute and irreversible . . . annihilation of slavery—root and branch—was even contemplated by the Congress. . . . To assume [otherwise] . . . is to mock at the victim smarting under a wrong which he knows and which all the world knows never would have been inflicted but for the fact that he or his kindred were bondsmen!"[76] Harlan's old friend Wayne MacVeagh termed the dissent "strong and well-reasoned."[77] Harlan's former colleague, Noah Swayne, who had left the Court in 1881, wrote the justice from New York that he had read the opinion "through without laying it down for a moment." It was, he declared, one of the "greatest" opinions in the Court's history and would "make a profound and lasting impression upon the Country."[78] "I fear you have exposed yourself," wrote another friend, who no doubt had seen news reports trumpeting a presidential ticket composed of Harlan and President Lincoln's son, Robert, "to the danger of being a candidate for the Presidency."[79]

And there were others. Justice William Strong, who had retired from the Court in 1880, was first inclined to side with the majority. But after reading Harlan's "*very* able opinion—the best you have ever written"—Strong began to have "great doubt. It may be," he told his former colleague, "that you are right. The opinion of the Court, as you said, is too narrow—sticks to the letter, while you aim to bring out the spirit of the Constitution."[80] Former President Hayes found the opinion in "every way noble" and reported that Mrs. Hayes had been "delighted both with *what* you said and the *way* you said it."[81] Later, Hayes wrote the justice that Lucy Hayes had argued with a lawyer about the dissent during a train trip. When asked who had gotten the better of the exchange, the indomitable "Lemonade Lucy" had assured her husband, "I talked the loudest."[82] Nor was support for the dissent confined to Harlan's friends and political associates. Roscoe Conkling, for example, read it "not only with admiration, but with surprise at its strength of position."[83]

Harlan may have been most gratified by the words of Frederick Douglass. In a published essay, the black leader praised the justice's "righteous and heroic stand . . . in defence of liberty and justice." He declared, "The marvel is that, born in a slave State, as he was, and accustomed to see the colored man degraded, oppressed and enslaved, and the white man exalted; surrounded by the peculiar moral vapor inseparable from the lessons of the late war and the principles of reconstruction, and, above all, that in these easy-going days he should find himself possessed of the courage to resist the temptation to go with the multitude."[84] Douglass wrote Harlan, moreover, that his opinion "should be scattered like the leaves of Autumn over the whole country, and be seen, read and pondered upon by every citizen of this country and . . . published in every newspaper and magazine in the land."[85]

Harlan mailed many copies of his dissent to friends around the country and apparently also suggested that they attempt to have local papers publish the entire opinion or lengthy extracts. The eccentric Judge Hammond assured him, for example, that he would have it published in at least one Memphis paper whose publisher had already asked the judge for an advance copy,[86] and others that made like offers.[87] Such efforts were not always successful. "Without the slightest intimation of your suggestion," a St. Louis friend had urged the editor of a local paper to publish the entire dissent, only to be told that he would were Harlan's opinion "not too long."[88] Many papers carried the full dissent or substantial excerpts, however, without pressure from Harlan or his surrogates.[89] Its appearance, as noted earlier, attracted numerous letters of praise from Americans both prominent and humble, black and white. The justice's daughter, Edith, would have been proud.

"The Wrong This Day Done"

Harlan sided with a majority of his brethren in certain racial discrimination and related civil rights cases. In *Ex Parte Yarbrough*,[90] decided the year after the ruling on the 1875 Civil Rights Act, a unanimous Court, speaking through Justice Miller, declared that the right of registered voters to participate in federal elections was an implicit attribute of national citizenship. The Court upheld the federal prosecutions of Ku Klux Klansmen who brutalized a black citizen seeking to exercise that right. Harlan also spoke for or joined the majority in several jury discrimination cases, at times on the side of the state. The same year the *Civil Rights Cases* were decided, he led the justices in striking down Kentucky laws excluding blacks from jury service.[91] When state courts refused to admit evidence supporting jury challenges,[92] or dismissed such claims on frivolous grounds,[93] he also concurred in the reversal of black defendants' convictions.

In other jury cases, however, Harlan limited access to federal habeas corpus proceedings and procedures for removing state cases into federal court as avenues of federal relief against discriminatory state jury practices.[94] In cases where no proof of discrimination was presented,[95] and even when a trial court found the evidence supporting a discrimination claim inadequate,[96] he also supported the state. Nor, without clear evidence of discriminatory application in specific cases, was he willing to look beyond the surface of racially neutral juror requirements to the obvious discriminatory intent underlying their adoption. In *Williams* v. *Mississippi* (1898),[97] for example, he joined the unanimous Court in rejecting the jury discrimination claims of a black defendant indicted and convicted of murder by all-white juries, even though jury service was limited to registered voters, and recently enacted poll tax and literacy requirements for voters had eliminated blacks from Mississippi's jury rolls.

Harlan's uniform concurrence with the majority in jury cases was hardly typical of his reaction to civil rights claims generally. In several voting rights cases unrelated to the jury discrimination issue, he did agree with the Court that challenges to state voter requirements which reached the Justices after the elections in question had taken place were moot and thus beyond their reach.[98] In 1903, however, he would break with the majority when it distinguished *Ex Parte Yarbrough* and voided a federal statute forbidding election bribery and intimidation where the language of the challenged law extended to private interference with state elections as well as the federal contests *Yarbrough* had involved.[99]

The same year, he dissented again in another suffrage case. Like other Alabama blacks, Jackson W. Giles had fallen victim to the restrictive voter requirements embodied in Alabama's 1901 constitution, a document adopted primarily to assure white supremacy at the polls. Under its dubious provisions, persons registered to vote under lenient standards in effect prior to 1903 remained voters for life, while future would-be voters were obliged to meet strict new requirements which, although racially neutral on their face, were amenable to discriminatory application and, in fact, were intended to serve that purpose. The undoubted impact of the new scheme, as Justice Holmes would later observe, was obvious: "The white men generally are registered for good under the easy test; and the black men are likely to be kept out in the future as in the past."[100]

When Giles and large numbers of blacks sought to register in Montgomery County in March, 1902, their applications were uniformly rejected, while all white applicants were registered. Giles petitioned a federal circuit court to order his name and those of over 5,000 other blacks added to the voting rolls, but the circuit court dismissed his complaint, and the Supreme Court, speaking through Justice Holmes, affirmed. Pleading the Court's impotence to deal effectively with Giles's complaint of a conspiracy by "the great mass of the white population [in Alabama] . . . to keep the blacks from voting," Holmes concluded for the majority that relief against such "great political wrong[s]" must come from Congress or the president, not the courts. The case, he asserted, posed another difficulty as well: If the Court declared Alabama's current scheme unconstitutional, how could it then use the same regulations to add names to the voter rolls? "[H]ow can we make the court a party to the unlawful scheme," asked Holmes, "by accepting it and adding another voter to its fraudulent lists?"[101]

Harlan's reaction to Holmes's strained logic would no doubt have made interesting reading. Harlan rested his dissent, however, on jurisdictional grounds. Complaints filed in federal circuit courts, he concluded, had to mention a specific amount of damages sought. Giles's suit had not; therefore, it was not properly before the courts for decision. But "to avoid misapprehension," Harlan also noted that in a proper case, in his judgment, "the plaintiff [would be] entitled to relief in respect of his right to be registered as a voter."[102]

Harlan generally also dissented from the Court's rulings in peonage and related cases. In *Clyatt* v. *United States* (1905),[103] a majority relied on what it considered to be a defective indictment to overturn the peonage convictions of two whites who had forced two black men to return to Georgia from Florida to work off a debt. The federal statute covered "every person who holds, arrests, returns, or causes to be held, arrested, or returned" another person for purposes of peonage. But the indictment charged the defendants only with "returning" their victims to a state of peonage, and Justice Brewer concluded for the majority that there was "not a scintilla of testimony" to support that charge. "That they were in debt, and that they had left Georgia and gone to Florida without paying that debt," declared Brewer, "does not show that they had been [previously] held in a condition of peonage, or were ever at work, willingly or unwillingly, for their creditor."[104]

Harlan obviously had no patience with such legalistic subtleties. The defendants had forced the victims to return to Georgia "against their will . . . to work out a debt." It was thus "going very far," in his judgment, "to hold in a case like this, disclosing barbarities of the worst kind against these negroes, that the trial court erred in sending the case to the jury."[105]

Hodges v. *United States*,[106] decided the following year, produced another Harlan dissent. Three white men had employed threats and violence in forcing black workers to quit their jobs at an Arkansas lumber mill. The Supreme Court, speaking again through Justice Brewer, overturned the defendants' convictions. The Thirteenth Amendment's "inciting cause," declared Brewer, "was the emancipation of the colored race"; its adoption was "not an attempt to commit that race to the care of the nation,"[107] or an effort to "constitute them wards of the nation." As free citizens, the defendants' victims were to take "their chances with other citizens in the states where they should make their homes."[108] The defendants had not subjected them to slavery or one of its badges, and they must thus look to the state courts for relief.

In his *Hodges* dissent, as in the *Civil Rights Cases*, Harlan termed the majority's reading of the Thirteenth Amendment's scope "entirely too narrow, and . . . hostile to the freedom established by the Supreme Law of the Land."[109] An inability to make contracts, he asserted, was "one of the insuperable incidents of slavery" at the time of the amendment's adoption, and continued to be an obstacle to true freedom for the former slaves and their descendants. "One who is shut up by superior or overpowering force, constantly present and threatening, from earning his living in a lawful way of his own choosing," he declared, was "as much in a condition of involuntary servitude as if he were forcibly held in a condition of peonage. . . . [A] combination or conspiracy to prevent citizens of African descent, solely because of their race, from making and performing . . . contracts, is thus in hostility to the rights and privileges that inhere in the freedom established by [the Thirteenth] Amendment."[110]

Yielding to precedent, Harlan decided not to dissent in a 1909 case decided on the basis of the *Hodges* ruling.[111] The previous year, however, he had again parted company with the majority. A 1907 Alabama statute, apparently intended to circumvent the federal ban on peonage, made a person's failure to fulfill a labor contract prima facie evidence of an intent to defraud, and a local rule of evidence prohibited testimony regarding the defendant's actual intent. In *Bailey* v. *Alabama*,[112] a black man indicted and jailed under the statute for obtaining $15 and then failing to perform the labor for which he had contracted, sought a writ of habeas corpus in the state courts. The state tribunals denied him relief, and the Supreme Court dismissed the appeal, Justice Holmes holding for a majority that Bailey's habeas corpus suit had been prematurely filed. At trial, Holmes reasoned, the prosecution might not rely on the presumption the statute created and instead might present evidence establishing fraudulent intent on the defendant's part, which clearly would be a crime.[113]

Harlan vigorously disagreed. Both Bailey and the attorney general of the United States, in an amicus curiae brief, had challenged the constitutionality of the Alabama statute. The Alabama supreme court had issued a final order sustaining the law, including the presumption it created, and rejecting the claim that the accused was imprisoned "not in punishment for crime, but really in liquidation of a debt." The Alabama court had not even intimated, moreover, that Bailey "took a 'short cut,' or pursued the wrong method to obtain his discharge." It was thus for Harlan "a curious condition of things" for the U.S. Supreme Court to "remain silent."[114]

On this occasion, Harlan's position ultimately prevailed. Following Bailey's conviction, the Supreme Court declared the Alabama law a violation of the Thirteenth Amendment. Holmes dissented; Harlan joined the majority.[115]

Harlan's most elaborate challenge to the perpetuation of involuntary servitude involved seamen, not blacks. In the mid-1890s, several merchant sailors had boarded the American bark, Arago, in San Francisco for a voyage to Washington state and several foreign ports. After becoming dissatisfied with their employment conditions, they left the ship at Astoria, Oregon. Authorities acting under federal law promptly arrested them and took them before a justice of the peace, who ordered the sailors jailed until the Arago was again ready to sail. Sixteen days later, a federal marshal placed them on board the Arago. When the vessel returned to San Francisco, the seamen were arrested and charged with refusing to work, which was a federal offense. A federal district court dismissed their petition for release on a writ of habeas corpus; the Supreme Court, over Justice Harlan's lone dissent, affirmed.

Citing longstanding English and American practice, Justice Henry Brown had no difficulty holding for the majority that the guarantees of the Bill of Rights and the Thirteenth Amendment were inapplicable to the laws governing the treatment of deserting seamen. "[A]n individual," declared Brown, could, "for a valuable consideration, contract for the surrender of his personal liberty for a definite time and for a recognized purpose, and subordinate his going and coming to the will of another during the continuation of the contract." Such agreements would not always necessarily be lawful, but "a servitude which was knowingly and willingly entered into could not be termed 'involuntary.'"[116]

In the Court's judgment, the special status of seamen under the law was in their best interest. Discipline, it was true, was "more stringently enforced" against them than in other fields of employment. But seamen were also given special protections "against the frauds and cruelty of masters, the devices of boarding-house keepers, and . . . the consequences of their own ignorance and improvidence." Congress, like the British parliament, had concluded that sailors were "as deficient in that full and intelligent responsibility for their acts which is accredited to ordinary adults, and as needing the protection of the law in the same sense in which minors and wards are entitled to the protection of their parents and guardians." The former slaves, Brown seemed to suggest, might no longer be in need of special protection, but seamen remained the "wards of admiralty."[117]

Harlan's reaction to the Court's rationale was as predictable as night following day. No court, he declared, would respect a contract by which a person agreed to become a slave, yet "[t]he condition of one who contracts to render personal services in connection with the private business of another [becomes] a condition of involuntary servitude from the moment he is compelled, against his will, to continue in such service." The other party to such an agreement might sue for breach of contract but could not subject a person to involuntary servitude. Under the Thirteenth Amendment's language, conviction for a crime was the only legitimate exception to its provisions. By condoning another exception for seamen, asserted Harlan, the Court was engaged in nothing less than "judicial legislation."[118]

Justice Harlan also found issue with other elements of the majority's rationale. He objected to the use of the phrase "supposed helpless condition" to describe sailors, arguing that it served as an "excuse for imposing upon them burdens that could not be imposed upon other classes without depriving them of rights that inhere in personal freedom."[119] He was equally scornful of Justice Brown's heavy reliance on British practice. The English had no real constitution, he stated. As Lord Bryce had put it, theirs were "ordinary laws, which could be repealed by parliament at any moment in exactly the same way as it can repeal a highway act or lower the duty on tobacco." The British system was thus no proper measure of governmental power in the United States. "Absolute, arbitrary power," exclaimed Harlan, "exists nowhere in this free land. The authority for the exercise of power by the congress of the United States must be found in the constitution. Whatever it does in excess of the powers granted to it, as in violation of the injunctions of the supreme law of the land, is a nullity, and may be so treated by every person."[120]

For Harlan, the greatest irony was the similarity of the treatment accorded seamen to the status of the former slaves. The petitioners, he pointed out, had been treated "somewhat as runaway slaves were in the days of slavery."[121] Now that the Court had condoned such a regime, the people could "look for advertisements, not for runaway servants . . . , but for runaway seamen. In former days, overseers could stand with whip in hand over slaves, and force them to perform personal service for their masters. While, with the assent of all, that condition of things has ceased to exist, we can but be reminded of the past, when it is adjudged to be consistent with the law of the land for freeman, who happen to be seamen, to be held in custody, that they may be forced to go aboard private vessels, and render personal services against their will."[122]

In force and eloquence, Harlan's defense of the rights of merchant sailors rivaled his dissent in the *Civil Rights Cases*. The previous year, however, he had written the opinion with which his career would be most closely associated—his *Plessy* dissent. The *Plessy* case was not Harlan's or the Court's first confrontation with state-mandated segregation in transportation. In *Hall* v. *DeCuir*,[123] decided the year after his appointment to the bench, the justice's nationalist tradition overrode his mounting concern for racial equality. In that case, he joined a unanimous tribunal in overturning damages that the Louisiana supreme court, acting under a Reconstruction-era statute, had awarded a black Louisiana woman denied admission to a steamship stateroom reserved for whites. Application of the law, Chief Justice Waite reasoned, thus interfered with interstate commerce, a matter within the exclusive control of Congress.

Harlan apparently agreed. Later, though, he was to take issue with his brethren's inconsistent application of the *DeCuir* precedent. In 1890, the Court upheld a Mississippi law requiring "equal, but separate" railroad accommodations for black and white passengers. Speaking for a seven–two majority, Justice Brewer distinguished *DeCuir* by concluding that the Mississippi statute applied solely to local commerce and that, in any event, any burden on interstate carriers which it imposed would be less severe than that at issue in *DeCuir*. Harlan, on the other hand, was "unable to perceive how . . . a state enactment requiring the separation of the white and black races on interstate carriers . . . is a regulation of commerce among the states, while a similar enactment forbidding such separation is not."[124]

Harlan found Mississippi's segregation statute an invalid regulation of interstate commerce "[w]ithout considering other grounds upon which, in my judgment, the statute in question might properly be held to be repugnant to the Constitution."[125] In *Plessy* v. *Ferguson*, he reached those "other grounds."

The story of Homer Plessy is familiar and has been well told elsewhere.[126] An 1890 Louisiana statute superseding the policy at issue in the *DeCuir* case required "equal but separate" railroad accommodations and obliged passengers to occupy cars or sections assigned only to members of their race. A New Orleans group of Creoles and blacks organized a committee to challenge the law. Only one-eighth black, but "colored" nevertheless in the eyes of Louisiana law, Homer Plessy agreed to initiate a test case in the organization's behalf. To avoid any question of state authority over interstate commerce, he purchased a ticket for a journey exclusively within Louisiana's borders. He also made certain that railroad personnel knew that he was a person of mixed race. On boarding a train, Plessy took a seat in a section reserved for white passengers. When he refused to move to the "colored only" section of the coach, he was forcibly ejected from the train, arrested, and taken to jail. In an effort to halt his trial, Plessy filed petitions challenging the constitutionality of the segregation statute he was charged with violating. When the state courts denied his claims, he won Supreme Court review of his case on a writ of error.

Eight justices, with Justice Brewer not participating, heard Plessy's claim that segregation laws stigmatize members of the black race in violation of the Thirteenth and Fourteenth Amendments. Seven justices joined the opinion of Michigan's Justice Brown in rejecting Plessy's arguments. A law, observed Brown, "which implies merely a legal distinction between the white and colored races—a distinction which is founded in the color of the two races, and which must always exist so long as white men are distinguished from the other race by color—has no tendency to destroy the legal equality of the two races, or re-establish a state of involuntary servitude."[127] Nor, in the majority's judgment, did such a provision violate equal protection. The Fourteenth Amendment was intended only "to enforce the absolute equality of the two races before the law," and not to "abolish distinctions based upon color, or to enforce social, as distinguished from political, equality, or a commingling of the two races upon terms unsatisfactory to either." Segregation laws had been "generally, if not universally, recognized" as within the scope of state police power, even in Massachusetts.[128] All state regulations had to be "reasonable," of course, but a state legislature could reasonably conclude that a policy of racial segregation would promote the "preservation of the public peace and good order."[129]

And what of Plessy's argument that segregation laws are based on racial stereotypes harmful to members of the minority race?

> We consider the underlying fallacy of the plaintiff's argument [declared Brown] to consist in the assumption that the enforced separation of the two races stamps the colored race with a badge of inferiority. If this be so, it is not by reason of anything found in the act, but solely because the colored race chooses to put that construction

upon it. . . . Legislation is powerless to eradicate racial instincts, or to abolish distinctions based upon physical differences, and the attempt to do so can only result in accentuating the difficulties of the present situation. If the civil and political rights of both races be equal, one cannot be inferior to the other civilly or politically. If one race be inferior to the other socially, the constitution of the United States cannot put them upon the same plane.[130]

For Harlan, the "underlying fallacy" in the majority's stance was its failure to grasp the central purpose of the Civil War, the constitutional revolution the war had spawned, or the harsh realities of quasi-slavery in the post-Reconstruction era. The war amendments, Harlan declared, had eliminated race as a legitimate basis for legislation or judicial decisions affecting civil rights. Thus, "[i]n view of the constitution, in the eye of the law, there is in this country no superior, dominant, ruling class of citizens. There is no caste here. Our constitution is color-blind, and neither knows nor tolerates classes among citizens. In respect of civil rights, all citizens are equal before the law."[131]

The state and the majority had assumed that laws requiring "separate but equal" facilities for whites and blacks treated both races equally. Harlan was incredulous. "Every one knows," he asserted, "that the statute in question had its origin in the purpose, not so much to exclude white persons from railroad cars occupied by blacks, as to exclude colored people from coaches occupied by or assigned to white persons. . . . The thing to accomplish was, under the guise of giving equal accommodations for whites and blacks, to compel the latter to keep to themselves while traveling in railroad passenger coaches. No one would be so wanting in candor as to assert the contrary."[132] And no one, he was certain, would be fooled by the Court's logic. "The thin disguise of 'equal' accommodations for passengers in railroad coaches," he wrote, "will not mislead any one, nor atone for the wrong this day done."[133]

Perhaps even more disturbing to the justice than the majority's refusal to look beyond the surface of "separate but equal" was the ruling's certain impact. The Court had accepted the notion that segregation laws might help to promote public peace and harmony. Harlan could not agree. "Sixty millions of whites are in no danger from the presence here of eight millions of blacks. The destinies of the two races, in this country, are indissolubly linked together, and the interests of both require that the common government of all shall not permit the seeds of race hate to be planted under the sanction of law. What can more certainly arouse race hate, what more certainly create and perpetuate a feeling of distrust between these races, than state enactments which, in fact, proceed on the ground that colored citizens are so inferior and degraded that they cannot be allowed to sit in public coaches occupied by white citizens?" For Harlan, the "sure guaranty of the peace and security of each race [was] clear, distinct, unconditional recognition" of the rights of all persons, regardless of race. Segregation laws and related racial controls, "cunningly devised to defeat legitimate results of the war," would "render permanent peace impossible, and . . . keep alive a conflict of races, the continuance of which must do harm to all concerned."[134] The Court's acceptance of such schemes meant that "[s]lavery, as an institution tolerated by law, would have disappeared from our country; . . . there would remain a power in the states, by sinister legislation, to . . .

place in a condition of legal inferiority a large body of American citizens, now constituting a part of the political community, called the 'People of the United
States.'"[135] Such complicity, Harlan prophesied, would, "in time, prove to be quite
as pernicious as the decision made by this tribunal in the Dred Scott Case."[136]

Constitutional Blind Spot

The Court's dismantling of Reconstruction had been largely completed before
Plessy was decided. Probably for that reason, the ruling and Justice Harlan's dissent
attracted little contemporary attention.[137] Even so, the justice's opinion was even
more moving and forceful than his dissent in the *Civil Rights Cases*, and much more
tightly reasoned. As a student of the *Plessy* case once suggested, Justice Brown's
opinion for the majority was "a compound of bad logic, bad history, bad sociology,
and bad constitutional law";[138] Harlan's dissent demolished the majority's rationale
on every front.

A close reading of the dissent also reveals the complicated nature of Harlan's
personal racial views—attitudes which might push his reaction to certain civil rights
claims in a different direction than the one he embraced in *Plessy* and the *Civil
Rights Cases*, among others. At one point in *Plessy*, for example, the justice asserted confidently, "Every true man has pride of race, and under appropriate circumstances, when the rights of others, his equals before the law, are not to be affected, it
is his privilege to express such pride and to take such action based upon it as to him
seems proper."[139] Later, he agreed that whites constituted "the dominant race in this
country . . . , in prestige, in achievements, in education, in wealth, and in power."
And although such an assertion could have been taken purely as a statement of historic fact rather than as reflecting feelings of racial superiority, Harlan immediately
followed it with the prediction that the white race would continue to be preeminent
if it "remains true to its great heritage, and holds fast to the principles of constitutional liberty." Only in the eyes of the law, he seemed to intimate, was there "no superior, dominant, ruling class of citizens" in the United States.[140]

Such passages prompt speculation whether the justice who denounced segregation in transportation, voting, places of public amusement, and the jury box might
have assumed a different stance in more sensitive areas of human interaction. Unfortunately, Harlan was never obliged to confront such matters squarely. The case
bearing most directly on the question, however, was to be *Cumming* v. *Richmond
County Board of Education*,[141] decided three years after *Plessy*. Pressed by black
citizens and the state's "separate but equal" law, the Augusta, Georgia, school board
opened the state's first public high school for blacks in 1880. The venture was apparently successful. In 1897, however, the board closed its black high school in the
face of a growing need for additional funds, its members said, for black grammar
schools.

Black parents then sued the school board and county tax collector, seeking an
injunction to block further spending for white high school education until funds for
black schools at that level were restored. Georgia Superior Court Judge Enoch Calloway refused to enjoin the tax collector. Citing the state's commitment to "separate

but equal," however, Judge Calloway did issue an order forbidding the school board to operate the white schools "until said board shall provide or establish equal facilities . . . for . . . colored children of high-school grades."[142] Georgia's highest court reversed Judge Calloway, and Senator George F. Edmunds carried the black parents' case to the Supreme Court. A unanimous tribunal, speaking through Justice Harlan, affirmed the state high court.

In arguing his clients' case before the justices, Senator Edmunds apparently had attacked Georgia's system of segregated education. But that contention had not been raised earlier; the plaintiffs had indicated, in fact, that they had no objection to "separate but equal." Harlan thus saw no "need [to] consider that question in [the] case."[143] Instead, he concluded for the brethren that the closing of the white high school would in no way provide relief for the black students and affirmed the Georgia supreme court on that narrow ground. "[T]he result" of a ruling granting the black parents the relief they sought, he declared, "would only be to take from white children educational privileges enjoyed by them, without giving to colored children additional opportunities."[144]

Harlan did suggest that a suit seeking a separate high school for black children might have raised "different questions." But he also stressed that public education was "a matter belonging to the respective states, and [that] any interference on the part of Federal authority with the management of such schools cannot be justified except in the case of a clear and unmistakable disregard of rights secured by the supreme law of the land."[145]

Shortly after Harlan's grandson joined the Court years later, Justice Felix Frankfurter discovered the *Cumming* case. A relatively consistent proponent of judicial self-restraint, who had dismissed the activist Harlan I as an "eccentric,"[146] Frankfurter was one of the justices most reluctant to encroach upon state control of public education in the *Brown* case.[147] From *Cumming* and presumably other evidence, he had formed a "hunch," he wrote the second Justice Harlan, that "Harlan I . . . would have sustained [school] segregation had the issue squarely come before the Court in his day."[148] Frankfurter found it hard to believe that a judge who considered segregated education unconstitutional could have written the Court's opinion in the *Cumming* case, particularly since Judge Calloway—"a true-blue southern Southerner"—had ruled against the segregation at issue there.[149]

In his reply, Harlan II agreed that "*Plessy* [provided] little basis for thinking that the old boy would have voted against school segregation." His reading of *Cumming*, as well as elements in his grandfather's background, led him to conclude, however, that the justice "would have been *against* segregation." Judge Calloway's opinion, he reminded Frankfurter, was "interesting," but not "contra segregation, only pro separate *but* equal."[150]

Characteristically, Frankfurter persisted with his campaign. In *Plessy*, he reminded the grandson, the grandfather had mentioned "about a score of times" that the segregation at issue involved use of the public highways.[151] The elder Harlan was hardly "persnickety as an ordinary rule, in restricting his opinion to the narrow scope of the facts of a case." His failure to refer at all to school segregation, or to use *Plessy* as a platform for attacking segregation laws generally, was thus for Frankfurter convincing, if not conclusive, evidence that Harlan I did not consider segregated public education unconstitutional. If a Georgia judge could find a basis for invalidating the school board's decision, he added, surely a judge of Harlan I's "intellectual habits" could have also, if indeed he opposed segregated schools:

> [W]hatever virtues may be attributed to Harlan I, no one, I submit, would credit—or charge—him with having been a close reasoner, more particularly, a writer who strictly confined himself to the narrow limits of a particular case. And even when it comes to what might be called a narrow adjudication, I submit that any judge who thought that the Constitution, as a legal proposition, is color blind, would at least have been able to reach the lawyer-like result . . . in not leaving colored high school children out in the cold.[152]

Harlan II also mentioned that his grandfather had done "an about-face on the Civil War Amendments."[153] Frankfurter was not impressed. Harlan I's initial opposition to Reconstruction had "aroused hostility to his appointment." And he would not have been the only judge, declared Frankfurter, "who, by his opinions, contradicted, however unconsciously, the ground of opposition to him."[154]

Frankfurter's arguments are well taken. Nor did Harlan's opposition, late in his career, to a state law requiring segregation in private schools resolve the issue. In a 1908 case,[155] Harlan vehemently condemned his native state's campaign against interracial education at Berea College as an "arbitrary . . . not to say cruel," interference with individual liberty, exclaiming, "Have we become so inoculated with prejudice of race that an American government, professedly based on the principles of freedom, and charged with the protection of all citizens alike, can make distinctions between such citizens in the matter of their voluntary meeting for innocent purposes simply because of their respective races?" He carefully pointed out, however, that his remarks had "no reference to regulations prescribed for public schools, established at the pleasure of the state and maintained at the public expense. No such question is here presented and it need not be now discussed."[156]

Whatever his precise feelings, later generations would view Harlan's *Plessy* dissent as a repudiation of all forms of state-mandated segregation. At least one of the justice's contemporaries sensed, moreover, its ultimate impact on the nation's destiny. Following the Court's decision, Chief Justice Fuller's former law partner, Henry M. Shepard, wrote to Harlan from Chicago to express his "gratification" at what the justice had written. "It will stand," Shepard predicted, "when the majority opinion will be forgotten."[157]

Liberty

John Harlan's Court contemporaries not only helped to dismantle the movement for racial equality and human dignity the Civil War and Reconstruction had begun; within two decades of the war's end, a majority had begun to convert the Fourteenth Amendment and other constitutional provisions into tools of *laissez faire*, shielding American commerce and industry from controls adopted by the voters' elected representatives.

In the *Slaughterhouse Cases* of 1873, the Supreme Court's first confrontation with the meaning of the Fourteenth Amendment, a majority had confined the amendment's reach largely to its historic racial context and refused to strike down a state law granting monopoly privileges to a New Orleans slaughterhouse concern. The amendment's guarantee against state laws abridging the privileges or immunities of U.S. citizens, Justice Miller reasoned for the majority, covered only a narrow range of rights enjoyed by citizens in their relations with the national government, its powers, and laws, rather than economic freedom and other basic rights of state citizenship. Resort to the amendment's equal protection and due process clauses was to no avail either. The former, according to the *Slaughterhouse* majority, was intended primarily to cover racial discrimination, not the sort of economic classification the challenged monopoly represented; and a state's grant of monopoly privileges to one business hardly amounted to a denial of due process.[1]

Munn v. *Illinois* (1877), decided the term preceding Justice Harlan's appointment, upheld a state law regulating grain elevator rates and reaffirmed the Court's reluctance to convert the Fourteenth Amendment into a significant safeguard of private property. Government clearly possessed broad power to regulate private enterprise in the public interest, Chief Justice Waite concluded, and those seeking relief for what they considered abuses of such authority "must resort to the polls, not to the courts."[2]

With changing personnel, however, the Court gradually discarded the *Slaughterhouse* and *Munn* precedents and embraced *laissez faire*. By the late 1880s, the justices were adopting the rhetoric of substantive due process—the notion that laws that unreasonably interfere with liberty and property violate due process required of the states by the Fourteenth Amendment, and of federal officials by the Fifth, just as much as unfair or arbitrary procedural practices.[3] In *Allgeyer* v. *Louisiana* (1897),[4] the Court struck down for the first time a state economic control on substantive due process grounds. Succeeding terms saw the doctrine applied to a host of business regulations, from wage and hour laws to pricing provisions.[5] In another line of cases, moreover, a majority of justices narrowly construed Congress's commerce and taxing powers, while also invoking the Tenth Amendment to invalidate federal economic controls held to encroach on the reserved powers of the states.[6]

Justice Harlan joined and even spoke for the Court in several such cases. At times, too, he privately applauded those promoting "protection to American industry."[7] But Harlan was also an admirer of the *Munn* decision, writing Chief Justice Fuller gleefully in 1891, "*Munn* v. *Illinois* is still in force, ready to do battle against all the Romans, however able or noble."[8] Someone with the Justice's Whig nationalist heritage, moreover, was unlikely to condone aggressive judicial restrictions on congressional power or exalt "states' rights." It was thus not surprising that Harlan generally opposed the Court's *laissez faire* leanings, especially its curbing of national authority.

Harlan and Money

While Harlan's Whig background clearly affected his position regarding the scope of federal regulatory power, his own financial experiences may also have had an impact on his thinking regarding corporate wealth and the degree to which government could and should regulate private property. Throughout his adult life following his father's death, Harlan seemed to be perennially in debt, constantly pressed by creditors, and on the brink of bankruptcy, while at the same time attempting to maintain the lifestyle expected of a prominent national figure.

The reasons for Harlan's chronic insolvency appear relatively obvious. His preCourt political activities undoubtedly detracted from his legal practice; the hard times regularly confronting the nation following the war meant, moreover, that he was often unable to collect the fees his clients owed him. According to family lore, in fact, he left Kentucky for Washington with $100,000 owed him in fees, most of which were never collected. The continuing financial plight of the *Louisville Commercial*, which he and other stockholders were forced to sell in 1879, was no help either.[9]

The justice's papers suggest, too, that he was an easy mark for relatives and friends. In the late 1860s, his cousin, Wellington Harlan, was involved in a bitter dispute with Harlan and other family members over the disposition of an estate.[10] But that difficulty was resolved, and Wellington sought loans from his cousin on several occasions.[11] When Wellington faced legal action for signing a friend's name to a note without his acquaintance's permission, he also turned to Harlan for help, pleading, "I am ruined and our name disgraced unless you come to my aid."[12]

Other relatives asking for Harlan's assistance included an aunt who requested funds for clothing;[13] a cousin who wanted money for "a splendid sewing machine.";[14] and Harlan Hiter's sister, who, it will be recalled, persuaded the justice to finance her brother's legal training. In fact, once when seeking assistance for "the sake of wife and little ones," Wellington Harlan conceded his cousin's "kinfolks" had caused him a "great deal" of (presumably financial) trouble. But Wellington assumed it would be "so easy out of your abundance" for Harlan to assist him in his "extremity."[15] Other relatives and friends apparently had the same impression.

Appointment to the bench and a fixed annual salary of $10,000 further complicated Harlan's precarious financial situation. Kentucky banks were soon hounding him for payment of notes. Gus Willson, among others, recommended that the justice simply refuse to renew any loans or pay additional interest.[16] And while Harlan apparently agreed to attempt to pay off 50 percent of the indebtedness that had prompted Willson's suggestion,[17] he continued to amass loans and fail to satisfy previous notes. In 1888, for example, an official of Louisville's German Security Bank berated a Washington attorney who had failed to secure a loan settlement from the justice. "If timid about it," the bank's officer, J.S. Barret, wrote, "return us the note and we will send it to an atty who is not afraid of the Justice and who will sue for us."[18] The lawyer shared the bank's letter with Harlan, and a settlement was ultimately reached.[19]

Harlan seemed aware, however, that his judicial position insulated him somewhat from the pressures of creditors, and he was willing to take advantage of his situation. In his will, Mrs. Harlan's father forgave a $10,000 loan to his son-in-law.[20] Later, however, Mallie's brothers, John Gilbert and George Shanklin, permitted the Shanklin estate to endorse a $5,000 note obtained by the justice from Louisville's Second National Bank. By 1880, the bank was pressing for payment and even initiated a suit against Harlan and the estate.[21] But the brothers assured the justice they were unconcerned. In one letter to Harlan, George Shanklin recommended that his brother-in-law simply "make the best terms you can with your creditors and get in a position to live comfortably with your family," adding, "don't bother about Mallie's property. I have 'raised' her to little purpose if she would not willingly sacrifice all else the world has to offer for the sake of those she loves!"[22]

It was hardly surprising, therefore, that as late as 1894 the brothers were being pressed about debts they had endorsed for Harlan. In that year, George Shanklin wrote his brother-in-law that the Kentucky National Bank was willing to wipe out a note for a relatively nominal payment. In reply, Harlan instructed the brothers "[i]n coming to an arrangement . . . not [to] assume to represent me or to speak for me. . . . As the matter now stands the Bank cannot annoy me. . . . The truth is that Judge Ballard, who was President of the Ky. Nat. Bank told me that the Bank would never bother me—had charged off the debt as lost—and that it would be content with whatever it got from your father's estate." At that point, Harlan wanted to avoid even acknowledging his debt. "I do not wish by any paper or release, to give [the bank] any additional capacity to annoy me."[23]

Even so, Harlan's persistent financial woes were a constant source of personal embarrassment and anxiety. Early in his judicial tenure, in fact, he considered resigning from the bench and returning to private practice in an effort to meet the demands of creditors. But family, friends, and even creditors dissuaded him from such a drastic step. In February of 1880, for example, his brother, James, cited the "inestimable value" his remaining on the Court would bring his family.[24] In a letter written in March of that same year, a Louisville bank official stressed that he and his colleagues possessed the "warmest friendship" for the Harlans, assured the justice that he would be "satisfied" with the proposal for resolving his debts that they were planning to offer, and urged Harlan not to think "for a moment of leaving the bench."[25]

Later that year, the justice wrote his old friend, Thomas W. Bullitt, now a bank representative seeking to collect yet another Harlan note, that he "[a]t one time . . . seriously considered" returning to private practice but had decided that the earnings from a Louisville practice would be insufficient to both support his family and meet his debts, which then amounted, he wrote, to more than $30,000, and that a move to a larger city was fraught with uncertainties as to "what I could accomplish." He should have sought the advice of friends earlier, he confessed, but his "pride" and "the hope that I could devise some scheme for my relief" had "held [him] back."[26]

Ten days later, the justice deeded two pieces of Louisville property to Bullitt for sale in the hope that the proceeds might substantially reduce his debts to the two banks Bullitt represented.[27] But the justice's financial burdens hardly subsided, and in succeeding years he continued to yearn for some arrangement that could provide him and his family financial security. When Gus Willson informed him in 1893, for example, that a prominent figure had been offered a lectureship at the University of Chicago, for a reported annual stipend of $25,000, Harlan's response was understandable, if crass. "If Rockefeller should make me such an offer, accompanied by a promise that in the event I became disabled by physical or other infirmity, from discharging my duties as lecturer I was to have a pension for life sufficient to maintain me, I should be greatly tempted to surrender my present position and accept his offer."[28]

By that point, however, Harlan had realized that his financial lot was permanently cast. "[I]t is hardly worth while to talk of such matters," he wrote Willson regarding the prospects for a lucrative lectureship, "because it is not likely that any such offer will be made to me."[29] In a letter to George Shanklin the following year, moreover, he seemed even more resigned to his financial fate. "I wish I had the money to pay off the old debts," he observed. "But I have not and never expect to have. It is too late for me to quit the Bench and go to the practice. If I could call back 10 years I would do so. So I have nothing to do but to 'jog along' in life, working hard, living economically, dying poor, and, finally, going—well, to Oak Hill Cemetery."[30]

Sadly, the justice's financial plight even strained his relations with his sons. Their offer to assist him in financing construction of the Euclid Avenue house the family occupied from the late 1880s obviously pleased him, and he apparently had no qualms about having his sons sign notes and, in James's case, put up property as surety for the venture. He took an active part, moreover, in overseeing the house's construction and pressing for the paving of Fourteenth Street out to Euclid Avenue.[31] But the newspaper publicity given the arrangement must have embarrassed him. A social note in a Danville, Kentucky, paper carried this account of his sons' generosity:

> The three boys of Justice John M. Harlan have presented that gentleman with a comfortable home in Washington City. Judge Harlan had become involved pecuniarily by endorsement for friends before his appointment to the Supreme Bench, and his fortune was swept away by these endorsements. He has three noble boys, who determined to prepare a home for the father and mother in Washington, and accordingly they bought a lot and erected a home for the Judge and his family as a token of their affection for them. It is a source of higher pleasure to be the father of such a lot of boys than to own a dozen palaces in Washington.[32]

In a letter accompanying the clipping, the justice's brother, James, indicated, "mention [had] been made by most of the Kentucky papers."[33]

Harlan bitterly resented the terms under which the sons wanted their parents to occupy the house. According to his account of the arrangement, the Harlans were to be entitled to live there throughout their lives, after which the property would revert to their sons and their sons' descendants. "Mama will thus have, in effect, only the right to use it during her life," the exasperated justice wrote John Maynard. "If during our lives it should for any reason be deemed by us prudent to give up the house and live elsewhere, the question as to what is to be done with it, or in what property its proceeds [are] to be invested, is to be determined by others, not by [us] . . . that which is occupied as our house is to belong, for all purposes of absolute control . . . , to others, not to her." Harlan was "utterly opposed to occupying any house upon such terms." They would be nothing more than "renters pure and simple," he declared, and he would not yield to any such "relation . . . [with] any of [his] children." Any house to which he contributed payments "must be dedicated for a home for Mama and to be absolutely hers, of which she is to be mistress, with uncontrolled power to dispose of it in her lifetime or by will as she pleases."[34]

Harlan suspected, correctly no doubt, that his sons feared the property might be lost to sale or mortgage if deeded to their mother. (His emphasis on securing the house for Mrs. Harlan may have been calculated to play on his sons' sympathies, but it may have simply reflected his realization that placing the house in his name would make it vulnerable to creditors.) He conceded, too, that "her or my necessities" might require disposal of the house at some point. He agreed that his sons should have a claim on the property to the extent of their "actual outlay," that they should "not . . . lose anything by the venture," and that title could be placed in the name of a trustee. But he insisted that Mrs. Harlan should have the right to dispose of the house "without the surveillance or control of any one." And if his sons could not accept such a condition, the property should be sold and the justice left "free to make my own arrangement for a home that will really belong to Mama."[35]

Eventually, the differences over the conditions under which the Harlans were to occupy the house were resolved, although the precise terms of the arrangement remain unclear. The strains the transaction created within the family hardly subsided, however. On at least one occasion, James resisted his father's proposal to have the mortgage on the house increased by between $7,000 and $8,000. "As it stands now," wrote James, the house "is an asset that some day may prove a great comfort to mother and the girls." But "[a] house overburdened with debt [was] no home at all."[36] In March of 1891, James complained to his father that his law practice was poor and asked the Justice to contribute a larger portion of the mortgage payments.[37] The next year, he reminded the justice that he was falling seriously behind in the contributions he had agreed to make.[38]

Nor was the Euclid Avenue house the only source of financial tensions between the Harlans and their sons. To relieve their father "from embarrassment," Richard and John Maynard had secured one of his notes with Louisville's German Security Bank, and then in 1889 were urged by an attorney for the bank to permit the sale of property connected with the note for a much lower price than they thought it should be worth.[39] A notation on a letter regarding the matter indicates, moreover, that the justice himself wrote the response which John Maynard sent the attorney, urging the bank to grant his father an "acquittance" from the debt and declaring that the elder Harlan had "no means whatever with which to meet the balance."[40]

Harlan's financial woes touched friends as well as family members. Eli Murray made him loans and endorsed notes,[41] for example, and Murray's brother, Logan, intervened in the justice's behalf with creditors.[42] Although the precise circumstances of the arrangement are unclear, a letter written to Harlan by a Washington bank indicates that Justice Field once endorsed his colleague's note for nearly $5,000, and that Field's nephew, Justice David Brewer, actually made monthly payments on a note for over $1,500 that the same bank had extended to Harlan and his son, Richard.[43]

Harlan's indebtedness to friends and banks may have accelerated his patronage and related efforts in their behalf. Harlan's support was probably decisive, for example, in Eli Murray's appointment as governor of the Utah territory. There is no evidence, however, that the justice's precarious finances led to any improper judicial behavior on his part. In fact, when Logan Murray offered Harlan's son, Richard, a single share of mining stock, the justice initially agreed that Richard could accept the gift, but soon changed his mind. He explained to his friend,

> I was . . . willing that Richard should accept it at the hands of an old friend for whom I cherished the warmest of affection, and between whom and myself there had existed for many years relations of the most intimate kind. But further reflection satisfied me that there were reasons why neither I nor any of my family should become interested in mining stocks. . . . There are now upon the docket of our Court several mining cases from the West, and we are likely for many years to have such cases before us. These cases may involve questions of great moment to all who are interested in mining property or mining stocks. If Richard should become the owner of any mining stocks it might be that his interests would be affected by our decision and that, too, without my knowledge, at the time, that such would be the result. I prefer that no such complications should exist and hence, with Richard's consent, return the certificate. . . . I am sure that you will concur with me in saying that a Judge should avoid even the appearance of evil. Come this way before [long], for I wish to talk to you about our "old Kentucky home."[44]

At the same time, the justice's money woes seem to have contributed to a deep skepticism, if not envy, of those possessing great wealth. In a letter to Gus Willson, he once vehemently declared,

The fact is the wealth of the country has for years evaded the payment of its fair share of taxes. That is the belief throughout the entire country, and it is well founded. It is a curious fact in my experience that I never knew a *very* rich man who was not astute in attempting to evade the payment of his proper share of taxes. . . . The fury of socialism is equaled by the fury with which mere millionaires, taking them as a class, and corporations, resent any attempt to make them pay their share of taxes. Many millionaires as they walk the streets, complain in their own minds that Tom, Dick and Harry whom they meet as they pass along, contribute nothing in the way of taxes to the Government. But those fellows forget that the men who are not able to pay taxes are those who, in time of trouble, give their lives to maintain their government and thereby protect the property of the well-to-do people of the country.[45]

As his letter to Willson suggests, Harlan's own precarious condition may have honed his sympathies for the poor and his sensitivity to their continuing struggle for survival—feelings he apparently first began to develop, it will be recalled, during his wartime service with lowly enlisted men. That affinity for society's unwashed and scorn for its wealthy may in turn have influenced the justice's response to laws enacted to curb corporate excess and relieve the plight of the poor.

The 1895 Trilogy

Only an undated portion of the justice's letter to Gus Willson survives. It was undoubtedly written, however, during the Court's monumental 1895 battle over Congress's power to tax income. Harlan's dissents in the income tax case, *Pollock* v. *Farmer's Loan & Trust Co.*[46] and his stance in two other cases of that eventful year[47] reflect the core of the justice's thinking regarding governmental authority over economic interests.

In early January of that year, the Court, in *United States* v. *E.C. Knight Co.*,[48] largely emasculated the Sherman Antitrust Act, passed by Congress in 1890 to control monopolies from restraining interstate commerce. The government had invoked the act in an effort to break up a trust that had gained control of 98 percent of the sugar refined in the United States. Speaking for the Court, Chief Justice Fuller deemed the sugar trust a monopoly over manufacturing rather than commerce and thus beyond the reach of the Sherman Act and Congress' interstate commerce power. Fuller naturally conceded that virtually complete control over the manufacture of a product would have a tremendous impact over interstate trade in the product. But such effects, declared Fuller, were only "indirect," not "direct," and extension of congressional authority to such practices would leave "comparatively little of business operations and affairs . . . for state control."[49]

Fuller's artificial distinctions between "manufacture" and "commerce," "direct" and "indirect" effects, and national and state power were to become principal weapons of those justices bent on shielding industry from governmental control. Harlan, the lone dissenter, was not impressed. If Congress could not reach the "stupendous combination" the sugar interests had conspired to create, he warned, it would possess virtually no "power to deal with gigantic monopolies holding in their grasp, and injuriously controlling in their own interest, the entire trade among the states in food products that are essential to the comfort of every household in the land."[50] He conceded that "the preservation of the just authority of the states is an object of deep concern to every lover of his country," but proclaimed national authority equally essential, both to the "safety of the states" and "to the attainment of the important ends for which that government was ordained by the people." That power, he declared, should not be given "an interpretation so rigid, technical, and narrow that those objects [could not] be accomplished."[51]

In Harlan's judgment, the sugar trust clearly lay within the scope of congressional power:

> Any combination . . . that disturbs or unreasonably obstructs freedom in buying and selling articles manufactured to be sold to persons in other states, or to be carried to other states,—a freedom that cannot exist if the right to buy and sell is fettered by unlawful restraints that crush out competition—affects, not incidentally, but directly, the people of all the states; and the remedy for such an evil is found only in the exercise of powers confided to a government which, this court has said, was the government of all, exercising powers delegated by all, representing all, acting for all.[52]

Nor would such exercises of national power interfere with state authority. No individual state after all, asserted Harlan, was any match for a monopoly of truly national scope.

As the legal citations accompanying his dissent indicate, Harlan's construction of congressional authority largely tracked that espoused by Chief Justice Marshall.[53] But his contempt and fear of great wealth were also clearly evident. "Men who form and control these combinations," he asserted at one point, ". . . will be satisfied with nothing less than to have the whole population of America pay tribute to them."[54] In another vehement passage, he condemned "overshadowing combinations . . . governed entirely by the law of greed and selfishness."[55]

The scorn the justice exhibited toward corporate greed in the sugar trust case was mild, however, in comparison with the fury the debate over the income tax brought bubbling to the surface. The Wilson Tariff Act, passed by Congress in 1894, had imposed a 2 percent tax on incomes exceeding $4,000. The act was to become effective on January 1, 1895. Previous rulings of the Supreme Court barred the federal courts from enjoining the collection of federal taxes. Instead, taxpayers were obliged to pay levies under protest, then sue for their return on the ground that the tax at issue was unconstitutional or otherwise invalid. William D. Gutherie, a young New York lawyer, hit on a scheme, however, for shortcutting this process. Stockholders were encouraged to sue companies to prevent payment of the tax. One Charles Pollock, a Massachusetts stockholder, filed suit against the Farmer's Loan & Trust Company of New York. Similar actions were brought by other stockholders against the Continental Trust Company, another New York firm, and a Pennsylvania company.[56]

Obviously, both the stockholders and the trusts wanted the tax invalidated. To avoid the appearance, if not the substance, of complicity, the companies retained able attorneys—led by James C. Carter, one of the outstanding members of the Supreme Court bar—to defend the law. Attorney General Richard Olney also argued in support of the tax, while a number of distinguished lawyers, including

Joseph H. Choate, former senator George F. Edmunds, and Harlan's former friend, Benjamin H. Bristow, challenged its validity. Following the failure to secure a favorable ruling in the lower courts, counsel for the stockholders carried the case to the Supreme Court where, in March, the justices heard an entire week of arguments in a courtroom packed with Washington notables.

On April 8, less than a month following oral argument, Chief Justice Fuller announced a decision invalidating portions of the Wilson Act. All the justices agreed, consistent with earlier rulings, that the law was unconstitutional to the extent that it taxed income from state and municipal bonds and thus offended principles of federalism. Over the dissents of Harlan and Justice White, a majority also struck down the tax the statute imposed on income from land, Fuller declaring that such levies were "direct" taxes required by the Constitution to be apportioned among the states according to population, rather than on the basis of the income amassed.[57] Ailing Justice Howell Jackson had not participated in the cases, however, and the eight remaining justices divided evenly on other issues raised in the litigation—specifically, whether a tax on income from personal property was also a direct tax subject to the apportionment requirement and whether the entire act should be voided as a result of the Court's decision regarding taxes on real estate income.[58]

In a lengthy dissent, Justice White saw no meaningful difference between a suit to restrain payment of a tax, which prior decisions prohibited, and the stockholder cases before the Court. White also challenged the majority's conclusion that taxes on real estate income were direct taxes subject to the apportionment requirement.[59] Justice Harlan limited himself to an unemotional two-page opinion concurring in White's dissent.[60]

But neither the Court nor Harlan was finished with the income tax. Opponents of the tax promptly filed a petition for rehearing, which the Court granted. On April 15, Justice Jackson, whose condition ranged from critical to guarded and who was being pressed to return to the Court or resign his seat, informed Chief Justice Fuller that he would participate in the second hearing.[61] Reargument of the cases began on May 6, again in a crowded courtroom, and lasted for three days. Then, the nation waited impatiently for the justices' decision.

Most impatient of all apparently was Justice Field, the income tax's most vehement opponent on the Court. On May 17, Field wrote Chief Justice Fuller to urge that the Court's decision be announced "as soon as practicable." The previous evening, Field had yielded to the advice of friends and injected an aching knee joint with carbolic acid. The result, he reported, had been "paroxysms of pain . . . so great, that I thought for some time that I should not be able to survive." Compounding his agony was "the thought that if I did not survive, our action in reference to the Income Tax cases would be entirely defeated." Field hoped that Fuller could announce the Court's decision the following Monday, May 20, even if additional time were needed for completion of the Chief Justice's opinion. "My hold upon life is too slight for me to trust, with any reasonable assurance," the anguished justice added, "to the certain continuance of it beyond a day."[62]

Field was to survive another four years, and the precise impact of his plea on the timing of the Court's decision is not known. That Monday, however, the chief justice delivered a five-to-four decision striking down the entire tax act before a courtroom crowded with spectators. Fuller consumed approximately fifty minutes in reading his opinion, but its gist was obvious: taxes on income from personal property, like those on real estate income, were unconstitutional unless apportioned among the states according to their population, rather than the distribution of income. Since the various provisions of the law constituted a single scheme of taxation, moreover, all must fall.[63]

Then it was Harlan's turn. Speaking forcefully and vehemently, gesturing and at times pounding the bench with his fist for emphasis, the justice vigorously challenged the majority's ruling and rationale. The decision, he declared, flew in the face of numerous rulings going back to the earliest days of the republic, including *Hylton* v. *United States* (1796),[64] holding excise taxes to be "indirect" rather than "direct" levies, and *Springer* v. *United States* (1881),[65] which had upheld an income tax assessed to finance the Civil War. But for Harlan the decision was more than simply an affront to long precedent. It also threatened national authority to deal effectively with developing emergencies and "tend[ed] to re-establish that condition of helplessness in which congress found itself during the period of the Articles of Confederation, when it was without authority . . . to lay and collect . . . taxes sufficient to pay the debts and defray the expenses of government, but was dependent in all such matters upon the good will of the states."[67]

Harlan was most indignant, however, at the "gross injustice to the many for the benefit of the favored," which the ruling represented. Requiring taxes to be apportioned among the states according to population would allow those with the greatest ability to pay, and arguably the greatest debt to the nation, to escape their fair share of tax burdens. He further argued:

> In the large cities or financial centers of the country there are persons deriving enormous incomes from the renting of houses that have been erected . . . for the sole purpose of being rented. Near by are other persons, trusts, combinations, and corporations, possessing vast quantities of personal property, including bonds and stocks of railroad, telegraph, mining, telephone, banking, coal, oil, gas, and sugar-refining corporations, from which millions upon millions of income are regularly derived. . . . And it is now the law, as this day declared, that under the constitution, . . . congress cannot tax [income from such property] . . . while it may compel the merchant, the artisan, the workman, the artist, the author, the lawyer, the physician, even the minister of the Gospel, no one of whom happens to own real estate, invested personal property, stocks, or bonds, to contribute directly . . . for the support of the government.[67]

Nor could the justice abide the claim of critics that the tax law "was an assault by the poor upon the rich," and its demise a victory for "the just rights of property against the advancing hosts of socialism." For him, the extensive exemptions granted large holdings of capital were conclusive evidence that Congress had no sympathy for "the pernicious theories of socialism," nor any desire "to despoil the rich."[68] In any event, the Court had no authority to make judgments on the wisdom or expediency of laws otherwise within congressional power to enact. If Congress went too far, in the eyes of the public, "the remedy for such abuses [was] to be found at the ballot box, and in a wholesome public opinion, which the representatives of the people will not long, if at all, disregard, and not in the disregard by the judiciary of powers that have been committed to another branch of the government."[69]

But the concluding paragraph of his opinion captured best Harlan's moral outrage:

> The practical effect of the decision to-day is to give certain kinds of property a position of favoritism and advantage inconsistent with the fundamental principles of our social organization, and to invest them with power and influence that may be perilous to that portion of the American people upon whom rests the larger part of the burdens of the government, and who ought not to be subjected to the dominion of aggregated wealth any more than the property of the country should be at the mercy of the lawless.[70]

Most of the nation's major newspapers, themselves associated with great wealth, praised the *Pollock* majority's wisdom. The New York *Tribune* thanked the Court for refusing to permit government "to be dragged into communistic warfare against rights of property," while the city's *Herald* predicted that "this particular form of populistic interference with individual rights will probably never be revived"; the *Philadelphia Inquirer* termed the decision "a fatal blow to an insidious form of communism," and the *New York Times*, alluding to the regional concentration of the nation's wealth, condemned the tax law as "sectional, aimed by the south and west against the north and east"; and numerous other papers echoed such sentiments.[71] But press reaction was by no means entirely one-sided. The New York *World* saw invalidation of the tax as "the triumph of selfishness over patriotism" and "another victory of greed over need." Many papers of the South and West were equally scornful of the majority's action.

Critics of the ruling directed some of their ire at the justice who had shifted his position on the tax between the Court's first and second rulings in the cases. On April 6, two days prior to announcement of the first decision, the *Chicago Tribune* had published a lengthy article purporting to detail the justices' debate over the tax law in the Court's conference room. The leak—widely attributed to Justice Harlan or his sons, although its source has never been established—claimed that Harlan, White, Henry Billings Brown, and George Shiras had voted in conference to sustain the act.[72] Since Jackson joined Harlan, White, and Brown in dissenting from the Court's second ruling, Court observers concluded that Shiras, one of the Court's best-liked if obscure members, had abandoned his initial support for the income tax. Subsequent research has shifted suspicion to other justices, including Justice Field's nephew, David Brewer.[73] But contemporary opponents of the majority's decision derisively tagged Shiras the "vacillating judge."

Most of the press commentary relating to specific justices, however, focused on Harlan and particularly on his courtroom demeanor during delivery of his May 20 dissent. The justice, one paper supportive of the majority exclaimed, "pounded the desk, shook his finger under the noses of the Chief Justice and Mr. Justice Field, turned more than once angrily upon his colleagues of the majority, and expressed his dissent from their conclusions in a tone and language more appropriate to a stump speech at a Populist barbeque than to an opinion on a question of law before the Supreme Court of the United States."[74] The New York *Tribune* added Justice

Horace Gray to the list of brethren toward whom the Justice had directed his ire.[75] *The Nation* scorned Harlan's "unbecoming . . . behavior" as an "harangue" and "escapade,"[76] while the *New York Times*, in a news story, termed the justice's dissent "little less than a stump speech crowded with inflammatory statements and thinly disguised sneers."[77] The *Times* and *Nation*, among other organs, charged, moreover, that Harlan, who was often mentioned in the press as a presidential prospect, had simply been stung by the "presidential bee."[78] Many other dailies and weeklies raised similar complaints.[79]

Such accounts enraged the justice. In a lengthy letter to his sons, James and John Maynard, he urged them not to become alarmed at the reports of "lying newspaper correspondents." He could never, he assured them, be rude to the chief justice who was "always courteous"; and any report that he had gestured in Fuller's face had "not the slightest foundation in truth." He had, he conceded, read a portion of his opinion directly to Justice Field, but only after being provoked.

> The fact is that Justice Field, who has acted often like a mad man during the whole of this contest about the income tax, bothered the Chief Justice on his left and Gray on his right, with sharp running comments on my opinion as it was being read. Offended by his unseemly conduct and discourtesy, I turned sharply towards him and read a part of my opinion directly at him. This was observed by many in the bar, and it was perhaps the occasion of the statement by the newspaper correspondents to the effect that I glared at some of my associates who were of the majority.[80]

Harlan admitted, too, that he had spoken in a loud, forceful voice and gestured often, but had no apologies for his behavior. "As this case was one of vast importance, I determined that I should be heard. So I read my opinion in a clear, distinct, audible tone of voice, which, I am told, rang through the court room so that everyone present heard each word of the opinion and took it for what it was worth. My voice and manner undoubtedly indicated a good deal of earnestness, and I am quite willing that it should have been so interpreted. I feel deeply about the case, and naturally the extent of my feeling was shown by my voice and manner." He was certain, moreover, that it was his message, not his demeanor, which had disturbed his critics. "The fact is, as I am constrained to believe, the dissent cut to the quick some that held contrary views, not because of any harshness of words used by me, but because of the exposure of the dangers that would follow the decision of the court."

Harlan's contempt for his press critics and their financial backers was at least as great as theirs for him. Edwin L. Godkin of the New York *Evening Post* and its weekly, *The Nation*, he sneered, "could not live without lying. . . . He is a low bred foreigner who has no sort of affection for this country or our institutions and is the mouthpiece of men in New York who care nothing for the country, and have no concern except for the handling of bonds and stocks." He labeled another journalist critic an "unmitigated scamp who loves money more than he does all else on earth." One of the papers "assail[ing]" the *Pollock* dissenters, he declared, was "really" owned by Southern Pacific Railroad President C. P. Huntington, "one of the monster swindlers of this age of money getting."[81]

Most galling of all to the justice was the charge that his dissent and courtroom demeanor smacked of politics. Such talk, he asserted, could impair his effectiveness as a judge, and he had agonized over how he could put a stop to it. Some years earlier, a "man from Kansas" had written to him regarding a Harlan presidential bid. "I not only said [in reply] that I would never accept political station," the justice assured his sons, "but expressed myself in favor of an amendment to the Constitution which would make a judge of the Supreme Court forever ineligible to any office of honor, trust, or profit, Federal or State." He wished that man "would, if alive, give [his letter] to the public."[82]

Harlan's critics were not the only ones who raised questions regarding the tenor of his dissent. When he sent William Howard Taft a copy, indicating that he might produce a lengthier revised version, the future chief justice responded that, based on "the little I have read of the case," he would probably have joined Harlan in dissent, especially in view of the strong precedent supporting characterization of the income tax as an "indirect" levy. Taft questioned, however, whether the justice should file "a longer or more elaborate opinion" as well as the tenor of Harlan's initial effort. "I hope it is not presuming in me," wrote the sixth circuit's chief judge, "to suggest that some of your expressions separated from the context are capable of being twisted into meanings which you would be the last to intend and are likely to be thus seized upon by unscrupulous persons to foment the very bitterness of controversy which I know both from your present opinion, and your lifelong views you strongly deprecate."[83] The revised opinion Harlan produced was somewhat more moderate in tone, moreover, than the version read in Court; it was perhaps for that reason that Justice Jackson termed the new effort "a great improvement [over] the opinion as announced from the Bench," adding: "I congratulate you on this dissent, which will fully vindicate the position of the minority, and will, I am sure, be regarded by the Bench and bar of the country as the soundest view of the question. It seems to me unanswerable."[84]

In fairness to Harlan, however, the ridicule heaped on his courtroom performance and the harsh tone of his oral dissent probably stemmed more from the fact, as the justice put it, that his views "cut [the opposition] to the quick" than from his demeanor. At least one press account noted that Justices Field and Gray "occasionally exchanged whispered comments" while Harlan was speaking.[85] Another article indicated that Gray was "evidently amused" by Harlan's dissent, "for his mouth every now and then twitched involuntarily, his eyes sparkled and his cheeks seemed half inclined to break into a smile."[86] Yet another observed that Justice White "made no attempt [while reading his dissent] to veil either his words or his feelings, and his criticism of the verdict, and by innuendo his associates, was savage. At times he disregarded the prepared opinion in front of him and interjected some extemporaneous expressions which added to the caustic assault he was making on the majority of the Court."[87] Yet only Harlan's conduct was the focus of scorn.

Whatever assessment his behavior in the cases deserves, those sympathetic with the justice's stance bolstered his spirits with letters of praise. A Kentuckian applauded his "honest indignation, and genuine patriotism";[88] another wrote of Harlan's "magnificent protest."[89] A member of the Virginia court of appeals to whom Harlan had written in defense of his conduct, assured the justice that he could "understand how earnestly you felt, how intensely wrought up you must have been," adding: "I, in common with many others, regard you as the ablest man now upon the court."[90] Many other letters were to like effect.

Several of Harlan's defenders were as contemptuous of corporate greed and the Court's protection of privilege as the justice had been. "One need not be a Socialist or a Populist, but merely an American," wrote the son of Oliver Morton, "to observe with keen regret and with something of a sense of humiliation, the incredible meanness of our rich, and their ignoble efforts to dodge taxation or to shift its burden upon a wage-earning class who are ever on the margin of penury. The solicitude of these opponents of the income tax concerning the Constitution is really exquisite."[91] One of the justice's law students expressed "admiration and respect" for his professor's "abilities, . . . broadmindedness, . . . pure Americanism and . . . personal character," but disdain for "artificial" constructions of the Constitution which enabled "[g]reedy aggregations of wealth [to] hide behind that instrument and cry 'unconstitutional.'"[92] And in a letter that Harlan shared with his sons, former Massachusetts Senator George Boutwell termed the majority's ruling "the greatest misfortune to the country since the days of secession, and with less prospect of a satisfactory outcome."[93]

For a time Harlan considered responding publicly to his critics, especially those who had charged him with presidential ambitions. His son, James, cautioned him, however, against such a course. The newspaper comments had been "so extreme" as to be "beyond the attention of reasoning men," in James's judgment, and "[i]t would . . . be a *capital* mistake to take any notice of them. The imputation that you have politics in mind," James conceded, was "most low and mean. But please do not for a moment think of denying them in print. That would be thoroughly a mistake. Let them howl on. You have both the confidence and respect of the country and all this talk will not change it."[94]

James also suggested that his father emphasize undesirable features of the law, particularly the numerous exemptions it had created, in the revised version of his dissent. James considered the Wilson Act a "bad law," apparently knew his father did, too, and recommended that the justice "say so" in his opinion, yet also stress the impropriety of judicial decisions on the wisdom of legislation, especially where the result was to deny "the general government a power of vast importance."[95] Harlan yielded to his son's counsel. The justice's revised opinion embodied to a degree James's suggestions. Bolstered perhaps by letters from admirers and the favorable reaction of many newspapers to his stance, he also dropped plans for a public rebuttal of his critics.

Even so, the Court's posture in a case decided one week after it had announced the second *Pollock* ruling no doubt convinced the justice, if indeed he needed further persuasion, that his brethren had become staunch defenders of economic privilege. During the depression of the 1890s, the Pullman railway car company had continued to pay its stockholders dividends while drastically curtailing the wages of its workers. Eventually, the employees struck, affiliating with the American Railway Union (ARU) and its controversial leader, Eugene V. Debs. Supporting the Pullman strike, ARU members refused to handle trains using Pullman cars. The railroads fired trainsmen participating in the boycott, provoking strikes in the Chicago area and throughout the nation. On July 2, 1894, Attorney General Olney ordered the U.S. attorney in Chicago to seek an injunction against Debs and other ARU leaders. Olney also prepared criminal conspiracy charges against the labor leaders and dispatched a force of 5,000 special deputy marshals to the railroads' assistance. When rioting erupted, President Cleveland, over the protests of Illinois Governor Peter Altgeld, sent federal troops to Chicago to restore order. Declaring the strike a combination in restraint of trade forbidden by the Sherman Act, the federal circuit court issued a broad injunction forbidding Debs and all other persons from further obstruction of railroad traffic. When Debs violated the order, he drew a six-month sentence for contempt of court. Debs then sought release through a petition for a writ of habeas corpus in the Supreme Court.[96]

Harlan probably harbored no sympathy with the Pullman Company's president, George Pullman, a former client with whom he had once had a dispute over fees.[97] Moreover, when John Maynard Harlan declined an offer to become associated with the Debs defense, his father urged him to reconsider. A lawyer, the justice argued, was "not required to share the convictions and feelings of his client, but only to see to it that his client [was] properly and fully defended." Harlan realized "how difficult" it would be for his son "to take Debs's case, when your views, as to the strike, were against his," but the justice insisted that "[e]very man, no matter how bad he is or what he may have done, [was] entitled to a lawyer." Besides, the justice pragmatically added, connection with the case offered certain advantages: "[Y]ou need now . . . to become known. A well prepared argument in such a case would do you much good."[98]

Given his nationalist leanings, the elder Harlan was not likely to side with Debs on the merits of the case. On May 27, the Court, speaking through Justice Brewer, upheld the injunction, and thus Debs's contempt citation, as an appropriate application of the Sherman Act. Harlan joined the unanimous decision without opinion.[99]

The irony of the Court's shifting conception of national power in the *Knight*, *Pollock*, and *Debs* cases—holding, in the first two suits, that it was largely powerless to control trusts and great wealth, yet ruling in the third case that it was a potent weapon against organized labor—was not lost on the justice. In a letter written to Judge W.A. Woods, trial judge in the *Debs* case, the day after the Supreme Court's decision was announced, Harlan speculated that "[n]o such disturbance as that raised by Debs [was] likely to arise again in this country." He then posed a question: "If Debs and his companions remain in jail during the summer, are they not likely to be regarded as martyrs by a large number of people?" Harlan considered the answer obvious and suggested that the conspiracy prosecutions be ended and the contempt citations dismissed against the labor leaders.

> Recent events . . . suggest that there may be wisdom in such a course. A construction of the Constitution which so narrows the power of the Genl. Government that, practically, it cannot compel rich landlords and the owners of *invested* personal property, to contribute to the support of the nation, and a construction so broad as that given in the Debs case, will not be understood by vast masses of people. The situation is one that is well calculated to increase the spirit of unrest and discontent in many parts, indeed, throughout all, of the country. I believe that generous action upon the part of the Govt. and the courts, at this time, would be of real service to the country. . . .[100]

Harlan's suggestion was never acted upon. Before mailing his letter to Woods, the justice read a defiant letter from Debs to a New York newspaper.[101] "He is not prudent," Harlan decided in a postscript to his letter. "It may be that you must move slowly just now."[102]

In later years, Harlan would continue to embrace a broad conception of national authority, especially in cases involving congressional exercises of the commerce power. At times, he joined the majority. In two important cases decided in 1897 and 1898, he joined the Court in upholding applications of the Sherman Act to railroad combinations.[103] The following year, a unanimous Court held the statute applicable to contractual arrangements tending to have a direct effect on interstate commerce,[104] and Harlan found himself again in the role of dissenter. When a majority denied certain fact-finding and rate-making powers to the Interstate Commerce Commission in 1897, for example, he vehemently complained in dissent that the Court's decision went "far to make that commission a useless body, and to defeat many of the important objects designed to be accomplished by the various enactments of Congress relating to interstate commerce."[105]

Federal and State Police Power

In addition to favoring a broad application of the Sherman Act and other exercises of congressional regulatory authority, Harlan also spoke in *Champion* v. *Ames*[106] for a five-four majority in condoning Congress' use of the commerce clause as a form of federal police power. In an 1895 statute, Congress prohibited the interstate shipment of lottery tickets. Critics argued that the Lottery Act was only superficially a regulation of interstate commerce; it was actually an attempt by Congress to regulate public morals, a matter within the reserved powers of the states. Drawing heavily again on the pronouncements of Chief Justice Marshall, Harlan rejected such contentions. If Congress's power over commerce, as Marshall had asserted, was "plenary," its authority allowed the exclusion of certain items from commerce. Nor had Congress invaded a reserved state power. "[T]he answer" to that argument, declared Harlan, was "that the power to regulate commerce among the states [had] been expressly delegated to Congress"; and Congress had not attempted to control lottery sales carried on exclusively within a single state, but only interstate transactions. Indeed, he asserted, the national legislature was merely trying to assist the states in enforcing their policies. "It said, in effect, that it would not permit the declared policy of the states, which sought to protect their people against the mischiefs of the lottery business, to be overthrown or disregarded by the agency of interstate commerce. We should hesitate long before adjudging that an evil of such appalling character, carried on through interstate commerce, cannot be met and crushed by the only power competent to that end."[107] The remedy for abuse of such power, he observed, as he had on earlier occasions, lay with the voters.[108]

In later cases, the Court extended the *Champion* precedent to permit the exclusion from interstate commerce of items that were inherently injurious to public health and safety[109] and those that, though harmless in themselves, were shipped interstate for what Congress considered to be inappropriate purposes.[110] But when Congress attempted to use its federal police power against child labor, the Court balked, distinguishing *Champion* and leaving the fate of children to the tender mercies of state assemblies. Harlan died long before *Hammer* v. *Dagenhart*[111] struck down the Child Labor Act. Had he been a member of the *Hammer* Court, however, he would undoubtedly have dissented from the majority's ruling, or helped to form a different majority in extending *Champion* to the exploitation of minors.

In general, Harlan was equally sympathetic to state exercises of police power and rejected substantive due process claims that such regulations "unreasonably" interfered with economic liberty. On occasion, the justice spoke or sided with a majority in such cases. When Pennsylvania banned the sale of oleomargarine as a public health measure and attempt to prevent fraud against would-be purchasers of dairy products, the Court, speaking through Harlan, upheld the statute, over Justice Field's lone dissent, as a valid exercise of the police power.[112] In *Jacobson* v. *Massachusetts*,[113] he was again the Court's spokesman in upholding a compulsory vaccination statute. In other cases he wrote or joined rulings affirming state antimonopoly regulations,[114] criminal sanctions against fraudulent grain transactions,[115] a city-granted monopoly over garbage collections,[116] and city assessments for street improvements.[117]

Not surprisingly, given the increasingly *laissez faire* thrust of the Court's economic rulings during Harlan's tenure, the justice often found himself in dissent from successful challenges to state business regulations. Justice Holmes's dissent from the majority's 1905 ruling in *Lochner* v. *New York*,[118] striking down on substantive due process grounds a New York law limiting the hours of work of bakery employees to no more than ten hours a day or 60 hours a week, remains the most widely quoted rebuttal to the judicial apostles of *laissez faire* and Social Darwinism. Arguably, however, Harlan's *Lochner* dissent was every bit as probing, eloquent, and forceful as Holmes's classic effort. Citing earlier cases, Harlan conceded that states could not "unduly interfere" with economic freedom and that the police power could not "be put forward as an excuse for oppressive and unjust legislation."[119] At the same time, he insisted that legislatures were entitled to "a large discretion" in determining what controls were necessary to preserve the public health, safety, and morals. "Granting," he declared, "that there is a liberty of contract which cannot be violated even under the sanction of direct legislative enactment, but [also] assuming, as according to settled law we may assume, that such liberty of contract is subject to such regulations as the state may reasonably prescribe for the common good and the well-being of society, . . . the rule is universal that a legislative enactment, Federal or state, is never to be disregarded or held invalid unless it be, beyond question, plainly and palpably in excess of legislative power."[120]

Judged by that deferential standard, the New York statute was to Harlan clearly constitutional.[121] "[A]ll know," Harlan asserted, that "the air constantly breathed by [bakery] workmen is not as pure and healthful as that to be found in some other establishments or out of doors."[122] What precise number of hours of work in a bakery would endanger an employee's health was "difficult to say," but hardly necessary to a ruling upholding the challenged law. It was sufficient to Harlan that the question was one "about which there [was] room for debate and an honest difference of opinion"[123] and that the line New York had drawn was based on "many reasons of a weighty, substantial character, based upon the experience of mankind, in support of the theory that, all things considered, more than ten hours' steady work each day, from week to week, in a bakery or confectionery establishment, may endanger the health and shorten the lives of the workmen, thereby diminishing their physical and mental capacity to serve the state and to provide for those dependent upon them."[124] The majority's decision invalidating the statute as a violation of due process, exclaimed Harlan, not only "enlarg[ed] the scope of the [Fourteenth Amendment] beyond its original purpose"; extended to statutes generally, it would "seriously cripple the inherent power of the states to care for the lives, health, and well-being of their citizens" and embroil the courts in improper judgments on the "justice or reason or wisdom" of statutes—judgments properly left to "the people's [elected] representatives."[125]

The deference which Harlan accorded the state police power extended to laws affecting interstate commerce and federal patents—domains over which the Constitution's framers had given Congress supreme lawmaking authority. Speaking for a unanimous Court in 1879, he upheld a Kentucky statute regulating the inspection and gauging of oils and fluids, even those processed under a federal patent. In exercising its patent power, the justice was certain, Congress had not intended to permit the sale of oil found by a state to be "unfit and unsafe for use." Nor did the congressional authority to regulate interstate commerce mean that the states had surrendered their police power over such subjects.[126]

In an 1896 case, Harlan spoke for the Court in upholding a Georgia statute that prohibited the operation of freight trains on Sunday. Employing a rationale similar to that invoked by the modern Court in upholding Sunday closing laws against religious establishment challenges,[127] Harlan characterized the regulation as an exercise of the state's "power to enact laws to promote the order and to secure the comfort, happiness, and health of the people," adding: "It is none the less a civil regulation because the day on which the running of freight trains is prohibited is kept by many under a sense of religious duty."[128] When a majority struck down Iowa restrictions on the shipment of intoxicating liquors into that state, Harlan dissented. Congress had not authorized the interstate commerce of such products, and Harlan was amazed that "the mere silence of congress upon the subject . . . [was] made to operate as a license to persons doing business in one state to jeopard[ize] the health, morals, and good order of another state, by flooding the latter with intoxicating liquors, against the expressed will of her people."[129] Harlan's position ultimately prevailed.

In 1890, Congress passed a law subjecting liquor shipments to the control of the state to which they were delivered immediately upon their arrival. The next year, the Court held that states, by virtue of the 1890 enactment, could now apply their prohibition laws to the sale of imported liquor, even if it was still in the original package in which it was shipped through interstate commerce.[130]

Despite his stance in numerous such cases, Harlan hardly rejected meaningful judicial scrutiny of economic controls or the substantive due process rationale on which such review was primarily based. In the late 1930s and 1940s, at the beginning of the Supreme Court's modern era, a growing majority of justices would largely dismantle the doctrines undergirding the Old Court's *laissez faire* precedents, including the substantive due process formula. Justice Hugo L. Black, who began a 34-year tenure on the Court in 1937, favored a complete repudiation of substantive due process and judicial rulings on the "reasonableness" of legislation.

While unwilling to adopt Black's stance outright, a majority of the modern Court defanged the doctrine, giving it only lip service in economic cases.[131] Since 1936, not a single economic regulation reviewed by the Court has fallen on substantive due process grounds, and only a single piece of regulatory legislation has succumbed to an equal protection challenge.[132]

Harlan, on the other hand, freely embraced substantive due process, but he accepted greater governmental interference with economic liberty than most of his colleagues were willing to tolerate. In fact, his opinion for the Court in *Mugler* v. *Kansas*[133] is considered one of the key elements in the Court's growing acceptance of economic due process following the adoption of the Fourteenth Amendment. Over Justice Field's dissent, the *Mugler* Court upheld a state liquor prohibition and acknowledged the paramount role of legislators in "determin[ing], primarily, what measures are appropriate or needful for the protection of the public morals, the public health, or the public safety."[134] Harlan, however, declared:

> It does not at all follow that every statute enacted ostensibly for the promotion of these ends is to be accepted as a legitimate exertion of the police powers of the state. There are, of necessity, limits beyond which legislation cannot rightfully go. While every possible presumption is to be indulged in favor of the validity of a statute, . . . the courts must obey the constitution rather than the law-making department of government, and must, upon their own responsibility, determine whether, in any particular case, these limits have been passed. . . . The courts are not bound by mere forms, nor are they to be misled by mere pretenses. They are at liberty, indeed, are under a solemn duty, to look at the substance of things, whenever they enter upon the inquiry whether the legislature has transcended the limits of its authority. If, therefore, a statute purporting to have been enacted to protect the public health, the public morals, or the public safety has no real or substantial relation to those objects, or is a palpable invasion of rights secured by the fundamental law, it is the duty of the courts to so adjudge, and thereby give effect to the constitution.[135]

Nor did Harlan simply give lip service to such a standard while invariably upholding regulatory legislation against substantive due process and related challenges. Indeed, he authored the Court's opinion in two major *laissez faire* rulings of his era. Speaking for a unanimous Court in *Smythe* v. *Ames* (1898),[136] he invalidated a Nebraska law regulating railroad rates. That decision was based on the relatively narrow ground that the restrictions imposed were so severe as to deny the railroads a "fair return" on their investment. In *Adair* v. *United States* (1908),[137] however, Harlan spoke for a majority in overturning a federal statute that forbade interstate carriers to discharge employees for their membership in a labor union. In dissent, Justice Holmes saw the law as a reasonable means for "prohibiting the more powerful party" to take advantage of the weaker in labor–management relations.[138] Both Holmes and Justice McKenna held, moreover, that Congress could have reasonably concluded that such a law was necessary to guard against strikes and related threats to the free flow of commerce. But Justice Harlan, in what arguably was a marked departure from his usual deferential stance in such cases, wrote of the "equality of right" enjoyed by employees and employers and termed "any legislation that disturbs that equality . . . an arbitrary interference with the liberty of contract which no government can legally justify in a free land."[139]

On occasion, he even dissented when a majority upheld a challenged regulatory statute. In an 1899 case, for example, the Court sustained a Kansas law requiring a reasonable attorney's fee to be included in judgments against railroad companies for damages caused by fire escaping from moving trains. In a dissent joined by three colleagues, Harlan found a denial of equal protection in any law that imposed such a requirement but gave railroads no right, when successful, to demand an attorney's fee from a losing party. "Suppose," he declared, "the statute in question had been so framed as to give the railroad corporation a special attorney's fee if successful in its defense, but did not allow such a fee to an individual plaintiff when successful. I cannot believe that any court, federal or state, would hesitate a moment in declaring such an enactment void."[140]

Arguably, however, the justice's position in such cases was uncharacteristic, explainable largely as a response to discrete aspects of the case, such as the discriminatory features of the fee statute and the extremely restrictive character of the rate regulation at issue in *Smythe* or, as in *Adair*, as a reflection of the rugged individualism common to those of Harlan's frontier background—an individualism suspicious of collectivist efforts to improve society. In the main, Harlan was deferential to governmental power over economic liberty, especially that wielded by national authorities. Such a stance was clearly consistent, moreover, with his Whig nationalist heritage, the feelings of vulnerability to shifting economic fortune his own precarious financial situation no doubt generated, and the concern for the underdog he had begun to develop during his wartime service with enlisted men—a sensitivity that the war's end had not erased. In 1876, the year before his appointment to the bench, a Kentucky judge had issued instructions, presumably to a jury, that an employee had the right "to moderately chastise a servant for failure to obey orders." Harlan was appalled. "This is curious law in these days of freedom and equality," he wrote an associate. "I have no doubt of the right of the employer to have ordered the servant from his premises, and upon her refusal to go his right to use such force as might be necessary to eject her. But the theory of moderate chastisement is bad law in these days."[141]

Harlan's Incorporation Campaign

Similar forces may have prompted the justice to champion a construction of the Fourteenth Amendment that, if adopted, would have subjected the states and their local governments to considerably more federal judicial scrutiny than his stance in economic cases generally tolerated. In the early days of the republic, the Supreme Court, speaking through Chief Justice Marshall, had held in *Barron* v. *Baltimore*[142] that the guarantees of the federal Bill of Rights (first eight amendments) were binding only on the national government, not the states. The movement for adoption of the Bill of Rights had been based on fear of national power; the First Amendment begins with the admonition that "Congress shall make no law." Marshall's position thus rested on firm ground. *Barron*'s effect, however, was to largely immunize from constitutional oversight the state and local officials with whom the individual regularly had the greatest contact.

The Reconstruction amendments enlarged the states' constitutional obligations. Indeed, as we have seen, the Court's construction of the Fourteenth Amendment— albeit arguably a perversion of its original purpose—had become a formidable weapon in the arsenal of *laissez faire* by the late 1890s. In case after case, however, a majority rejected contentions that the Fourteenth Amendment incorporated some or all the provisions of the Bill of Rights, making those fundamental guarantees binding on the states;[143] not so Justice Harlan.

Beginning with his dissent in *Hurtado* v. *California* (1884),[144] Harlan embraced the incorporation argument for the balance of his career. Joseph Hurtado was brought to trial for murder on an information or accusation of the prosecution rather than a grand jury indictment. The Fifth Amendment requires a grand jury in all serious federal cases, but the Court upheld Hurtado's conviction and death sentence against the claim that his Fourteenth Amendment right to due process had been violated. The Fifth Amendment, Justice McKenna reasoned for the Court, included not only provision for the grand jury but also a due process clause virtually identical in language to that of the Fourteenth Amendment. Logically, therefore, due process alone could hardly be held to embody the right to a grand jury.

Justice Harlan filed a lone dissent. Due process, he asserted, had the same meaning under the Fifth and Fourteenth Amendments. The adoption of similar language by the framers of the Fourteenth Amendment "was not accidental, but evince[d] a purpose to impose upon the states the same restrictions, in respect of proceedings involving life, liberty, and property, which had been imposed upon the general government."[145] Those requirements, according to earlier rulings and commentaries, included "settled usages and modes of proceedings existing in the common and statute law of England before the emigration of our ancestors . . . and which [were] shown not to have been unsuited to their civil and political condition by having been acted on by them after the settlement of this country."[146] Given its long history in Britain and the United States, the grand jury was for Harlan surely among such guarantees, especially in capital cases.

Nor was the justice impressed with the majority's conclusion that due process could not be construed to embody the grand jury since the Fifth Amendment embodied both guarantees:

> It seems to me that too much stress is put upon the fact that the framers of the constitution made express provision for the security of those rights which at common law were protected by the requirement of due process of law, and, in addition, declared, generally, that no person shall "be deprived of life, liberty, or property without due process of law." The rights, for the security of which these express provisions were made, were of a character so essential to the safety of the people that it was deemed wise to avoid the possibility that congress, in regulating the processes of law, would impair or destroy them. Hence, their specific enumeration in the earlier amendments of the constitution, in connection with the general requirement of due process of law, the latter itself being broad enough to cover every right of life, liberty, or property secured by the settled usages and modes of proceedings existing under the common and statute law of England at the time our government was founded.[147]

The majority's logic, Harlan added, "would lead to results . . . inconsistent with the vital principles of republican government," for it meant that the Fourteenth

Amendment must be read to exclude not only the grand jury but also the right to a speedy and public trial by an impartial jury, safeguards against double jeopardy and compulsory self-incrimination, and other Bill of Rights guarantees long associated with the concept of due process.

> If the argument of my brethren be sound, those rights—although universally recognized at the establishment of our institutions as secured by that due process of law which for centuries had been the foundation of Anglo-Saxon liberty—were not deemed by our fathers essential to the due process of law prescribed by our Constitution; because,—such seems to be the argument,—had they been regarded as involved in due process of law they would not have been specifically and expressly provided for, but left to the protection given by the general clause forbidding the deprivation of life, liberty, and property without due process of law.[148]

Of the majority's insistence that the Constitution was intended for "an undefined and expanding future" and that due process thus should not "be so interpreted as . . . to deny to the law the capacity of progress and improvement," Harlan was equally incredulous. It was difficult for him "to perceive anything in the system of prosecuting human beings for their lives, by information [rather than grand jury], which suggests that the state which adopts it has entered upon an era of progress and improvement in the law of criminal procedure."[149]

Harlan's stance was not to prevail, however. In 1892, a majority in *O'Neil* v. *Vermont*[150] upheld a sentence of over 54 years at hard labor for a Vermont defendant convicted of liquor law violations and declined on procedural grounds to decide whether such a severe verdict constituted cruel and unusual punishment, a practice forbidden by the Eighth Amendment. Five years later, Harlan spoke for a unanimous Court in construing the Fourteenth Amendment's due process clause to require states to provide just compensation for private property taken for public use, but he did so without any mention whatever of his incorporation thesis or the Fifth Amendment provision imposing an identical standard on federal officials.[151]

Maxwell v. *Dow*[152] continued the trend, reaffirming *Hurtado*'s rejection of the grand jury in state cases and also upholding eight-member state trial juries, despite previous decisions construing the Sixth Amendment jury guarantee to mandate 12-member panels. In *Patterson* v. *Colorado* (1907),[153] the Court, speaking through Justice Holmes, declined to decide whether the Fourteenth Amendment embodied a freedom of speech "similar to that in the 1st," but concluded that "even if we were" to make such an assumption, that guarantee "main[ly]" reached only prior restraints on expression rather than "the subsequent punishment of such [freedom] as may be deemed contrary to the public welfare."[154] (In dissent, Justice Harlan insisted that the First and Fourteenth Amendments reached both prior restraints and subsequent punishments and that "[t]he public welfare cannot override constitutional privileges."[155]) Finally, in *Twining* v. *New Jersey* (1908),[156] a majority rejected extension to the states of the Fifth Amendment ban on compulsory self-incrimination. Justice Brewer joined Harlan's *O'Neil* dissent "in the main,"[157] and Justice Field, furious at the harsh sentence meted to O'Neil, wrote a separate dissent including the guarantee against cruel and unusual punishments among the requirements of Fourteenth Amendment due process.[158] But both justices soon parted whatever company they had shared with Harlan, who remained his era's lone consistent advocate of incorporation.

The justice's admirers, however, were to be as persistent in their praise of his stance as his brethren were determined to reject it. The day after the Court announced its decision in *Maxwell* v. *Dow*, for example, Maxwell's attorney, J.W.N. Whitecotton, wrote to the justice of his confidence "that the intention of the framers of the XIV Amendment was to extend the operation of the first eight Amendments as limitations upon the powers of the States." Harlan's dissent, Whitecotton assured the justice, was "a great comfort to me in my defeat"; the majority's ruling was a "great mistake on fundamental grounds, and one that will yet rise to vex the people in some future time." Whitecotton asked the justice for a photograph, which he planned to frame and put on his desk "as a constant reminder, that there is still left one judge, who believes that the Constitution of the United States is a protection to the personal rights of the citizen against the mad folly of State legislatures." The lawyer hoped Harlan's life could be spared many years, "as 'a voice crying in the wilderness.'"[159]

Fraternity

The dismantling of Reconstruction and triumph of *laissez faire* were to be the major developments on the Supreme Court during Justice Harlan's lengthy tenure. But the rise of American imperialism, especially U.S. acquisition of Alaska, Puerto Rico, the Philippines, and Hawaii, also presented the high bench, and Harlan personally, with a variety of international, economic, and human rights challenges. Harlan's reaction to each would be as mixed as his responses to the racial and regulatory cases that dominated the Court's agenda during the Gilded Age.

The Bering Sea Arbitration

Harlan's first involvement in disputes growing out of America's thirst for territorial expansion stemmed from the purchase of Alaska from Russia in 1867. That controversy would take him away from the Court, immerse him in the complexities of international law and politics for nearly a year, and, not entirely coincidentally, satisfy his longtime desire to tour Europe. In 1870, the United States had granted a private company limited sealing rights on the Pribilof Islands, a small group of Bering Sea islands included in the Alaska purchase that served as the breeding grounds for fur seals. As the value of sealskin increased, vessels from other nations, especially Canada, began pelagic or open-sea sealing beyond the three-mile limit of U.S. jurisdiction. Amid growing fears that the pelagic sealing might soon decimate the herds, U.S. officials claimed that Russia had possessed exclusive jurisdiction over the Bering Sea, that Great Britain and other nations had acquiesced in Russian control of the area, and that Russia's rights had passed to the United States with the Alaskan cession. When Great Britain refused to accept American authority, U.S. vessels seized a British sealing schooner in 1886. Judicial proceedings were instituted at Sitka, the vessel was condemned, and the ship's master and mate were imprisoned and fined. Other seizures followed the next year.[1]

Not surprisingly, the British government vehemently protested the American action. President Cleveland's secretary of state, Thomas F. Bayard, just as vigorously defended U.S. dominion over the sea. Initial efforts at negotiation proved fruitless, and Cleveland's first term ended without a resolution of the dispute. On assuming his duties in Benjamin Harrison's cabinet, Secretary of State James G. Blaine, like Bayard before him, sought an international agreement on the issue and arranged a British–Russian–American conference in Washington for that purpose. The Washington conference and subsequent exchanges of correspondence failed to bring an end to the controversy. In 1890 an Anglo–American arbitration treaty referred the matter to a seven-member international tribunal. Scheduled to convene in Paris, the tribunal was to be composed of two American members, two British delegates, one member each from France and Italy, and a seventh delegate representing Sweden and Norway. Under the terms of the treaty, the arbitrators were to address five issues. Four turned on Russian–U.S. assertions of exclusive jurisdiction over seal fishing in the Bering Sea and the extent to which Great Britain had acquiesced in such authority. The fifth involved a justification for U.S. control, which the Harrison administration had recently formulated. In preparing a defense of American interests, administration officials had discovered little evidence to support exclusive Russian—and thereby American—jurisdiction over the sea. Secretary of State Blaine planned to argue that since the Pribilof Islands, a U.S. possession, served as the seals' breeding grounds, the seal herds were U.S. property and subject to its protection on the open sea.

One day in the spring of 1892, President Harrison sent for Justice Harlan. Following the usual exchange of pleasantries, the president asked his friend to become one of the American representatives on the arbitration tribunal. While honored by Harrison's request, Harlan was reluctant to leave his family for the extended period that service on the panel would entail. On learning that the president expected his family to accompany him to Europe, however, the justice eagerly accepted the assignment. His eldest son, Richard, was then traveling in Europe with his wife and sister, Laura. The president's offer would enable the Harlans, their daughter, Ruth, and granddaughter, Edith, to tour the continent at government expense—a not inconsiderable lure for the perennially strapped justice.[2]

The justice's son, James, was appalled at the president's selection of H. W. Blodgett, a veteran U.S. district judge and an old family friend, as one of the counsel to argue the nation's case before the tribunal. Blodgett's appointment, James wrote his father, was "almost grotesque." The judge had "no presence . . . is . . . painful to listen to . . . and physically disabled." His rough exterior, James was certain, would "frighten the Italian arbitrators. They will take him for a bear."[3] But the U.S. counsel also included James C. Carter of New York, the leader of the American bar, and E. J. Phelps, President Cleveland's minister to London and, like Carter, a lawyer of national repute. Joining Harlan as an American member of the tribunal, moreover, was Senator John T. Morgan of Alabama, acknowledged Democratic leader of the Senate on international matters. Other members of the tribunal were at least equally distinguished.

To allow himself ample time to study the voluminous records pertinent to the tribunal's work—and to give his family the opportunity for extensive travel—Harlan booked passage on a French liner departing August 6, well in advance of the tentative date for the proceedings to begin. As the departure date approached, he arranged to rent his Washington home to Justice Brewer;[4] developed contingency plans with his former law partner, Gus Willson, and others for any emergency that might arise during his stay abroad;[5] and endured a bit of good-natured ribbing from his friends. Harlan wrote William Howard Taft that Justice Brewer was convinced his colleague would "return from Europe wearing a wig of curled hair, and declining to speak in any except the French language." The justice had assured Brewer, a native Kansan, that "a Kansas man was not qualified to speak of foreign affairs."[6]

On August 6, Harlan and his family sailed from New York to the French seaport of Le Havre, and then traveled to Paris. After several days in the French capital, they journeyed by train to Switzerland, where they joined Richard, his wife, and Laura. Harlan's original plan had been to miss the Supreme Court's entire 1892–1893 term. But for reasons now obscure, although probably related to the Court's docket, he left his family in Montreux in September and returned to Washington for the Court's opening session in October. When the justices adjourned for their Christmas recess, he returned to Europe and joined his family in Paris.[7]

In February, following his return to Europe, Harlan and his family spent ten days in London, where he heard the venerable English statesman William Gladstone speak in the House of Commons in support of Irish home rule. Gladstone's speech, the justice later wrote his friend Eli Murray, "was a very remarkable display by a man eighty-four years of age," and the prime minister was "quite as remarkable as" Clay and Webster had been in their day. The bill, he declared, would probably win passage in the House of Commons but be rejected by the titled gentry of the House of Lords. "In time," he predicted, fervently if inaccurately, the British would "dispense with the House of Lords and have a Senate composed of untitled persons," as well as "a Supreme Court with power to pass upon the validity of Acts of legislation with reference to the fundamental principles which make up what we call 'Anglo-Saxon liberty.'" Such a development might be "far in the future," but "the final result will be an enlargement of the principles of popular government."[8] Harlan obviously relished such a possibility.

Travel and social events, all later detailed in Mrs. Harlan's memoirs,[9] would consume a fair portion of Harlan's time in Europe. Before his initial departure for Paris, however, he had assured William Howard Taft that "if hard work will suffice to make me thoroughly acquainted with all that is to be known in reference to the seal fisheries, that work will be bestowed upon every question involved in the Arbitration."[10] He was apparently true to his word. Notes and materials in the justice's papers indicate that he became thoroughly familiar not only with the legal issues the tribunal was to confront but also with seals, sealing, and the growing risks of the valuable animals' extinction, as well as the cruelty with which sealers hunted their prey. Among his papers, for example, was the following 1729 sealer's account of his grim sport: "[I]f we had mind to have some sport with him, which we called Lion-baiting, usually six, seven or eight or more of us, would go with a Half Pike in his hand, and so prick him to death; which commonly would be sport for two or three hours before we could conquer him."[11]

The justice was determined to review and decide the issues before the tribunal fairly and dispassionately. "I may say to you," he confided to Eli Murray, "that the work which I have in hand is the most serious that has ever been committed to me. The average American will assume that the Arbitrators designated by our country will decide every question submitted to them in favor of our Government, overlooking the fact that we sit as Judges obliged by the highest principles of honor to determine the case in all it aspects according to the principles of law and justice. At any rate I take this view of my position, and do not permit myself to doubt that the other Arbitrators will look at the matter in the same way."[12]

Tribunal proceedings began in late March. By mid-April, in a letter to Chief Justice Fuller, Harlan wrote, "This business has now got complete possession of me. It is with me, in all my waking hours and wherever I go."[13] The ill health of one of the British arbitrators at times delayed the tribunal's progress.[14] At one point early in the proceedings, moreover, the eccentric Justice Field threatened to ask Harlan to honor a promise to return to Washington were there "any trouble" in a pending railroad case.[15] Gradually, however, the representatives amassed an impressive record and moved toward a decision.

The tribunal announced its ruling on August 15, 1893. Several days earlier, Senator Morgan sent Harlan a note expressing his "high appreciation of your services to the cause of justice, truth and your country."[16] Harlan immediately reciprocated. "One of the pleasantest reflections I have in connection with the work here," he wrote the Alabamian, "is that you, an ex-Confederate soldier, and I, an ex-Union soldier, have sat side by side, in a foreign land, in a Tribunal of Arbitration constituted for the solution of important questions. . . . [M]y association with you in this great work will always be remembered by me as one of the most delightful events of my life."[17]

The two American arbitrators would part company, though, on most of the questions the tribunal confronted. On the four issues relating to American claims of exclusive jurisdiction over the Bering Sea, Justice Harlan alone joined a majority of the court in rejecting U.S. contentions. Perhaps because it was the only justification for American control of the seal fisheries advanced by a Republican president, the justice did agree with Senator Morgan that the United States possessed proprietary rights over the fur seals of the Pribilof Islands, even beyond the three-mile limit. But the United States lost that battle as well.[18]

Not only were the U.S. claims rejected; the United States was also directed to pay Great Britain nearly a half million dollars in damages. Even so, the venture was not a complete U.S. defeat. Under a protective regulation that was to remain in force until 1908, pelagic sealing was forbidden within a 60-mile zone around the Pribilof Islands for a specified period each year.

Harlan remained convinced that the United States held property rights over the seals of the Bering Sea and devoted a substantial portion of his lengthy opinion in the case to a defense of that proposition.[19] At the same time, he realized that the sealing restrictions the tribunal had imposed were about all U.S. officials could have realistically expected. "The fact is," he wrote Gus Willson several days after the tribunal's decision was announced, "that all pelagic sealing should have been prohibited. But the neutral arbitrators having held that the U.S. did not *own* the seals, and that the taking of those seals in the high seas, admittedly destructive to the race, was a *right* under international law, they could not be induced to go any further than they did."

Under the regulations, he added, sealers could use firearms against their prey only in
February, March, and April; and only the last half of April was a good hunting period.[20] Judge Blodgett agreed: "[I]f the regulations are enforced," he assured Harlan,
"the profits of pelagic sealing will be so precarious that few will engage in it."[21]

Whatever the ultimate impact of the tribunal's work, Justice Harlan's participation further enhanced his national reputation. In June of 1894, over 2,000 persons—
"applaud[ing] to the last pair of hands"—packed Chicago's Central Music Hall to
hear his account of the sealing dispute and the tribunal's work.[22] Somewhat ironically, the victorious British were also impressed with the justice. "To Judge Harlan,
of the Supreme Court of the United States," wrote one correspondent for an English
magazine, "especial credit is due. Considering the peculiarities of popular opinion
in the States, and the dependency of all United States officials for reputation and
popularity on the zeal with which they fight the battles of the Republic in accor-
dance with the wishes and desires of the masses of its citizens, no slight moral
courage was necessary to join the majority of his [tribunal] colleagues in practically
giving a verdict in favour of England upon questions which so nearly affected the
vanity of our American cousins."[23]

"The Dred Scott of Imperialism!"

The Bering Sea dispute involved significant questions of American economic interest and the reach of U.S. authority over its territorial possessions and their natural
wealth. By far the most important legal issues growing out of U.S. territorial expansion, however, were to involve the constitutional status of the territories, especially
the degree to which individual rights guaranteed by the Constitution extended to
territorial inhabitants. In short, did the Constitution follow the flag?

It was uncertain how Justice Harlan might respond to such a question. His insistence on the extension of Bill of Rights safeguards to contiguous U.S. territories
suggested that he would also assume such a stance with respect to outlying possessions. His record in racial discrimination cases amply demonstrated, moreover, his
empathy for the underdog. As we have already seen, however, the justice's racial attitudes and judicial record in race cases were much more complicated than a review
of his major civil rights dissents might suggest.

Nor were such questions aroused purely by his complex feelings regarding the
former slaves. While at Princeton, Harlan's son, James, decided to participate in a
debate on the Chinese Exclusion Act of 1882, which had suspended all immigration
of Chinese laborers into the United States for a ten-year period. As he had on other
debate topics, the justice prepared a draft argument for his son in support of the
statute. He suggested the following "line of thought:"

> [W]e are not bound, upon any broad principle of humanity to harm our own country
> in order to benefit the Chinese who may come here. . . . [I]f, by the introduction of
> Chinese labor we [jeopardize] our own laborers, why not restrict the immigration of
> Chinese. The Chinese are of a different race, as distinct from ours as ours is from the
> negro. Suppose there was a tide of immigration [of] . . . African savages. Would we
> not restrict their coming? Would we desist because they are human beings and upon

the idea that they have a right to better their condition? . . . [They] will not assimilate to our people. If they come, we must admit them to citizenship, then to suffrage. What would become of the country in such a contingency[?] . . . [W]e have an opportunity to test the question whether it is safer to let down the bars and permit unrestricted immigration. The Chinese [already] here will, in that time [during which immigration is prohibited], show of what stuff they are made. Our policy is to keep this country . . . under *American* influence. Only Americans, or those who become such by long stay here, understand *American* institutions.[24]

Harlan may simply have been outlining a debate strategy for James rather than his own views. Indeed, he encouraged his son to "go into that debate, & talk out as if you didn't care for the result."[25] But he made no effort to separate his own position from the arguments he was advancing.

Other bits of evidence also suggest that the justice was hardly free of ethnocentric attitudes. In his *Plessy* dissent, Harlan referred uncritically to the Chinese as "a race so different from our own that we do not permit those belonging to it to become citizens of the United States."[26] Moreover, the person who booked return passage for the justice following the Harlan family's initial voyage to Europe for the Bering Sea proceedings had assured Harlan, it will be recalled, that the vessel on which he was to sail "will not carry immigrants on this trip."[27]

The justice's spotty record in racial discrimination and related cases not involving the former slaves is equally instructive. In 1884, he filed a vigorous dissent when a majority first refused to hold that American Indians no longer affiliated with a tribe were U.S. citizens under the Fourteenth Amendment; then permitted a state to deny them the vote. Under the amendment's grant of citizenship to "[a]ll persons born or naturalized in the United States, and subject to the jurisdiction thereof," he asserted, American Indians who broke all tribal ties and became fully subject to federal and state laws were citizens. By holding to the contrary, the majority, in his judgment, had in effect rewritten the amendment to extend citizenship only to "persons born subject to the jurisdiction of, or naturalized in, the United States."[28] Not surprisingly given his stance in the *Hurtado* case, he also dissented, albeit without opinion, when his eight colleagues refused to extend the Fifth Amendment right to a grand jury to tribal proceedings.[29]

In a number of opinions Harlan liberally construed the rights of Chinese laborers. Speaking for a majority in an 1884 case involving the Chinese Exclusion Act, he held that provisions of the statute making a Chinese worker's certificate of identification the "only evidence permissible to establish his right to re-entry" into the United States could not be applied against laborers who had established proper residence under a valid treaty, yet had left the country before the exclusion act was adopted.[30] Later, when the Court could find no statutory authority to justify federal prosecution of a band of California men who had driven a group of Chinese aliens from their homes and places of business and held them captive on a steamboat barge, Harlan dissented. Declaring that "denial by the State of the equal protection of the laws to persons within its jurisdiction may arise as well from the failure or inability of the state authorities to give that protection, as from unfriendly enactments," the justice embraced the broad conception of congressional authority he had advanced four years earlier in the *Civil Rights Cases*.[31]

But Harlan's stance in such cases was hardly consistent. In *United States* v. *Jung Ah Lung*,[32] a Chinese laborer robbed of his identification certificate by Chinese pirates was denied reentry at the port of San Francisco. There was no doubt that he had been issued a proper permit, and the exclusion act specifically prohibited only reentry *by land* without a certificate. A majority held, therefore, that the law did not forbid reentry *by vessel* without a certificate. Joined by Justices Field and Lamar, Harlan dissented, asserting that Congress could not have intended one rule for reentry by land and another by water. The theft of Jung Ah Lung's certificate, the justice added, was merely "his misfortune."[33]

In the leading case of *United States* v. *Wong Kim Ark*,[34] Harlan joined Chief Justice Fuller's dissent when a majority held that a child born in the United States of permanent resident Chinese nationals was a citizen from birth under the Fourteenth Amendment. Fuller's reading of the congressional debates over the amendment's adoption had convinced him that persons "subject to any foreign power" were not subject to U.S. jurisdiction and thus were not citizens within the amendment's meaning. Children of Chinese subjects, like their parents, owed allegiance to the Chinese emperor, whose laws required decapitation for anyone renouncing that allegiance. Since the children of Chinese parents could not legally renounce their allegiance, they were subject to a foreign power and thus excluded from Fourteenth Amendment citizenship.

Harlan apparently accepted Fuller's rationale. But his stance in the *Wong Kim Ark* case might also reflect a reluctance to extend citizenship to a "race, as distinct from ours as ours is from the negro." Indeed, Fuller himself had asserted in his dissent that the Chinese did not want to become U.S. citizens and that the Court's ruling would tear up "parental relations by the roots."[35]

Conceivably, Harlan's ambitions for his son, James, might have influenced his position regarding the constitutional status of American colonial possessions and their inhabitants. The justice was convinced that his son, John, would achieve prominence at the bar. "He is cut out for a practicing attorney—ready for any emergency which arises in the progress of a trial," Harlan wrote Gus Willson from Paris as he prepared for the Bering Sea proceedings. But he believed that James had "more caution and sagacity" than his brother, "and ought some time not far distant to be upon the bench."[36] When Judge Blodgett resigned his Chicago district judgeship in 1892, James wrote to his father for advice on whether he should "consent" to become a candidate for Blodgett's seat.[37] The justice was obviously pleased at such a prospect and gratified when many prominent Illinois lawyers and judges, including three members of the state supreme court, wrote the president to endorse James's candidacy.[38] Nor did Harlan cease his efforts when Blodgett's seat went to another hopeful. Neither he nor James showed any enthusiasm for a movement to win James's selection as the Supreme Court's reporter of opinions.[39] But the justice did engage in several subsequent campaigns to win his son's appointment to a judgeship.[40] Those further efforts also failed. Then, in late 1900, President McKinley nominated James to be attorney general of Puerto Rico.

McKinley's choice immediately aroused controversy, as did his selection of a son of Justice McKenna to another Puerto Rican post, and not surprisingly. In the aftermath of the Spanish-American War, the United States found itself in possession of a colonial empire consisting of the former Spanish possessions of Guam, Puerto

Rico, and the Philippines, as well as the republic of Hawaii. The new American empire immediately raised political and legal issues. McKinley won a second term in 1900, but only in the face of anti-imperialist sentiment in his own party and the nation generally. At the time of James's nomination as Puerto Rico's attorney general, moreover, the first wave of the so-called *Insular Cases* was moving toward a decision before Harlan and his brethren. The president's critics suspected that his selection of James for a territorial position was designed to win the justice's support for the administration's position in the insular litigation.[41]

Such concerns proved entirely unfounded. The first three of the cases—*De Lima* v. *Bidwell*,[42] *Dooley* v. *United States*,[43] and *Downes* v. *Bidwell*[44]—arose essentially from efforts by American tobacco and sugar producers to preserve their tariff protections from the products of the newly acquired territories. Argument in the cases consumed nearly a week in early January of 1901; the Court announced its decisions on May 27. In the *De Lima* case, a majority held that Puerto Rico was no longer a foreign country and that goods imported from there to the mainland could not be subjected to existing tariffs on imports from other nations. Justice Harlan joined that ruling as well as the decision in the *Dooley* case that goods imported from the mainland to Puerto Rico were, for the same reason, also immune from existing tariffs. Harlan vigorously dissented, however, from a badly divided majority's conclusion in *Downes* that, although no longer a foreign country, Puerto Rico had not yet become a part of the United States. Its imports to the mainland could thus be taxed at whatever rate Congress chose to impose, despite the constitutional requirement that federal tax rates be uniform "throughout the United States."

The decisions in *De Lima* and *Dooley* were difficult to reconcile with the ruling in *Downes*, and only Justice Brown joined all three. The conclusion in the first two, that existing tariff laws were no longer applicable to trade between Puerto Rico and the mainland, was relatively easy to accept. The status accorded the territory in *Downes* was another matter. Speaking only for himself, Justice Brown found comfort in the scant attention given territories in the Constitution. Brown conceded that Congress had been liberal in extending constitutional provisions to the nation's contiguous territories, but he insisted that "there [was] nothing in the Constitution itself, and little in [its] interpretation," to justify the assertion that the document followed the flag "by its own force." That "silence," in Brown's judgment, "preclud[ed] the idea that the Constitution attached to these territories as soon as acquired, and [dictated that] unless such interpretation be manifestly contrary to the letter or spirit of the Constitution, it should be followed by the judicial department."[45] For Brown, the acquisition and regulation of territories were essentially political matters best left to Congress. He predicted that "the annexation of outlying and distant possessions" would present "grave questions [arising] from differences of race, habits, laws and customs of the people, . . . which [might] require action on the part of Congress that would be quite unnecessary in the annexation of the contiguous territory inhabited only by people of the same race, or by scattered bodies of native Indians."[46] Brown obviously opposed judicial tampering with such delicate judgments.

A false step at this time might be fatal to the development of what Chief Justice Marshall called the American empire. Choice in some cases, the natural gravitation of small bodies towards large ones in others, the result of a successful war in still others, may bring about conditions which would render the annexation of distant possessions desirable. If those possessions are inhabited by alien races, differing from us in religion, customs, laws, methods of taxation and modes of thought, the administration of government and justice, according to Anglo-Saxon principles, may for a time be impossible, and the question at once arises whether large concessions ought not to be made for a time, that ultimately our own theories may be carried out, and the blessings of a free government under the Constitution extended to them. We decline to hold that there is anything in the Constitution to forbid such action.[47]

Brown could see "no middle ground" between his view that the power to acquire territory implied authority to determine the status of its inhabitants, and the opposing contention that a territory's people, "whether savage or civilized," automatically became U.S. citizens, entitled to all constitutional guarantees immediately on the territory's acquisition.[48] At the same time, the author of *Plessy* was not prepared to deny all rights to the "alien races" of newly acquired possessions. Instead, he drew a "distinction between certain natural rights enforced in the Constitution by prohibitions against interference with them, and what may be termed artificial or remedial rights which are peculiar to our own system of jurisprudence," suggesting that the former might extend to territorial inhabitants, while the latter would not. He left unclear the precise scope of these fundamental and merely formal rights and the reach of congressional power over them.[49] But he had no doubt that the Constitution's revenue provisions, including the requirement of uniform tax rates, had no application to the newly acquired territories in the absence of congressional action. A provision of the Foraker Act, passed by Congress to provide a temporary civil government for Puerto Rico, imposed a special 15 percent duty on products imported from the island to the mainland. Despite the uniformity clause, Brown sustained the tariff.

Two other members of the *Downes* majority also filed opinions. Justice White, joined by Justices McKenna and George Shiras, attempted to sidestep the issue of whether the Constitution followed the flag. White reasoned that treaty provisions did not automatically incorporate a newly acquired possession into "the American family," and that Congress alone could decide when a new territory became a full part of the United States, subject to all applicable constitutional provisions. Since the treaty under which Puerto Rico had been acquired from Spain did not specifically incorporate the territory into the United States, the Constitution, concluded White, was not yet applicable to Puerto Rican affairs. In a brief separate opinion, Justice Gray adopted White's rationale: "If Congress is not ready to construct a complete government for the conquered territory," observed Gray, "it may establish a temporary government, which is not subject to all the restrictions of the Constitution."[50]

Justices Harlan, Brewer, and Peckham joined in the dissenting opinion Chief Justice Fuller filed in *Downes*. Originally, Harlan later confided to William Howard Taft, he had planned to write no opinion in any of the insular cases. But Justice Brown had "said some things" in his *Downes* opinion which Harlan "was unwilling to pass without explicitly referring to them." He was "sorry to say," and knew Taft would be shocked to learn, "that the greater part of my dissent was written on the Sabbath, with my wife's consent. I stayed away from church to do the work. Horrible! But my ox was in the ditch, and had to be gotten out in some way."[51]

His *Downes* dissent, Harlan wrote Taft, "express[ed] views about which I feel strongly." Readers of his opinion would have no doubt on that point. Were Brown's thinking to acquire majority support on the Court, Harlan declared, "[w]e will . . . pass from the era of constitutional liberty guarded and protected by a written constitution into an era of legislative absolutism."[52] Nations "unrestrained by written constitutions" could exercise despotic power over their territories, but not a government controlled by "fundamental law."

> To say otherwise is to concede that Congress may, by action taken outside the Constitution, engraft upon our republican institutions a colonial system such as exists under monarchical governments. Surely such a result was never contemplated by the fathers of the Constitution. If that instrument had contained a word suggesting the possibility of a result of that character it would never have been adopted by the people of the United States. The idea that this country may acquire territories anywhere upon the earth, by conquest or treaty, and hold them as mere colonies or provinces,—the people inhabiting them to enjoy only such rights as Congress chooses to accord them,— is wholly inconsistent with the spirit and genius, as well as with the words, of the Constitution.[53]

In his *Downes* opinion, Justice Brown had written soothingly of the safeguards extended territorial inhabitants through "certain principles of natural justice inherent in Anglo-Saxon character, which need no expression in constitutions or statutes to give them effect or to secure dependencies against legislation manifestly hostile to their interests."[54] Harlan was not consoled. The Constitution's framers had not been willing to rest "their safety" upon such a shaky foundation. "They believed that the establishment here of a government that could administer public affairs according to its will, unrestrained by any fundamental law and without regard to the inherent rights of freemen, would be ruinous to the liberties of the people by exposing them to the oppressions of arbitrary power." Instead, they enumerated in a written constitution the powers of the national government. "It will be an evil day for American liberty," asserted Harlan, "if the theory of a government outside of the supreme law of the land finds lodgment in our constitutional jurisprudence."[55] He was equally incredulous of Brown's suggestions that certain provisions of the Constitution would apply to the newly acquired territories, while others would not. Nothing in the Constitution's language or "sound rules of interpretation" supported such a notion.[56]

Consistent with his own ethnocentrism, Harlan agreed that the nation's territorial policies should depend in part on "[w]hether a particular race will or will not assimilate with our people, and whether they can or cannot with safety to our institutions be brought within the operation of the Constitution." But such considerations properly should be brought to bear, he insisted, at the time of a territory's acquisition. "A mistake in [such judgments] . . . cannot be made the ground for violating the Constitution or giving full effect to its provisions. The Constitution is not to be obeyed or disobeyed as the circumstances of a particular crisis in our history may suggest the one or the other course to be pursued. The People have decreed that it shall be the supreme law of the land at all times."[57]

Harlan gave brief attention to Justice White's argument that a territory acquired by treaty or conquest could become incorporated into the United States only with the express consent of Congress. He realized that congressional approval was necessary for a territory to be admitted to statehood, but he could not fathom how a U.S. territory having a civil government established by Congress was "not, for all purposes of government by the nation, under the complete jurisdiction of the United States, and therefore a part of, and incorporated into, the United States, subject to all the authority which the national government may exert over any territory or people."[58] Nor could Harlan accept the intimations of both Brown and White that the United States must be permitted to "exert all the power that other nations are accustomed to exercise" if ours was to become a world power. "If our government needs more power than is conferred upon it by the Constitution," he declared, "that instrument provides the mode in which it may be amended and additional power thereby obtained. The People of the United States who ordained the Constitution never supposed that a change could be made in our system of government by mere judicial interpretation. They never contemplated any such juggling with the words of the Constitution as would authorize the courts to hold that the words 'throughout the United States,' in the taxing clause of the Constitution, do not embrace a domestic 'territory of the United States.' . . . This is a distinction which I am unable to make, and which I do not think ought to be made when we are endeavoring to ascertain the meaning of a great instrument of government."[59]

The Court's pro-imperialist stance and inconsistencies in its rulings drew considerable public scorn. The decisions had come close on the heels of McKinley's 1900 defeat of William Jennings Bryan, who had sought to make imperialism a campaign issue. The connection was too close for Finley Peter Dunne's Mr. Dooley to pass. "[N]o matter whether the Constitution follows th' flag or not," remarked Dooley, "th' Supreme Coort follows th' iliction returns."[60] Justice Brown's status as the classic swing vote in the cases led to the almost equally well-circulated observation "that four of the judges said the constitution did follow the flag, that four of them said it did not follow the flag, and one said, 'It sometimes follows the flag and sometimes does not, and I will tell you when it does and when it does not.'"[61]

Justice Harlan's stance was not universally applauded, even among his close friends. "I do not wish to reason about the Insular cases or the opinion," Gus Willson wrote the justice. "I know it represented your best feeling and best thought and I do not expect to have the faintest influence on your opinion, but I am always sorry when any opinion or any influence in this country hinders, hampers or drags on the full and complete power of this country to own any property or territory that any other country in the world can own. . . . I should not be willing to belong to a country that could not, in case it deemed it proper, exercise all the National powers, authority and rights that any other country can exercise, and I believe not merely in the legality, but in the desirability of holding Porto Rico, The Hawaiian Islands and the Phillipines [sic] Archipelego [sic] and in exercising all the necessary powers to regulate the people who happen to be tenants of these possessions."[62]

At the time the cases were being argued, moreover, William Howard Taft, who had been appointed by President McKinley as president of the commission charged with organizing a civil government for the Philippines and in 1901 would become the islands' governor, had shared with the justice his doubts regarding extension of the jury trial and related constitutional provisions to the newly acquired territories. "The truth is," wrote Taft, "that there are not more than three or four men in the islands who can be trusted as judges of the superior courts, and if that be the case you can readily see that juries made from much less likely material will be completely subject to the highest bidder."[63]

Harlan's stance attracted widespread acclaim from anti-imperialist quarters, however. Gus Willson enclosed in his letter to the justice a letter from a Cincinnati lawyer—"the best hearted and wrongest headed man I ever knew"[64]—who praised Harlan's "great, gloriously and truly American opinion."[65] A prominent New York lawyer shared with Harlan his recent law review article in which he, too, had been "weak enough to assume and to advocate, somewhat dogmatically, . . . that the Constitution follows the flag."[66] Another New York attorney expressed the hope that the *Downes* decision would prove to be "the Dred Scott of Imperialism!"[67] Senator Morgan, Harlan's Bering Sea tribunal colleague, applauded the justice's "mental and moral honesty."[68] And William Jennings Bryan, among others, suggested that Harlan become the Democrats' 1904 presidential candidate.[69]

The reaction of Harlan's son, James, to the Justice's insular stance is not clear. The Justice's papers do make obvious, however, that both father and son viewed the Puerto Rican appointment as a stepping stone to judicial office and were deeply disappointed when nothing materialized in that direction. Shortly before his assassination in September of 1901, President McKinley had indicated his plan to nominate James for a district judgeship in Illinois when one was created. In March of 1902, Justice Harlan asked William Howard Taft to speak to President Roosevelt in his son's behalf, sharing with the new president McKinley's intentions, the endorsements James had received on previous occasions[70]—and the justice's plans to retire once his son had become a judge. Following a meeting with Roosevelt, Taft wrote Harlan that he "was not greatly encouraged" at James's prospects. He had not mentioned, he added, "what was suggested in our conversation in respect of your intentions when James should be settled."[71]

Harlan's reaction to Taft's disappointing news was no surprise. "It has been a costly experiment for James," he declared in a cordial but frank reply to his friend, "to surrender—indeed, to lose—a fine, growing practice to take a place in which he could win no reputation, and which has a salary not more than one third of what he was earning at his profession."[72]

James was even more upset. The justice had considered it inappropriate to ask Taft for details of his conversation with Roosevelt, and Taft had volunteered no information. But James suggested several possible explanations for the frustrating turn of events. He doubted that his father's "judicial attitude on insular questions" had affected Roosevelt's thinking. He assured his father that, were that the case, "it relieves my own mind not only from all sense of disappointment but from all anxiety," adding: "If that is their point of view I am entirely content not to have an honor at the hands of the administration." His recent battles over the use of San Juan harbor with a steamship company known to have "strong friends in Washington" could have had some impact on the president. But that dispute, he had decided, "amounts to nothing here and ought not to there."[73]

Ultimately, James laid blame for the situation at Taft's feet. He refused to believe that Roosevelt had not appreciated his work or was "so small as to bear" his father "any resentment" for his insular dissent. Taft's failure to relate, even "in a general way," the nature of his conversation with Roosevelt could only mean, James decided, that his father's friend simply had "not take[n] the matter up seriously with the President." After all, James reasoned, Taft had no personal responsibility for what Roosevelt had told him and must have known that the justice "would take it in a manly way, however disagreeable" it might have been to him. But if Taft had failed "to carry out what he voluntarily undertook to do" in James's behalf, he would naturally "not [be] inclined to face that responsibility." James could see "no other plausible explanation" for Taft's perplexing letter and considered his conduct "churlish in the extreme [and] . . . unpardonable." He urged his father not to be distressed by the situation, however. "I am ready to return to my practice," he declared, "if any is left and if not to fight it out in my profession. I am not going to let any disappointment sour me or worry me, and I hope that you will not worry on my account."[74]

James would remain at his post as Puerto Rico's attorney general for another year and a half, corresponding with his father regularly about developments there. To circumvent a local provision that limited the suffrage to taxpayers, hundreds of islanders had purchased for a few cents a one-day license as vegetable vendors. Had the issue been raised before him, James wrote his father, "I probably should have been compelled to hold that such peddlers licenses did not come within the spirit or the letter of the [voter requirement]." But the question, he seemed happy to report, had not come to his office. "[T]he general result," he added, "probably will be universal suffrage."[75] Other letters focused on related matters.[76]

In late 1903, however, James returned to Chicago and established a practice with his brother, John. John alone signed a card announcing the partnership. The card mentioned James's service in Puerto Rico. An announcement signed by both brothers, John explained to their father, "could not well refer to [that fact] . . . without seeming ostentatious." At the same time, John thought it "advisable for business reasons to recall [it] to people's minds . . . for in the course of time our business with Porto Rico should pros[per]."[77] James's frustrating colonial service was thus put to advantage after all.

Nor was his tenure in Puerto Rico to be James's only federal post. In 1905, he was again in contention for a federal judgeship in Illinois. Newspapers soon reported that his appointment would complicate his brother John's campaign to become Chicago's mayor. In a letter to Taft, Harlan dismissed such concerns as the "merest humbug." He also shared with the future president a letter he had recently received from a New York telegraph operator who had "been handling some telegrams about the judgeship"—messages indicating that railroad interests were actually behind opposition to James's nomination. Harlan conceded, "Of course the operator does not commend himself by betraying telegrams that go through his hands." He considered the operator's letter clear evidence, though, "that the Railroads are hunting for a Judge who they believe will stand by them in their contests about rates." The recent Washington visit of the general counsel for one railroad to lobby in behalf of another hopeful for the position lent "some force," Harlan added, to his suspicions.[78]

For whatever reason, James again failed to win a judgeship. The following year, however, President Roosevelt appointed him to a seat on the Interstate Commerce Commission—albeit not without difficulty. "I am having a little trouble about your son James," Roosevelt confided to the justice in late June. "There is a good deal of feeling, I find, against putting on the Interstate Commerce Commission a man whose father on the Supreme Court will pass on his actions. I have been a little puzzled about it."[79]

Harlan rushed immediately to his son's defense. In a letter to the president, the justice expressed "surprise" that anyone would consider his position a legitimate barrier to James's appointment. James would be only one of seven commissioners; Harlan, but one of nine justices. And the possibility that a justice would be influenced by the position his son held was for Harlan "entitled to no consideration whatever. It should be assumed," he declared, "that each Justice of the Supreme Court recognizes the responsibilities attached to his high position, and, in deference, to his conscience will do his duty fearlessly, without fear or favor, and regardless of the personnel of the tribunal whose official action comes under his examination." No one had objected when Justice Field's nephew, Justice Brewer, joined him on the Court. Harlan could not understand why his "natural ambition to see [James] on the Federal Bench [could] not be gratified, except by my retiring from my position on the Supreme Bench." Earlier, it will be recalled, Harlan had suggested to Taft that he would retire once James secured a judgeship. Now, he adamantly opposed such a course. "My self respect, to speak of no other aspect of the matter, forbids such an announcement. . . . My retirement from the Bench must depend, as I know you wish it to depend, absolutely on my own judgment as to what, in my opinion the public interests and my own sense of duty may require at the particular time."[80]

Roosevelt's reply was respectful but firm. He was not certain, he wrote, that "I made myself quite clear in my last letter." There was a good chance that the recently adopted Hepburn Act, which enlarged the Interstate Commerce Commission's powers, would be challenged in the courts. Several senators "of high standing," he explained, had protested that were such a case brought to the Supreme Court, "it would not look well to have a son of one of the justices holding an office under an act upon the constitutionality of which his father, as one of the justices, was to pass." Roosevelt was not ready to indicate what weight he would give such arguments or to name the senators in question. "But it is a matter," he observed, that "I have to consider."[81]

Fortunately, on this occasion the justice prevailed. In early September, Roosevelt shared with the elder Harlan his "very real pleasure" at appointing James to the commission. He had thoroughly considered the objections senators had raised, but had concluded that they did not justify denying James the post. "I need not say," added Roosevelt, "how glad I was to be able conscientiously to come to this conclusion."[82]

James would enjoy a long tenure on the commission. In 1905, William Howard Taft had again failed to secure a judgeship for his friend's son.[83] As president, however, Taft would appoint James to a second term on the commission.[84]

The justice would continue to pursue a judgeship for his son for the balance of his life. In 1910, the year before his death, he wrote Horace H. Lurton, a recent Taft appointee to the Supreme Court, of his interest in a seat for James on the Commerce Court. "My ambition," wrote Harlan, "is that he occupy a *judicial* position. He can make [a] reputation as a Judge; for he is an excellent lawyer, and possesses the judicial temperament in a high degree."[85] But James was never to occupy a judicial seat.

Harlan was equally persistent and unsuccessful in pursuing full constitutional status for the noncontiguous territories and their inhabitants. Dissenting in *Hawaii* v. *Mankichi*,[86] decided in 1903, he favored habeas corpus relief for a defendant denied a grand jury and convicted of manslaughter by 9 of 12 jurors, rather than the unanimous verdict required in federal cases under the Sixth Amendment right to trial by an impartial jury. A majority, speaking through Justice Brown, reasoned that Congress, by the resolution annexing Hawaii to the United States, had not intended to extend all constitutional rights to the territory's inhabitants but merely those of a "fundamental" character, among which the rights at issue naturally were not included. Harlan joined an opinion of Chief Justice Fuller disputing the majority's reading of congressional intent.[87]

Characteristically, however, he also filed a separate dissent reiterating the position he had embraced in *Downes* and calling for full and immediate application of the Bill of Rights to the outlying possessions. "[I]t has been announced by some statesmen that the Constitution should be interpreted to mean not what its words naturally, or usually, or even plainly, import, but what the apparent necessities of the hour, or the apparent majority of the people, at a particular time, demand at the hands of the judiciary. I cannot assent," he declared, "to any such view of the Constitution."[88] In other cases, he pressed the same themes, but to no avail.[89]

As in most other areas in which he fought a losing battle on the Court, the Justice maintained his sense of humor. In early 1904, the William Howard Tafts were invited to the Harlans's Washington home for lunch. As the day approached, Harlan extended his friend the following "instructions:"

> Remember that you need not be accompanied by a Troop of Cavalry, having a commander whose coat will be so short behind that it will not conceal his *fundamental* parts. If you approach our humble habitation "outside of the Constitution," rely upon it that, once within the walls of our house, you will be under the Constitution, without the slightest danger of your being deprived of any right "except by due process of law." And when you sit down at our table, you will be accorded that position of preference which is due to the Ex-Sovereign of twelve millions of "*Subjects*." If a common Associate Justice of the Supreme Court of the United States should claim that he is entitled to preference by reason of his being one of the *heads* of a co-equal Department of the Government of the United States, he will be promptly reminded that this country has become a world-power, and its officers, however high, are of no consequence in the presence of one who has recently ruled millions of subjects, if not by divine right, by the supreme will of Congress.[90]

His Brother's Keeper

From his 1883 dissent in the *Civil Rights Cases* to his championing of full citizenship for the "alien races" of the noncontiguous territories at the turn of the century, Justice Harlan had compiled a judicial record perhaps best described as a powerful, if uneven, treatise on moral responsibility, brotherhood, and solicitude for the underdog. His troubling relationship with his brother, James, over the same period, while in many ways understandable, was quite another matter.

Two years Harlan's senior and the only brother to witness his elevation to the supreme bench, James Harlan may have been the justice's intellectual superior. One eulogy published at his death in 1897 termed James "a distinguished and honored lawyer, regarded by most of his associates as endowed with higher talents than his eminent brother."[91] Another, entitled "An Exceptional Man" and written by Mallie Harlan's brother, John Shanklin, characterized him as "a man of remarkable intellectual grasp and . . . power of analysis," adding: "He could detect a flaw in any legal proceedings at the most cursory glance and his critical taste and knowledge of literature made him a valuable counselor in laying down courses of reading for the young. Scarcely an author of any language could be named with whose writings he was not familiar and whose style he could not accurately describe."[92] Following a period in Evansville, Indiana, James had moved his practice to Harrodsburg and then Frankfort before settling in Louisville in 1868. In 1872, he was appointed to an unexpired term as vice-chancellor of the city's principal equity court, and in August of that year, he was elected to a full term.[93] When his brother won appointment to the Supreme Court, James resigned his judgeship and formed a practice with John's former partner, Gus Willson.

The justice, Willson wrote Harlan's son, Richard, years later, had been "inclined to advise [Willson] against" joining James in law practice.[94] The reason for Harlan's concern was not difficult to fathom. As Willson explained to Richard, "James Harlan was a lovable man and learned lawyer but could not let liquor alone."[95] James's thirst had always been considerable, but the untimely death of his wife, Amelia, in 1876 pushed him over the brink. In time, he became a hopeless alcoholic and an opium and morphine addict as well.

In part, no doubt, out of regard for Justice Harlan, Gus Willson did his best to hold the partnership together. As James steadily lost ground in his battles with his vices, though, Willson found their continued professional association increasingly untenable. "The Judge has been in a very bad condition," Willson wrote Justice Harlan in 1879. "I cannot help grave apprehension as to his case and am very much worried as to our business and our future arrangements. I need him as a partner and love him as a friend but this thing means destruction of business and all prospects. . . . I think I ought to say that the next recurrence must end our partnership. But I shall do as you think right in the matter."[96]

Justice Harlan apparently encouraged his friend to continue the partnership; Willson, himself torn between loyalty to James and frustration over the damage his drinking was doing to their practice, acquiesced. For brief periods, James remained sober and was even appointed as a temporary chancery judge. But his condition—and Willson's—gradually became desperate. James's return to the bench was cut short when he became intoxicated while presiding over a trial, forcing the closing of court.[97] A former Harlan family retainer was instructed to follow him day and night and sleep at his doorway while he was in bed, alerting Willson to any problem.[98] On more than one occasion, James was found wandering about at night in a rainstorm, soaking wet and only partially clothed.[99] "As he is going now he will be in the gutter and penniless before the summer is over," Willson wrote the justice in July of 1880, "unless he is taken charge of at once and held in."[100]

At Willson's suggestion, the Harlans invited James to spend part of that summer with them on the seashore at Block Island, Rhode Island. The change was invigorating, and James seemed committed to reform on his return to Louisville. He joined a church and assured his brother in a September letter, "I am fully persuaded of my duty . . . , and hope by shaping out a new line of life, avoiding places of amusement and becoming active in Church work, to get the better of my weakness."[101] For a brief time even Gus Willson was optimistic, writing Justice Harlan that James "had worked steadily and hard" ever since joining the church.[102] Soon, though, James fell back into his old pattern—brief periods of sobriety followed by embarrassing and extended binges.[103] In the spring of 1882, Gus Willson ended their partnership.[104]

For the next several years, James managed to survive in Louisville on the meager earnings of his law practice and the charity of others, including his brother's gifts of cash and clothing. He often expressed the hope, however, that he could establish a new life in a major city or in the West,[105] and in 1887 he settled briefly in Kansas.[106] The following year, he migrated to the Oklahoma territory. There, his circumstances were to become even more pitiful than those that had driven him from Kentucky. Initially, he wrote his brother optimistically of establishing a successful law practice or securing a government post there.[107] Increasingly, though, his letters to the justice and others focused on the misery of his existence. In letter after letter, he complained of the virtual loss of his eyesight, as well as lice-infested sleeping quarters and exposure to the elements,[108] and pleaded with his brother for clothes and money, including funds for a mail-order remedy that claimed to cure opium addiction.[109]

Justice Harlan, his son, Richard, and other relatives provided James with clothing and funds. But fearful that his brother might use the money simply to support his vices, the justice sometimes mailed the funds to a local postmaster, with instructions that they be used for James's support. The postmaster had warned Harlan against sending money directly to his brother, explaining that James would "send [for] and get opium as fast as he can pay for it."[110] But James bitterly resented that arrangement and scorned the postmaster as "a bankrupt, with scarcely a meal ahead."[111] James bemoaned, too, his brother's indifference toward him, hinted at suicide, and made veiled threats to expose his situation—the pauper-like existence of a Supreme Court justice's brother—to the public at large. "You have done your best to degrade me," he complained in one letter. "It is cruel and mean to treat me in this way. . . . You can't do worse than you have done if you were my enemy. God knows I don't deserve such treatment."[112] Whether maliciously or not, he also regularly praised, in his letters to the justice, the charity extended to him by others, especially their mulatto half-brother, Robert Harlan.[113]

Justice Harlan's support of his brother was apparently quite limited. Harlan's own perennial financial problems, as well as the natural concern that any funds sent to James would only go to his habits, no doubt help to explain the justice's parsimony. But the motivations underlying Harlan's behavior toward James were much more complicated than that; indeed, they were a complex mixture of pity, contempt, impatience, and embarrassment.

As a young man, John Harlan had been a leader in the Frankfort chapter of the Younger Brothers of Temperance. With the passage of time, he had become decidedly more tolerant of liquor, often favoring friends, even presidents, with a case of

Kentucky's finest.[114] But he remained forever fearful of demon rum and the misery it could inflict. When his son, John, seemed oblivious to its dangers, the justice reminded him that there were, "on both sides of your house, some melancholy instances of ruin coming from the use of stimulants." Urging "total abstinence," he declared that he "would be a much stronger man, mentally and physically, than I am, if I had never used strong drink, or wines, or tobacco."[115]

The devout Presbyterian never lost his disdain for those who had an excessive thirst. James, as the justice's letter to John indicated, was not the only family member vulnerable to alcoholism. His cousin, Wellington, had been dismissed from his government position as storekeeper at a distillery for drinking at his post.[116] James's son, Henry, was an alcoholic, too. In 1889, Henry had faced discharge from his government post for drunkenness and sought his uncle's aid. The justice's response was harsh and uncompromising:

> You are correct in supposing that I had heard your habits were not good, and you do not say in your letter that you abstain entirely from drinking. You only say that the reports about you are exaggerated, and that you are not *a drunkard*. Frankness compels me to say that your case is a hopeless one, if you touch strong drink *at all*. One drop is evidence to me that you are destined to a drunkard's grave at an early day, and, supposing that you now and then drank, I had concluded that it was a waste of time for me to follow after you as I have often others, and try to save you from ruin. . . . I am unwilling to lose any time in helping any one who has deliberately or recklessly set out upon a road that he knows leads to ruin. I have made up my mind that if one of my sons ever contracts the habit of drinking, to break off all connection with or responsibility for him, and never allow him to come into my presence. The truth is that the public have dealt too leniently with those who are dissipated. The worst man in the community is the married man, who, with knowledge of the bad influence of strong drink deliberately enters upon a career of dissipation, and brings his family down to poverty and disgrace. The man drinks in the belief that somebody, particularly the women of his family, will treat him kindly and tenderly, and see that he does not want for anything. It is all because the drunkard deliberately declines to exert his will-power, and refuse to drink. My creed from now forward is to let such a drinker go his own way and destroy himself if he will do it.[117]

Whether Harlan ever wrote his brother such a letter is not known. In one of her letters to James, however, Mallie Harlan urged her brother-in-law to "realize how hopeless the talk of helping you seems unless you can change your whole course of life."[118] The available evidence suggests, moreover, that Justice Harlan reacted to his brother's addictions in much the same way he responded to Henry's difficulties. Several months prior to the justice's appointment to the Bering Sea tribunal, James had returned to Kentucky, where he lived for a time at an abbey maintained by a religious order.[119] Shortly before his departure for Europe, Justice Harlan wrote Gus Willson that his brother's "relapses give me great pain," but added, "there is nothing that I can do. Nor can I abandon my duties and plans to go to him." Should James die while Harlan was abroad, Willson was to see that he was "decently buried" in the family plot at Frankfort, "with as little expense as possible."[120]

Several months earlier, when Willson suggested that a visit to the Harlans in Washington might help his former partner, the justice replied that he "should like to see" his brother, but had a concern: "[Y]ou will understand how embarrassing it would be to me and to my family, if he should get off the track while here."[121] In an 1894 letter regarding the possibility of placing James in Washington's Garfield Hospital, where the justice was a board member, or in the Harlans's home, such concerns surfaced again. "[A]s I have young daughters in society," Harlan wrote Willson, "I could not in justice to them, to say nothing of my wife have James here to be recognized on the streets, in his condition, as an inmate of my house. He knows well that there has never been a moment when I was not willing to share all I have with him, & to have him with me, all his & my days, if his life had been such as to have admitted of his being invited here."[122]

On returning to Kentucky from Oklahoma, James had continued to bemoan his existence and his brother's neglect of him, plead for funds, predict his imminent demise, and hint at taking his own life. His complaints, like earlier ones, were not without substance. As before, Justice Harlan provided James with limited financial support. Prior to sailing for Paris in December of 1892, for example, the justice gave Gus Willson six checks of $20 each for his brother's monthly support during the first half of 1893.[123] After James left the abbey, moreover, the justice for a time paid for his brother's lodging at an inexpensive Louisville hotel.[124] By 1895, however, James had been placed in the Kentucky Home for the Aged and Infirm, an almshouse outside Louisville, with his brother's reluctant approval. "It is distressing beyond all conception," Harlan had written Willson, "that a brother of mine should be in an Alms House. But what can be done to prevent such a thing[?] If he were put in some good Hospital, and was supplied with money, it would only make matters worse, and it is certain as we live that a large part of the money I would send him would get into Henry's hands and encourage *him* to continue his indefensible course."[125]

As Justice Harlan prepared to visit Louisville in the summer of 1895 for a reunion of Civil War veterans, Willson purchased a suit and accessories for James with money the justice provided. Wilson, and presumably Harlan, hoped that Captain J. K. Westfall, superintendent of the almshouse to which James had been confined, might bring the justice's brother to the reunion. But when Westfall wrote Harlan at Willson's request, the justice did not respond. A perplexed Willson then contacted Harlan, urging him to write Westfall. "He has really been very kind to the Judge," wrote Willson, "and knows you very well and felt somewhat hurt about the matter."[126]

Whether James attended the reunion is not known. But if he did, it was to be one of his last personal contacts with his brother. It was the old man's habit to walk down to the almshouse depot each day to get a newspaper dropped off by an afternoon train. On June 15, 1897, he was struck by a passing train and killed instantly. Two days later, he was buried at Frankfort. Justice Harlan, papers reported, had arrived that morning for the funeral.[127]

The impact Justice Harlan's relationship with James may have had on his professional work is, of course, impossible to assess with any precision. One or more of several lines of influences can be suggested, though. Harlan's disdain for those, like his brother, who suffered the consequences of behavior over which they had some degree of control may have heightened the justice's sympathy for those plagued with burdens for which they bore no responsibility. Or some unconscious sense of guilt over his treatment of his brother may have intensified his efforts in behalf of the former slaves and other victims of an imperfect society. Or the sheer human tragedy that James's life reflected may have exerted an influence on the justice's response to those seeking the Court's protection. Yet Harlan's relationship with James, like his complicated racial attitudes and his willingness to use his position to avoid financial responsibilities, contrasted markedly with his judicial record.

Whatever the reality of their relationship, however, contemporary newspaper reports of the justice's treatment of James were generous and sympathetic. Drawing largely on Gus Willson's testimony, the Louisville *Courier-Journal* provided the following profile of the brothers' relationship in its report of James's death:

> Justice Harlan always looked after his unfortunate brother with great solicitude. He constantly furnished him money through Mr. A. E. Willson. Until three years ago Justice Harlan provided for him at the Enterprise Hotel, when the old man went to the county alms-house against his brother's protest. Capt. Westfall, the keeper, was an old friend of the family, and Judge Harlan was warmly attached to him. Justice Harlan kept [James] supplied constantly with all that he needed and with many little comforts besides. Last week Justice Harlan made a flying trip to Louisville and spent most of his time with his brother, and when he departed left money with Mr. Willson to provide for his every want. [Justice Harlan] at one time expressed a desire to take his brother to his home in Washington, but his friends here strongly opposed such a course, as Judge Harlan's mental and physical condition and the fact that he was with his old friend, Capt. Westfall, made him more content where he was.[128]

Twilight

Whatever Harlan's treatment of his brother, he and Mrs. Harlan were unusually devoted parents, as much in the twilight years of their lives as before. The justice's constant promotion of his son, James, has already been recounted. John's difficulties at Princeton had been deeply disappointing, but Harlan clearly recognized his son's legal talents and took an active interest in his professional career and political activities, offering encouragement, advice, and optimistic predictions as, for example, during John's successful campaign to secure a seat on Chicago's city council and his losing bids to become its mayor. As a devout Presbyterian lay leader, Harlan probably admired most his eldest son, Richard, for his choice of a ministerial career. When Richard secured an administrative post at George Washington University, where his father taught law classes for nearly 20 years, the justice's hand in the school's choice was clearly evident.[1] The justice's papers contain many lengthy letters between the elder Harlans and their sons.

The Harlans were equally solicitous grandparents. Following the untimely death of their daughter, Edith, in 1882, it will be recalled, they had elected to raise their granddaughter, Edith, as their own child. In 1901, they presented Edith to Washington society at a tea in their Euclid Avenue home. Five years later, President Roosevelt, cabinet members, diplomats, and other Washington elites witnessed her wedding in the New York Avenue Presbyterian Church, the Harlan family's local congregation where Edith's mother had been married years before.[2] Neither Richard and his wife, Margaret, nor James and Maud Harlan were to have children. But John and his wife, Elizabeth, presented his parents with three granddaughters and, in 1899, a grandson, the future Justice John Marshall Harlan. "The only trouble about your grandson having your name," a friend wrote the elder Harlan several months after the child's birth, "is that he may suffer from 'standing in the shadow of a great name.'"[3]

The justice's interest in his grandchildren, like that in his sons and their wives, was genuine and deep. He wrote his eldest granddaughter, Elizabeth, or "Lysbeth," as she was more often called, lengthy letters. In one, he mentioned a forthcoming White House dinner. "Grandma, I suppose, will be taken out by the President and I will go out with Mrs. Roosevelt. I wonder if you will ever preside at the White House. Who can tell[?]"[4] In another, written on Abraham Lincoln's birthday, he promised to send Elizabeth a book on the late president's "marvelous career." "Just to think," he exclaimed; "a man born in a log cabin, [who] was even a rail-splitter and common flatboatman, and yet became President."[5] Harlan delighted in teasing Elizabeth and other family members, not always with their approval. "[W]e . . . must get closer together," he joked to his granddaughter on one occasion. "Ruth is the only one at whom I can poke fun. [The others] say I am a tease. But that is a mistake. It is not teasing—it is fun."[6]

Summers, especially, were a time for Harlan family gatherings. As soon as the Court recessed for the summer, the Harlans sought escape from the sweltering Washington heat on the seashore or in the mountains. For most of the justice's years on the bench, their summer destinations varied, although Block Island was clearly the family's favorite. But beginning in 1897, the year of his brother's death, the justice and his family made Pointe-au-Pic, Quebec—a breathtakingly beautiful village on the lower St. Lawrence, more commonly called Murray Bay—their permanent summer residence. Richard had first vacationed at Murray Bay in 1896 and was so impressed with the spot that in 1900 his wife, Margaret, bought a tract of land there on which they built a cottage. Eventually, the elder Harlans also built a large house on a high bluff overlooking the area, naming it "Braemead." John and his growing family rented a house there as well. Justice and Mrs. Harlan, their daughters and sons' wives, and John's children spent most of every summer in Murray Bay. The Harlan brothers visited as frequently as their careers would permit, and their parents also played host to an assortment of guests. Several prominent Canadians and Americans, most notable among them William Howard Taft, as well as visitors from other countries, also vacationed there, and the Harlans quickly grew to cherish the area. "I do not believe," the justice often remarked to Mallie, that "there is a more beautiful spot on God's earth."[7]

Harlan's enthusiasm for the game of golf, to which his son, Richard, introduced him on his first trip to Murray Bay, was to become as great as his affection for Pointe-au-Pic. The justice would never become a champion golfer, but his addiction to the game became so avid that his brethren began referring to him as "the golfer" in their summer correspondence. Several year's after his father's death, Richard would devote a lengthy magazine article to the justice's love of the sport.[8] Watched closely by international galleries of spectators, Harlan and his sons were regular participants in Murray Bay golf matches, challenging all comers to competition. In one letter to Taft, for example, the justice goaded the "Father of the Filipinos, the Builder of the Panama Canal and the Slayer of Boss Cox [to] add to [his] titles by becoming the Slayer of Judges and Senators who think they can play golf, but can do no more than play *at* the game."[9]

Harlan quickly became a familiar figure on the links of the Chevy Chase country club outside Washington; a hole the justice once miraculously made in a single stroke would be dubbed "Harlan's Hole." Not surprisingly, given his perennial financial woes, he at times wrangled over club charges, once urging the club treasurer to "[p]lease . . . not let the Golf Professional labor under the impression that I have any clubs at the Caddy-House, else he will make another charge for cleaning that which he does not clean."[10] But he struck an impressive figure on the course. In his later years, the justice had become increasingly careless in his attire. "This morning," observed one reporter who spotted him eating in a hotel dining room during circuit duties in Detroit, "he wore a wing collar that was four or five sizes too large for him, and his white stiff-bosomed shirt was also quite 'roomy,' to say the least. The bosom flapped loosely. His trousers were badly wrinkled and bagged from under his Prince Albert [coat]. He wore a silk tie and carried a heavy, old-fashioned walking cane."[11] His golf uniform was quite a different matter, as the following press description makes obvious: "He usually appears in a coat of scarlet, with Scotch plaid trousers. He is especially elaborate in his hosiery, which is like a rainbow winding around his well-shaped calves. A bright cap crowns this gay costume, though he prefers to play bareheaded."[12]

The Justice, speaking with gusto and in a voice one journalist compared to the "double bass in a pipe organ,"[13] had always been a consummate storyteller. Now, his conversations sparkled with golf anecdotes. His favorite perhaps involved an Episcopal clergyman, one of his frequent companions on the Chevy Chase links. The cleric had missed a drive completely. He was thoroughly frustrated but not a word escaped his lips. Finally, the justice spoke: "Doctor Skerrett, the things you didn't say were something awful. That was the most profane silence I ever heard!"[14]

Golf tales by and about the justice, as well as other humorous stories about the popular jurist, continued to make their way regularly into the press. One of the more delightful anecdotes involved his well-known distaste for automobiles. Inherently suspicious of modern "contraptions," he resisted for years having a telephone installed in his home. Although several of the brethren bought electric automobiles and Justice McKenna drove a gas-powered vehicle, Harlan detested autos and the hazards they posed. One day, he and Justice White were walking up Pennsylvania Avenue on their way home from Court. Suddenly, as a newspaper later described it, "an automobile came whizzing around a corner and Justice Harlan was saved from possible injury by Justice White, who dragged him out of harm's way." Harlan was furious. Once he had recovered his composure, he remarked to White:

> Let me make a prophesy. Some day a real man from the West, from the plains—from that section of the country where men do not permit other men to trifle with their feelings—some day such a man will come to Washington. He will walk down Pennsylvania Avenue, just as you and I are walking.
>
> As he starts across the street an automobile will come bowling along at breakneck speed, and come within an inch of taking off a leg.
>
> It will be an old story with the driver but a new one with the man from the West. That particular man from the West will pull his shooting iron from his pocket and fill the reckless driver full of holes, and judge though I am, I believe the man from the West will get off scott free.[15]

Publication of the story in numerous papers attracted new Harlan admirers. A police magistrate and ex-justice of the peace praised his "manly position."[16] A "humble sinner from the South," then residing in Philadelphia, informed the justice that he "enforce[d] with my pistol almost weekly what I consider reasonable rules of the road," and lamented the "automobilists' indifference to most individuals' rights."[17]

When not dodging automobiles, golfing, or immersed in the Court's business, the aging justice also continued to indulge his abiding interests in religion and politics. As in the past, he taught a men's Bible class at the New York Avenue church, which he also served as elder. He and Wallace Radcliffe, the minister serving the congregation in the justice's later years, were particularly close. When dissident church members attempted to oust Radcliffe, Harlan vigorously defended his friend against his detractors.[18]

At Murray Bay, the family attended a church in which, eventually, Anglican services were held one Sunday and Presbyterian services the next. One Sunday, his grandson, John, attended an Anglican service, conducted in Latin. "How was church?" his grandfather asked on his return. "Oh, it was all right," John replied. "The minister dressed in a sheet and spoke Chinese."[19] From 1900 until his death, the justice served the Murray Bay church as one of its two trustees, playing a major role in securing funding for extensive improvements in its facilities. "Most of us remember well," a member of the congregation later recalled, "the tall, distinguished and venerable figure of Mr. Justice [Harlan] as he stood on Sunday mornings under the birch tree near the door at the end of the church welcoming with his kindly, genial presence the entering" worshipers.[20] Following the justice's death, members placed an inscription at the church entrance in his memory.

Harlan continued to be prominent in national Presbyterian circles. When a denominational committee drafted proposed revisions in church doctrine, he questioned a number of the suggested modifications in correspondence with Princeton scholar Henry van Dyke.[21] In 1905, he served as Vice-Moderator of the denomination's General Assembly, held that year at Winona Lake, Indiana. Like most such occasions, the proceedings were as much about public affairs as ecclesiastical concerns, especially those sessions in which the justice participated. During a debate over racial segregation within the church, he vigorously objected to suggestions that blacks as a race were more prone to crime than whites. Such talk, he declared, amounted to nothing less than the "baseless fostering of race prejudice."[22] While supporting increased funding for mission work, moreover, he expressed regret that the United States had become a world power. He asserted,

We have gone so far that a government founded on the right of human beings to be governed by their own consent, is governing millions of human beings, substantially by the sword, without their consent. We have tacked upon our republican system a colonial system, covering races who are practically our subjects—can never be our fellow-citizens. I am not making an argument; I am simply stating conditions, and in the face of those conditions I want to say that we cannot accept the position of a world power without accepting its responsibilities. If we are so rich and strong that no man dares to lay hands on us, then let us meet our responsibilities like men, and use our riches and our strength to spread the church of Christ all over the world.

The justice devoted most of his General Assembly efforts toward a longstanding goal: a campaign to establish a Presbyterian national cathedral in Washington, D.C.

In February, he had circulated a letter outlining such a project to numerous Presbyterian clerics and laypersons throughout the country.[23] Now, he defended his plan on the assembly floor. Opponents attacked the proposal as symptomatic of the denomination's general drift toward formalism and ritual, but Harlan rose "spiritedly," by one account, to its defense. "I despise," he declared, "ceremonies and forms in the Christian Church." He had no desire, he insisted, for a "cathedral" in any prelatic sense; in fact, he preferred the phrase "Presbyterian minister" to the term "cathedral" in describing his goal. He simply wanted "a plain, old-fashioned, large Presbyterian church" that would "fairly represent the nobility and commanding power of Presbyterianism in the United States."

At Harlan's urging, the assembly overwhelmingly endorsed his project. The justice then returned to Washington and persuaded his New York Avenue congregation and another local church to merge, forming a potential nucleus for the national facility he envisioned. Apart from the concerns of other local congregations regarding the project's possible impact on their membership, the Washington opposition had essentially the same objections as those raised at Winona Lake—and got the same response, if a bit more colorfully stated, from Harlan. "I am tooth and toenail against frills in a church," he assured one gathering. "[E]xalted ministerial position has no weight with me whatever, but I do think that Presbyterianism should have the proper dignity in Washington, the capital of the nation, and I think this new church should have the approval of every man in the city, Presbyterian or any other denomination."[24] The justice was persuasive. Both congregations approved the merger, and the Washington presbytery, governing body for the local churches, gave the project its unanimous endorsement.

In politics, the justice continued to intervene in patronage matters, particularly in behalf of friends. In 1901, for example, he wrote President Roosevelt in support of a Kentucky native who was fearful of losing an internal revenue position in Texas.[25] As in the past, his efforts were generally successful, but not always. His lobbying for a Civil War veteran, for instance, drew the following response from Roosevelt: "[M]y experience in these cases is generally that it is simply impossible for many of the veterans now to give the service necessary. I am sure that the average head of a department wishes to favor the veterans, but he often has work that *must* be done by younger men."[26]

Harlan's campaigns to secure a federal judgeship for his friend, Gus Willson, were nearly as frequent and intensive as his efforts in behalf of his son, James—and equally fruitless. When Willson made a successful 1907 bid to become a one-term Kentucky governor, however, the justice successfully enlisted William Howard Taft to campaign in the candidate's behalf,[27] and also expressed the wish that he could join them—"'unbeknownst,' as I am on the bench."[28] But Taft and other prominent national Republicans never considered Kentucky as important to the party's national fortunes or as politically promising as Harlan did. During Taft's victorious 1908 presidential campaign against William Jennings Bryan, the justice recommended that the Republican candidate schedule an extensive series of speaking engagements in the blue-grass state. Taft's response was prompt and blunt. "If I were running for governor of Kentucky, your suggestions as to where I ought to go in the State would be valuable, but as my campaign managers are not likely to permit me to make a speech anywhere your suggestion that I [speak] . . . in about a dozen different places in Kentucky hardly meets with the exigencies of the present situation. . . . [I]f I did so in Kentucky I should have to do so in Maryland, North Carolina, Tennessee and Missouri, and that is beyond the ability of any man except Bryan."[29]

The justice's connections to electoral politics were not limited to the campaigns of others. On several occasions, and as late as the eve of the 1904 presidential race, it will be recalled, Harlan had been widely endorsed for the presidency. During his last years, various Kentuckians urged him to retire from the bench and return to his native state as a candidate for governor or for a U.S. Senate seat. In 1906, for example, talk of a Harlan gubernatorial campaign had become so widespread that the justice sent Gus Willson a letter explaining his reasons for declining such a race. He had found the "numerous and cordial expressions" of support for his candidacy "most gratifying . . . [and] highly prized," he wrote, but the time and energy required for a statewide campaign and four years in office, if elected, were an insurmountable obstacle to his candidacy. "Please, therefore, as opportunity may be presented," he asked Willson, "inform my Kentucky friends that they must not think of me in connection with political station."·Presumably with Harlan's approval—and no doubt consistent with Willson's own gubernatorial ambitions—the justice's former law partner promptly had the letter published in state papers.[30]

The justice may have had mixed feelings about foregoing such efforts. The next year, Kentucky newspapers carried stories that Harlan might become a Senate candidate. In another letter to Willson, he declared that "the idea of my retiring from the Bench and going into the Senate is out of the question." Willson was instructed to "[s]ay, if required, that I will never have any office except the one I have now." But Harlan also added, wistfully perhaps, "No opportunity will come for such a thing as that to happen."[31]

Whatever his attitude toward his judicial position, the Court's senior Justice was to be the object of numerous honors during his last decade. In October of 1902, a highly flattering biographical profile by the columnist Savoyard appeared in many papers;[32] and in 1906, James B. Morrow wrote another widely publicized tribute to the justice.[33] In December of 1902, Washington's Willard Hotel was the setting for a banquet hosted by the Supreme Court bar in honor of Harlan's completion of a quarter century on the bench. The justice's old friend, Wayne MacVeagh, presided, while President Roosevelt and other dignitaries toasted the honored guest and his military, political, and judicial record. Justice Brewer, however, provided the evening's most memorable quote. In a gentle dig at his longtime colleague, Brewer assured his audience that Harlan "goes to bed every night with one hand on the Constitution and the other on the Bible, and so sleeps the sweet sleep of justice and righteousness." But Brewer said more, and his words perhaps captured best the justice's own perception of his constitutional philosophy:

> He believes in the Constitution as it was written; that the Constitution as it was must be the Constitution as it is, and the Constitution as it shall be, unless and until the American people shall, in the way they have appointed, amend its provisions. To him it is no rope of sand to be broken by every legislative mandate, nor cord of rubber to be stretched by any tension of popular feeling, but a strong cable, binding this Government in all its movements and activities to those eternal principles of justice, lib-

erty, and equality without which the fathers believed that no free republic could ever endure and prosper.[34]

The Harlans's golden wedding anniversary in 1906 provided another occasion for tributes to the venerable justice. The following year, New York's Kentuckians Society hosted a banquet at the Plaza Hotel in honor of Harlan's thirtieth year on the Court. In a somewhat rare display of pique, given the circumstances, the justice had declined a similar invitation two years earlier, by one account, because "other guests" were also to be honored and the society member designated to invite the justice was "deaf as a post."[35] In 1906, however, when the Kentuckians decided to honor Harlan alone, the justice accepted. In remarks delivered at the banquet, he stressed his kinship with his native state but also declared, characteristically, "We are . . . something far more than Kentuckians," adding: "[W]hat would it mean to us to be Kentuckians if we were not also or rather first of all, Americans, whose allegiance to the Nation in matters of general concern is above allegiance to any State, just as the Constitution of the United States, with respect to all national objects, is above the Constitution of any State. . . . The best friends of State rights . . . are not those who habitually denounce as illegal everything done by the General Government, but those who recognize the Government of the Union as possessing all the powers granted to it in the Constitution . . . ; for, without a General Government possessing controlling power in relation to matters of national concern, the States would have no prestige before the world and would be in perpetual conflict with one another."[36]

The justice's remarks may have been prompted in part by recent outbreaks of nightrider violence in Kentucky. During his gubernatorial campaign that year, black leaders had complained to Gus Willson about his and his party's recent record on race relations, comparing the candidate unfavorably to Harlan and other Republicans. Willson had drafted, but not mailed, hot replies, scorning his detractors' "absurd appeals" and declaring that he did "not believe in favors to the colored people, but in fair play."[37] Perhaps partly to associate himself with the *Plessy* dissenter's aura, however, Willson invited Harlan to visit Kentucky shortly after his inauguration as governor for another round of tributes to the nation's most venerable defender of civil rights. Harlan readily accepted. Willson, after all, was probably his most intimate personal friend, as familiar as anyone perhaps with the justice's weaknesses as well as his strengths. Harlan realized, too, that the governor was virtually powerless to cope with racial violence in his state. Harlan had written his friend several months before his visit,

> If the local authorities will not or cannot move effectively, I do not see that you can do much under your limited powers. The last legislature was criminally negligent in not heeding your demand for such changes in the existing laws as would enable you to meet the crisis, and to suppress lawlessness. The laws regulating changes of [trial] venue should have [been] so amended as to make it the duty of the court, on the application of either party, to send the case to some [area] . . . where a trial could be had that would not be dominated by the excitement prevailing in the locality where the lawlessness existed. You should have been given all the money and all the armed force that the emergency demanded.[38]

Harlan visited Kentucky as Governor Willson's guest at Thanksgiving. Whatever his, or Willson's, motivations for his return to his "Old Kentucky Home," the justice did not use the occasion as an opportunity for a discourse on race relations in his native state. Instead, he devoted the trip primarily to nostalgic reunions with old friends, social gatherings, newspaper interviews, and innocuous speechmaking, including an address at Transylvania University, where he praised great—and unreconstructed—jurists of the state's past, most notably his mentors, Thomas Marshall and George Robertson.[39] Just two weeks earlier, however, he had hardly minced words when his brethren upheld the use of Kentucky regulations to forbid interracial education at Berea College. Vehemently dissenting in that case, it will be recalled, he had scorned the legislation's "cruel" character and obvious inconsistency "with the great principle of the equality of citizens before the law."[40]

Glowing tributes and flattering newspaper profiles were obviously high points of the justice's last years on the bench. There were also to be major disappointments. But by that stage of his life no doubt, Harlan had become accustomed to losing the great constitutional battles he waged on the Court. Even so, continued defeat must have been a bitter pill, particularly with the growing realization that his days were numbered.

Harlan was to suffer more personal setbacks as well. By 1910, he had been teaching law at Columbian University (later renamed George Washington University) for nearly two decades. His course subjects were wide-ranging. In 1891, when he first began teaching, for example, he served as "Professor of the Federal Jurisprudence of the United States, of Domestic Relations, of Commercial Law, and of the Law of Evidence."[41] He also lectured from time to time at other institutions, especially the University of Virginia.[42] Not surprisingly, his teaching was heavily oriented toward constitutional law, for which he prepared detailed lectures intended for eventual publication in a casebook or treatise on the subject.[43]

By all accounts, Harlan was an extremely popular professor, early as well as late in his career. A Washington correspondent's 1895 newspaper profile of the justice offered the following description of Professor Harlan and his classroom:

> [H]is lectures are so popular that the gallery of the college auditorium, open to outsiders, is nearly always crowded to the doors, and many of his attentive listeners are ladies. . . . Promptly at 7 o'clock Justice Harlan enters and takes his seat on the platform. His appearance is greeted with cheer after cheer from the students and visitors. He must . . . wait a minute or two before he can make his voice heard above the clamor of approval. Then his great force, clad most frequently in evening dress [as are many spectators], rises amid the hisses of the boys for silence, and by the time he has uttered his familiar greeting—"young gentlemen of the law class"—the dropping of a pin can almost be heard, so still is the room and close the attention paid him, which continues to the end of the lecture, though interrupted with popular applause, or laughter, at the frequent fine points scored, and witty thrusts. . . . The Constitution of the United States is his most fruitful subject, and his lectures thereon . . . are magnificent. His words make one bubble over with enthusiastic patriotism. . . . He also takes time to answer whatever questions may be handed him in writing by the students, and also to administer a quiz or two on matters previously gone over.[44]

If the letters in the justice's papers are typical, Harlan's students revered their professor. An undated memorandum, perhaps written for the justice's son, Richard, when he was planning to write a biography of his father, describes, for example, Harlan's near-violent rebuke of students involved in a shoving and scuffling match outside his class. "We received a lecture that was smoking hot," the student recalled, and "so entirely effective I do not believe we ever again disturbed Judge Harlan." Yet the student had "no recollection that any of us harbored the slightest ill-feeling against him on account of it. . . . [W]e all loved the old judge so well we could not entertain any feeling of injury for what he righteously said to us about it."[45]

Harlan obviously relished his role as teacher, and, given his persistent financial difficulties, undoubtedly was grateful for the additional income it afforded. At its highest point, his stipend amounted to $4,000 annually. When his commitment to the university was reduced in 1903 from four hours of weekly lecturing to two, however, the justice was asked to take a $1,000 reduction in income.[46] In 1910, a new dean, E. G. Lorenzen, asked the university's law faculty to contribute to a salary fund for a departmental secretary[47] and, shortly thereafter, to accept a potentially severe salary cut. Citing budget constraints, Lorenzen proposed that faculty members agree to be paid only half their annual salaries in the usual monthly installments, the balance to be paid, to the extent funds were available, at the end of the academic year, after the law department had made a substantial contribution toward meeting the university's debt.[48]

Harlan was vacationing at Murray Bay when Lorenzen's proposals reached him. Although he asked for more advance notice on any "further demands" and stressed that his "means [were] very limited," the justice reluctantly agreed to contribute to the secretarial fund. But the salary proposal offended him deeply, and not purely for financial reasons. The month before, Harry Snow, the husband of one of Mrs. Harlan's cousins, had been named acting president of the university. In recent months and for reasons the Harlans were unable to fathom, Snow's wife, Margaret, had severed relations with them, refusing to visit their home and, as Harlan later put it, "talk[ing] about us everywhere."[49] The day of her husband's selection as George Washington's acting administrator, Mrs. Snow wrote Justice Harlan a bizarre letter. Her husband, she declared, "will have *saved* [the university], if it is saved," despite "the results of *extreme* idiocy *on the part of every one connected with it.*" But the Harlans were her principal target. "You all thought," she wrote, that "we were to be patronized when we came here. *Why*, only you know. My father, *who made law*, . . . was greater than all the judges who ever sat on the bench put together."[50]

The proposed salary reduction, following on the heels of Mrs. Snow's letter and an apparent cut in the salary of the justice's son, Richard, who was a member of the university administrative staff, added to Harlan's growing disenchantment with the university and its treatment of him. His volatile son, John, was even more infuriated. John insisted that his father reject any further reduction in salary or uncertainty in its payment. "[Y]ou have been the drawing card at the law school," he wrote the justice on learning of Lorenzen's proposal, "and they should pay you well." Any wavering on his father's part, he warned, "would be seized upon by that crazy woman and her cowed husband and a wrong face put upon it to others."[51]

Whether the justice attempted further negotiation with George Washington officials is not known, but several days after receiving his son's letter, he wrote the university's trustees that he would formally resign from the faculty on his return to

Washington in the fall. A board member acknowledged receipt of Harlan's letter "with much regret," but agreed that it was "both wise and just for you to husband your strength."[52] "This is a mistake," Harlan quickly shot back. He added:

> My health is good and I had intended to continue my work as Lecturer on Constitutional Law as long as it was possible to do so. . . . No, my course of action was . . . due . . . wholly to other causes. My surroundings had become very disagreeable. The Chairman of the Executive Committee had without cause become hostile to every member of my family and to myself. His wife was writing unfriendly letters about us in many directions. The husband, of course, knew of these letters and originally or subsequently approved, or failed to control her action. Besides, the unjust action taken in reference to my son's salary was largely due to him as Trustee and as Chairman of the Executive Committee. To this I may add, that I did not like the proposition made in reference to my own salary [either]."[53]

In a letter to another member of the law faculty, in which he reproduced Mrs. Snow's letter, Harlan reiterated his complaints, termed Snow "wholly unequal to the place he holds," and predicted the university's decline under Snow's leadership. The colleague agreed with the justice's assessment and expressed doubt "whether, unless some of [Snow's] schemes are thwarted by saner minds, the affairs of the corporation will be materially improved under his management."[54] Harlan also shared his concerns with others connected with the university. In September, however, he formally resigned his position.[55] The law department's annual report of that year applauded his willingness to give students "the benefit of his great learning and eminent personality," adding: "Cherishing above all else the constitution of his country, Mr. Justice Harlan regarded it both a duty and a pleasure to awaken in the hearts of students a like love and reverence."[56] But apparently no movement developed to retain his services.

Harlan deeply regretted his estrangement from the university's students, and the failure of George Washington's officialdom to accommodate his concerns must have been a severe blow to his pride. A decision by his old friend, William Howard Taft, in December of that year, however, would be even more devastating to the justice.

During his lengthy tenure on the bench, Harlan had been witness to numerous appointments, retirements, and deaths among the brethren. He was unfailingly gracious on such occasions. When Horace Gray died in 1902, for example, he had written to Chief Justice Fuller that "[w]ith all his peculiarities of manner, [Gray] was at heart a just and fearless man."[57] When Charles Evans Hughes was appointed to replace Justice Brewer in 1910, Harlan telegraphed his new colleague that "[t]he country [was] to be congratulated upon" Hughes's selection.[58]

On at least one occasion, Harlan had attempted to nudge a colleague into retirement, albeit to no immediate avail. By the mid-1890s, Justice Field, as Hughes would delicately put it, had "tarried too long on the bench,"[59] with brief periods of remarkable lucidity increasingly overshadowed by episodes of senility. Finally, a member of the Court recalled that Field himself had been a member of a committee of the brethren charged with persuading Justice Robert C. Grier to retire in 1870, after Grier's mind had wandered dangerously during the justices' consideration of the first of the important *Legal Tender Cases*.[60] Justice Harlan was selected to remind Justice Field of the Grier incident in the hope that Field, too, might decide to retire. Justice Hughes would later recount Harlan's version of the ensuing encounter with the venerable and irascible Field:

> [Harlan] went over to Justice Field, who was sitting alone on a settee in the robing room apparently oblivious of his surroundings, and after arousing him gradually approached the question, asking if he did not recall how anxious the Court had become with respect to Justice Grier's condition and the feeling of other Justices that in his own interest and in that of the Court he should give up his work. Justice Harlan asked if Justice Field did not remember what had been said to Justice Grier on that occasion. The old man listened, gradually becoming alert and finally, with his eyes blazing with the old fire of youth, he burst out: "Yes! And a dirtier day's work I never did in my life!" That was the end of that effort of the brethren of the Court to induce Justice Field's retirement. . . .[61]

When Field finally did agree to retire in 1897, however, he asked Harlan to review a draft of the letter announcing his decision.[62]

In March of 1910, Justice Brewer had died, to be replaced by Hughes. On July 4 of that year, Melville Fuller, the justice with whom Harlan had perhaps been closest, also died, giving President Taft the opportunity to fill the Court's center seat. Within a day of Fuller's death, the White House began to receive letters and telegrams recommending Harlan for the chief justiceship. Much of that effort originated with Kentuckians. From Massachusetts, where he was vacationing, for example, Governor Willson assured the president that the Justice was "universally beloved," adding: "Everybody would be glad, nobody could be sorry to see him promoted before retiring."[63] Supportive letters came in from around the nation, and while many sounded the sentimental theme Willson had struck, others praised Harlan's record, particularly his commitment, as one admirer put it, to the constitutional principles of Chief Justice Marshall.[64] In September, moreover, the *New York Times* reported that friends of the justice had approached Taft with a proposal that the president choose Harlan on the understanding that he would retire before the end of Taft's administration so that Justice Hughes could then be moved to the Court's center seat.[65]

As the Court's senior justice, Harlan had become acting chief justice on Fuller's death, pursuing that role with typical gusto. But often in recent years, especially in letters to Gus Willson, Harlan had speculated about retirement. In one lengthy 1906 letter, he had even considered specific dates, such as the occasion of his completion of 30 years on the bench or the date of his golden wedding anniversary that very year. In the same letter, he conceded that he was "not as *keen* for" the Court's work as he once had been.[66] When newspapers began carrying articles about his possible selection as Fuller's replacement, moreover, he had assured his friend, Horace Lurton, that the lobbying in his behalf was "without my knowledge or procurement," adding: "I do not suppose that I will be thought of."[67] And in a letter written in late July, he had informed Justice William Day that the campaign in his behalf had been instigated by "some enthusiastic friends of mine at Louisville," acting "without my knowledge and without consulting me." He had asked them to "forebear" further such efforts and thought that they had acceded to his wishes. "Of course," he added, "the President will never think of me in connection with this matter. My years forbid his consideration of my name, even if he had no other objections." Enclosed with the letter was a copy of a letter Harlan had written President Taft, endorsing Day for Fuller's seat. "Now, do not growl," the justice soothed. "What I have done will do you no harm."[68]

With but little cynicism on the reader's part, Harlan's letter to Taft in Day's behalf could have been construed as a brief for its author. True, much of the letter was devoted to Day's qualifications, but it was also a defense of Harlan's view "that an Associate Justice ought, as a general rule, to succeed a Chief Justice . . . unless, in the judgment of the President, he was disqualified for the position by advanced years, or by ill health." In fact, he cited Day's tenure as support for his appointment. "His experience as a Judge would enable him to take up the work of the Court where the late Chief Justice left it, and go right ahead without any delay or any friction whatever. He would not be under the necessity of becoming trained in details, upon the handling of which with ease and promptness so much depends. He is already fully informed as to the manner in which the business of the Court is transacted." If a justice with Day's relatively brief tenure (seven years) was well prepared for the post, Harlan might have added (but of course could not), what about a justice with nearly 33 years on the bench?

In fairness to Harlan, his reference to "advanced years" as a barrier to elevation of a sitting justice obviously could have applied to his own situation. But if he indeed was attempting to make his own case through a letter written ostensibly in Day's behalf, he need not have wasted his time. The deaths of Fuller and Brewer had given Taft two vacancies to fill; the death of Justice Peckham the year before had provided another opportunity; and Justice William H. Moody, who suffered from crippling rheumatism, resigned in 1910 following the enactment by Congress of special legislation extending him retirement benefits.

Before these fortuitous, albeit sad, developments occurred, the president had becoming increasingly disgruntled with the Court and its aging membership. In a 1909 letter, Taft confided his frustrations to Horace Lurton, his old associate from the sixth circuit court: "The condition of the Supreme Court is pitiable, and yet those old fools hold on with a tenacity that is most discouraging. Really the Chief Justice is almost senile; Harlan does no work; Brewer is so deaf that he cannot hear and has got beyond the point of the commonest accuracy in writing his opinions; Brewer and Harlan sleep almost through all the arguments. I don't know what can be done. It is most discouraging to the active men on the bench."[69]

Ironically, given this harangue against the Court's "old fools," Taft gave Lurton the seat created by Peckham's death, making the 65-year-old jurist—who would be dead less than five years later—the oldest person ever appointed to the Court.[70] The president's selection of a chief justice, however, would be entirely consistent with the sentiments he had shared with Lurton. On December 12, 1910, just two days after Justice Harlan's thirty-third anniversary on the bench, Taft nominated Harlan's old antagonist, Edward Douglass White, to fill the Court's center seat.

Harlan had told others that his age alone was an insurmountable barrier to his appointment as chief justice. Even so, Taft's rebuff was a devastating blow. In a Christmas Day letter to Gus Willson, Harlan made no mention of the president by name. In reply to a letter Willson had written to him, however, he observed, "I agree to all you say about that man. He has gone out of my life entirely and will, I am sure, never come back. Certainly not, unless he satisfactorily explains what he has done and omitted to [do]. He has cast a shadow over the few years that remain to me in this life. I hope he will meet the political fate he deserves. If possible, I will avoid meeting him altogether. I will have to meet him on some occasions, and while I will not be rude to him, he shall see that I do not care to meet or talk with him on any subject."[71]

En route from Murray Bay to Washington the following fall, Harlan would encounter the journalist son of a friend in the lobby of New York's Belmont Hotel. During their conversation, the reporter revealed after the justice's death, Harlan displayed no bitterness toward President Taft. But with "mellow pathos in his voice" and a lump in his throat, he "frankly avowed his disappointment" that the chief justiceship had gone to White. "I hope no friend of mine importuned the President to make me chief justice," Harlan had said. "That office is too great to be scrambled for. I had hoped, though, that the President would let me round out my career as chief justice. It would have given me an opportunity for work that would have prolonged my life." The justice could not understand Taft's concern about his age. "I am only 78. That ought not to indicate old age and uselessness." Nor could he condone the president's disregard of their long association. "It once was my privilege to be of some little service to Mr. Taft when he was a young judge," he told his friend's son, a wave of sadness sweeping across his face. "I had thought that he understood me better than he seemed to."[72]

Whatever the impact of Taft's decision on Harlan's spirits, they had by no means been broken entirely. In his last years as before, the justice had continued to defend a broad conception of the congressional commerce authority. In 1908, for example, he had dissented when a majority struck down the Federal Employers' Liability Act of 1906, which had effectively nullified the fellow servant defense used by railroads to defeat employee injury claims.[73] Within months of the president's elevation of White, moreover, the old man had taken on all his brethren, and especially the new chief justice, in one last fierce defense of his commerce power jurisprudence against overwhelming odds. Citing common-law practice and other precedents, Justice White—a staunch defender of Louisiana sugar interests before his appointment to the bench—had argued that the Sherman Act's ban on "every combination" in restraint of interstate trade realistically was intended to reach only "unreasonable" or "undue" burdens on commerce. In 1877, a majority, speaking through Justice Peckham in *United States* v. *Trans-Missouri Freight Association*,[74] had refused to embrace this "rule of reason," leaving White to embrace it in dissent. In an opinion announcing the Court's decision in the famous *Northern Securities* case of 1904,[75] Justice Harlan had also rejected White's thesis. But Harlan would not have been able to secure majority support for dissolution of the railroad holding company without the vote of Justice Brewer. Although he agreed with White, Brewer formed the majority because he considered the Northern Securities Company an "unreasonable" restraint on trade.[76] In a dissent joined by Chief Justice Fuller and Associate Justices White and Peckham, moreover, Justice Holmes had opposed any construction of the Sherman Act that would allow "the universal disintegration of society into single men, each at war with all the rest, or even the prevention of all further combinations for a common end."[77] An extreme, literal interpretation of the statute, declared Holmes, would mean that "a partnership between two stage drivers who had been competitors in driving across a state line, or two merchants once engaged in rival commerce among the states, . . . is a crime. . . . I should regard calling such a law a regulation of commerce as a mere pretense. It would be an attempt to reconstruct society."[78]

With Justice Brewer's critical vote, Harlan had managed to defeat the efforts of J. P. Morgan, James J. Hill, and other magnates of the day to maximize their grip over the nation's railways. But a different *Northern Securities* majority had also embraced Justice White's "rule of reason," further emasculating the Sherman Act. Now, during Harlan's final year on the Court, the new chief justice would have the satisfaction of advancing his position in two significant antitrust cases. In the first, decided on May 15, 1911, White delivered a 20,000-word opinion sustaining dissolution of the Standard Oil trust.[79] In the second, decided two weeks later, he again spoke for the Court in breaking the American Tobacco trust.[80] In his opinions in both cases, however, White emphasized that the Sherman Act reached only "unreasonable" restraints on trade and disposed of previous decisions rejecting such a construction of the law by concluding that those cases had involved combinations of an "undue" or "unreasonable" character, whatever the language of their opinions.[81]

Justice Harlan naturally concurred in the Court's smashing of the trusts. In each case, however, he dissented from his brethren's endorsement of the "rule of reason." Perhaps because his old antagonist, White, father of the "reasonableness" standard, had spoken for the Court, and President Taft, who originally had opposed White's thesis, had come to accept it, the justice's opinions were particularly vehement.

Near the opening of his *Standard Oil* opinion, Harlan drew an analogy between the slavery against which the Civil War amendments were directed and "another kind of slavery sought to be fastened on the American people; namely, the slavery that would result from aggregations of capital in the hands of a few individuals and corporations controlling, for their own profit and advantage exclusively, the entire business of the country, including the production and sale of the necessities of life."[82] Recognizing the evils this modern form of slavery posed for the nation's citizens, Congress had expressly forbidden in the Sherman Act "any" and "every" combination in restraint of interstate and foreign commerce. Harlan pointed out that the Court had for years "expressly declined to indulge in judicial legislation, by inserting in the act the word 'unreasonable' or any other word of like import."[83] Had Congress wished, it could have acted to overturn the Court's construction of the statute. "But at every session of Congress since the [*Trans-Missouri*] decision [rejecting White's reasonableness standard] . . . , the lawmaking branch of the government, with full knowledge of that decision, has refused to change the policy it had declared, or to so amend the act of 1890 as to except from its operation contracts, combinations, and trusts that *reasonably* restrain interstate commerce."[84] The Court's willingness to do what Congress had refused to do was for Harlan simply part and parcel of a "most harmful tendency" then "abroad in our land . . . to bring about the amending of constitutions and legislative enactments by means alone of judicial construction."[85] On this occasion, in Harlan's view, the judiciary's usurpation of legislative authority was likely to produce particularly dire consequences. As written, he declared, the Sherman Act "prescribed a simple, definite rule that all could understand, and which could be easily applied by everyone wishing to obey the law." Under the Court's new construction, however, "we are to have, in cases without number, the constantly recurring inquiry—difficult to solve by proof— whether the particular contract, combination, or trust involved in each case is or is not an 'unreasonable' or 'undue' restraint of trade."[86]

Harlan's *American Tobacco* opinion paralleled his rationale in the oil trust case— albeit more succinctly. The Court's insistence that earlier cases had actually applied a "rule of reason" while appearing to reject it, the justice wryly observed, surprised him "quite as much as would a statement that black was white or white was black."[87]

The justice's courtroom delivery of his *Standard Oil* dissent rivaled his perfor- mance in the *Income Tax Cases*. Earlier, he had complained to his new colleague, Justice Hughes, about the serenity of the Court, asserting that there were too few dissents. Hughes's biographer, drawing on an interview with his subject, later re- ported, "As if to demonstrate his point, [Harlan] brought his service to a conclusion with a tirade against the Standard Oil decision that almost rattled the benches in the staid old courtroom. His tongue loosened by whiskey, he bellowed bitter invectives that caused his brethren to blush with shame."[88] "He went far beyond his written opinion," Hughes himself would recall, behaving in a manner his new colleague "thought most unseemly. It was not a swan song but the roar of an angry lion."[89] The next morning, Justice McKenna encountered Senator Philander C. Knox of Pennsylvania, attorney general in the McKinley cabinet, on a trolley car. "What do you think of the Court now?" asked McKenna. "Well," replied Knox, "I should hate to use any such language about the Court as it said about itself yesterday."[90]

Whatever his demeanor or the reactions of his brethren, however, Harlan's posi- tion garnered considerable favor with the public and the press. "Justice Harlan Re- veals Evils of the Decision," read one headline; "Harlan Tells How Court Has Spiked Anti-Trust Law," declared another. The *Minneapolis Tribune* called Harlan the "Grandest Old Man in America, If Not the World." And *The Commoner*, William Jennings Bryan's organ, exclaimed, "There will be rejoicing in Wall Street, but . . . sadness in the homes of the masses," adding: "The decision explains . . . why Justice White was made chief justice instead of Justice Harlan."[91] But a Columbus, Ohio, newspaper perhaps captured best the sentiments of Harlan's ad- mirers and the Court's critics:

> Having read what the Supreme Court did to the Standard Oil company, it is well to consider what it did to the rest of us.
>
> And by the way, what did it do to the Standard Oil company? Why, it merely said that the work of the S.O. was too coarse and must be refined a bit. It said that trusts were all right and restriction of trade was all right, and stifling competition was all right—so long as it wasn't carried to an unreasonable extent.
>
> The S.O. had gotten three feet into the trough and two seems to be the reasonable limit. . . . And any other monopoly can flourish so long as it is not too utterly hoggish for a majority of the lawyers on the United States Supreme bench to stomach it.[92]

Even some of those who applauded the Court's decision seemed dubious of its rationale. *Wall Street Journal* editor William P. Hamilton admitted, for example, that the majority had "read into the Sherman law an amendment that never could have passed the Congress."[93] Distressed by Harlan's arguments, the New York *Herald* simply suggested that dissenting opinions should no longer be published.[94] And the *New York Times*, which had often disagreed with the Justice over the years, declared in a flattering profile that "[f]ew men in American public life have been . . . so tenacious of principle. Regardless of the consequences . . . with an eye single to the right as he sees it, he will keep to his course."[95]

The *Times* also predicted that Harlan's trust opinions would be "among the last, if not the last, important dissents that Harlan [would] deliver."[96] That speculation was to be more prophetic than its author knew. Amid debate over the trust rulings, the Harlans had escaped to Murray Bay. Mrs. Harlan would later pronounce her husband's summer there that final year of his life a "most delightful one." He was seemingly in good health, his spirits were excellent, and "[o]n most days in good weather he had his game of golf, generally playing the full eighteen holes . . . sometimes entering the various tournaments, and enjoying it all to the full."[97]

Harlan had always been the picture of health, a powerful, robust man rarely afflicted with even brief periods of illness. But he was now 78. He had a massive appetite, and his weight at times approached 300 pounds, although with exercise he often kept it considerably lower—a fact he took pride in and pointed out to the truly substantial William Howard Taft. The Washington heat of the previous spring had taken its toll. When in July a representative of the publishing house, Charles Scribner's Sons, expressed continued interest in a book project he and the justice had been discussing,[98] Harlan begged off making any immediate commitment. "I have not been entirely well since I came here," he reported. "I think I am now 'out of the woods' and am feeling better every day. But I have not quite recovered from the exhausting heat of last spring to say positively what I can do about that book."[99] In an August letter from Murray Bay to his friend Blackburn Esterline, moreover, he complained of having been "somewhat weakened" by an attack of indigestion.[100]

Within a week of his letter to Esterline, the justice wrote a Supreme Court staff member that he was again feeling well and that, in fact, "everything [was] lovely" with him.[101] On his return from Canada, he and his son, John, spent a week in New York before being joined by Mrs. Harlan and Ruth for several more days there. While in New York, the justice and Mrs. Harlan visited President Grant's tomb. Harlan recalled Grant's "great service to the country" and mused whether those in the "Great Beyond" retain any memory of worldly life. Mrs. Harlan later recalled that "he seemed in imagination to have entered already into the peace and rest of the Great Hereafter."[102]

The Court's fall term was scheduled to begin on Monday, October 9. The previous Wednesday, the Harlans had returned to their Euclid Avenue home, where the justice began immediately to prepare his study table for the Court's work. He had been stricken with a severe cold during his stopover in New York, but he nevertheless went to the Capitol on Monday for the noon convening of the term—a brief session limited to the admission of new members to the Supreme Court bar and the submission of motions. "It was gratifyingly remarked by several of the older members of the Bar," the justice's secretary, J. E. Hoover, would later write Harlan's son, Richard, "how fresh and well your dear Father looked, which was true. He exhibited as much vim and alertness in all that went on as any of the younger members of the Bench."[103]

The justice himself was more concerned about Mrs. Harlan than about his own health. "My condition is very good," he wrote Governor Willson the day the Court convened, "but Mrs. Harlan is still disturbed about her eyes. They do not pain her, but she sees very indistinctly and must rely upon my girls entirely for reading." He had not lost his sense of humor. To illustrate a point, he recalled for his old friend the story of the man who, on spotting a calf whose tail was sticking in a hole, exclaimed, "I will be D—— if I can tell how that calf got through that hole." Neither had he lost his interest in politics. "[A]fter the next Presidential election," he predicted, "the Republican Party will never be heard of again. It will go out of existence as certainly as the old Whig Party went out of existence when the Democratic Party got possession of the country."[104]

Had he lived to witness the splitting of his party and Woodrow Wilson's defeat of Taft the following year, Harlan might have concluded that his prediction was coming true. But his letter to Gus Willson was to be one of the last, if not the last, of his life. The next morning, he discussed the needs of Washington's Garfield Hospital with two other board members[105] and then went to the Capitol for another session of the Court, apparently in good health. At the luncheon that day, however, as the justice's secretary later delicately put it to Richard Harlan, he "partook of more than he had usually been in the habit of taking at such times. This apparent overloading of the stomach seemed to have a depressing effect upon him during the remainder of the day."[106]

Harlan remained on the bench until the chief justice adjourned the session at 4:30. When he attempted to leave the bench, the Court reporter and a page were obliged to assist him to the marshal's office, where a taxicab was summoned. When he arrived home, accompanied by Justice McKenna, Mrs. Harlan immediately telephoned the family physician. Discovering that his patient's temperature was 103 degrees, the doctor concluded that Harlan was suffering from acute bronchitis. The next morning, his fever had virtually disappeared; but by afternoon it had climbed above 103 degrees. Gradually, his condition worsened, developing into pneumonia, and Harlan lapsed into a coma. Richard and his wife were in Europe, but John and James rushed to join their mother and sisters at their father's bedside. At about 6 a.m. on Saturday, October 14,[107] the old man roused enough to murmur, "Goodbye, I'm sorry I kept you all waiting so long." Then, he died.[108]

The following Monday, with Harlan's chair draped in heavy black crepe, the Supreme Court convened just long enough to adjourn out of respect for his memory. The next day, a private funeral attended only by family members was held at the Harlans's home. Later, the justice's colleagues, Governor Willson, and many others packed his New York Avenue church for public services. Marching on foot, members of his Bible class then followed his hearse out to Rock Creek Cemetery.[109] Nationalist to the end, Harlan was to be buried there rather than in the family plot in Frankfort.

At least one newspaper used the justice's death as an occasion to champion mandatory retirement of federal judges, contending that Harlan, "[d]espite his very great ability, his unquestioned integrity and his wonderful grasp of great problems," should have retired "several years ago."[110] A Vicksburg, Mississippi, editor concluded, "[I]f some of Justice Harlan's early legal opinions had been declared to be the law of the land all the old doctrines of the reconstructionists and carpetbaggers would have been enforced and the country would have probably passed through a race war." He praised the fact that "White, and not Harlan, was properly made chief justice."[111] Georgia demagogue Tom Watson, writing in the *Jeffersonian*, declared that he preferred the Protestant Harlan over the Catholic White, but only because the new chief justice "*was* a Jesuit and *was* willing to go down upon his creaky old knees to buss the dago's flipper."[112] And the Louisville *Courier-Journal*, despite the justice's repeated and well-known protests to the contrary, reported that he had resigned his Civil War commission "rather than continue his support of what he regarded as an unconstitutional usurpation of power."[113]

The justice would no doubt have viewed favorably, however, most of the comment on his passing. William Randolph Hearst, in a signed eulogy, termed him "the last of the Constitutionalists" and applauded his unalterable opposition "to the usurpation of power on the part of the Supreme Court and to the encroachments of the court upon the power of Congress and the president."[114] Many other editors and publishers followed suit, and admirers spoke of raising $1 million for a Presbyterian temple dedicated to the justice's memory.[115] The Supreme Court bar and bar groups in Kentucky and elsewhere conducted memorials.[116]

President Taft eventually appointed Mahlon Pitney to an undistinguished tenure in Harlan's seat, but early speculation focused on other prospects, including Utah's George Sutherland. "If one servilely and meanly attentive to the predatory rich is wanted for the supreme bench, to rattle around in the shoes of noble, brilliant Justice Harlan and write opinions that are 'unreasonable,'" a Utah paper editorialized, "then we nominate our own dear George. Do we hear a second?"[117] (Sutherland would make it to the Court in 1922, becoming one of its most reactionary members.)

In death, even the justice's chronic insolvency had an ennobling effect. Harlan left no will. According to the petition his son, James, filed with a District of Columbia court to become the administrator of his father's estate, the justice left only $7,200 in life insurance and a personal estate of $5,700. As a safeguard against creditors, his Washington and Murray Bay homes were in Mrs. Harlan's name; he had no other real estate.[118]

Various newspapers carried such information as well as the testimony of Albert Rosenthal, a Philadelphia artist, before a congressional committee. Rosenthal had offered to sell Harlan a portrait he had painted of the justice as part of a series on all the brethren. "I'm too poor to buy it," Harlan had replied. "When I married I borrowed $1,000 to marry on, and every year when I cast up my accounts I find I still owe that thousand."[119] Such anecdotes merely enhanced the justice's image, however. More than one paper reported that Harlan had died "poor but honest."[120] "[W]ho ... would not prefer to have been John Marshall Harlan," asked the Louisville *Courier-Journal*, "than to have been a millionaire?"[121]

The justice probably would have found most touching, though, the sentiments expressed during a December 11 gathering in his memory at Washington's Metropolitan A.M.E. Church. Harlan's family was invited[122] but apparently did not attend. President Taft, Theodore Roosevelt, and other politicians, as well as several of Harlan's colleagues, offered letters rather than their presence. But prominent blacks from various states and territories journeyed to Washington to pay homage to the "Great Dissenter." A resolution adopted that night proclaimed that Christianity for Harlan "meant present, practical fatherhood of God, and brotherhood of man." As a justice, it added, Harlan had "emphasized the duty of the favored to the ill-favored; of the strong to the weak."[123]

Epilogue

The years immediately following Justice Harlan's death were not particularly happy ones for his family. His son, Richard, and Richard's wife, Margaret, were touring Europe when the elder Harlan died. Family members attributed their travels to Margaret's health. In truth, however, the couple had left the country at the urging of Richard's brothers to avoid embarrassing questions about a trust Margaret's father had established for each of his three daughters. Richard had been made one of the trustees and given virtually unlimited discretion over matters relating to Margaret's inheritance; eventually, he had become sole trustee. By 1909, his wife's trust had been almost completely depleted, largely as a result of his unwise investments. Members of Margaret's family—who stood to inherit the balance of the trust at her death, since she and Richard had no children—were pressing the justice's son for an accounting, and Richard was frantic. At Christmas that year, he had revealed the situation to his wife and brothers. In a desperate effort to avoid scandal and the anguish it would cause their parents, not to mention the embarrassment, the Harlan sons devised a scheme. With funds provided by James, including a portion put up in exchange for all Margaret's property except personal effects, they replenished a part of the trust and prepared a false accounting to cover the balance. The elder Harlans presumably never learned of the affair, and the brothers' ruse placated Margaret's family for a time. Ultimately, though, the scheme provoked lawsuits among the brothers and Margaret that would not be resolved until the late 1920s. The entire episode, examined in some detail in my biography of the second Justice Harlan,[1] permanently damaged the brothers' relations.

In January of 1912, a Kentucky congressman introduced legislation to provide Mrs. Harlan a pension equal to her husband's salary ($13,500) at the time of his death.[2] In an effort to supplement the pension and other income, the justice's widow wrote her memoirs of their lives together.[3] But her effort was never published. In July of 1916, Mallie Harlan suffered a broken hip in a fall at the family's Murray Bay summer home. In early October, she was brought back to her Washington residence at 1833 M Street, the Euclid Avenue family home having been sold following the justice's death. There, at midnight on October 9, just days before the fifth anniversary of her husband's death, she died.[4]

The Harlans's daughters, Laura and Ruth, continued to live in Washington and never married. Laura would serve as social secretary to the wives of Presidents Harding and Coolidge, as well as a number of diplomatic and cabinet wives.[5] Their mother had established a trust for Laura and Ruth,[6] but Laura Harlan would achieve the financial success that had eluded her father, becoming a prominent Washington real estate broker.[7] By contrast, John Maynard Harlan, the son who most closely resembled his father in appearance and temperament, would be nearly penniless at his death in 1934.[8]

Meanwhile, Justice Harlan had largely faded from the nation's memory. In 1915, Professor Floyd B. Clark, a political scientist, published a competent analysis of the justice's constitutional views.[9] Issues of the *American Law Review* in 1912 and 1917 carried detailed summaries of his dissents.[10] But the author of the first summary article, Harlan's old colleague Justice Henry Brown, author of the *Plessy* majority opinion, predicted that Harlan's dissents would "probably share the general fate and will not result in many changes in the law."[11] The biography the justice's son, Richard, intended to write never materialized. And by 1947, Justice Felix Frankfurter, an avowed enemy of Harlan's thesis that the Fourteenth Amendment incorporated the Bill of Rights, confidently dismissed his predecessor as a mere "eccentric."[12]

Even the appointment of the justice's grandson to the nation's highest tribunal in 1955 was not without irony. Both justices were Republicans, but while Harlan I had remained committed to the party's historic roots in the struggle for human dignity, Harlan II would be closely associated with its later image as protector of economic privilege. Harlan II made his impressive legal reputation as a Wall Street lawyer, defending the Du Pont brothers and other commercial giants of the sort his grandfather had often scorned. Once on the Court, moreover, Harlan II became a disciple of Felix Frankfurter and, indirectly, a critic of the first Justice Harlan's judicial record. He opposed application of the Bill of Rights to the states; generally favored narrow readings of civil liberties guarantees; accepted the creative role judges play in constitutional construction while eschewing attacks on "judicial legislation"; and championed limits to judicial power based on the individual judge's commitment to self-restraint rather than an elusive search for literal meaning, as he characterized his grandfather's judicial approach.[13]

In fact, among members of the modern Supreme Court, the first Justice Harlan's constitutional philosophy and approach to specific issues would most closely resemble the jurisprudence of Hugo Lafayette Black, who was the principal judicial antagonist of Harlan II and Justice Frankfurter. Justice Black displayed a portrait of Harlan I in his chambers, maintained warm personal relations with his grandson, and was convinced that the Blacks and Harlans were distant relations. Even Black's jurisprudence differed in a number of important respects, moreover, from the elder Harlan's thinking. Black, for example, rejected substantive due process entirely, while Harlan I embraced that controversial doctrine as a device for protecting individual freedom from "unreasonable" governmental interference, albeit less enthusiastically than most of his brethren. Arguably, too, Black went much further than his illustrious forebear in attempting to bind judges to relatively fixed constitutional interpretations limiting the scope of judicial discretion.[14]

In decisional trends, if not subtle doctrinal shadings, however, the first Justice Harlan's jurisprudence was to experience a triumphant rebirth on the modern Court. At his death, an admiring Ohio newspaper editor had asserted that the Justice was simply far ahead of his times. "He was really too great for the Supreme Court," the editor had declared; "a seat upon that august bench handicapped him rather than helped him. He was so far in advance of the other justices in thought and mental make-up that he was usually in the minority in his opinions. . . . [But] the dissenting opinions of Justice Harlan [will] invariably come to be the opinions of the court later on."[15]

Those words would prove prophetic. In a 1949 law review article, a lawyer and a law student wrote of Justice Harlan's "Coming Vindication" in race relations cases.[16] In a 1953 rejoinder to Justice Frankfurter, another student examined Harlan's career in light of recent judicial developments and asked, "How 'Eccentric' Was Mr. Justice Harlan?"[17] And in the fall of 1955, Henry J. Abraham, who was then at the beginning of a distinguished career as one of the nation's foremost Supreme Court and constitutional scholars, published a lengthy list of Harlan dissents that had already become law via judicial decisions, congressional legislation, and constitutional amendments.[18]

Naturally, Harlan's *Plessy* opinion, recently vindicated in the *Brown* case,[19] led Professor Abraham's list. But also included were the justice's dissents in other railroad segregation cases,[20] the *Sugar Trust Case*,[21] litigation restricting state liquor controls,[22] the *Lochner* case[23] the merchant marine slavery case,[24] and the *Income Tax Cases*.[25] In the 1960s, moreover, the Warren Court, often over the forceful dissents of Harlan II, extended most Bill of Rights guarantees to the states,[26] embraced the first Justice Harlan's broad construction of the Thirteenth Amendment as a weapon against private forms of racial discrimination;[27] and came close to endorsing the assertion Harlan had so vigorously advanced in the *Civil Rights Cases* that Congress is empowered to punish private interferences with Fourteenth Amendment rights, despite the emphasis on "state" action in the amendment's language.[28]

Of course, no majority opinion of the Court has yet adopted Harlan's rationale in the *Civil Rights Cases*. Nor has the modern Court been willing to hold, as Harlan repeatedly urged, that all the rights of the Bill of Rights are encompassed within the Fourteenth Amendment's meaning and are thus binding on the states as well as the federal government. Instead, a majority has consistently embraced various versions of "selective incorporation," imposing only "fundamental" Bill of Rights guarantees on state governments and their local counterparts.[29] In the *Brown* case, moreover, the justices based their rejection of state-mandated segregation in the public schools largely on the inherently adverse impact of such education on minority children, and not on Justice Harlan's eloquent plea in *Plessy* for a "color-blind" Constitution. Indeed, the willingness of the Court in more recent years to uphold a variety of affirmative action programs obviously flies in the face of Harlan's broad assertion, as critics of such arrangements regularly contend.[30]

It is not even certain that Harlan would have joined the *Brown* decision, despite his defense of a "color-blind" Constitution. His racial attitudes, after all, were in many ways consistent with those of most white southerners of his day. The memoirs of his wife, presumably more progressive in matters of race than her husband, are filled with racial stereotypes—loving and affecting but stereotypical, nevertheless. And it is more than possible that both the justice and Mrs. Harlan personally believed that blacks constituted an inherently inferior race. Harlan's relationship with his mulatto half-brother, Robert, moreover, would remain limited, largely political rather than intimately familial, and apparently somewhat condescending. As a political candidate, even after his conversion to Republicanism and the goals of Reconstruction, it must also be remembered, Harlan had continued to support segregated public schools. And while that stump stance may have reflected the politician's prudence rather than personal conviction, he of course had spoken for the Court years later in dodging the issue when it came before the justices in the *Cumming* case. Harlan might not have been able, therefore, to join the Supreme Court's most profound contribution to the second Reconstruction, just as the modern Court has never embraced significant elements of his jurisprudence.

Whether Harlan would have joined modern civil liberties developments that the justices of his era were not obliged to confront is even more problematic. Seemingly oblivious to the charges of "judicial legislation" that exercises of substantive due process invariably raise, though quick to charge his brethren with such abuse of their power in other contexts, the justice freely embraced that formula to rule on the reasonableness of economic controls. The modern Court has employed essentially the same calculus in grafting onto the Constitution abortion and related privacy rights mentioned nowhere in the document's text.[31] But the rock-ribbed Presbyterianism—which no doubt contributed to Harlan's complex relationship with his brother, James—might have made it impossible for him to agree to such modern uses of substantive due process. Similarly, while Harlan vigorously advocated extension of the Bill of Rights, including its procedural guarantees, to the states—and, for that matter, also joined the first Supreme Court case excluding illegally seized testimonial evidence from judicial proceedings[32]—his judicial record furnishes little indication of the stance he might have assumed in modern cases that have significantly expanded the rights of suspects and defendants in criminal cases.[33]

Not only may Harlan's current image as a major precursor of modern expansions of civil liberties law be somewhat overdrawn; certain elements of his enigmatic personal life stand in marked contrast to the idealized visions the justice's name evokes among admirers relatively unfamiliar with the complexities of his life and personality. Although understandable, especially given his religious leanings, Harlan's treatment of his brother, James, conflicts with the humanitarian themes that dominate his judicial opinions, as does his relationship with his half-brother, Robert. His handling of personal finances is similarly troubling. One may applaud his apparent refusal to profit from his political influence and judicial office, yet be disturbed by his willingness to use them in evading his obligations to creditors.

Such personal shortcomings, however, may simply demonstrate the obvious— that flawed human beings are responsible for civilization's advances as well as its retrogressions. Whatever connection exists between Justice Harlan's jurisprudence and modern conceptions of civil rights and liberties, moreover, one thing is quite certain: Justice Harlan was a major inspiration for the second Reconstruction, and not merely among Supreme Court Justices of the *Brown* era.

Just as Justice Harlan was the principal judicial defender of the first Reconstruction, Thurgood Marshall, as chief counsel for the National Association for the Advancement of Colored People (NAACP), was perhaps the most profoundly significant figure in the modern struggle for racial justice. During recent Supreme Court ceremonies held in Justice Marshall's memory, Constance Baker Motley, senior U.S. district judge for the southern district of New York, reminisced about her longtime association with the late civil rights advocate and jurist as a member of the NAACP's legal staff. During those remarkable and often frustrating times, Judge Motley revealed, Harlan I and his judicial opinions, especially his *Plessy* dissent, were a constant source of encouragement for Marshall:

> Marshall had a "Bible" to which he turned during his most depressed moments. . . . Marshall would read aloud passages from Harlan's amazing dissent. I do not believe we ever filed a major brief in the pre-*Brown* days in which a portion of that opinion was not quoted. Marshall's favorite quotation was, "Our Constitution is color-blind." . . . It became our basic creed. Marshall admired the courage of Harlan more than any Justice who has ever sat on the Supreme Court. Even Chief Justice Earl Warren's forthright and moving decision for the Court in *Brown* did not affect Marshall in the same way. Earl Warren was writing for a unanimous Supreme Court. Harlan was a solitary and lonely figure writing for posterity.[34]

That moral example, an inspiration to Marshall and other leaders of the modern civil rights movement, was the enigmatic first Justice Harlan's greatest legacy.

Notes

Preface

1. Civil Rights Cases, 109 U.S. 3, 25 (1883).
2. Ibid., pp. 61–62.
3. Plessy v. Ferguson, 163 U.S. 537, 559 (1896).
4. See, for example, Hurtado v. California, 110 U.S. 516, 538 (1884).
5. See, for example, Downes v. Bidwell, 182 U.S. 244, 375 (1901).
6. See, for example, United States v. E.C. Knight Co., 156 U.S. 1, 18 (1895).
7. Quoted in Francis Biddle, *Mr. Justice Holmes* (New York: Scribner's, 1942), p. 111.
8. A transcript of remarks delivered at the dinner is in the John Marshall Harlan Papers, University of Louisville, hereinafter cited as HPUL.
9. Adamson v. California, 332 U.S. 46, 62 (1947) (Frankfurter, J., concurring).
10. See, for example, Benton v. Maryland, 395 U.S. 784 (1969).
11. See, for example, Brown v. Board of Education, 347 U.S. 483 (1954).
12. Jones v. Alfred H. Mayer Co., 392 U.S. 409 (1968).
13. United States v. Guest, 383 U.S. 745 (1966).
14. See, for example, NLRB v. Jones & Laughlin Corp., 301 U.S. 1 (1937).
15. Compare, for example, Lochner v. New York, 198 U.S. 45 (1905) (Harlan, J., dissenting), with Adair v. United States, 208 U.S. 161 (1908) (Harlan, J.).
16. See, for example, West Coast Hotel Co. v. Parrish, 300 U.S. 379 (1937).
17. A summary of the survey findings can be examined in Henry J. Abraham, *Justices and Presidents,* 3d ed. (New York: Oxford, 1992).
18. Cumming v. Richmond Co. Board of Education, 175 U.S. 528 (1899).
19. Adair v. United States, 208 U.S. 161 (1908).
20. Jones v. Commonwealth, 64 Ky. 34 (1866).
21. Commonwealth v. Palmer, 65 Ky. 570 (1866).
22. Bowlin v. Commonwealth, 65 Ky. 5 (1867).
23. *Louisville Daily Journal,* November 1, 1864.
24. Speed S. Fry to William Brown, November [illegible date], 1877, on file in the records of the U.S. Senate Committee on the Judiciary proceedings regarding Harlan's nomination to the Supreme Court, National Archives, Washington, D.C.

25. Tinsley E. Yarbrough, *John Marshall Harlan: Great Dissenter of the Warren Court* (New York: Oxford, 1992), pp. 35–41.

26. John M. Harlan to George W. Shanklin, November 19, 1894, John Marshall Harlan Papers, Library of Congress, hereinafter cited as HPLC.

27. J. S. Barret to T. W. Neill, January 26, 1888, HPLC.

28. John M. Harlan to Augustus E. Willson, July 23, 1892, HPUL.

29. John M. Harlan to Henry Harlan, July 10, 1889, HPUL.

30. John M. Harlan to Augustus E. Willson, December 11, 1894, HPUL.

31. Robert James Harlan to John M. Harlan, November 5, 1871, HPLC.

32. Malvina Shanklin Harlan, *Some Memories of a Long Life: 1854–1911* (1915), a transcript of which is in the HPLC.

33. John Bates to John M. Harlan, September 22, 1892, HPUL.

Chapter 1   Beginnings

1. Elizabeth Davenport Harlan to John Marshall Harlan, June 2, 1893, HPLC. The description of family physical characteristics is drawn from an undated autobiographical typescript in HPLC.

2. This discussion is drawn from typewritten and handwritten genealogical narratives and charts in HPLC. For an extremely thorough genealogy of the Harlan family, see Alpheus H. Harlan, *History and Genealogy of the Harlan Family* (Baltimore: Gateway Press, 1987, orig. pub. by Lord Baltimore Press, 1914).

3. Until a few years ago, portions of the walls of the "Old Stone House" were still standing. By the summer of 1992, however, they had been removed by the current owner of the property, the stone purchased for use in construction of a wall on the estate of Kentucky Governor Brereton Jones. So much for historic preservation.

4. James S. Greene, III, *Major Silas Harlan: His Life and Times* (1963), p. i. A copy of this privately published work is in HPLC.

5. James Harlan to Charles Lanaman, September 3, 1858, Charles Lanaman Papers, The Filson Club Historical Society, Louisville, Ky., contains a succinct summary of James Harlan's career. Numerous typescript autobiographical accounts of Justice Harlan's life, in HPLC, also contain extensive material on the justice's father. An autobiographical letter written by Justice Harlan in July of 1911, shortly before his death, and hereinafter cited as Autobiographical Letter, is particularly helpful. See also the entry on James Harlan in the *Dictionary of American Biography*, vol. 4, part 2, p. 267.

6. James Harlan to Thomas B. Stevenson, April 27, 1851, William Lindsay Papers, University of Kentucky Archives, Lexington, Ky.

7. A copy of the petition is in the Thompson Family Papers, University of Kentucky Archives, Lexington, Ky.

8. James Harlan to Charles Lanaman, September 3, 1858.

9. Alex H. H. Stuart to James Harlan, March 27, 1851, HPLC.

10. Autobiographical Letter.

11. James Harlan to Alex H. H. Stuart, April 5, 1841, HPLC.

12. Alex H. H. Stuart to James Harlan, April 15, 1851, HPLC.

13. Alex H. H. Stuart to James Harlan, May 27, 1851, HPLC.

14. Autobiographical Letter.

15. James Harlan to Charles Lanaman, September 3, 1858.

16. Autobiographical Letter.

17. James Harlan to John J. Crittenden, June 29, 1850, HPUL. In addition to Fletcher v. Peck, 6 Cr. 87 (1810), Harlan cited Marshall's construction of the contract clause in Dart-

mouth College v. Woodward, 4 Wheat. 518 (1819). HPUL contains numerous other opinions drafted by James Harlan during his tenure as Kentucky's attorney general.

18. Henry Clay to James Harlan, August 5, 1848, HPLC.

19. Autobiographical Letter.

20. James Harlan to James B. Clay, August 23, 1855, HPLC.

21. This account is drawn from an autobiographical typescript written by Justice Harlan, on file in HPLC.

22. James Harlan to unnamed, June 18, 1855, University of Kentucky Archives, Lexington, Ky.

23. Nathaniel Refus to James Harlan, July 24, 1857, HPLC.

24. D. Howard Smith to James Harlan, August 4, 1851, HPLC.

25. James Harlan to D. Howard Smith, August 5, 1851, HPLC.

26. Malvina Harlan, *Some Memories of a Long Life.*

27. The deed, from Elizabeth Barrett to David Graham, dated June 18, 1834, is in HPLC.

28. Malvina Harlan, *Some Memories of a Long Life.*

29. Henry Clay to James Harlan, January 26, 1850, HPLC.

30. Henry Clay Harlan to Orlando Brown, August 14, 1849, Orlando Brown Papers, The Filson Club Historical Society, Louisville, Ky.

31. Malvina Harlan, *Some Memories of a Long Life.*

32. Noted in Loren Beth, *John Marshall Harlan: The Last Whig Justice* (Lexington: University Press of Kentucky, 1992), p. 12.

33. Wendell P. Dabney, *Cincinnati's Colored Citizens: Historical, Sociological and Biographical* (New York: Negro Universities Press, 1970, orig. pub. in 1926 by Dabney Publishing Co.), p. 131.

34. James W. Gordon, "Did the First Justice Harlan Have a Black Brother?" *Western New England Law Review* 15 (1993): 159–238.

35. Author's telephone interview with Roberta Harlan Nabrit, March 31, 1992, Washington, D.C.

36. Paul McStallworth, "Robert James Harlan," in *Dictionary of American Negro Biography*, eds. Rayford W. Logan and Michael R. Winston (New York: W.W. Norton, 1982), p. 287.

37. *Cincinnati Enquirer*, September 22, 1897.

38. See, for example, William J. Simmons, *Men of Mark: Eminent, Progressive and Rising* (New York: Arno Press, 1968, orig. pub. in 1887), p. 613. The deed of emancipation, from the Franklin County Court order book, is reprinted in Gordon, "Did the First Justice Harlan Have a Black Brother?" p. 159, n. 1.

39. The scrapbook is in the Kentucky Historical Society, Frankfort, Ky.

40. *Cincinnati Enquirer*, September 22, 1897.

41. Arthur M. Schlesinger, Jr., *The Age of Jackson* (Boston: Little, Brown & Co., 1945), pp. 212–13, discusses the controversy surrounding Johnson.

42. O. S. Poston to John Marshall Harlan, July 9, 1868, HPLC.

43. An unidentified clipping summarizing Poston's background is in the Harlan family scrapbook, on file in the Kentucky Historical Society, Frankfort, Ky.

44. *Cincinnati Enquirer*, September 22, 1897. Except where otherwise indicated, this discussion of Robert Harlan is based on this obituary and on McStallworth, "Robert James Harlan"; Simmons, *Men of Mark*; *Ohio State Journal*, April 26, 1886; *Colored Sentinel* (Cincinnati, Ohio), September 5, 1885. See generally also Willard Gatewood, *Aristocrats of Color: The Black Elite* (Bloomington, Ind.: Indiana University Press, 1990).

45. Gordon, "Did the First Justice Harlan Have a Black Brother?" p. 174.

46. A copy of the order is in ibid., p. 159, n. 1.

47. Gordon, "Did the First Justice Harlan Have a Black Brother?" p. 176.

48. Charles Theodore Greve, *Centennial History of Cincinnati and Representative Citizens* (Chicago: Biographical Publishing Co., 1904), p. 242.

49. Dabney, *Cincinnati's Colored Citizens*, p. 25.

50. Data regarding Robert Harlan's positions and residences, as well as those of his son, are available in various volumes of the Cincinnati city directory.

51. Robert Harlan, Jr., to Benjamin Harrison, August 11, 1888, Benjamin Harrison Papers, Library of Congress.

52. Robert Harlan, Jr., to William Howard Taft, July 12, 1927, William Howard Taft Papers, Library of Congress.

53. Robert Harlan, Jr., to William Howard Taft, May 27, 1908, Taft Papers.

54. Robert Harlan, Jr., to William Howard Taft, August 1, 1908, Taft Papers.

55. G. C. Hall to Robert Harlan, Jr., August 8, 1908, Taft Papers.

56. William Howard Taft to Robert Harlan, Jr., August 16, 1908, Taft Papers.

57. Robert Harlan, Jr., to William Howard Taft, July 1, 1913, Taft Papers.

58. Robert Harlan, Jr., to William Howard Taft, July 10, 1913, Taft Papers.

59. Robert Harlan, Jr., to William Howard Taft, July 3, 1917, Taft Papers.

60. Their correspondence is in the Taft Papers.

61. Brown v. Bd. of Education, 347 U.S. 483 (1954), 349 U.S. 294 (1955).

62. This material is drawn from the funeral program of Robert Jackson Harlan, who died December 26, 1989, newspaper clippings, and related material provided me by Roberta Harlan Nabrit.

63. Robert J. Harlan to John M. Harlan, May 22, 1956, John Marshall Harlan II Papers, Seeley G. Mudd Manuscript Library, Princeton University.

64. Correspondence relating to efforts to secure Harlan a position in the U.S. attorney's office are in ibid.

65. *Washington Post*, March 10, 1957.

66. Author's undated telephone conversation with Barrett Prettyman, Jr., Washington, D.C.

67. Author's undated telephone conversation with Eve Harlan Dillingham, Redding, Conn.

68. Author's undated telephone conversation with Edith Harlan Powell, New York, N.Y.

69. Robert Harlan, Jr., to William Howard Taft, March 21, 1929, Taft Papers.

70. Ibid.

71. Robert Harlan to Frederick Douglass, July 1, 1889, Frederick Douglass Papers, Library of Congress.

72. Robert Harlan to Frederick Douglass, October 2, 1890, Douglass Papers.

73. Robert Harlan to John Marshall Harlan, June 9, 1873, HPLC.

74. Robert Harlan to John Marshall Harlan, March 28, 1876, HPLC.

75. Robert Harlan to John Marshall Harlan, March 7, 1877, HPLC.

76. William Cheek and Aimee Lee Cheek, *John Langston and the Fight for Black Freedom, 1829–65* (Urbana: University of Illinois Press, 1989), *passim,* discusses the Walls and their background, as well as Langston's. Robert Ewell Greene, *Black Defenders of America: 1775–1973* (Chicago: Johnson Publishing Co., Inc., 1974), pp. 96–97, carries a brief profile of Captain Wall's Civil War activities.

77. Thomas F. Miller to John Marshall Harlan, August 21, 1871, HPLC.

78. Benjamin H. Bristow to John Marshall Harlan, September 2, 1871, HPLC.

79. Benjamin H. Bristow to John Marshall Harlan, September 5, 1871, HPLC.

80. Benjamin H. Bristow to John Marshall Harlan, September 18, 1871, HPLC.

81. Charles P. Pennebaker to Benjamin Bristow, September 19, 1871, HPLC.

82. Robert Harlan to John Marshall Harlan, November 5, 1871, HPLC.

83. William W. Belknap to John Marshall Harlan, September 9, 1871, HPLC.

84. Robert Harlan to John Marshall Harlan, November 5, 1871.

85. A number of studies of Harlan's pre-Court life and career were excellent sources of insight and primary materials, including David G. Farrelly, "Harlan's Formative Period: The Years before the War," *Kentucky Law Journal* 46 (1958): 367–406, and "A Sketch of John Marshall Harlan's Pre-Court Career," *Vanderbilt Law Review* 10 (1957): 209–25; Louis Hartz, "John M. Harlan in Kentucky, 1855–1877: The Story of his Pre-Court Political Career," *Filson Club History Quarterly* 14 (1940): 17–40; Alan F. Westin, "John Marshall Harlan and the Constitutional Rights of Negroes: The Transformation of a Southerner," *Yale Law Journal* 66 (1957): 637–710; Thomas L. Owen, "The Pre-Court Career of John Marshall Harlan" (M.A. Thesis, University of Kentucky, 1970).

86. Quoted in L. F. Johnson, *The History of Franklin County, Ky.* (Frankfort: Roberts Printing Co., 1912), p. 112.

87. *Louisville Commercial*, April 19, 1882.

88. Ibid.

89. Walter A. Groves, "Centre College—The Second Phase, 1830–1857," *Filson Club History Quarterly* 24 (1950): 317.

90. The list is in HPLC.

91. Quoted in Groves, "Centre College," p. 328.

92. Ibid., p. 327.

93. Ibid., pp. 328–29.

94. Sayre's position is summarized in an autobiographical transcript, in HPLC.

95. Malvina Harlan, *Some Memories of a Long Life.*

96. Quoted in John D. Wright, Jr., *Transylvania: Tutor to the West* (Lexington: Transylvania University, 1975), p. 144.

97. Frankfort *Semi-Weekly Commonwealth*, February 1, 1867.

98. Autobiographical Letter.

99. Quoted in George Robertson, *Scrap Book on Law and Politics, Men and Times* (Lexington: A. W. Elder, 185), p. 193.

100. Quoted in ibid., p. 245.

101. Quoted in ibid., p. 330.

102. Ibid.

103. Quoted in ibid., p. 335.

104. Ibid.

105. Henry Clay Harlan to Orlando Brown, August 14, 1849, Orlando Brown Papers, The Filson Club Historical Society, Louisville, Ky.

106. Henry Clay to James Harlan, October 4, 1849, HPLC.

107. An 1858 newspaper firm advertisement lists John's name in bold letters; the firm's St. Clair Street Frankfort address; James, Jr., and W.L. in much smaller print; and several prominent political figures, including James, Sr., as those to whom firm business could be referred. Frankfort *Tri-Weekly Commonwealth*, September 17, 1858.

108. The records of Harlan's law practice, including the transactions cited in the text, are in HPUL and HPLC.

109. This account is drawn from an autobiographical typescript in HPLC.

110. Malvina Harlan, *Some Memories of a Long Life.*

111. Ibid.

112. Ibid.

113. Ibid.

114. Ibid.

115. Ibid.

116. An autobiographical typescript describing Harlan's activities as adjutant general is in HPLC.

117. Harlan's account of his initiation and later activities in the Know-Nothing movement is in an autobiographical typescript in HPLC. Unless otherwise indicated, this discussion is drawn from Harlan's typescript. Agnes Geraldine McGann, *Nativism in Kentucky to 1860* (Washington, D.C.: Catholic University of America, 1944), chs. 3–6, is an interesting discussion of the movement in Kentucky.

118. Harlan's opinions and Robertson's letter are printed in the Lexington *Observer and Reporter*, July 29, 1857, a Know-Nothing newspaper.

119. McGann, *Nativism in Kentucky*, pp. 92–113; *Louisville Times*, August 1, 5, 1855.

120. Copies of the platform appeared frequently in Kentucky newspapers, including the Frankfort *Tri-Weekly Commonwealth*, July 23, 1855.

121. Ibid.

122. Frankfort *Tri-Weekly Commonwealth*, July 10, 1855.

123. Lexington *Observer and Reporter*, July 25, 1855.

124. *Louisville Daily Journal*, July 29, 1856.

125. *Louisville Daily Journal*, July 4, 1856.

126. Frankfort *Tri-Weekly Commonwealth*, May 21, 1856.

127. An autobiographical typescript of Harlan's involvement in the 1859 congressional race is in HPLC. Unless otherwise indicated, the following account of the campaign is drawn from this typescript and a Harlan memorandum, dated March 1, 1908, also in HPLC.

128. Frankfort *Weekly Kentucky Yeoman*, May 21, 1859.

129. Frankfort *Tri-Weekly Yeoman*, June 21, 1859.

130. Paris *Western Citizen*, June 10, 1859.

131. Paris *Western Citizen*, May 27, 1859.

132. Frankfort *Tri-Weekly Yeoman*, July 23, 1859; Farrelly, "Harlan's Formative Period," p. 400.

133. Paris *Western Citizen*, June 10, 1859.

134. Paris *Western Citizen*, June 10, 1859; Louisville *Weekly Journal*, June 3, 1859.

135. Ibid.

136. Frankfort *Tri-Weekly Yeoman*, May 24, 1859.

137. Lexington *Statesman*, undated, quoted in Frankfort *Tri-Weekly Yeoman*, May 28, 1859.

138. Paris *Western Citizen*, July 8, 1859. The charge was initially raised in the Louisville *Democrat*, June 29, 1859.

139. Paris *Western Citizen*, May 27, 1859.

140. Frankfort *Tri-Weekly Commonwealth*, July 29, 1859. Ballard's explanation was contained in a letter to Harlan, dated July 8, 1859, and reprinted in ibid.

141. *Kentucky Statesman*, July 19, 1859.

142. *Washington Post*, October 26, 1902, based, it should be noted, on Harlan's account.

143. Paris *Western Citizen*, June 10, 1859.

144. The intermediaries were Kentucky Governor Charles S. Morehead, Davis's friend, and Simms's second, James B. Beck, another influential Kentuckian.

145. An elaborate exchange of correspondence outlining the Davis–Simms dispute and the negotiations leading to its settlement is reprinted in the Frankfort *Tri-Weekly Yeoman*, June 23, 1859. In the letter that Simms had considered a challenge to duel, dated June 11, 1859, Davis had written Harlan's opponent: "For your language in reference to myself at

Ruddel's Mills, yesterday, you will name some day and time, when and where, we can adjust this matter without interruption."

146. Louisville *Daily Courier*, August 11, 1859, reprinting what were purported to be official returns.

147. Louisville *Daily Journal*, July 27, 1859.

148. Frankfort *Tri-Weekly Commonwealth*, August 8, 1859.

149. *Lexington Statesman*, undated, quoted in Frankfort *Tri-Weekly Yeoman*, August 13, 1859.

150. Unidentified newspaper clipping, November 23, 1908, in the Augustus E. Willson Papers, The Filson Club Historical Society, Louisville, Ky.

Chapter 2   War

1. Quoted in Owen, "The Pre-Court Career of John Marshall Harlan."

2. Autobiographical typescript in HPLC.

3. James A. Rawley, *Turning Points of the Civil War* (Lincoln: University of Nebraska Press, 1966), pp. 11, 150.

4. Thomas Speed, *The Union Cause in Kentucky* (New York: G.P. Putnam's Sons, 1907), p. vii. The quote is from Justice Harlan's foreword to the book.

5. Rawley, *Turning Points of the Civil War*, p. 15.

6. E. Merton Coulter, *The Civil War and Readjustment in Kentucky* (Chapel Hill: University of North Carolina Press, 1926), p. 248.

7. Louisville *Daily Journal*, January 10, 1861; Owen, "The Pre-Court Career of John Marshall Harlan."

8. Harlan's explanation for the move is contained in an autobiographical typescript in HPLC.

9. Malvina Harlan, *Some Memories of a Long Life*.

10. H. Levin, *The Lawyers and Lawmakers of Kentucky* (Chicago: Lewis Publishing Co., 1892), p. 163.

11. Ibid. For another account of the case, albeit without reference to Bullock, see Alfred Pirtle, "My Early Soldiering Days," in the Alfred Pirtle Papers, The Filson Club Historical Society, Louisville, Ky.

12. Malvina Harlan, *Some Memories of a Long Life*.

13. Coulter, *The Civil War and Readjustment in Kentucky*, pp. 93–97.

14. John Marshall Harlan to Joseph Holt, March 11, 1861, Holt Family Papers, Library of Congress.

15. Ibid.

16. Autobiographical Letter.

17. Malvina Harlan, *Some Memories of a Long Life*.

18. Quoted in Rawley, *Turning Points of the Civil War*, p. 22.

19. Quoted in Coulter, *The Civil War and Readjustment in Kentucky*, p. 38.

20. Autobiographical Letter.

21. This portion of Harlan's autobiographical summaries is reprinted in Speed, *The Union Cause in Kentucky*, pp. 116–21.

22. See the entry on Prentice in the *Dictionary of American Biography*, vol. 8, part 1, pp. 186–87.

23. Louisville *Daily Journal*, April 1, 1861.

24. Unless otherwise indicated, this discussion is drawn largely from an autobiographical typescript in HPLC.

25. Louisville *Daily Journal*, July 30, 1861.

26. Paul Shipman Drane to Richard D. Harlan, November 12, 1930, HPLC. Drane was Shipman's nephew. Other pertinent correspondence includes Richard D. Harlan to Paul Shipman Drane, November 26, 1930, HPLC.

27. Paul D. Shipman to John Marshall Harlan, October 16, 1903, HPLC.

28. See Robert Emmett McDowell, *City of Conflict—Louisville in the Civil War: 1861–1865* (Louisville: Louisville Civil War Round Table, 1962), pp. 35–36, for a profile of Buckner.

29. Ibid., p. 36.

30. In an autobiographical typescript in HPLC, Harlan refers to the unit as the Crittenden *Union* Zouaves. But his undated commission, also on file in HPLC and signed by Mayor Delph, refers only to the Crittenden Zouaves. Harlan's reference may have been to the unit's political and military leanings, rather than to its formal name.

31. For a more detailed summary of the legislation than that presented here, see Coulter, *The Civil War and Readjustment in Kentucky*, pp. 86–87.

32. Unless otherwise indicated, this discussion of the "Lincoln Guns" episode is drawn from ibid., pp. 88–89; Daniel Stevenson, "General Nelson, Kentucky, and Lincoln Guns," *Magazine of American History* 10 (August, 1883): 115–39; and Justice Harlan's account, reprinted in Speed, *The Union Cause in Kentucky*, pp. 119–21.

33. Frankfort *Tri-Weekly Commonwealth*, May 11, 1861, quoted in Coulter, *The Civil War and Readjustment in Kentucky*, p. 88.

34. Harlan described his home guard activities and relationship with General Sherman in an autobiographical transcript, on file in HPLC, on which this discussion is largely based.

35. Basil W. Duke, *Reminiscences of General Basil W. Duke, C.S.A.* (New York: Doubleday, Page & Co., 1911), p. 76.

36. Ibid., p. 77.

37. Malvina Harlan, *Some Memories of a Long Life*.

38. Ibid.

39. Louisville *Daily Journal*, September 27, 1861.

40. One of Harlan's accounts of his service with the Tenth Kentucky Volunteers is reprinted in Speed, *The Union Cause in Kentucky*, pp. 195–99. Other accounts are included in his Autobiographical Letter and in other typescripts dealing with specific wartime incidents and battles, all of which are on file in HPLC. Except where otherwise indicated, this discussion is based upon those materials.

41. For official reports relating to Harlan's involvement in the Mill Springs engagement, see the account of Colonel Mahlon D. Mason and Harlan's own report in *The War of the Rebellion: A Compilation of the Official Records of the Union and Confederate Armies*, Series I, vol. 7, pp. 83–86, 88–90.

42. *The War of the Rebellion*, Series I, vol. 16, part 2, p. 236.

43. John Marshall Harlan to James Harlan, September 17, 1862, HPLC.

44. For Harlan's report of his pursuit of Morgan's raiders, see *The War of the Rebellion*, Series I, vol. 20, part 1, pp. 134–41. The commendation, issued by Brigadier-General Speed S. Fry, a longtime friend but future political foe, is reprinted in ibid., p. 141.

45. Champ Clark, *My Quarter Century of American Politics*, vol. 2 (New York: Harper & Brothers, 1920), pp. 64–65.

46. Ibid., p. 65.

47. *The War of the Rebellion*, Series I, vol. 7, pp. 89–90.

48. Speed, *The Union Cause in Kentucky*, pp. 196–97.

49. John Marshall Harlan to James Harlan, September 17, 1862, HPLC.

50. This statement is taken from an autobiographical typescript in HPLC. The account that appeared in the Autobiographical Letter, which Harlan wrote shortly before his death, is more sanguine regarding the family's financial situation. His father, he wrote, had "the largest practice of any lawyer in Kentucky and the support of my Mother and the family depended on the right handling of the business left by him. . . . I was connected with my father in business and alone knew of what was necessary to be done in order to preserve from loss or waste what he had fairly earned by hard work in his profession."

51. Louisville *Daily Journal*, March 11, 1863; Frankfort *Tri-Weekly Commonwealth*, March 13, 1863.

52. A copy of the resignation letter is included in the Autobiographical Letter. A copy of the memorandum of acceptance is in HPUL.

53. Louisville *Daily Journal*, January 5, 1863.

54. Louisville *Daily Journal*, March 11, 1863.

55. The brothers' appointment was made on March 14, 1863. A copy of the announcement appears in the Frankfort *Tri-Weekly Commonwealth*, March 16, 1863, as does an announcement of their partnership. According to the most complete Harlan genealogy, Harlan, *History and Genealogy of the Harlan Family*, p. 274, their brother, William Lowndes, did not die until March 23, 1868. In the account of his father's death that appeared in his Autobiographical Letter, however, John Harlan stated that his "three oldest brothers," one of whom was William, were already deceased at the time of his father's death.

56. Frankfort *Tri-Weekly Commonwealth*, April 27, 1863.

57. Frankfort *Tri-Weekly Commonwealth*, March 18, 1863.

58. Louisville *Daily Journal*, March 20, 1863.

59. *The War of the Rebellion*, Series I, vol. 7, pp. 89–90.

60. Summary of Harlan's remarks, Louisville *Daily Journal*, March 20, 1863.

61. Robert O. Bryan to John Marshall Harlan, March 28, 1863, HPLC.

62. Malvina Harlan, *Some Memories of a Long Life*.

63. Owen, "The Pre-Court Career of John Marshall Harlan." This unpublished master's thesis is the most thorough study of Harlan's pre-Court political career to appear to date.

64. Frankfort *Tri-Weekly Commonwealth*, April 1, 1863.

65. *Louisville Daily Commercial*, July 8, 1863.

66. Frankfort *Tri-Weekly Commonwealth*, September 4, 1863.

67. Clark, *My Quarter Century of American Politics*, vol. 2, pp. 63–64.

68. Harlan's autobiographical typescript account of the raid is in HPLC, but see also the Louisville *Daily Journal*, June 13, 1864. Harlan's description has the incident occurring in the fall of 1864, but the newspaper account and Harlan's version probably dealt with the same event.

69. Owen, "The Pre-Court Career of John Marshall Harlan."

70. O. S. Poston to John Marshall Harlan, January 18, 1864, HPLC.

71. Owen, "The Pre-Court Career of John Marshall Harlan."

72. For a discussion of military occupation of Kentucky, see Coulter, *The Civil War and Readjustment in Kentucky, passim*.

73. Harlan's New Albany speech is reprinted in Matilda Gresham, *Life of Walter Quintin Gresham, 1832–1895*, vol. 1 (Chicago: Rand McNally & Co., 1919), pp. 823–25.

74. Frankfort *Tri-Weekly Commonwealth*, September 30, 1864.

75. Louisville *Daily Journal*, September 24, 1864.

76. Louisville *Daily Journal*, undated, quoted in Frankfort *Tri-Weekly Commonwealth*, October 12, 1864.

77. Ibid.

78. Frankfort *Tri-Weekly Commonwealth*, October 12, 1864.

79. Louisville *Daily Journal*, November 1, 1864.

80. H. C. McLeod to John Marshall Harlan, May 8, 1865, HPLC.

81. Lexington *Observer and Reporter*, June 10, 1865. Colonel Combs had written Harlan on behalf of the Conservative Unionists of Woodford County, urging him to run for Congress.

82. Frankfort *Tri-Weekly Commonwealth*, July 28, 1865.

83. Ibid.

84. Coulter, *Civil War and Readjustment in Kentucky*, p. 282; Johnson, *History of Franklin County*, p. 163.

85. 64 Ky. (1 Bush) 34 (1866).

86. 65 Ky. (2 Bush) 5 (1867).

87. The records of the *Bowlin* case and the others discussed in this section are on file in the Kentucky Department of Archives, Frankfort, Ky.

88. Bowlin v. Commonwealth, 65 Ky. at 21.

89. John M. Palmer, *Personal Reflections of John M. Palmer: The Story of an Earnest Life* (Cincinnati: The Robert Clarke Company, 1901), p. 242.

90. 65 Ky. (2 Bush) 570 (1866).

91. Ibid., p. 575. While this discussion has focused exclusively on Harlan's civil rights-related caseload as attorney general, HPLC and HPUL contain numerous opinions and other documents relating to his tenure in that office. For a biography of General Palmer, see George T. Palmer, *A Conscientious Turncoat: The Story of John M. Palmer, 1817–1900* (New Haven: Yale University Press, 1941).

92. Cincinnati *Weekly Gazette*, March 21, 1866.

93. A detailed summary of Harlan's Glascow remarks is in the *Cincinnati Commercial*, July 20, 1866.

94. Lexington *Observer and Reporter*, February 24, 1866.

95. Louisville *Daily Journal*, July 20, 1866.

96. Owen, "The Pre-Court Career of John Marshall Harlan."

97. Louisville *Daily Courier*, July 17, 1866.

98. Louisville *Daily Courier*, July 18, 1866.

99. Owen, "The Pre-Court Career of John Marshall Harlan."

100. Hartz, "John M. Harlan in Kentucky," p. 25.

101. Louisville *Daily Courier*, July 18, 1866.

102. *Cincinnati Gazette*, December 1, 1866.

103. Frankfort *Semi-Weekly Commonwealth*, February 1, 1867.

104. Ibid.; Coulter, *The Civil War and Readjustment in Kentucky*, pp. 316–17.

105. Coulter, *The Civil War and Readjustment in Kentucky*, p. 319.

106. *Louisville Daily Democrat*, March 8, 1867.

107. *Louisville Daily Democrat*, March 9, 1867.

108. John Marshall Harlan to John B. Bruner, March 11, 1867, John B. Bruner Papers, The Filson Club, Louisville, Ky.

109. *Louisville Daily Democrat*, May 2, 1867.

110. *Louisville Daily Democrat*, May 2, 1867.

111. *Louisville Daily Democrat*, July 24, 1867.

112. B. S. Sinclair to John Marshall Harlan, November 30, 1867, HPLC.

Chapter 3   Redemption

1. For a profile of Judge Newman, see Levin, *The Lawyers and Lawmakers of Kentucky*, pp. 770–71.

2. Wellington Harlan to John Marshall Harlan, January 21, 1868, HPLC.

3. Frankfort *Weekly Commonwealth*, March 20, 1868.

4. Frankfort *Weekly Commonwealth*, July 24, October 2, 23, 1868.

5. W. H. Wadsworth to John Marshall Harlan, November 27, 1868.

6. Ulysses S. Grant to John Marshall Harlan, November 4, 1869, Ulysses S. Grant Papers, Library of Congress.

7. John Marshall Harlan to "Lou," July 12, 1870, HPLC.

8. Frankfort *Weekly Commonwealth*, January 10, 1868.

9. Georgetown *Weekly Times*, January 15, 1868.

10. John Bennett to John Marshall Harlan, August 16, 1870, May 11, 1870, HPLC.

11. T. G. Kyle to John E. Newman, August 2, 1870, HPLC.

12. John E. Newman to Edward Hilpp, June 20, 1868, reprinted in Frankfort *Weekly Commonwealth*, June 24, 1868.

13. Ross A. Webb, *Benjamin Helm Bristow: Border State Politician* (Lexington: University Press of Kentucky, 1969), is an estimable Bristow biography. For a brief profile, see his entry in the *Dictionary of American Biography*, Vol. 2, part 1, pp. 55–56.

14. Benjamin H. Bristow to John Marshall Harlan, September 22, 1866, HPLC.

15. John Marshall Harlan to Benjamin Bristow, September 22, 1866, HPLC.

16. Benjamin H. Bristow to John Marshall Harlan, November 20, 1866, HPLC.

17. Benjamin H. Bristow to John Marshall Harlan, January 3, 1867, HPLC.

18. The Harlan collections and the Benjamin Helm Bristow Papers, Library of Congress, are replete with such letters.

19. Benjamin H. Bristow to John Marshall Harlan, March 10, 1872, HPLC.

20. Benjamin H. Bristow to John Marshall Harlan, May 4, 1873, HPLC.

21. Benjamin H. Bristow to John Marshall Harlan, December 24, 1870, HPLC. Bristow's attack on Sumner, it should be noted, was made in the context of the latter's opposition to President Grant's plan to annex Santo Domingo, and not in reference to Sumner's Reconstruction stance.

22. Benjamin H. Bristow to Horace Morris, et al., February 1, 1875, Bristow Papers.

23. Berea College v. Kentucky, 211 U.S. 45 (1908).

24. Benjamin H. Bristow to John G. Fee, May 15, 1876, Bristow Papers.

25. Benjamin H. Bristow to John Marshall Harlan, January 11, 1875, HPLC.

26. John Marshall Harlan to Benjamin H. Bristow, September 16, 1871, Bristow Papers.

27. John Marshall Harlan to Benjamin H. Bristow, September 27, 1871, Bristow Papers.

28. Gabriel C. Wharton to Benjamin H. Bristow, September 24, 1871, Bristow Papers.

29. See, for example, D. Howard Smith to John Marshall Harlan, February 6, 1869, HPLC.

30. John Mason Brown to John Marshall Harlan, November 25, 1870, HPLC.

31. S. W. Haney to John Marshall Harlan, November 21, 1870, HPLC.

32. According to a notation attached to ibid.

33. Gabriel C. Wharton to Benjamin H. Bristow, October 1, 1871, Bristow Papers.

34. John Marshall Harlan to Benjamin H. Bristow, September 27, 1871, Bristow Papers.

35. Harlan to Bristow, September 27, 1871.

36. John Marshall Harlan to Benjamin H. Bristow, September 29, 1871, Bristow Papers.

37. Benjamin H. Bristow to John Marshall Harlan, September 27, 1871, HPLC.

38. John Marshall Harlan to Benjamin H. Bristow, August 10, 1874, Bristow Papers.

39. John Marshall Harlan to Benjamin H. Bristow, August 28, 1874, Bristow Papers.

40. George H. Williams telegram to John Marshall Harlan, February 11, 1873, HPLC.

41. Westin, "John Marshall Harlan and the Constitutional Rights of Negroes," p. 664, n. 97.

42. For a general discussion of the struggle in Kentucky, see Coulter, *The Civil War and Readjustment in Kentucky*, pp. 394–99; for an examination of the church litigation in which Harlan was to become embroiled, see Ronald W. Eades, *Watson v. Jones: The Walnut Street Presbyterian Church and the First Amendment* (Louisville: Archer Editions Press, 1982), and *History of the Supreme Court of the United States*, vol. VI, *Reconstruction and Reunion, 1864–88, Part One,* by Charles Fairman (New York: Macmillan, 1971), pp. 895–917.

43. Watson v. Jones, 80 U.S. 666 (1872).

44. 65 Ky. (5 Bush) 110 (1868).

45. Gartin v. Perrick, 68 Ky. (5 Bush) 110 (1868).

46. Watson v. Avery, 66 Ky. (5 Bush) 635 (1868).

47. *History of the Supreme Court*, p. 908.

48. Eads, *Watson v. Jones*, pp. 34–35. Numerous briefs, letters, and other materials connected with the Walnut Street case and related church suits are in HPLC.

49. HPLC and the Bristow Papers contain numerous letters reflecting such frustrations.

50. Benjamin H. Bristow to John Marshall Harlan, March 19, 1871, HPLC.

51. Benjamin H. Bristow to John Marshall Harlan, April 4, 1871, HPLC.

52. John Marshall Harlan to Benjamin H. Bristow, April 4, 1872, Bristow Papers.

53. John Marshall Harlan to Benjamin H. Bristow, April 15, 1872, Bristow Papers.

54. 80 U.S. at 678.

55. Ibid., p. 676.

56. John Marshall Harlan to Benjamin H. Bristow, April 15, 1872, Bristow Papers.

57. Frankfort *Semi-Weekly Commonwealth*, February 22, 1867.

58. Noted in Westin, "John Marshall Harlan and the Constitutional Rights of Negroes," p. 664, n. 97.

59. John Marshall Harlan to W. C. Matthews, October 5, 1869, HPUL.

60. See, for example, John Marshall Harlan to Robert J. Breckinridge, October 6, 23, November 16, December 5, 1866, Breckinridge Family Papers, Library of Congress.

61. For a Breckinridge profile, see *Dictionary of American Biography*, vol. 2, part 1, pp. 10–11.

62. *Louisville Commercial*, December 29, 1869.

63. See, for example, John Marshall Harlan to B. N. Perrick, July 21, 1873, HPUL; John Marshall Harlan to W. W. Gardner, July 21, 1873, HPUL.

64. John Marshall Harlan to H. V. Boynton, July 23, 1873, HPUL.

65. A copy of the purchase agreement is in HPUL.

66. James Hardin to John Marshall Harlan, February 16, 1870, HPLC.

67. *Louisville Daily Commercial*, May 18, 1871.

68. Ibid.

69. The *Louisville Daily Commercial*, June 3, 1871, included a transcript of the candidates' remarks.

70. See, for example, Louisville *Courier-Journal*, July 28, 1871.

71. Quoted in *Louisville Commercial*, November 1, 1877.

72. Ibid. In several newspaper transcripts of this statement, including the *Commercial*'s version of his Vanceburg speech, Harlan is quoted as saying he would rather be viewed as "right than *in*consistent." *Louisville Daily Commercial*, June 3, 1871 (emphasis added).

73. *Louisville Daily Commercial*, July 29, 1871.

74. *Louisville Daily Commercial*, July 29, 1871.

75. *Louisville Daily Commercial*, July 29, 1871.

76. *Cincinnati Gazette*, June 3, 1871.

77. *Louisville Daily Commercial*, June 3, 1871.

78. Ibid.

79. Ibid.

80. See, for example, *Louisville Daily Commercial*, June 18, 1871.

81. J. D. Duncan to Editors, *Commercial*, June 7, 1871, HPLC.

82. John Marshall Harlan to W. A. Meriwether, July 7, 1871, HPLC.

83. Benjamin H. Bristow to John Marshall Harlan, July 23, 1871, HPLC.

84. Benjamin H. Bristow to John Marshall Harlan, July 28, 1871, HPLC.

85. *Cincinnati Gazette*, July 21, 22, 1871.

86. Louisville *Courier-Journal*, July 28, 1871.

87. W. H. Perrin, et al., *Kentucky: A History of the State* (Louisville: F. A. Battey, 1888), p. 479.

88. *New York World*, undated, quoted in *Kentucky Yeoman*, August 17, 1871.

89. *Cincinnati Gazette*, August 9, 1871.

90. John Marshall Harlan to John B. Bruner, August 26, 1871, Bruner Papers.

91. *Cincinnati Gazette*, August 9, 1871.

92. Harlan's account of the gesture is recounted in the autobiographical typescript dealing with his Know-Nothing and other pre-Court political activities, in HPLC.

93. Benjamin H. Bristow to John Marshall Harlan, June 8, 1872, HPLC.

94. Benjamin H. Bristow to John Marshall Harlan, June 18, 1872, HPLC.

95. *Louisville Commercial*, July 28, 1872.

96. Malvina Harlan, *Some Memories of a Long Life*.

97. From the autobiographical typescript of Harlan's pre-Court political activities, HPLC.

98. Ibid.

99. John Marshall Harlan to J. G. Hatchitt, July 15,1873, HPUL.

100. John Marshall Harlan to Thomas Kyle, April 5, 1873, HPUL.

101. John Marshall Harlan to T. Flippen, April 4, 1873, HPUL.

102. Samuel R. Smith to John Marshall Harlan, January 30, 1874, HPLC; J.B. Bowman to John Marshall Harlan, January 5, 1874, HPLC.

103. Louisville *Courier-Journal*, May 13, 1875.

104. John Marshall Harlan to O. S. Poston, May 17, 1875, HPUL.

105. John Marshall Harlan to Thomas E. Burns, May 17, 1875, HPUL. Numerous letters in a similar vein are in HPUL.

106. Such correspondence is in HPUL.

107. John Marshall Harlan telegram to Benjamin H. Bristow, May 22, 1875, Bristow Papers.

108. Benjamin H. Bristow to James Harlan, June 9, 1875, HPLC.

109. Benjamin H. Bristow to James Harlan, June 11, 1875, HPLC.

110. Benjamin H. Bristow to W. A. Meriwether, June 9, 1875, Bristow Papers.

111. Thomas A. Ridgeway to E. F. Winslow, June 22, 1875, HPLC.

112. E. F. Winslow to John Marshall Harlan, June 23, 1875, HPLC.

113. Benjamin H. Bristow to John Marshall Harlan, July 5, 1875, HPLC.

114. D. C. Swan Wintersmith to John Marshall Harlan, May 22, 1875, HPLC.

115. John Marshall Harlan to D. C. Swan Wintersmith, May 25, 1875, HPLC.

116. John Marshall Harlan to M. Stevenson, May 25, 1875, HPUL.

117. Louisville *Courier-Journal*, July 7, 1875.

118. *Daily Louisville Commercial*, June 29, 1875.

119. From an unidentified 1875 newspaper account, quoted in *Louisville Commercial*, November 1, 1877.

120. Ibid.

121. From Harlan's account in the autobiographical typescript of his pre-Court activities, HPLC.

122. Ibid.

123. *Daily Louisville Commercial*, June 29, 1875.

124. From an 1875 campaign speech quoted in *Louisville Commercial*, November 1, 1877.

125. Louisville *Courier-Journal*, April 26, 1903; *Cincinnati Enquirer*, November 14, 1908.

126. In a marginal notation on a newspaper account of the story, which McCreary apparently delighted to tell, *Cincinnati Enquirer*, November 14, 1908.

127. Such concerns are the principal topic of numerous Bristow letters in HPLC.

128. Benjamin H. Bristow to John Marshall Harlan, September 4, 1874, HPLC.

129. Such entreaties are a regular theme of Harlan letters in the Bristow Papers.

130. John Marshall Harlan to Benjamin H. Bristow, November 16, 1870, Bristow Papers.

Chapter 4   Reward

1. The Harlan Papers are replete with correspondence relating to such efforts.

2. John Marshall Harlan to Marshall Jewell, January 17, 1876, HPUL.

3. Quoted in John Marshall Harlan to George A. Armstrong, January 19, 1876, HPUL.

4. Ibid.

5. Quoted in John Marshall Harlan to Marshall Jewell, July 1, 1876, HPUL.

6. Ibid.

7. See, for example, John Marshall Harlan to Marshall Jewell, July 7, 1876, HPUL.

8. Augustus E. Willson to Richard D. Harlan, April 11, 1930, HPLC. In 1930–31, Justice Harlan's son, Richard, wrote Willson in connection with research for a biography of his father, which never materialized.

9. John Marshall Harlan to James C. Lewis, September 23, 1869, HPUL. See *Dictionary of American Biography*, Vol. 10, part 2, p. 312, for a biographical profile of Willson. The Augustus Everett Willson Papers, The Filson Club Historical Society, Louisville, Ky., include several biographical profiles.

10. Benjamin H. Bristow to John Marshall Harlan, April 8, 1873, HPLC.

11. Willson to Richard D. Harlan.

12. Benjamin H. Bristow to John Marshall Harlan, December 16, 1875, HPLC.

13. Augustus E. Willson to John Marshall Harlan, February 7, 1876, HPLC.

14. John Marshall Harlan to J. H. Reno, December 17, 1875, HPUL.

15. William Cassius Goodloe to John Marshall Harlan, January 4, 1876, HPLC.

16. J. H. Wilson to John Marshall Harlan, December 22, 1875, HPLC.

17. Henry V. N. Boynton to John Marshall Harlan, January 30, 1876, HPLC.

18. John D. Baldwin to John Marshall Harlan, February 15, 1876, HPLC.

19. H. G. Petner to John Marshall Harlan, February 11, 1876, HPLC.

20. *New York Times*, March 12, 1876.

21. This tabulation is drawn from E. Bruce Thompson, "The Bristow Presidential Boom of 1876," *Mississippi Valley Historical Review* 32 (1945): 5–6. For another discussion of the Bristow-Harlan roles in the 1876 election, see Webb, *Benjamin Helm Bristow*, ch. 9.

22. For references to others connected with the Bristow effort, see Thompson, "The Bristow Presidential Boom of 1876," pp. 5–15.

23. Ibid., p. 3.

24. D. H. Chamberlain to John Marshall Harlan, May 10, 1876, HPLC.

25. Joseph Harmon to Benjamin H. Bristow, May 5, 1876, HPLC.

26. Thompson, "The Bristow Presidential Boom of 1876," pp. 8–9.

27. Madison, Wisconsin, *Herald*, April 8, 1876.

28. New York *Herald*, March 18, 1876.

29. Thompson, "The Bristow Presidential Boom of 1876," p. 15.

30. H. V. Boynton, "The Whiskey Ring," *North American Review* 123 (1876): 280ff.

31. Benjamin H. Bristow to John Marshall Harlan, June 2, 1876, HPLC.

32. Stanley Matthews to John Marshall Harlan, March 14, 1876, HPLC.

33. John Marshall Harlan to Benjamin H. Bristow, April 21, 1876, Bristow Papers.

34. Benjamin H. Bristow to John Marshall Harlan, May 3, 1876, Bristow Papers; Webb, *Benjamin Helm Bristow*, p. 230.

35. Benjamin H. Bristow to M. C. Garber, Jr., April 14, 1876, HPLC.

36. Webb, *Benjamin Helm Bristow*, p. 231.

37. John W. Finnell to John Marshall Harlan, May 13, 1876, HPLC.

38. J. G. Hatchitt to John Marshall Harlan, May 2, 1876, HPLC.

39. John Marshall Harlan to Carl Schurz, May 6, 1876, summarized in Harlan to Schurz, May 9, 1876, HPLC.

40. Benjamin H. Bristow to John Marshall Harlan, April 17, 1876, Bristow Papers.

41. Benjamin H. Bristow to John Marshall Harlan, May 21, 1876, HPLC.

42. Benjamin H. Bristow to Luke P. Poland, May 21, 1876, HPLC.

43. J. H. Wilson to John Marshall Harlan, May 18, 1876, HPLC.

44. John Marshall Harlan to Walter Q. Gresham, May 25, 1876, Walter Q. Gresham Papers, Library of Congress.

45. Ibid.

46. Thompson, "The Bristow Presidential Boom of 1876," pp. 19–20; *New York Times*, June 1, 1876.

47. Benjamin H. Bristow to John Marshall Harlan, May 3, 1876, Bristow Papers.

48. Thompson, "The Bristow Presidential Boom of 1876," p. 20.

49. Benjamin H. Bristow to J. H. Wilson, June 11, 1876, Bristow Papers.

50. Ibid.

51. Quoted in Thompson, "The Bristow Presidential Boom of 1876," p. 21.

52. Bristow to Wilson.

53. Ibid.

54. C.B. Chapman telegram to John Marshall Harlan, June 12, 1876, HPLC.

55. E.F. Madden to John Marshall Harlan, June 12, 1876, HPLC.

56. The statements, dated June 12, 1876, are in the Bristow Papers.

57. *New York Times*, June 16, 1876.

58. Webb, *Benjamin Helm Bristow*, p. 244.

59. Ibid., p. 241.

60. William C. Cochran to his mother, June 18, 1876, Rutherford B. Hayes Papers, Hayes Library, Fremont, Ohio.

61. Ibid.

62. John Marshall Harlan to Benjamin H. Bristow, June 19, 1876, HPLC.

63. Ibid.

64. Ibid.

65. Matilda Gresham, *Life of Walter Quintin Gresham: 1832–1895*, 2 vols. (Chicago: Rand McNally & Co., 1919), II: 459.

66. Thompson, "The Bristow Presidential Boom of 1876," p. 28, n. 110.

67. Gresham, *Life of Walter Quintin Gresham*, II: 823.

68. Benjamin H. Bristow to John Marshall Harlan, June 16, 1876, HPLC.

69. Benjamin H. Bristow to John Marshall Harlan, June 20, 1876, HPLC.

70. Webb, *Benjamin Helm Bristow*, pp. 251, 253.

71. S. C. Weir to John Marshall Harlan, June 19, 1876, HPLC.

72. John Marshall Harlan to Rutherford B. Hayes, June 21, 1876, Hayes Papers.

73. John Marshall Harlan to Rutherford B. Hayes, July 10, 1876, Hayes Papers.

74. Edward F. Noyes to John Marshall Harlan, July 13, 1876, HPLC.

75. John Marshall Harlan to Edward F. Noyes, July 14, 1876, HPUL.

76. John Marshall Harlan to James G. Blaine, August 5, 1876, HPUL.

77. See, for example, John Marshall Harlan to T. O. Shackleford, September 4, 1876, HPUL.

78. John Marshall Harlan to John D. White, July 14, 1876, HPUL. See also, for example, John Marshall Harlan to Alphonso Taft, July 28, 1876, HPUL; John Marshall Harlan to John D. White, July 28, 1876, HPUL.

79. Noted in Harlan to Shackleford.

80. See, for example, John Marshall Harlan to W. M. Randolph, partial letter bearing no date, HPUL.

81. John Marshall Harlan to W. R. Holloway, October 4, 1876, HPUL.

82. *New York Times*, November 6, 1876.

83. James M. Comly to Rutherford B. Hayes, January 8, 1877, Hayes Papers.

84. W. D. Bickham to Rutherford B. Hayes, February 14, 1877, Hayes Papers.

85. Carl Schurz to Rutherford B. Hayes, February 17, 1877, Hayes Papers.

86. Bland Ballard to John Marshall Harlan, February 26, 1877, Hayes Papers.

87. January 17, 1877, entry in Hayes's diary, Hayes Papers.

88. Oliver P. Morton to Rutherford B. Hayes, March, 1877, but otherwise undated, Hayes Papers.

89. Richard Smith to Rutherford B. Hayes, March 3, 1877, Hayes Papers.

90. William Henry Smith narrative, August 8–9, 1890, Hayes Papers.

91. William Dennison to John Marshall Harlan, March 16, 1877, HPLC.

92. Murat Halstead to Benjamin H. Bristow, March 5, 1877, Bristow Papers.

93. This description is based on the report of the Louisiana Commission, dated April 21, 1877, and reprinted in the *Cincinnati Commercial*, April 22, 1877, and on Charles R. Williams, *The Life of Rutherford Birchard Hayes*, 2 vols. (Columbus: Ohio State Archaeological and Historical Society, 1928), II: ch. 28.

94. William M. Evarts to Commissioners, April 2, 1877, Hayes Papers.

95. Walter Q. Gresham to John Marshall Harlan, March 28, 1877, HPLC.

96. John W. Finnell to John Marshall Harlan, April 4, 1877, HPLC.

97. Summarized in Williams, *The Life of Rutherford Birchard Hayes*, II: 58–59.

98. George Foster to John Marshall Harlan, April 9, 1877, HPLC.

99. E. L. Weber to Commissioners, April 10, 1877, Hayes Papers.

100. A copy of Hunt's undated report is in HPLC.

101. The HPLC contain numerous materials related to such activities.

102. John Marshall Harlan to Benjamin H. Bristow, April 13, 1877, Bristow Papers.

103. Commissioners' telegram to Rutherford B. Hayes, April 18, 1877, Hayes Papers.

104. Commissioners' telegram to Rutherford B. Hayes, April 20, 1877, Hayes Papers.

105. Williams, *The Life of Rutherford Birchard Hayes*, II: 60.

106. Quoted in ibid., II: 65.

107. T. De S. Tucker to John Marshall Harlan, June 11, 1877, Hayes Papers. Harlan forwarded Tucker's letter to the president with his recommendations. John Marshall Harlan to Rutherford B. Hayes, June 16, 1877, Hayes Papers.

108. John W. Finnell to John Marshall Harlan, April 27, 1877, HPLC.

109. Several copies of Harlan's one-day diary are in the justice's papers. For a printed

version, see David G. Farrelly, "John M. Harlan's One-Day Diary, August 21, 1877," *Filson Club History Quarterly* 24 (1950): 158–68. Harlan planned to make regular entries, but apparently wrote only the August 21 narrative.

110. Ibid.

111. Ibid. The handwritten draft of the telegram is in the Bristow Papers.

112. "Harlan's One-Day Diary."

113. William Dennison to John Marshall Harlan, March 22, 1877, HPLC. The letter was erroneously addressed to "General James Harlan."

114. Benjamin H. Bristow to William Dennison, March 16, 1877, Bristow Papers.

115. H. V. Boynton to Benjamin H. Bristow, April 3, 1877, Henry Van Ness Boynton Papers, Hayes Library.

116. H. V. Boynton to Benjamin H. Bristow, April 8, 1877, Boynton Papers.

117. Discussed in Benjamin H. Bristow to John Marshall Harlan, April 11, 1877, Bristow Papers.

118. John Marshall Harlan to Benjamin H. Bristow, April 9, 1877, Bristow Papers.

119. John Marshall Harlan telegram to Benjamin H. Bristow, April 11, 1877, Bristow Papers.

120. Bristow to Harlan, April 11, 1877.

121. John Marshall Harlan to Benjamin H. Bristow, April 13, 1877, Bristow Papers.

122. H. V. Boynton to John Marshall Harlan, April 15, 1877, Boynton Papers.

123. Numerous such letters are in the Bristow and Boynton papers.

124. Samuel Miller to William Pitt Ballinger, March 18, 1877, quoted in Charles Fairman, *Mr. Justice Miller and the Supreme Court, 1862–1890* (New York: Russell & Russell, 1939), p. 352.

125. Samuel Miller to William Pitt Ballinger, May 6, 1877, quoted in ibid.

126. Ibid.

127. John Marshall Harlan telegram to W. K. Rogers, May 26, 1877, Hayes Papers.

128. John Marshall Harlan to Stanley Matthews, May 28, 1877, Hayes Papers.

129. Stanley Matthews to W. K. Rogers, May 29, 1877, Hayes Papers.

130. John Marshall Harlan to John Sherman, June 4, 1877, Hayes Papers.

131. Fairman, *Mr. Justice Miller and the Supreme Court*, p. 356.

132. This discussion is based on "Harlan's One-Day Diary."

133. Augustus E. Willson to John Marshall Harlan, August 25, 1877, HPLC.

134. Lewis Dembitz to Rutherford B. Hayes, September 26, 1877, Hayes Papers.

135. Supporting letters numbering in the hundreds are in the Hayes Papers.

136. Thomas C. Jones, et al., to the president, September 8, 1877, Hayes Papers; William Lindsay, et al., to the president, September 7, 1877, Hayes Papers.

137. James B. McCreary to John Marshall Harlan, September 10, 1877, HPLC.

138. *Washington Post*, February 5, 1916.

139. A. H. Siegfried to Rutherford B. Hayes, September 27, 1877, Hayes Papers.

140. E. B. Martindale to Rutherford B. Hayes, September 25, 1877, Hayes Papers.

141. See, for example, Wayne MacVeagh to Rutherford B. Hayes, October 8, 1877, Hayes Papers.

142. James Harrison to Rutherford B. Hayes, September 22, 1877, Hayes Papers.

143. See, for example, Charles W. Fairbanks to Rutherford B. Hayes, September 31 [sic], 1877, Hayes Papers.

144. C. B. Lawrence to John Marshall Harlan, October 20, 1877, HPLC.

145. H. V. Boynton to Benjamin H. Bristow, August 15, 1877, Boynton Papers.

146. John W. Finnell to John Marshall Harlan, October 12, 1877, HPLC.

147. Numerous letters in HPLC provide evidence of such dedication.

148. Rutherford B. Hayes to William Henry Smith, September 29, 1877, Hayes Papers.

149. William Henry Smith to Rutherford B. Hayes, October 3, 1877, Hayes Papers.

150. Samuel Miller to William Pitt Ballinger, October 8, 1877, quoted in Fairman, *Mr. Justice Miller and the Supreme Court*, p. 361.

151. Wayne MacVeagh to John Marshall Harlan, October 3, 11, 1877, HPLC.

152. See, for example, *Louisville Commercial*, October 11, 1877.

153. Handwritten note, on Treasury Department stationery, to Rutherford B. Hayes, October 10, 1877, Hayes Papers. The signature on the note is illegible. A brief clipping reporting the president's decision was attached.

154. William Henry Smith to Rutherford B. Hayes, October 10, 1877, Hayes Papers.

155. W. K. Rogers to William Henry Smith, October 11, 1877, Hayes Papers.

156. Wayne MacVeagh to John Marshall Harlan, October 13, 1877, HPLC.

157. Samuel Miller to William Pitt Ballinger, October 13, 1877, quoted in Fairman, *Mr. Justice Miller and the Supreme Court*, p. 363.

158. John Marshall Harlan to Rutherford B. Hayes, October 19, 1877, Hayes Papers.

159. Robert M. Kelley telegram to John Marshall Harlan, October 17, 1877, HPLC.

160. L.Q.C. Lamar telegram to Henry Watterson, October 17, 1877, HPLC.

161. John Marshall Harlan to Benjamin H. Bristow, September 29, 1871, Bristow Papers.

162. John W. Finnell to John Marshall Harlan, October 17, 1877, HPLC.

163. See, for example, Sterling B. Toney to John Marshall Harlan, October 18, 1877, HPLC; Stewart L. Woodford to Rutherford B. Hayes, October 18, 1877, Hayes Papers; W. B. Woods to Rutherford B. Hayes, October 19, 1877, Hayes Papers.

164. Frederick T. Stone to John Marshall Harlan, October 20, 1877, HPLC.

165. For interesting discussions of the nomination and confirmation battles, see "Document: The Appointment of Mr. Justice Harlan," *Indiana Law Journal* 29 (1953): 46–74; Loren P. Beth, "President Hayes Appoints a Justice," *Yearbook 1989, Supreme Court Historical Society* (Washington, D.C.: Supreme Court Historical Society, 1989), 68–77.

166. For a profile of Conkling, see *Dictionary of American Biography*, Vol. 2, part 2, pp. 346–47.

167. Justin Morrill to Rutherford B. Hayes, August 25, 1877, Hayes Papers. For a profile of Edmunds, see *Dictionary of American Biography*, Vol. 3, part 2, pp. 24–27.

168. George F. Edmunds to Benjamin H. Bristow, October 27, 1877, Bristow Papers.

169. Melville W. Fuller to Hannibal Hamlin, October 29, 1877, in Senate judiciary committee records on the Harlan nomination, National Archives, Washington, D.C., hereinafter cited as Senate Records.

170. John Ledwick to S. J. Kirkland, November 17, 1877, Senate Records.

171. William Brown to George F. Edmunds, November 19, 1877, Senate Records.

172. *War of the Rebellion*, Series I, vol. 20, part 1, p. 141.

173. Benjamin H. Bristow to John Marshall Harlan, June 12, 1874, HPLC.

174. Speed S. Fry to John Marshall Harlan, March 13, 1876, HPLC.

175. Speed S. Fry to John Marshall Harlan, March 6, 1877, HPLC.

176. Wellington Harlan to John Marshall Harlan, November 20, 1877, HPLC.

177. Fry to Harlan, March 6, 1877.

178. Speed S. Fry to William Brown, November [illegible date], 1877, Senate Records.

179. Wellington Harlan to John Marshall Harlan, November 20, 1877, HPLC.

180. W. H. Painter to George F. Edmunds, undated, Senate Records. Although the letter was undated, the receipt stamp bore the date, November 4, 1877.

181. H. V. Boynton Statement Touching Gen. Harlan, November 13, 1877, Senate Records.

182. James Speed telegram to George F. Edmunds, November 1, 1877, Senate Records.

183. James Speed to George F. Edmunds, November 10, 1877, Senate Records.

184. Bluford Wilson telegram to David Davis, October 19, 1877, Senate Records.

185. Bland Ballard telegram to David Davis, October 17, 1877, Senate Records.

186. Oliver P. Morton to John Marshall Harlan, December 8, 1872, Senate Records.

187. Augustus E. Willson to Richard D. Harlan, April 11, 1930, HPLC.

188. John W. Finnell to John Marshall Harlan, November, 1877, but otherwise undated, HPLC.

189. *Louisville Commercial*, November 1, 1877.

190. William Brown to George F. Edmunds, November 21, 1877, Senate Records.

191. The letter, dated October 31, 1877, is printed, with annotations, in "Document: The Appointment of Mr. Justice Harlan," pp. 60–68.

192. Thomas L. Crittenden to John Marshall Harlan, November 1, 1877, HPLC.

193. John Marshall Harlan to Rutherford B. Hayes, October 31, 1877, Hayes Papers.

194. Stewart L. Woodford to John Marshall Harlan, November 2, 1877, HPLC.

195. Wayne MacVeagh to John Marshall Harlan, November 13, 1877, HPLC.

196. Thomas L. Crittenden to John Marshall Harlan, November 21, 1877, HPUL.

197. *New York Times*, November 25, 1877.

198. *New York Times*, November 28, 1877.

199. James Beck to John Marshall Harlan, November, 1877, but otherwise undated, HPUL.

200. Augustus E. Willson telegram to John Marshall Harlan, November 29, 1877, HPUL.

201. Drawn from handwritten note, HPUL.

202. Malvina Harlan, *Some Memories of a Long Life*.

203. James H. Embry to John Marshall Harlan, December 3, 1877, HPLC. Since the committee and floor action were unrecorded, no official records of the votes survive. The paucity of records has led some to the incorrect conclusion that Harlan initially received a recess appointment to the Court. See Arthur Krock to Arthur John Keeffe, February 27, 1963; John S. Castellano to John Marshall Harlan II, undated; Arthur John Keeffe to Arthur Krock, March 8, 1963; John S. Castellano to Arthur Krock, undated; Alan F. Westin to John Marshall Harlan II, April 2, 1963, HPLC, and published materials cited in this correspondence.

204. Samuel M. Breckinridge to Joseph C. Breckinridge, December 4, 1877, Breckinridge Family Papers, Library of Congress.

205. H. V. Boynton to Benjamin H. Bristow, January 8, 1878, Bristow Papers.

206. See Rutherford B. Hayes telegrams to Benjamin H. Bristow, January 15, 16, 1878, Bristow Papers.

207. John Marshall Harlan telegram to Morrison Waite, December 3, 1877, Morrison Waite Papers, Library of Congress.

208. John Marshall Harlan to H. J. Stites, et al., December 6, 1877, HPLC.

209. John Marshall Harlan to George Pullman, January 3, 1878, HPLC.

210. Malvina Harlan, *Some Memories of a Long Life*.

Chapter 5   Washington

1. James S. Harlan to James Harlan, March 30, 1879, HPUL.

2. Malvina Harlan, *Some Memories of a Long Life*.

3. The Harlan papers contain many such invitations.

4. Malvina Harlan, *Some Memories of a Long Life*.

5. See partial letter of Henry W. Jessup, undated, HPUL.

6. J. H. McCullogh to John Marshall Harlan, August 5, 1891, HPUL.

7. John Marshall Harlan to J. H. McCullogh, August 6, 1891, HPUL.

8. Malvina Harlan, *Some Memories of a Long Life*.

9. Ibid.

10. Ibid.

11. This description is drawn from several unidentified clippings and *The Columbian Call*, January 9, 1896.

12. Malvina Harlan, *Some Memories of a Long Life*.

13. The Hayes papers include correspondence between Edith and then ex-President Hayes. See, for example, Rutherford B. Hayes to Edith Harlan, April 16, 1881; Edith Harlan to Rutherford B. Hayes, July 9, 1881.

14. Malvina Harlan, *Some Memories of a Long Life*.

15. Unidentified obituary for Edith Harlan Child, undated, HPUL.

16. Unidentified, undated clipping, HPUL.

17. John Marshall Harlan to James S. Harlan, August 6, 1882, HPLC.

18. John Marshall Harlan to "Dear Boys," November 9, 1882, HPLC.

19. John Marshall Harlan to Richard D. Harlan, two telegrams, November 12, 1882, HPLC. Interestingly, a phrenological reading, done in Frankfort on March 16, 1866, and carefully preserved in the family papers, had warned Edith that she "really . . . must take better care of [her] health, making that paramount." The reading is in HPUL.

20. Wellington Harlan to John Marshall Harlan, January 10, 1883, HPLC.

21. John Marshall Harlan to James S. Harlan, November 25, 1882, HPLC.

22. See, for example, Frank Child to Edith Child, October 3, 1893, HPLC.

23. HPLC and HPUL include many such letters.

24. Richard received his degrees in 1881, 1884, and 1885; James and John Maynard in 1883 and 1884, respectively.

25. John Marshall Harlan to James S. Harlan, September 11, 1880, HPLC.

26. John Marshall Harlan to James S. Harlan, November 23, 1880, HPLC.

27. John Marshall Harlan to James S. Harlan, January 11, 1881, HPLC.

28. Undated, unidentified obituaries of George W. Shanklin are in the Harlan family scrapbook, Kentucky Historical Society.

29. John Marshall Harlan to James S. Harlan, April 23, 1883, HPLC.

30. A. R. Spofford to John Marshall Harlan, April 21, 1883, HPLC.

31. John Marshall Harlan to James S. Harlan, February 13, 1883, HPLC.

32. John Marshall Harlan to James S. Harlan, February 9, 1882, HPLC.

33. John Marshall Harlan to James S. Harlan, January 11, 1881, HPLC.

34. John Marshall Harlan to James S. Harlan, September 15, 1880, HPUL.

35. John Marshall Harlan to James S. Harlan, October 8, 1881, HPLC. Presumably, Harlan also wrote John Maynard directly; but the available sources include no such correspondence.

36. Ibid.

37. John Marshall Harlan to James S. Harlan, October 8, 1881, HPLC. This was the second of two letters written to James on October 8.

38. Ibid.

39. John Marshall Harlan to James S. Harlan, February 15, 1882, HPLC.

40. For more detailed profiles of the brothers, see Yarbrough, *John Marshall Harlan*, pp. 4–9, 36–39.

41. For a memorial to Harlan Cleveland, see *The Court Index* (official paper of the Hamilton County, Ohio, courts), January 18, 1907, HPLC.

42. Laura H. Thornton to John Marshall Harlan, July 27, 1895, HPLC.

43. Henry St. George Tucker to John Marshall Harlan, undated, HPUL.

44. William L. Wilson to John Marshall Harlan, May 16, 1900, HPUL.

45. Harlan Hiter to John Marshall Harlan, June 9, 1900, HPUL.

46. Harlan Hiter to John Marshall Harlan, June 13, 1900, HPUL.

47. Samuel Miller to William Pitt Ballinger, December 25, 1880, quoted in Fairman, *Mr. Justice Miller and the Supreme Court*, p. 370.

48. John Marshall Harlan to Benjamin Harrison, August 27, 1888, Benjamin Harrison Papers, Library of Congress.

49. John Marshall Harlan to James S. Harlan, May 25, 1882, HPLC.

50. L. Hord to John Marshall Harlan, April 28, 1879, HPUL.

51. E. C. Bohne to John Marshall Harlan, August 5, 1879, HPUL.

52. J. B. Hawley to John Marshall Harlan, May 22, 1879, HPUL.

53. See, for example, R. L. Phythian to John Marshall Harlan, April 12, 1880; George W. Brown to John Marshall Harlan, December 7, 1879, HPUL.

54. John Marshall Harlan to C. G. Sims, November 13, 1879, HPUL.

55. See, for example, John Marshall Harlan to Rutherford B. Hayes, January 14, 18, 1880, and several undated letters, Hayes Papers.

56. Eli Murray to John Marshall Harlan, March 18, 1880, Hayes Papers.

57. John Marshall Harlan to Rutherford B. Hayes, July 3, 1879, Hayes Papers. See, for example, R. Gudgell to John Marshall Harlan, July 31, 1879,

58. HPUL; J. G. Barret to John Marshall Harlan, July 31, 1879, HPUL; John Mason Brown to John Marshall Harlan, July 31, 1879, HPUL; Wellington Harlan to John Marshall Harlan, August 27, 1879, HPUL.

59. John Marshall Harlan to Rutherford B. Hayes, July 31, 1879, Hayes Papers.

60. John Marshall Harlan to Rutherford B. Hayes, August 4, 1879, Hayes Papers.

61. John Marshall Harlan to Rutherford B. Hayes, August 26, 1879, Hayes Papers.

62. John Marshall Harlan to Rutherford B. Hayes, September 1, 1879, Hayes Papers.

63. Ibid.

64. J. W. Barr to John Marshall Harlan, April 12, 1880, HPUL.

65. Theodore B. Tracie to John Marshall Harlan, June 3, 1878, HPLC.

66. James T. Buckner to John Marshall Harlan, May 5, 1881, Hayes Papers.

67. John Marshall Harlan to Augustus E. Willson, January 9, 1889, Willson Papers. Harlan's letter to Harrison, also dated January 9, 1889, is in the Harrison Papers.

68. Rutherford B. Hayes to W. D. Bickham, June 25, 1876, Hayes Papers.

69. See, for example, Rutherford B. Hayes to Lucy Hayes, March 30, August 10, 1878, Hayes Papers.

70. See, for example, John Marshall Harlan to Rutherford B. Hayes, June 15, 1880, January 5, 1881, Hayes Papers.

71. John Marshall Harlan to Rutherford B. Hayes, May 18, 1880, Hayes Papers.

72. In an 1880 note, undated, Harlan invited Garfield to an evening game of whist at the home of Justice William Strong. James A. Garfield Papers, Library of Congress.

73. John Marshall Harlan to James A. Garfield, December 6, 1880, Garfield Papers. See also the justice's letter of October 29, 1880, in the same collection.

74. See, for example, John Marshall Harlan telegrams to Morrison Waite, August 16, 17, 26, 1881, Garfield Papers.

75. John Marshall Harlan to Benjamin Harrison, December 25, 1888, Harrison Papers.

76. See John E. Semonche, *Charting the Future: The Supreme Court Responds to a Changing Society, 1890–1920* (Westport, Conn.: Greenwood Press, 1978), pp. 8–9, for a detailed description of the Capitol facilities.

77. This description is drawn from "John Marshall Harlan," *Literary Digest*, October 28, 1911, pp. 725–26, and from unidentified newspaper and magazine clippings in HPLC and HPUL.

78. John Marshall Harlan to Melville Fuller, undated, Melville Fuller Papers, Library of Congress.

79. John Marshall Harlan to Morrison Waite, January 7, 1878, Waite Papers.

80. 95 U.S. 670 (1878).

81. First National Bank v. Insurance Co., 95 U.S. 673 (1878).

82. United States v. Clark, 96 U.S. 37 (1878).

83. The summary is drawn from a tabulation in HPLC.

84. John Marshall Harlan to Morrison Waite, December 15, 1877, Waite Papers.

85. John Marshall Harlan to Morrison Waite, undated, Waite Papers.

86. John Marshall Harlan to Melville Fuller, undated, Fuller Papers.

87. John Marshall Harlan to James S. Harlan, June 19, 1883, HPLC.

88. John Marshall Harlan to Mrs. Morrison Waite, July 23, 1883, Waite Papers.

89. John Marshall Harlan to Morrison Waite, July 31, 1883, Waite Papers.

90. Charles Williams, *Diary and Letters of Rutherford B. Hayes* (Columbus, Ohio: Ohio State Archeological and Historical Society, 1924), 4: 461.

91. John A. Campbell to John Marshall Harlan, September, 1881, specific date illegible, HPUL. A letter written Campbell by Harlan, August 23, 1881, and mentioned in Campbell's letter, could not be located.

92. Willard L. King, *Melville Weston Fuller: Chief Justice of the United States, 1888–1910* (New York: Macmillan Co., 1950), p. 132.

93. John Marshall Harlan to Melville Fuller, April 23, 1888, Fuller Papers.

94. John Marshall Harlan telegram to Melville Fuller, May 1, 1888, Fuller Papers.

95. John Marshall Harlan to Melville Fuller, May 11, 1888, Fuller Papers.

96. Mark DeWolfe Howe (ed.), *Holmes-Pollock Letters*, 2d ed, 2 vols. (Cambridge, Mass.: Harvard University Press, 1961), II: 7–8, quoting a letter of April 5, 1919.

97. Charles Evans Hughes, *The Autobiographical Notes of Charles Evans Hughes*, ed. David J. Danelski and Joseph S. Tulchin (Cambridge, Mass.: Harvard University Press, 1973), p. 168. Hughes was chief justice from 1930 to 1941.

98. Ibid., p. 170.

99. See, for example, Merlo J. Pusey, *Charles Evans Hughes*, 2 vols. (New York: Columbia University Press, 1963), I: 277.

100. John Marshall Harlan to Melville Fuller, undated, Fuller Papers.

101. John Marshall Harlan to Augustus E. Willson, March 9, 1880, John Marshall Harlan Papers, The Filson Club Historical Society, Louisville, Ky.

102. Many such letters are in the papers of Harlan's contemporaries, cited elsewhere in the study.

103. John Marshall Harlan to Joseph P. Bradley, February 23, 1889, HPUL. Bradley served on the Court from 1870 to 1892.

104. Quoted in King, *Melville Weston Fuller*, p. 175.

105. Ibid., pp. 175–76. Charles Henry Butler, a Harlan relative, succeeded Davis and served as the Court's reporter 1902–16.

106. Hughes, *The Autobiographical Notes of Charles Evans Hughes*, p. 170.

107. John Marshall Harlan to Morrison Waite, July 31, 1883, Waite Papers.

108. I have made no attempt to profile each of the many justices with whom Harlan served. For such information, see general period studies of the Court, such as Semonche, *Charting the Future*, and appropriate volumes of the *History of the Supreme Court of the United States*; Henry J. Abraham's comprehensive and excellent study of Supreme Court appointments, *Justices and Presidents*; biographies of Harlan contemporaries, including those cited in this book; and appropriate encyclopedic entries.

109. Copies of Harlan speeches are in HPUL and HPLC.

110. Louis Brownlow, *A Passion for Politics: The Autobiography of Louis Brownlow, First Half* (Chicago: University of Chicago Press, 1955), pp. 345–46.

111. Ibid., pp. 346–47.

112. E.E.L. Taylor to Richard D. Harlan, May 26, 1930, HPUL.

113. Almon C. Kellogg to Richard D. Harlan, May 27, 1930, HPUL.

114. Samuel Hill to John Maynard Harlan, June 11, 1929, HPUL.

115. J. M. Dickinson to John Marshall Harlan, March 10, 1928, HPUL.

116. John Marshall Harlan to Thomas Drummond, May 6, 1878, HPUL.

117. John Marshall Harlan to Morrison Waite, June 4, 1878, Waite Papers.

118. John Marshall Harlan to Rutherford B. Hayes, July 22, 1879, Hayes Papers.

119. James Harlan to John Marshall Harlan, December 14, 1880, HPUL.

120. James Harlan to John Marshall Harlan, December 14, 1880, HPUL.

121. King, *Melville Weston Fuller*, pp. 157–58.

122. Quoted in ibid., p. 158.

123. See, for example, Succession v. Esbri, 200 U.S. 103 (1905); Perez v. Fernandez, 202 U.S. 80 (1905).

124. John Marshall Harlan to John Maynard Harlan, August 20, 1888, Harlan Family Papers, in the possession of Roger A. Derby, Jr., Warrenton, Va. Mr. Derby is Harlan I's great-grandson.

125. John Marshall Harlan to John Maynard Harlan, August 10, 1888, Harlan Family Papers.

126. S. V. Pinney to John Marshall Harlan, May 18, 1878, HPLC.

127. John Marshall Harlan to James S. Harlan, May 26, 1884, HPLC.

128. See, for example, John V. Farwell to John Marshall Harlan, May 15, 1901, HPUL; John Maynard Harlan to John Marshall Harlan, May 23, 1901, HPUL.

129. *Indianapolis News*, July 15, 1887.

130. *In Re* Coy, 31 Fed. Rep. 794 (1887). Coy was indicted under Sections 5440 and 5511 of the federal Revised Statutes.

131. *In Re* Coy, 127 U.S. 731, 753054 (1888).

132. See, for example, *Ex Parte* Siebold, 100 U.S. 371 (1880).

133. Matilda Gresham, in her biography of her husband, *Life of Walter Quintin Gresham*, II: 484–86, discusses the *Coy* case but, like much of her work, can hardly be considered entirely objective, since Judge Gresham had refused to allow Coy's prosecution prior to Harlan's involvement in the case.

134. The letter, dated October 24, 1888, is reprinted in ibid., II: 604. See ibid., II: ch. 38, for a lengthy discussion of the incident, and Allan Nevins, *Grover Cleveland: A Study in Courage* (New York: Dodd, Mead & Co., 1934), pp. 436–37, for a brief summary.

135. Nevins, *Grover Cleveland*, p. 436.

136. Gresham, *Life of Walter Quintin Gresham*, II: 606.

137. W. A. Woods to John Marshall Harlan, December 25, 1888, HPLC.

138. John Marshall Harlan to W. A. Woods, December 30, 1888, HPLC.

139. John Marshall Harlan to W. A. Woods, January 11, 1889, HPLC.

140. Quoted in Gresham, *Life of Walter Quintin Gresham*, II: 613.

141. Quoted in ibid.

142. Unidentified clipping, HPLC.

143. Noted in Gresham, *Life of Walter Quintin Gresham*, II: 614.

144. Solomon Claypool to John Marshall Harlan, January 15, 1889, HPLC.

145. See, for example, W. A. Woods to John Marshall Harlan, February 13, 25, 1889, HPLC.

146. A copy of the materials is in HPLC.

147. W. A. Woods to John Marshall Harlan, October 13, 1890, HPLC.

148. John Marshall Harlan to W. A. Woods, December 24, 1888, HPLC.

149. George F. Edmunds to Benjamin Harrison, January 8, 1889, Harrison Papers.

150. W. Hallett Phillips to John Marshall Harlan, undated, HPLC.

151. John Marshall Harlan to Melville Fuller, December 13, 1892, Fuller Papers.

152. Horace H. Lurton to John Marshall Harlan, April 23, 1900, HPUL.

153. John Marshall Harlan to E.S. Hammond, April 25, 1900, HPUL.

154. Unidentified clipping, HPLC.

155. Walter Q. Gresham to John Marshall Harlan, May 14, 1891, HPLC.

156. *Chicago Herald*, undated, HPLC.

Chapter 6   Equality

1. See especially the Civil Rights Cases, 109 U.S. 3 (1883).

2. Ibid.

3. See, for example, Williams v. Mississippi, 170 U.S. 213 (1898). But see also Yick Wo v. Hopkins, 118 U.S. 356 (1886).

4. *Ex Parte* Yarbrough, 110 U.S. 651 (1884).

5. Plessy v. Ferguson, 163 U.S. 537 (1896).

6. James Harlan to D. Howard Smith, April 5, 1851, HPLC.

7. Malvina Harlan, *Some Memories of a Long Life*.

8. Quoted in Speed Fry to William Brown, November [illegible date], 1877, Senate Records.

9. *Louisville Commercial*, November 1, 1864.

10. *Louisville Daily Commercial*, June 3, 1871.

11. John Marshall Harlan to William Howard Taft, April 1, 1892, Taft Papers.

12. John Marshall Harlan to W. R. Holloway, October 4, 1876, HPUL.

13. Unidentified clipping, HPUL.

14. The manuscript for the untitled, undated work is in HPLC.

15. Malvina Harlan, *Some Memories of a Long Life*.

16. Ibid.

17. Ibid. For a brief account of the second Justice Harlan's relationship with his messenger, see Yarbrough, *John Marshall Harlan*, pp. 233–35.

18. Malvina Harlan, *Some Memories of a Long Life*.

19. Ibid.

20. Robert Harlan, Jr., to William Howard Taft, July 3, 1917, Taft Papers.

21. O. S. Poston to John Marshall Harlan, July 9, 1868, HPLC.

22. John G. Weir to John Marshall Harlan, March 18, 1874, HPLC.

23. James Poindexter to John Marshall Harlan, November 24, 2877, HPLC.

24. John Marshall Harlan to Frederick Douglass, June 4, 1888, Douglass Papers.

25. John Marshall Harlan to Frederick Douglass, May 1, 1888, Douglass Papers.

26. John Marshall Harlan to Frederick Douglass, July 29, 1889, Douglass Papers.

27. William S. McFeely, *Frederick Douglass* (New York: Norton, 1991), p. 382.

28. John Marshall Harlan to John Maynard Harlan, December 9, 1888, Harlan Family Papers.

29. *New York Times*, December 14, 1879.

30. James S. Harlan to John Marshall Harlan, December 14, 1879, HPUL.

31. John Maynard Harlan to John Marshall Harlan, October 21, 1883, HPUL.

32. Ibid.

33. Ibid.

34. Richard D. Harlan to William Howard Taft, June 17, 1910, Taft Papers.

35. Unidentified clipping in HPUL.

36. As a member of one of Montgomery, Alabama's most distinguished law firms, Judge Rives had defended the racial status quo. Following his son's death, however, his racial views, by the judge's own account, underwent a dramatic transformation. As a fifth circuit jurist, he voted to outlaw segregation on Montgomery's buses and participated in numerous other civil rights rulings. For profiles of Judge Rives, see Jack Bass, *Unlikely Heroes* (New York: Simon and Schuster, 1981), pp. 69–77; Tinsley E. Yarbrough, *Judge Frank Johnson and Human Rights in Alabama* (University, Ala.: University of Alabama Press, 1981), ch. 4.

37. John Marshall Harlan to James S. Harlan, November 25, 1882, HPLC.

38. 100 U.S. 303 (1880).

39. Virginia v. Rives, 100 U.S. 313 (1880).

40. *Ex Parte* Virginia, 100 U.S. 339 (1880).

41. 103 U.S. 370 (1881).

42. Quoted in ibid., p. 394.

43. Ibid., p. 397.

44. Ibid., p. 396.

45. 106 U.S. 583 (1882).

46. 106 U.S. 629, 644 (1883).

47. The criminal suits were United States v. Stanley, from Kansas; United States v. Nichols, from Missouri; United States v. Ryan, the San Francisco case; and United States v. Singleton, the New York prosecution. The damage suit was Robinson and Wife v. Memphis and Charleston R.R.

48. George F. Edmunds to John Marshall Harlan, December 1, 1882, HPUL.

49. Civil Rights Cases, 109 U.S. 3 (1883).

50. Ibid., p. 14.

51. Ibid., p. 20.

52. Ibid., pp. 24–25.

53. Ibid., p. 25.

54. An extensive scrapbook in the HPUL includes numerous clippings and other materials relating to the cases. Except where otherwise indicated, this discussion is drawn from those sources.

55. Walter Thomas to John Marshall Harlan, October 16, 1883, HPUL.

56. James Lawson to John Marshall Harlan, October 16, 1883, HPUL.

57. Partial, unidentified letter, October 19, 1883, HPUL.

58. T. W. Donaldson to John Marshall Harlan, October 17, 1883, HPUL.

59. John W. Finnell to John Marshall Harlan, October 25, 1883, HPUL.

60. Wager Swayne to John Marshall Harlan, October 24, 1883, HPUL.

61. Dred Scott v. Sandford, 19 Howard 393 (1857).

62. Malvina Harlan, *Some Memories of a Long Life.*

63. Ibid.

64. 109 U.S. at 26.

65. Ibid.

66. Ibid., p. 36.

67. Ibid., p. 48.

68. Ibid., pp. 50–51.

69. Ibid., p. 54.

70. Ibid., pp. 58–59.

71. Ibid., p. 59.

72. Ibid., pp. 61–62.

73. Crandall v. Nevada, 6 Wallace 35 (1868).

74. New York *Daily Tribune*, November 22, 1883.

75. New York *Daily Tribune*, November 21, 1883.

76. W. Wallace Brown to John Marshall Harlan, December 17, 1883, HPUL.

77. Wayne MacVeagh to John Marshall Harlan, November 20, 1883, HPUL.

78. Noah H. Swayne to John Marshall Harlan, November 20, 1883, HPUL.

79. Melville M. Bigelow to John Marshall Harlan, November 24, 1883, HPUL.

80. Harlan quoted Strong's impressions, given him verbally, in an undated letter to Mrs. Harlan, HPUL.

81. Rutherford B. Hayes to John Marshall Harlan, November 28, 1883, HPUL.

82. Rutherford B. Hayes to John Marshall Harlan, January 19, 1884, HPUL.

83. Roscoe Conkling to John Marshall Harlan, December 27, 1883, HPUL.

84. *American Reformer*, December 8, 1883.

85. Frederick Douglass to John Marshall Harlan, November 27, 1883, HPUL.

86. E. S. Hammond to John Marshall Harlan, November 11, 1883, HPUL.

87. Such letters are in HPUL.

88. George H. Shields to John Marshall Harlan, November 10, 1883, HPUL.

89. See, for example, the letter to Harlan from his cousin, John M. Butler, November 24, 1883, HPUL.

90. 110 U.S. 651 (1884).

91. Bush v. Kentucky, 107 U.S. 110 (1883) (Harlan, J.).

92. Carter v. Texas, 177 U.S. 444 (1900).

93. Rogers v. Alabama, 192 U.S. 226 (1904).

94. *In Re* Wood, 140 U.S. 278 (1891) (Harlan, J.); Andrews v. Swartz, 156 U.S. 272 (1895) (Harlan, J.); Gibson v. Mississippi, 162 U.S. 565 (1896) (Harlan, J.).

95. Murray v. Louisiana, 163 U.S. 101 (1896); Brownfield v. South Carolina, 189 U.S. 426 (1903); Martin v. Texas, 200 U.S. 316 (1906); Franklin v. South Carolina, 218 U.S. 161 (1910).

96. Thomas v. Texas, 212 U.S. 278 (1909).

97. 170 U.S. 213 (1898).

98. Mills v. Green, 159 U.S. 651 (1895); Jones v. Montague, 194 U.S. 147 (1904); Selden v. Montague, 194 U.S. 153 (1904).

99. James v. Bowman, 190 U.S. 127 (1903).

100. Giles v. Harris, 189 U.S. 475, 483 (1903).

101. Ibid., p. 486.

102. Ibid., p. 487.

103. 197 U.S. 207 (1905).

104. Ibid., p. 222.

105. Ibid., p. 223.

106. 203 U.S. 1 (1906).

107. Ibid., p. 16.

108. Ibid., p. 20.

109. Ibid., p. 37.

110. Ibid., pp. 34, 38.

111. United States v. Powell, 212 U.S. 564 (1909).

112. 211 U.S. 452 (1908).

113. Ibid., p. 455.

114. Ibid., pp. 458, 459.

115. Bailey v. Alabama, 219 U.S. 219 (1911).

116. Robertson v. Baldwin, 165 U.S. 275 (1897).

117. Ibid., pp. 287–88.

118. Ibid., p. 301.

119. Ibid., p. 299.

120. Ibid., p. 296. '

121. Ibid., p. 288.

122. Ibid., p. 303.

123. 95 U.S. 485 (1878).

124. Louisville, N.O. & T. Ry. Co. v. Mississippi, 133 U.S. 587, 594 (1890) (Harlan, J., dissenting).

125. Ibid., pp. 594–95.

126. The definitive study is Charles A. Lofgren, *The Plessy Case: A Legal–Historical Interpretation* (New York: Oxford University Press, 1987).

127. Plessy v. Ferguson, 163 U.S. 537, 543 (1896).

128. Ibid., p. 544.

129. Ibid., p. 550.

130. Ibid., pp. 551–52.

131. Ibid., p. 559.

132. Ibid., p. 557.

133. Ibid., p. 562.

134. Ibid., pp. 560–61.

135. Ibid., pp. 563–64.

136. Ibid., p. 557.

137. The justice's papers include no files on the case and few references to it.

138. Robert J. Harris, *The Quest for Equality: The Constitution, Congress, and the Supreme Court* (Baton Rouge: Louisiana State University Press, 1960), p. 101.

139. 163 U.S. at 554.

140. Ibid., p. 559.

141. 175 U.S. 528 (1899).

142. Quoted in ibid., p. 535.

143. Ibid., p. 543.

144. Ibid., p. 544.

145. Ibid., p. 545.

146. Adamson v. California, 332 U.S. 46, 62 (1947) (Frankfurter, J., concurring).

147. For a recent discussion of Frankfurter's involvement in that litigation, see James F. Simon, *The Antagonists: Hugo Black, Felix Frankfurter and Civil Liberties in Modern America* (New York: Simon and Schuster, 1989), pp. 211–26.

148. Felix Frankfurter to John Marshall Harlan II, July 6, 1956, Harlan II Papers.

149. Ibid.

150. John Marshall Harlan II to Felix Frankfurter, July 12, 1956, Harlan II Papers.

151. Felix Frankfurter to John Marshall Harlan II, July 18, 1956, Harlan II Papers.

152. Felix Frankfurter to John Marshall Harlan II, July 31, 1956, Harlan II Papers.

153. Harlan II to Frankfurter, July 12, 1956.

154. Frankfurter to Harlan II, July 31, 1956. For a fuller account of this exchange, see Yarbrough, *John Marshall Harlan*, pp. 121–23.

155. Berea College v. Kentucky, 211 U.S. 45 (1908).

156. Ibid., p. 69.

157. Henry M. Shepard to John Marshall Harlan, July 14, 1896, HPLC.

Chapter 7 Liberty

1. Slaughterhouse Cases, 83 U.S. 36 (1873).

2. Munn v. Illinois, 94 U.S. 113, 134 (1877).

3. See, for example, Mugler v. Kansas, 123 U.S. 623 (1887) (Harlan, J.).

4. 165 U.S. 578 (1897).

5. See, for example, *Lochner* v. *New York*, 198 U.S. 45 (1905).

6. See, for example, United States v. E.C. Knight Co., 156 U.S. 1 (1895).

7. John Marshall Harlan to Benjamin Harrison, November 3, 1888, Harrison Papers.

8. John Marshall Harlan to Melville Fuller, September 9, 1891, Fuller Papers.

9. A copy of the sale agreement is in HPLC.

10. Pertinent documents are in HPLC.

11. See, for example, Welllington Harlan to John Marshall Harlan, February 12, 1872, HPLC.

12. Wellington Harlan to John Marshall Harlan, March 16, 1874, HPLC.

13. Unidentified letter, HPUL.

14. Unidentified letter, HPUL.

15. Wellington Harlan to John Marshall Harlan, March 18, 1874, HPUL.

16. Augustus E. Willson to John Marshall Harlan, June 22, 1880, HPLC.

17. Augustus E. Willson to John Marshall Harlan, June 26, 1880, HPLC.

18. J. S. Barret to T. W. Neill, January 26, 1888, HPLC.

19. T. W. Neill to John Marshall Harlan, March 24, 1888, HPLC.

20. A copy of John Shanklin's will, dated October 16, 1875, is in HPLC.

21. Materials relating to the loan, including a copy of the complaint, are in HPLC.

22. George W. Shanklin to John Marshall Harlan, July 16, 1880, HPLC.

23. John Marshall Harlan to George W. Shanklin, November 19, 1894, HPLC.

24. James Harlan to John Marshall Harlan, February 21, 1880, HPUL.

25. James A. Leech to John Marshall Harlan, March 17, 1880, HPUL.

26. John Marshall Harlan to Thomas W. Bullitt, October 17, 1880, HPUL.

27. John Marshall Harlan to Thomas W. Bullitt, October 27, 1880, HPUL.

28. John Marshall Harlan to Augustus E. Willson, March 13, 1893, HPUL.

29. Ibid.

30. John Marshall Harlan to George W. Shanklin, November 19, 1894.

31. See John Marshall Harlan to John Maynard Harlan, June 8, 10, 11, 1888, Harlan Family Papers.

32. Danville *Advocate*, May 20, 1887.

33. James Harlan to John Marshall Harlan, May 24, 1887, HPLC.

34. John Marshall Harlan to John Maynard Harlan, March 31, 1889, Harlan Family Papers.

35. Ibid.

36. James S. Harlan to John Marshall Harlan, undated, HPUL.

37. James S. Harlan to John Marshall Harlan, March 31, 1891, HPUL.

38. James S. Harlan to John Marshall Harlan, April 27, 1892, HPUL.

39. For correspondence relating to that transaction, see Newton G. Rogers to John Maynard Harlan, May 17, 1889, HPLC; John Maynard Harlan to Newton G. Rogers, June 12, 1889, HPLC.

40. Harlan to Rogers.

41. After Murray's death, it should be noted, his widow attempted to collect on a debt the justice had actually paid years before. See, for example, Owsley & Motley, Attorneys, to John Marshall Harlan, August 11, 1898, HPLC; Augustus E. Willson to John Marshall Harlan, October 15, 1898, HPLC; Augustus E. Willson to James S. Barret, October 18, 1898, HPLC; Augustus E. Willson to John Marshall Harlan, October 23, 27, 1898, HPLC.

42. See, for example, Augustus E. Willson to John Marshall Harlan, June 26, 1880, HPLC.

43. Riggs & Co. to John Marshall Harlan, December 20, 1892, HPLC.

44. John Marshall Harlan to Logan Murray, February 9, 1881, HPUL.

45. John Marshall Harlan to Augustus E. Willson, undated, HPUL.

46. 157 U.S. 429, 652 (1895); 158 U.S. 601, 638 (1895).

47. United States v. E.C. Knight Co., 156 U.S. 1, 18 (1895); *In Re* Debs, 158 U.S. 564 (1895).

48. 156 U.S. 1 (1895).

49. Ibid., p. 17.

50. Ibid., p. 19.

51. Ibid.

52. Ibid., p. 33.

53. Harlan drew heavily, for example, on Marshall's opinions in McCulloch v. Maryland, 4 Wheat. 316 (1819), and Gibbons v. Ogden, 9 Wheat. 1 (1824).

54. Ibid., p. 43.

55. Ibid., p. 44.

56. Except where otherwise indicated, this discussion is based on King, *Melville Weston Fuller*, ch. 15; Carl Brent Swisher, *Stephen J. Field: Craftsman of the Law* (Hamden, Conn.: Archon Books, 1963), ch. 15; David G. Farrelly, "Justice Harlan's Dissent in the Pollock Case," *Southern California Law Review* 24 (1951): 175–82; and an address, "The Revolution of 20th May, 1895," by Henry H. Ingersoll, read before the Tennessee Bar Asasociation, July, 1895, a copy of which is in HPUL.

57. See Article I, Section 2 of the Constitution.

58. Pollock v. Farmer's Loan & Trust Co., 157 U.S. 429 (1895).

59. 157 U.S. at 608.

60. Ibid., p. 652.

61. Howell Jackson to Melville Fuller, April 15, 1895, Fuller Papers. Jackson died on August 8, 1895.

62. Stephen J. Field to Melville Fuller, May 17, 1895, Fuller Papers.

63. Pollock v. Farmer's Loan & Trust Co., 158 U.S. 601 (1895).

64. 3 Dall. 171 (1796).

65. 102 U.S. 586 (1881).

66. 158 U.S. at 671. These and subsequent passages are taken from the published version of Justice Harlan's opinion, rather than the version delivered in Court. The Justice revised his original effort prior to publication. See, for example, Howell Jackson to John Marshall Harlan, June 25, 1895, HPLC. The press, however, ran lengthy extracts of his oral presentation. Copies of many are in HPUL.

67. Ibid., pp. 672–73.

68. Ibid., pp. 674–75.

69. Ibid., p. 680.

70. Ibid., p. 685.

71. These quotations are drawn from clippings in HPUL.

72. *Chicago Tribune*, April 6, 1895.

73. For summaries of such theories, see King, *Melville Weston Fuller*, pp. 205–206; Nevins, *Grover Cleveland*, pp. 778–79.

74. New York *Sun*, May 22, 1895.

75. New York *Tribune*, May 21, 1895.

76. "Justice Harlan's Harangue," *The Nation*, May 30, 1895, p. 417.

77. *New York Times*, May 21, 1895.

78. Ibid.; "Justice Harlan's Harangue," p. 417.

79. Numerous clippings are in HPUL; see also Farrelly, "Justice Harlan's Dissent in the Pollock Case," pp. 177–78.

80. John Marshall Harlan to James and John Maynard Harlan, May 24, 1895, HPUL. A published version of the letter is in Farrelly, "Justice Harlan's Dissent in the Pollock Case," pp. 178–81.

81. Ibid.

82. Ibid.

83. William Howard Taft to John Marshall Harlan, May 27, 1895, HPUL.

84. Howell Jackson to John Marshall Harlan, June 25, 1895, HPLC.

85. New York *Tribune*, May 21, 1895; Farrelly, "Justice Harlan's Dissent in the Pollock Case," pp. 178–81.

86. Unidentified clipping, HPUL.

87. Unidentified clipping, HPUL.

88. Will Lyons to John Marshall Harlan, May 21, 1895, HPUL.

89. B. O. Flower to John Marshall Harlan, May 21, 1895, HPUL.

90. James Keith to John Marshall Harlan, May 24, 1895, HPUL.

91. Oliver Morton to John Marshall Harlan, May 21, 1895, HPUL.

92. H. C. Evans to John Marshall Harlan, May 27, 1895, HPUL.

93. George B. Boutwell to John Marshall Harlan, June 18, 1895, reprinted in John Marshall Harlan to "My dear Boys," June 20, 1895, HPUL.

94. James S. Harlan to John Marshall Harlan, May 2[illegible], 1895, HPUL.

95. Ibid.

96. For accounts of the Pullman strike, see Nevins, *Grover Cleveland*, ch. 33; Semonche, *Charting the Future*, pp. 72–73.

97. See, for example, John Marshall Harlan to George M. Pullman, January 3, 1878; George M. Pullman to John Marshall Harlan, April 6, 1878, HPLC.

98. John Marshall Harlan to John Maynard Harlan, July 16, 1894, HPLC. See also the Justice's second letter of the same date to his son.

99. *In Re* Debs, 158 U.S. 564 (1895).

100. John Marshall Harlan to W. A. Woods, May 28, 1895, HPUL.

101. New York *Herald*, May 28, 1895.

102. Harlan to Woods.

103. United States v. Joint Traffic Association, 171 U.S. 505 (1898); United States v. Trans-Missouri Freight Association, 166 U.S. 290 (1897).

104. Addyston Pipe & Steel Co. v. United States, 175 U.S. 211 (1899). Harlan, it should also be noted, occasionally joined rulings refusing to extend the Sherman Act's reach. See, for example, Anderson v. United States, 171 U.S. 604 (1898), excluding from the act's coverage an association of cattle brokers; and W.W. Montague & Co. v. Lowry, 193 U.S. 38 (1904), exempting a combination of wholesale title, mantel, and grate dealers. His position in such cases probably reflected his acquiescence in the *Knight* precedent.

105. ICC v. Alabama Midland Ry., 168 U.S. 144, 176 (1897).

106. 188 U.S. 321 (1903).

107. Ibid., pp. 357–58.

108. Ibid., 363.

109. See, for example, Hipolite Egg Co. v. United States, 220 U.S. 45 (1911), upholding the exclusion of impure foods and drugs from interstate traffic.

110. See, for example, Hoke v. United States, 227 U.S. 308 (1913), upholding the Mann Act ban on the interstate transportation of women for immoral purposes.

111. 247 U.S. 251 (1918).

112. Powell v. Pennsylvania, 127 U.S. 678 (1888).

113. 197 U.S. 11 (1905).

114. German Alliance Ins. Co. v. Hale, 219 U.S. 270 (1911) (Harlan, J.).

115. House v. Moyes, 219 U.S. 270 (1911) (Harlan, J.); Booth v. Illinois, 184 U.S. 425 (1902) (Harlan, J.).

116. Gardner v. Michigan, 199 U.S. 325 (1905) (Harlan, J.).

117. City of Detroit v. Parker, 181 U.S. 399 (1901); Walston v. Nevin, 121 U.S. 578 (1888).

118. 198 U.S. 45 (1905).

119. Ibid., p. 66.

120. Ibid., p. 68.

121. Justices White and William Rufus Day dissented, along with Harlan and Holmes.

122. Ibid., p. 70.

123. Ibid., p. 72.

124. Ibid.

125. Ibid., pp. 73–74.

126. Patterson v. New Jersey, 97 U.S. 501, 505 (1879).

127. See McGowan v. Maryland, 366 U.S. 420 (1961).

128. Hennington v. Georgia, 163 U.S. 299, 304 (1896).

129. Bowman v. Chicago & N.W. Ry. Co., 125 U.S. 465, 515 (1888). In Leisy v. Hardin, 135 U.S. 100, 125 (1890), Harlan and Justice Brewer joined Justice Gray's dissent.

130. *In Re* Rahrer, 140 U.S. 545 (1891).

131. For a discussion of the Court's and Black's developing positions, see Tinsley E. Yarbrough, *Mr. Justice Black and His Critics* (Durham: Duke University Press, 1988), pp. 48–55.

132. Morey v. Doud, 354 U.S. 457 (1957). The *Morey* decision was in effect overruled in New Orleans v. Dukes, 427 U.S. 297 (1976).

133. 123 U.S. 623 (1887).

134. Ibid., p. 661.

135. Ibid., p. 661.

136. 169 U.S. 466 (1898).

137. 208 U.S. 161 (1908).

138. Ibid., p. 191.

139. Ibid., p. 175.

140. Atchison, T. & S. F. R. Co. v. Matthews, 174 U.S. 96, 112 (1899).

141. John Marshall Harlan to J.H. Reno, July 31, 1876, HPLC.

142. 7 Peters 243 (1833).

143. See, for example, Hurtado v. California, 110 U.S. 516 (1884); O'Neil v. Vermont, 144 U.S. 323 (1892); Maxwell v. Dow, 176 U.S. 581 (1900); Twining v. New Jersey, 211 U.S. 78 (1908).

144. 110 U.S. 516, 538 (1884).

145. Ibid., p. 541.

146. Ibid., p. 543, quoting Murray's Lessee v. Hoboken, 18 Howard 272, 277 (1856).

147. Ibid., p. 550.

148. Ibid., p. 548.

149. Ibid., p. 553.

150. 144 U.S. 323 (1892).

151. Chicago, B. & Q. R. Co. v. Chicago, 166 U.S. 226 (1897).

152. 176 U.S. 581 (1900).

153. 205 U.S. 454 (1907).

154. Ibid., p. 462.

155. Ibid., p. 465.

156. 211 U.S. 78 (1908).

157. 144 U.S. at 371.
158. Ibid., p. 337.
159. J.W.N. Whitecotton to John Marshall Harlan, February 27, 1900, HPLC.

Chapter 8 Fraternity

1. Except as otherwise indicated, this discussion is drawn from G. H. Knott, "The Behring Sea Arbitration," *American Law Review* 27 (1893): 684–707; *Harper's Encyclopaedia of United States History*, s.v. "Bering Sea Arbitration," by John Watson Foster. Foster was U.S. agent to the tribunal established to resolve the dispute.

2. Malvina Harlan, *Some Memories of a Long Life*. For correspondence relating to Harlan's appointment, see James G. Blaine to John Marshall Harlan, June 1, 1892, HPLC; William Wharton to John Marshall Harlan, June 6, 1892, HPLC; John Marshall Harlan to Secretary of State, June 20, 1892, HPLC.

3. James S. Harlan to John Marshall Harlan, May 12, 1892, HPUL.

4. Malvina Harlan, *Some Memories of a Long Life*.

5. See, for example, John Marshall Harlan to Augustus E. Willson, June 28, August 5, 1892, HPUL.

6. John Marshall Harlan to William Howard Taft, May 2, 1892, Taft Papers.

7. Harlan to Willson, June 28, 1892; John Marshall Harlan to Eli Murray, February 15, 1893, HPUL.

8. Harlan to Murray, February 15, 1893.

9. Malvina Harlan, *Some Memories of a Long Life*.

10. John Marshall Harlan to William Howard Taft, May 29, 1892, Taft Papers.

11. The extract, in HPUL, is from volume 4 of *Dampier's Voyages*, published in London.

12. Harlan to Murray, February 15, 1893.

13. John Marshall Harlan to Melville Fuller, April 16, 1893, Fuller Papers.

14. See, for example, John Marshall Harlan to Melville Fuller, April 24, 1893, Fuller Papers.

15. Stephen Field to Melville Fuller, March 31, 1893, Fuller Papers.

16. John T. Morgan to John Marshall Harlan, August 9, 1893, HPUL.

17. John Marshall Harlan to John T. Morgan, August 10, 1893, HPUL.

18. A copy of the award made by the tribunal follows Knott, "The Behring Sea Arbitration," pp. 699–707.

19. *New York Times*, January 1, 1894, contains extensive excerpts from his opinion.

20. John Marshall Harlan to Augustus E. Willson, August 20, 1892, HPUL.

21. H. W. Blodgett to John Marshall Harlan, August 21, 1893, HPUL.

22. *Chicago Evening Post*, June 7, 1894.

23. "International Courts of Arbitration and the Behring Sea Commission," *Concord*, October, 1893, p. 170.

24. John Marshall Harlan to James S. Harlan, January 21, 1883, HPLC.

25. Ibid.

26. Plessy v. Ferguson, 163 U.S. at 561.

27. James A. Bates to John Marshall Harlan, September 22, 1892, HPUL.

28. Elk v. Wilkins, 112 U.S. 94, 121 (1884).

29. Talton v. Mayes, 163 U.S. 376 (1896).

30. Chew Heong v. United States, 112 U.S. 536 (1884).

31. Baldwin v. Franks, 120 U.S. 678, 700 (1887).

32. 124 U.S. 621 (1888).

33. Ibid., p. 639.

34. 169 U.S. 649 (1898).

35. Ibid., p. 726.

36. John Marshall Harlan to Augustus E. Willson, February 16, 1893, HPUL.

37. James S. Harlan to John Marshall Harlan, May 19, 1892, HPUL.

38. Ibid.; see, for example, John Scholfield to Benjamin Harrison, November 12, 1892, HPUL.

39. John Marshall Harlan to Melville Fuller, August 4, 1898, Fuller Papers.

40. For evidence of such efforts, see, for example, John Marshall Harlan to Melville Fuller, March 20, 1893, Fuller Papers; W. A. Woods to John Marshall Harlan, December 15, 1898, HPUL; Robert Rae to John Marshall Harlan, January 31, 1899, HPUL; Robert Rae to William McKinley, February 6, 1899, HPUL.

41. *New York Times*, January 12, 1901.

42. 182 U.S. 1 (1901).

43. 182 U.S. 222 (1901).

44. 182 U.S. 244 (1901).

45. 182 U.S. at 286.

46. Ibid., p. 282.

47. Ibid., pp. 286–87.

48. Ibid., p. 279.

49. Ibid., p. 283.

50. Ibid., p. 346. For more thorough discussions of the opinions of majority justices, including the sources of their thinking, see, for example, King, *Melville Weston Fuller*, ch. 20; Semonche, *Charting the Future*, pp. 135–41.

51. John Marshall Harlan to William Howard Taft, July 22, 1901, Taft Papers.

52. 182 U.S. at 379.

53. Ibid., p. 380.

54. Ibid., p. 280.

55. Ibid., pp. 381, 382.

56. Ibid., p. 383.

57. Ibid., p. 384.

58. Ibid., p. 389.

59. Ibid., pp. 386–87.

60. Quoted in King, *Melville Weston Fuller*, p. 269.

61. William Howard Taft took delight in quoting that assessment of the cases in his letter to Harlan, dated October 21, 1901, Taft Papers.

62. Augustus E. Willson to John Marshall Harlan, June 20, 1901, HPLC.

63. William Howard Taft to John Marshall Harlan, January 7, 1901, Taft Papers.

64. Willson to Harlan, June 20, 1901.

65. Charles B. Wilby to Augustus E. Willson, undated, HPLC.

66. Seymour D. Thompson to John Marshall Harlan, June 28, 1901, HPLC.

67. Richard Warren Barkley to John Marshall Harlan, May 28, 1901, HPLC.

68. John T. Morgan to John Marshall Harlan, May 28, 1901, HPLC.

69. New York *Evening Post*, June 15, 1901.

70. John Marshall Harlan to William Howard Taft, undated, Taft Papers.

71. William Howard Taft to John Marshall Harlan, March 24, 1902, Taft Papers.

72. John Marshall Harlan to William Howard Taft, March 28, 1902, Taft Papers.

73. James S. Harlan to John Marshall Harlan, undated, HPUL.

74. Ibid.

75. James S. Harlan to John Marshall Harlan, November 19, 1902, HPUL.

76. Such correspondence is in HPUL.

77. John Maynard Harlan to John Marshall Harlan, January 8, 1904, HPUL. The announcement is also in HPUL.

78. John Marshall Harlan to William Howard Taft, undated, Taft Papers. The operator's letter, signed "Operator," is also in the Taft Papers.

79. Theodore Roosevelt to John Marshall Harlan, June 28, 1906, Theodore Roosevelt Papers, Library of Congress.

80. John Marshall Harlan to Theodore Roosevelt, July 5, 1906, Roosevelt Papers.

81. Theodore Roosevelt to John Marshall Harlan, July 21, 1906, Roosevelt Papers. Roosevelt did not specifically mention the Hepburn Act, which became law on June 29, 1906; but that was obviously the statute to which he referred.

82. Theodore Roosevelt to John Marshall Harlan, September 3, 1906, Roosevelt Papers.

83. See, for example, James S. Harlan to William Howard Taft, March 4, 1905, Taft Papers.

84. James S. Harlan to William Howard Taft, December 8, 1911, Taft Papers.

85. John Marshall Harlan to Horace H. Lurton, July 3, 1910, HPUL.

86. 190 U.S. 197 (1903).

87. Ibid., p. 221.

88. Ibid., p. 241.

89. See, for example, Dorr v. United States, 195 U.S. 138, 154 (1904) (dissenting); Trono v. United States, 199 U.S. 521, 535 (1905) (dissenting).

90. John Marshall Harlan to William Howard Taft, February 4, 1904, Taft Papers.

91. *Louisville Times*, undated, HPLC.

92. *Evansville Courier*, June 17, 1897.

93. John Marshall Harlan telegram to Benjamin H. Bristow, March 2, 1872, Bristow Papers. For a campaign advertisement, see *Louisville Commercial*, July 28, 1872.

94. Augustus E. Willson to Richard D. Harlan, April 11, 1930, HPLC.

95. Ibid.

96. Augustus E. Willson to John Marshall Harlan, March 24, 1879, HPUL.

97. Augustus E. Willson to John Marshall Harlan, May 19, 1880, HPUL.

98. Augustus E. Willson to John Marshall Harlan, June 24, 1880, HPUL.

99. Augustus E. Willson to John Marshall Harlan, July 5, 1880, HPUL.

100. Ibid.

101. James Harlan, Jr., to John Marshall Harlan, September 14, 1880, HPUL.

102. Augustus E. Willson to John Marshall Harlan, September 24, 1880, HPUL.

103. See, for example, James Harlan, Jr., to John Marshall Harlan, February 25, 1882, HPUL.

104. James Harlan, Jr., to John Marshall Harlan, July 17, 1882, HPUL.

105. See, for example, James Harlan, Jr., to John Marshall Harlan, October 20, 1886, HPLC.

106. During his Kansas sojourn, James resided in Kansas City and Quenemo. See, for example, James Harlan, Jr., to John Marshall Harlan, August 26, 1887, May 12, 1888, HPUL.

107. James Harlan, Jr., to John Marshall Harlan, July 17, 1888, HPUL.

108. See, for example, James Harlan, Jr., to unknown, October 4, 1890, HPLC; James Harlan, Jr., to John Marshall Harlan, undated, HPLC.

109. See, for example, James Harlan, Jr., to John Marshall Harlan, February 1, 1891, HPLC.

110. W. W. Acers to John Marshall Harlan, May 6, 1891, HPLC.

111. James Harlan, Jr., to John Marshall Harlan, April 11, 1891, HPLC.

112. James Harlan, Jr., to John Marshall Harlan, undated, HPLC. Many other such letters are also in HPLC.

113. See, for example, James Harlan, Jr., to John Marshall Harlan, April 11, 1891, HPLC.

114. See, for example, Theodore Roosevelt to John Marshall Harlan, December 26, 1906, Roosevelt Papers.

115. John Marshall Harlan to John Maynard Harlan, February 7, 1894, HPLC.

116. A. M. Swope to John Marshall Harlan, January [illegible date], June 26, 1880, HPUL.

117. John Marshall Harlan to Henry Harlan, July 10, 1889, HPUL.

118. James Harlan quoted this passage from a letter he had received from Mrs. Harlan in his letter to her on March 22, 1891, HPLC.

119. James Harlan, Jr., to John Marshall Harlan, January 19, 1892, HPUL.

120. John Marshall Harlan to Augustus E. Willson, July 23, 1892, HPUL.

121. John Marshall Harlan to Augustus E. Willson, April 27, 1892, HPUL.

122. John Marshall Harlan to Augustus E. Willson, December 11, 1894, HPUL.

123. John Marshall Harlan to Augustus E. Willson, December 14, 1892, HPUL.

124. Augustus E. Willson to Richard D. Harlan, April 30, 1930.

125. Harlan to Willson, December 11, 1894.

126. Augustus E. Willson to John Marshall Harlan, August 31, 1895, HPLC.

127. Louisville *Courier-Journal*, June 16, 1897; *Frankfort Roundabout*, June 19, 1897; unidentified clipping in Harlan Family Scrapbook, Kentucky Historical Society.

128. Louisville *Courier-Journal*, June 16, 1897.

Chapter 9   Twilight

1. As noted previously, the Harlan sons' careers and difficulties are treated in greater detail in Yarbrough, *John Marshall Harlan, passim.*

2. Washington *Star*, May 17, 1906; New York *Herald*, May 18, 1906. Edith married Erastus Corning, Jr., of Albany, New York.

3. J. M. Dickinson to John Marshall Harlan, October 14, 1899, HPUL. For discussions of Harlan II's sisters, Elizabeth, Janet, and Edith, see Yarbrough, *John Marshall Harlan, passim.*

4. John Marshall Harlan to Elizabeth Harlan, January 31, 1905, Harlan Family Papers.

5. John Marshall Harlan to Elizabeth Harlan, February 12, 1905, Harlan Family Papers.

6. Harlan to Elizabeth, January 31, 1905.

7. Malvina Harlan, *Some Memories of a Long Life.* Documents and related materials dealing with the ultimate disposition of the Murray Bay property following the justice's death are in the Harlan Family Papers.

8. Richard D. Harlan, "Justice Harlan and the Game of Golf," *Scribner's Magazine,* November, 1917, pp. 626–35.

9. John Marshall Harlan to William Howard Taft, November 18, 1905, Taft Papers.

10. John Marshall Harlan to Charles J. Bell, April 24, 1911, HPLC.

11. *Detroit News*, June, [no date] 1911, in HPLC.

12. Unidentified clipping, HPLC.

13. Louisville *Courier-Journal*, February 4, 1906.

14. Quoted in Richard Harlan, "Justice Harlan and the Game of Golf," p. 635.

15. Chicago *Inter-Ocean*, December 30, 1910.

16. Fred Beisswanger to John Marshall Harlan, December 31, 1910, HPUL.

17. W. F. Arnold to John Marshall Harlan, January 2, 1911, HPUL. The letter was addressed to "Henry" Harlan.

18. See, for example, W. B. Robison to John Marshall Harlan, March 29, 1900; Harlan to Robison, March 31, 1900; Wallace Radcliffe to John Marshall Harlan, April 4, 1900, HPUL.

19. I also included this story, drawn from an interview with Harlan's granddaughter, Janet Harlan White, in my biography of Harlan II, *John Marshall Harlan*, p. 10. I have attempted to avoid using the same anecdotes in both books but could not resist this one exception to my rule.

20. From a copy of *The Murray Bay Protestant Church, 1867–1917*, undated and apparently privately published, in HPLC.

21. See Henry van Dyke to John Marshall Harlan, January 30, 1902, HPUL.

22. Except where otherwise indicated, this discussion is based on a summary of Assembly proceedings published in *The Interior*, a church organ, on file in HPLC.

23. A copy of the letter, dated February 13, 1905, is in HPUL.

24. Quoted in unidentified clipping, HPLC.

25. John Marshall Harlan to Theodore Roosevelt, October 12, 1901, Roosevelt Papers.

26. Theodore Roosevelt to John Marshall Harlan, December 15, 1902, Roosevelt Papers.

27. See, for example, John Marshall Harlan to Augustus E. Willson, July 18, 1907, Willson Papers.

28. John Marshall Harlan to Augustus E. Willson, August 22, 1907, Willson Papers.

29. William Howard Taft to John Marshall Harlan, July 3, 1908, Taft Papers.

30. An unidentified clipping, apparently from a letter dated December 7, 1906, is in HPLC.

31. John Marshall Harlan to Augustus E. Willson, April 22, 1907, Willson Papers.

32. See, for example, *Washington Post*, October 26, 1902.

33. See, for example, *Washington Post*, February 25, 1906.

34. A transcript of the evening's proceedings, as well as many other pertinent materials, are in HPUL.

35. John R. Dunlap to R. M. Kelly, October 24, 1907, HPLC.

36. A copy of the justice's remarks and other pertinent materials are in HPLC.

37. Augustus E. Willson to John H. Frank, June 22, 1907, Willson Papers. See also Augustus E. Willson to E. W. Chenault, July 5, 1907, Willson Papers.

38. John Marshall Harlan to Augustus E. Willson, August 24, 1908, Willson Papers.

39. Many newspaper clippings and other materials relating to the trip are in HPLC and HPUL.

40. Berea College v. Kentucky, 211 U.S. at 69.

41. Minutes of the university board of trustees' annual meeting, dated June 15, 1891, on file in HPLC, record the appointment.

42. Raleigh Cellinor to John Marshall Harlan, April 25, 1896, HPUL.

43. For correspondence related to his book project, see, for example, John F. Dillon to John Marshall Harlan, August 12, 1908, HPUL; John Marshall Harlan to Charles Henry Butler, August 7, 1908, HPLC. In a doctoral dissertation, "The Republic According to John Marshall Harlan: Race, Republicanism, and Citizenship" (1989), a modified version of which is now in preparation for publication, Linda Carol Przybyszewski devotes considerable attention to an analysis of Harlan's lectures. Arguably, however, his judicial opinions offer considerably greater insight into his judicial and constitutional philosophy.

44. Unidentified clipping, HPUL.

45. Undated, typescript recollections of Enoch Aquila Chase, a Washington lawyer, in HPLC.

46. Charles Nelhany to John Marshall Harlan, July 7, 1903, HPUL.

47. E. G. Lorenzen to John Marshall Harlan, June 22, 1910, HPLC.

48. E. G. Lorenzen to John Marshall Harlan, June 27, 1910, HPLC; see also Walter C. Clephane to John Marshall Harlan, June 25, 1910, HPLC. Clephane, another member of the faculty, summarized the terms in his letter to Harlan.

49. John Marshall Harlan to Walter C. Clephane, July 29, 1910, HPLC.

50. Margaret Snow to John Marshall Harlan, May 26, [1910], HPUL.

51. John Maynard Harlan to John Marshall Harlan, July 19, 1910, HPLC.

52. A. B. Browne to John Marshall Harlan, July 26, 1910, HPLC.

53. Harlan to Browne, July 29, 1910.

54. Walter C. Clephane to John Marshall Harlan, August 1, 1910, HPLC.

55. John Marshall Harlan to Board of Trustees, September 12, 1910, HPLC.

56. A copy of the department's statement was sent to Harlan by the university secretary. Richard Cobb to John Marshall Harlan, January 6, 1911, HPLC.

57. John Marshall Harlan to Melville Fuller, September 18, 1902, Fuller Papers. After a stroke had left Gray partially paralyzed, he resigned contingent on the appointment of a successor. Gray died before the Senate had confirmed President Roosevelt's nomination of Justice Holmes to replace him.

58. John Marshall Harlan telegram to Charles Evans Hughes, April 26, 1910, HPLC.

59. Hughes, *The Supreme Court of the United States*, p. 75.

60. Hepburn v. Griswold, 75 U.S. 603 (1870).

61. Hughes, *The Supreme Court of the United States*, p. 76.

62. For an interesting discussion of the complicated series of events that led to Field's retirement, see King, *Melville Weston Fuller*, pp. 222–27.

63. Augustus E. Willson telegram to William Howard Taft, July 6, 1910, Taft Papers.

64. Letters supporting Harlan's selection are in HPLC and HPUL, the Taft Papers, and the Harlan file in the national archives.

65. *New York Times*, September 5, 1910.

66. John Marshall Harlan to Augustus E. Willson, September 25, 1906, HPLC. See also, for example, John Marshall Harlan to Augustus E. Willson, June 16, 1907, Willson Papers.

67. John Marshall Harlan to Horace H. Lurton, September 12, 1910, Horace H. Lurton Papers, Library of Congress.

68. John Marshall Harlan to William R. Day, July 22, 1910, HPUL; John Marshall Harlan to William Howard Taft, July 11, 1910, Taft Papers.

69. William Howard Taft to Horace H. Lurton, May 22, 1909, Taft Papers.

70. For a discussion of considerations leading to Lurton's selection, which Taft called the "chief pleasure of my administration," see H.F. Pringle, *The Life and Times of William Howard Taft*, 2 vols. (New York: Farrar & Rinehart, 1939), 1: 530-31.

71. John Marshall Harlan to Augustus E. Willson, December 25, 1910, Willson Papers. Willson's earlier letter to Harlan could not be located.

72. *Los Angeles Examiner*, October 20, 1911.

73. Employers' Liability Cases, 207 U.S. 463 (1908).

74. 166 U.S. 290 (1897).

75. Northern Securities Co. v. United States, 193 U.S. 197 (1904).

76. Ibid., p. 360 (Brewer, J., concurring).

77. Ibid., p. 407.

78. Ibid., p. 410. Justice White, joined by the other dissenters, filed a separate dissent focusing on the "reasonableness" of the Northern Securities scheme.

79. Standard Oil Co. v. United States, 221 U.S. 1 (1911).

80. United States v. American Tobacco Co., 221 U.S. 106 (1911).

81. For a more thorough discussion of White's position, see Robert B. Highsaw, *Edward Douglass White, Defender of the Conservative Faith* (Baton Rouge: Louisiana State University Press, 1981), pp. 91–96.

82. 221 U.S. at 83.

83. Ibid., p. 91.

84. Ibid., p. 92.

85. Ibid., p. 105.

86. Ibid., p. 103.

87. 221 U.S. at 191.

88. Merlo J. Pusey, *Charles Evans Hughes*, 2 vols. (New York: Columbia University Press, 1963), 1: 283.

89. Hughes, *Autobiographical Notes of Charles Evans Hughes*, p. 170.

90. Charles Henry Butler, *A Century at the Bar of the United States* (New York: G.P. Putnam's Sons, 1942), p. 169.

91. HPLC and HPUL contain much such material, most of it undated and otherwise unidentified.

92. *Columbus Citizen*, May 17, 1911.

93. Quoted in "A Review of the World," *Current Literature*, July, 1911, p. 1.

94. Noted in ibid.

95. *New York Times*, June 4, 1911.

96. Ibid.

97. Malvina Harlan, *Some Memories of a Long Life*.

98. Robert Bridges to John Marshall Harlan, July 21, 1911, HPUL.

99. John Marshall Harlan to Robert Bridges, July 24, 1911, HPUL.

100. John Marshall Harlan to Blackburn Esterline, August 12, 1911, HPUL.

101. A Harlan letter of August 16, 1911, quoted in James D. Maher to John Marshall Harlan, August 18, 1911, HPUL.

102. Malvina Harlan, *Some Memories of a Long Life*.

103. J. E. Hoover to Richard D. Harlan, October 11, 1911, HPUL.

104. John Marshall Harlan to Augustus E. Willson, October 9, 1911, HPUL.

105. Malvina Harlan, *Some Memories of a Long Life*.

106. Hoover to Richard Harlan.

107. Malvina Harlan, *Some Memories of a Long Life*.

108. Several newspaper accounts carried this version of Harlan's last words, but Mrs. Harlan's memoirs make no mention of them.

109. *New York Times*, October 17, 18, 1911.

110. Unidentified clipping, HPUL.

111. An undated editorial of the *Vicksburg Herald*, summarized in the Memphis *Commercial Appeal*, October 18, 1911.

112. Thomason, Ga., *Jeffersonian*, October 19, 1911.

113. Louisville *Courier-Journal*, October 17, 1911.

114. *Los Angeles Examiner*, October 16, 1911.

115. *New York Times*, October 17, 1911.

116. Newspaper accounts and transcripts of such proceedings are in HPLC and HPUL.

117. *Ogden City Standard*, October 28, 1911.

118. New York *Sun*, January 16, 1912.

119. Recounted in several unidentified clippings.

120. See HPLC.

121. Undated clipping, HPUL.

122. Shelby J. Davidson to James S. Harlan, December 2, 1911, HPUL.

123. *Washington Post*, undated, in HPUL.

Epilogue

1. Yarbrough, *John Marshall Harlan*, pp. 35–40.

2. *New York Times*, January 17, 1912.

3. Malvina Harlan, *Some Memories of a Long Life.*

4. *New York Times*, October 10, 1916.

5. *New York Times*, March 6, 1921, August 23, 1923.

6. A memorandum prepared for Mrs. Harlan's descendants in 1948 by the second Justice Harlan, then a Wall Street lawyer, describes the arrangements for Laura and Ruth. The memorandum was written in the late 1940s, at the time of the family's disposal of the Murray Bay property, which had been made available for Laura and Ruth as part of the trust provisions. The memorandum and documents relating to the property's disposition are in the Harlan Family Papers.

7. Author's interviews with Edith Harlan Powell, May 12, 15, 1989, New York. Mrs. Powell is the youngest sister of the second Justice Harlan.

8. See Yarbrough, *John Marshall Harlan*, pp. 39–41.

9. Floyd B. Clark, *The Constitutional Doctrines of Justice Harlan* (Baltimore: The Johns Hopkins Press, 1915).

10. Henry B. Brown, "The Dissenting Opinions of Mr. Justice Harlan," *American Law Review* 46 (May-June, 1912): 321–52; Thomas J. Knight, "The Dissenting Opinions of Justice Harlan," *American Law Review* 57 (July-August, 1917): 481–506.

11. Brown, "The Dissenting Opinions of Mr. Justice Harlan," p. 352.

12. Adamson v. California, 332 U.S. 46, 62 (Frankfurter, J., concurring).

13. For analyses of Harlan II's jurisprudence, see, for example, Norman Dorsen, "The Second Mr. Justice Harlan: A Constitutional Conservative," *New York University Law Review* 44 (1969): 249; J. Harvie Wilkinson III, "Justice John M. Harlan and the Values of Federalism," *Virginia Law Review* 57 (1971): 1185; Yarbrough, *John Marshall Harlan*, chs. 5–9.

14. Analyses of Justice Black's thinking, and his conflicts with the Frankfurter-Harlan approach to constitutional construction, abound. More recent efforts include James F. Simon, *The Antagonists: Hugo Black, Felix Frankfurter and Civil Liberties in Modern America* (New York: Simon and Schuster, 1989); Mark Silverstein, *Constitutional Faiths: Felix Frankfurter, Hugo Black, and the Process of Decision-Making* (Ithaca, New York: Cornell University Press, 1984); Yarbrough, *Mr. Justice Black and His Critics.*

15. *Dayton News*, October 14, 1911.

16. Richard F. Watt and Richard M. Orlikoff, "The Coming Vindication of Mr. Justice Harlan," *Illinois Law Review* 44 (1949): 13.

17. Edward F. Waite, "How 'Eccentric' Was Mr. Justice Harlan?" *Minnesota Law Review* 37 (1953): 173.

18. Henry J. Abraham, "John Marshall Harlan: A Justice Neglected," *Virginia Law Review* 41 (1955): 871, 890–91.

19. Brown v. Bd. of Education, 347 U.S. 483 (1954); 349 U.S. 294 (1955).

20. E.g., Louisville, N.O. & Texas Ry. v. Mississippi, 133 U.S. 587 (1890), overruled by Morgan v. Virginia, 328 U.S. 373 (1946).

21. United States v. E.C. Knight Co., 156 U.S. 1 (1895), overruled by NLRB v. Jones & Laughlin Steel Corp., 301 U.S. 1 (1937).

22. Leisy v. Hardin, 135 U.S. 100 (1889), nullified by adoption of the Twenty-First Amendment.

23. Lochner v. New York, 198 U.S. 45 (1905), overruled by Bunting v. Oregon, 243 U.S. 426 (1917), among other cases.

24. Robertson v. Baldwin, 165 U.S. 275 (1897), rectified by adoption of the 1915 Seamen's Act.

25. Pollock v. Farmers' Loan and Trust Co., 158 U.S. 601 (1895), nullified by ratification of the Sixteenth Amendment.

26. See, for example, Duncan v. Louisiana, 391 U.S. 145 (1968).

27. Jones v. Alfred H. Mayer Co., 392 U.S. 409 (1968).

28. See the various opinions filed in United States v. Guest, 383 U.S. 745 (1966).

29. See, for example, Palko v. Connecticut, 302 U.S. 319 (1937); Duncan v. Louisiana.

30. See, for example, Henry J. Abraham, "Some Post-*Bakke*, *Weber*, and *Fullilove* Reflections on Reverse Discrimination," *University of Richmond Law Review* 14 (1980): 373.

31. See especially, of course, Roe v. Wade, 410 U.S. 113 (1973).

32. Boyd v. United States, 116 U.S. 616 (1886).

33. E.g., Mapp v. Ohio, 367 U.S. 643 (1961); Miranda v. Arizona, 384 U.S. 436 (1966).

34. The memorial proceedings, conducted at the Supreme Court on November 15, 1993, and to be published later, were telecast on C-SPAN on November 24, 1993.

Bibliographical Note

The John Marshall Harlan Papers at the Library of Congress and the University of Louisville were the primary sources of research for this study. Largely available in microfilm and arranged chronologically as well as by a number of separate subject headings, these collections afford excellent insight into the justice's historic roots, family life, personality, interpersonal relations, education, professional life, Civil War service, political career, and judicial tenure. Unfortunately, they include separate files for only the *Civil Rights Cases* of 1883 and a few other major cases in which Harlan participated, obliging the researcher to seek additional such materials in the justice's correspondence with his colleagues and other contemporaries as well as in related sources. But those materials are a rich source of anecdotal research relating to the justice's service on the Court.

The collections also include Harlan's autobiographical typescripts on a variety of topics, as well as the unpublished memoirs of his wife, Malvina Shanklin Harlan, entitled *Some Memories of a Long Life*. Other Harlan papers were available, moreover, from separate sources. Harlan files in the possession of the justice's great-grandson, Roger A. Derby, offered much material on Harlan's children, their relations with their parents and each other, and the family's Murray Bay, Quebec, summer home, as well as on other subjects. The Kentucky Historical Society in Frankfort is a repository for a number of Harlan papers, including a thick family scrapbook of unknown origin, as is The Filson Club Historical Society of Louisville. The papers of the second Justice Harlan in the Seeley G. Mudd Manuscript Library at Princeton University were also helpful, especially in providing a crucial lead to a descendant of Harlan I's mulatto half-brother, Robert Harlan. That descendant, Roberta Harlan Nabrit, provided clippings and other valuable materials relating to her ancestor. Equally helpful were numerous conversations with Roger Derby and other Harlan family members, including the second Justice Harlan's sister, Edith Harlan Powell, and his daughter, Eve Harlan Dillingham.

Of additional archival sources, the Kentucky Department of Archives furnished the records of several race-related cases that Harlan handled as the state's attorney general. The National Archives in Washington contain materials relative to the justice's appointment to the Supreme Court in 1877, as well as letters unsuccessfully urging his selection as chief justice in 1910.

The papers of Harlan contemporaries were also extremely helpful. All are cited in the notes to the text. Among the most fruitful, however, were the collections of the justice's law partners and close political associates, Benjamin H. Bristow and Augustus E. Willson, on file at the Library of Congress and The Filson Club Historical Society, respectively; the Library of Congress papers of Harlan's Supreme Court contemporaries, Morrison R. Waite and Melville W. Fuller; the papers of President Rutherford B. Hayes at the Hayes presidential library in Fremont, Ohio; the papers of Presidents Ulysses S. Grant, James A. Garfield, Benjamin Harrison, Theodore Roosevelt, and William Howard Taft, available on microfilm from the Library of Congress; and the Library of Congress papers of Frederick Douglass.

Newspapers were another important primary source. The Harlan papers themselves contain many clippings. But collections of Kentucky, Ohio, and national newspapers were examined at the Library of Congress, Kentucky Historical Society, University of Kentucky, Kentucky Department of Archives, the Cincinnati Historical Society, the Cincinnati Public Library, and The Filson Club Historical Society.

Until recently, book-length studies of Justice Harlan were virtually nonexistent, despite his developing stature as one of the Supreme Court's "great" jurists. Shortly after the justice's death, Floyd B. Clark examined his career in *The Constitutional Doctrines of Justice Harlan* (Baltimore: The Johns Hopkins Press, 1915). Over 20 years ago, Frank B. Latham wrote *The Great Dissenter: John Marshall Harlan, 1833–1911* (New York: Cowles, 1970), a book intended for juvenile audiences. But Loren P. Beth's solid work, *John Marshall Harlan: The Last Whig Justice*, published by the University Press of Kentucky in 1992, was the first major biography to appear.

Numerous excellent journal articles are devoted to the justice. Among the best are Henry J. Abraham, "John Marshall Harlan: A Justice Neglected," *Virginia Law Review* 41 (1955): 871–90; David G. Farrelly's "Harlan's Formative Period: The Years Before the War," *Kentucky Law Journal* 46 (1958): 367–406, part of a symposium issue devoted to the justice, and "A Sketch of John Marshall Harlan's Pre-Court Career," *Vanderbilt Law Review* 10 (1957): 209–25; Louis Hartz, "John M. Harlan in Kentucky, 1855–1877: The Story of his Pre-Court Political Career," *Filson Club Historical Quarterly* 14 (1940): 17–40; James W. Gordon, "Did the First Justice Harlan Have a Black Brother?" *Western New England Law Review* 15 (1993): 159–238; Alan F. Westin, "John Marshall Harlan and the Constitutional Rights of Negroes, The Transformation of a Southerner," *Yale Law Journal* 66 (1957): 637–710; Henry B. Brown, "The Dissenting Opinions of Mr. Justice Harlan," *American Law Review* 46 (1912): 321–53; Thomas J. Knight, "The Dissenting Opinions of Justice Harlan," *American Law Review* 51 (1917): 481–506; Richard F. Watt and Richard M. Orlikoff, "The Coming Vindication of Mr. Justice Harlan," *Illinois Law Review* 44 (1949): 13–40; Edward F. Waite, "How 'Eccentric' Was Mr. Justice Harlan?" *Minnesota Law Review* 37 (1953): 173–87; and Florian Bartosic,

"The Constitution, Civil Liberties and John Marshall Harlan," *Kentucky Law Journal* 46 (1958): 407–447, another entry in the symposium issue cited above. Numerous other studies are cited in the notes to this book. But easily as valuable as the published works is Thomas L. Owen, "The Pre-Court Career of John Marshall Harlan" (M.A. Thesis, University of Kentucky, 1970).

Index